Canadian Public-Sector Financial Management
2nd Edition

Andrew Graham

Queen's Policy Studies Series
School of Policy Studies, Queen's University
McGill-Queen's University Press
Montreal & Kingston • London • Ithaca

SCHOOL OF
Policy Studies

Publications Unit
Robert Sutherland Hall
138 Union Street
Kingston, ON, Canada
K7L 3N6
www.queensu.ca/sps/

Library and Archives Canada Cataloguing in Publication

Graham, Andrew (Andrew Bryan), author
    Canadian public-sector financial management / Andrew Graham.
– 2nd edition.

(Queen's policy studies series)
Includes bibliographical references and index.
Issued in print and electronic formats.
ISBN 978-1-55339-426-6 (pbk.). – ISBN 978-1-55339-427-3 (epub).
– ISBN 978-1-55339-428-0 (pdf)

    1. Finance, Public – Canada – Management. 2. Finance, Public –
Canada. I. Title. II. Series: Queen's policy studies series

HJ9921.G73 2014   352.4'0971   C2014-901971-8
                                       C2014-901972-6

Dedication

Tom Plunkett – A Leader in Canadian Public Administration

This book is dedicated to the memory of a great leader in public administration in Canada. As director of the School of Public Administration (1977–84 and 1990–92) at Queen's University, Tom Plunkett nurtured the Master of Public Administration program to national prominence. His prior experience as a city manager and government consultant informed his teaching and research, and inspired his students. His academic work has stood the test of time. Above all, he was a relentless advocate of sound public management.

In his honour, the School of Policy Studies has created The Thomas Plunkett Executive-in-Residence Endowment Fund. Support from this fund enables senior practitioners with a distinguished record of achievement in public administration in Canada, preferably at the municipal level, or in the broader public sector, to spend a period of time as fellows at the School of Policy Studies at Queen's University. At the request of the author, proceeds from the sale of this text will be directed to this fund.

Contents

List of Figures

Chapter 4

Chapter 5

Chapter 6

Chapter 7

Chapter 8

Chapter 9

Chapter 10

Chapter 11

Acknowledgements for the Second Edition

In 2012, on a tour of Italy, we found ourselves on a walk through Venice, stopping at the old market and counting houses in the Rialto Market, once used by Luca Pacioli, the codifier of double-entry bookkeeping. I became quite excited to be where so much of what we do in financial management today actually began. At that point I was reminded that I just may have gone a bit too far with this interest and perhaps I needed a life. Still, reflecting over a glass of wine on a lovely piazza nearby, to be so close to the origins of debits and credits, who could ask for more? Such is the intensity that can follow an enthusiastic interest in what some would see as arcane.

The venture of producing this text, now in its second edition, has been one of learning and fellowship. As I noted in my first edition, I came to this by accident and without perhaps the full qualifications associated with such ventures. Of course, the experience of years of public administration with significant financial responsibilities does count and I freely admit does show up in the text. So, too, does the growing awareness of the needs of students, new to public administration, and those with experience approaching their first actual budget responsibility. Over the many years of teaching in this area, I realized that fear of finance is a real issue for a lot of people. One of the objectives of this book is to rid them of at least a bit of it.

As the first edition was taken up by colleagues across the country and adopted for use in many university public-sector financial management courses, a small group of users developed. Some of us shared testing, case- and classwork material. Some provided some great advice for this edition, some of which I have taken up where space permitted. Some found mistakes. Who would have thought that might happen? To everyone who provided both feedback and encouragement, thank you.

One increasing source of feedback and learning for me has been my students. Typically I teach this material in our summer term, a time that permits both full- and part-time students to mix in classes. It is a great time, quite intense, and a lot of fun. Students bring so many experiences and perceptions to the text content and our class discussions. Their ideas and advice guided my re-edit and additions all along the way. For instance, even though I saw this myself, the stories of the emerging budget pressures, and the need to improve budget cutting and reallocation skills, informed the new chapter on that topic.

Along the way, the text got taken up by a number of non-educational groups. I always intended it for use well outside the classroom as a useful resource to the young professional skilled in many areas, but, once again, with a fear of finance and about to take on managerial responsibilities. However, as life will often do, at one point I found myself, with the help of a resourceful research assistant, recasting the text for an international NGO to be used in emerging public administrations in far-off parts of the world. I owe those with the vision to take something they found useful and challenge me to make it culturally relevant elsewhere.

My colleagues at the School of Policy Studies have been invaluable. I want to thank Dr. Kim Nossal, director and Lynn Freeman, assistant director, for their unwavering support in seeing me through this edit; production and release. And, of course, Mark Howes and Val Jarus have been invaluable in moving this forward. This time round, Anne Holley-Hime provided supportive but much needed editorial guidance. I also want to thank Ian Clark of the University of Toronto for linking my text and all my work in financial management to the exciting emergent *Atlas of Public Policy and Management*. I have a strong belief that we all grow if we share, not protect, our work, and Ian and Les Pal's exceptional work and my modest linkage to it are important to that view. I thank them both.

Finally, as before, my wife, Katherine Graham, has as always been a strong supporter, even when I wax eloquent about debits and credits under the ancient arches of the Rialto Market.

Andrew Graham

Introduction to the Second Edition

"It's All about the Money"[1] … It's Still All about the Money

In reflecting back over the six years since this text was first published, a lot has changed in public-sector financial management, much of it for the good. This text was written to fill a gap – there is no other Canadian text that deals specifically with financial management, particularly from the focus of the practitioner. The focus for many years in public administration teaching has been on the politics of budgets, a different but worthy area of study as well. However, many of my students, and those surveyed by their respective schools after graduation, identified the need to improve their financial management skills. It is heartening, therefore, to see so many schools of public administration across the country using this text as they rise to meet this need.

The text was intended for both classroom use and as a reference guide for practitioners. It still is. I well recall the point in my own public service career when, upon promotion, I found myself being a budget manager for the first time. In the sink-or-swim learning environment, I swam, with a little help. Luckily, I found a colleague who would show me the ropes. Luckily, I had financial advisors who would take the time to explain things to the newbie. Luckily, I had a boss with a tolerant view, at least at the outset. This book was written with that experience in mind, not just because it was mine, but because, throughout my public service career and in the years teaching at Queen's, I heard versions of it time and time again. So, for the upcoming public servant who finds herself being called a budget manager or responsibility centre manager, here is a little help to get on board.

In this Introduction, I would like to reflect on what has developed in public-sector financial management since the first edition, set out the broad framework for financial management in government and the broader public sector, and address the characteristics of what being a literate financial manager are. This later topic is one that has arisen many times in my teaching, in individual discussions, and with senior government officials across the country. I felt that it needed to be better described than it has been to date.

Developments in Public-Sector Financial Management

Since the publication of the first edition, we have seen some turbulent times in government. We have also seen some developments in the craft of financial management come to fruition. While a long time in development, the results of such changes as the movement to accrual are now evident and have begun to have an impact on public policy decisions. The following are some of the developments of note:

- **Surges in Spending:** The Great Recession, that broke in 2008 and linger still, presented major challenges to everyone. Governments responded with all the public policy tools they had, including a major infusion of public spending to stimulate the economy. The successful delivery of that program strained financial management capacity, but proved its strength in the final analysis.
- **Retrenchment and Deficits:** The deficit created by this surge left many governments seeking ways to reduce spending. Added to this was the impact of new accrual accounting that firmly places future liabilities such as pensions on the books. This increased the understanding of the real deficit situation of virtually all governments.
- **Systematic Spending Reviews:** Canada, along with a few other countries, began to see the results in terms of program cuts and spending reductions in targeted areas of the spending review process.
- **Accrual Takes Hold:** Many years in the making, the conversion to full accrual accounting in government started to produce results, some of them not so pleasant, but still needed, as in the pension issue noted above.
- **IFRS Replaces GAAP – In Places:** The International Financial Reporting Standards, which replace country-based GAAP, are now being applied to parts of the public sector. For the program manager, this means very little. For the financial expert, it means a lot.

- **Government Delivery Agencies Grow:** Governments continue the trend, now more pronounced, of using special delivery agencies at arm's length from traditional departments to deliver specific services. This has proven to be a stress on normal accountability and reporting regimes. It has also caused concern about what is, and what is not, in the government reporting entity for financial reporting.
- **More Contract and Financing Tools:** Governments have adopted more strategic approaches to major contracting leading to complex and dynamic arrangements that have to be well informed by expert financial analysis on the government side. Similarly, governments have developed new financing schemes that involve private capital investments. More and more, these ways of doing business mean that financial literacy and expertise within government have to improve.
- **Controllership Pays Off:** Major efforts by governments to improve financial management continue to show results. The emergence of quarterly financial statements in the past few years is a good example.
- **Big Data:** The growth of finance-based analytics and its application to providing new tools for financial management has begun to be seen in government. As financial systems produce more and more information, being able to mine it for trends, and analysis through new techniques, will affect what tools managers have to manage their increasingly scarce or threatened resources.

What does all this mean? Many of these developments have been years in the making and are only coming to notice now. For this text, changes have been made to adapt to some. For instance, there is now a chapter on budget reductions and reallocation. Taken together, they reinforce a theme that drove the creation and structure of this text: the effective management of financial resources is a core part of virtually every program manager's and organizational leader's job.

The Framework for Financial Management: A Public Policy Implementation Focus

The public sector of Canada is a large and important part of the social, economic, and fiscal landscape of this country. Taken at its broadest possible definition, it encompasses a wide range of public activities, some under the title of government, core, broader and contracted, and some under the title of the voluntary, nonprofit, or third sector.[2]

The successful delivery of public services, be they policies, regulations, direct client services, or payments of some kind, depends on the resources available. While the

term resources embraces many elements – people, time, attention, focus, and capacity – in the end, the amount of money available to deliver the program is the key variable for success. In that sense, it is all about the money.

Effective management of these funds by the managers responsible is the principal focus of this book. As the cycle of public policy outlined in **Figure 0.1** shows, there is more to the public sector than simply spending money, and it all begins with public policies. An array of tools has evolved to deliver public goods under the overall umbrella of the public sector, be it government, near-government agencies, wholly independent public organizations, fully independent nonprofit organizations and private sector firms.[3]

This text is organized to address the elements of this framework, which is represented diagrammatically in **Figure 0.2**. Accounting for the proper expenditure of funds is not only an element of good management: it is essential to good government and good governance of the public enterprise. It is also where governments are most heavily scrutinized and where they can get into a great deal of trouble. The Centre for First Nations Governance drives this point home very well:

> Financial Management Capacity ensures that our good work is not derailed by an inability to plan for, monitor, and account for financial resources. Financial capacity permits long-term, multi-year planning and proactive decision making. Effective financial management permits communities to plan beyond the arbitrary end of a fiscal year or a federal funding cycle and instead to plan for generations.[4]

FIGURE 0.1
Public Policy and Resource Cycle

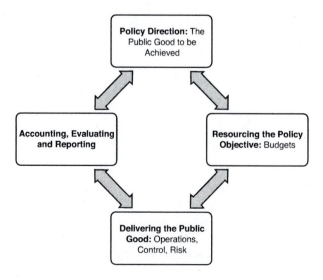

FIGURE 0.2
The Framework for Public-Sector Financial Management

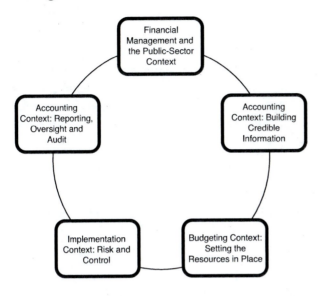

Public policy drives how the public sector operates. Without it, no measure of public activity would make any coherent sense. However, it rarely ends there. Otherwise, we would have no end of interesting public-policy pronouncements, but little or no action to bring them to life. Furthermore, so much of the effectiveness of any policy turns on matching resources to policy aspirations. It is often called "delivering on promises." This process is continuous. Policy direction may be the notional start of the cycle of resourcing and accounting, but time does not stand still and seldom is one policy ever implemented on its own. Policy is also reformulated by the experience of operations and assessment of results. The loop is continuous and can move in both directions.

There is no shortage of good ideas in the public realm. There is equally no shortage of advocates for specific policies or courses of action, but there is a shortage of resources to get things done. This is a remorseless fact of public administration. Further, neither policy decisions, nor allocations of resources to support them, are made in isolation. There is a continual and fierce competition among departments of governments for both policy attention and resources. For any actor in the public sector, it is vital both to have an understanding of how governments balance their objectives and allocate funds to them, and to know both the formal and informal decision-making systems for budgetary allocation. Succeeding within those systems is often a measure of one's success in obtaining resources on behalf of a program or policy initiative.

The challenge does not end there. Just getting the money is the first step. It has to be spent for the purposes intended according to the rules. Results have to be achieved. Accounts have to be rendered of both performance and compliance for the public policy good and for the resources themselves. There has to be a continuous refinement of the policy, public good, or program to make it more effective and efficient, which can involve resource reallocations and outright reductions.

Getting funds approved by whatever authorizing body to perform some measure of public good is the start of the financial-management cycle that this text examines. Not all public-sector managers need to be accountants to do their jobs. (This text will certainly not qualify you as one.) Nevertheless, effective management of funds requires an understanding of basic accounting language and tools.

All public-sector managers are financial managers to some degree. For instance, they may have direct authority and responsibility for spending funds, approving expenditures and contracts, being concerned with the policies that allocate them, or being responsible for monitoring their use from a range of perspectives, e.g., as the client or the organization, or in an external oversight role. Each of these roles in the delivery of public goods has a financial aspect.

There are tools we will look at so that managers at all levels within public-sector organizations can effectively spend and account for the resources they are responsible for. These tools include technical information based on accounting principles, program information and control mechanisms to ensure that the funds are being spent, properly monitored, and accounted for.

Funds do not spend themselves. Decisions must be made and actions taken. Procedures must be put in place to make sure that spending happens. Cost controls and the avoidance of over-expenditure through effective management practices are vital aspects of financial management. Effective control requires an understanding of how to build and use financial reports even if you do not do this yourself. It also puts financial management squarely into the realm of human relations, organizational behaviour, interpersonal relations, deal-making, and deal-breaking. It requires a constant eye on the public and political implications of poor management of funds allotted.

Such managerial behaviours are all part of a cycle of control of public funds. The ability to demonstrate, in terms both of procedures and of results, that you are in control of your resources is essential to creating public confidence. Establishing such measures of management control that are consistent with risk, material importance, and clarity go to the heart of both internal and external accountability.

Integral to public-sector management is a continuing cycle of accountability. All public-sector organizations have both internal and external accountability mechanisms to both justify and control their funds. This drives two key elements of public accountability: that funds are expended for the purposes for which they were budgeted, and that the manner in which they are spent follows legal rules set out to avoid fraud or misuse of public monies.

While the issue of control often centres on questions of misuse of funds, it is more complex than that. It also deals with the equitable distribution of funds, the efficacy of the program itself, and the all-important capacity of the public organization to link financial performance with actual program results. Adherence to rules and procedures in the public sector is a guarantee to the public that it can have some confidence in the public-sector entity that holds some part of its trust. Further, there is a reasonable expectation that financial results also bear some connection to program results. Thus, financial management becomes a further part of the greater accountability to deliver on policy objectives.

Accountability also has many internal-to-government dimensions. In measurement and evaluation, the issue of profit and loss is seldom material in assessing the performance of a public-sector institution, but the question of being within budget certainly is.

Financial information becomes of interest for other reasons. For example, the public, or politicians representing them, will often be concerned with the equity issue. Did we get our share? Such debates and interests pervade public discourse. They find their substance in reported financial data.

In that context, financial information often serves as a surrogate for other performance data. Often non-financial performance data are unavailable. The expected program outcomes cannot be readily measured. Many governments do not do a good job of reporting on performance, and financial information is often the clearest data that come forward on a regular basis.

This practice does not mean that financial information presents a full picture.

Although the accounting profession sets high standards for its work, there is also a tendency to treat all financial information as absolute. Think twice about that. The capacity to cook the books is limited by transparency and good audit in the public sector. However, as we shall see, issues of recognition and reporting cycles have to be understood in order to interpret financial information.

This brings us back to policy formulation, where it began in **Figure 0.1.** There is, then, a full circle of elements to financial management in the public sector. The size of the organization and the scope of its activities will dictate the degree to which this circle is complex or simple. Regardless of size, all agencies spend other people's money. They must do so effectively and efficiently and be prepared to answer for it at the end. **Figure 0.3** shows how this book is organized to address the framework topics.

FIGURE 0.3
Organization of the Text

Ch. 1 – Financial Management in the Public Sector	
The Accounting Context	Ch. 2 – Public-Sector Accounting Principles
	Ch. 3 – Financial Statements
	Ch. 4 – Accrual Accounting and Budgeting
The Budgeting Context	Ch. 5 – Budgets: What They Are and What They Do
	Ch. 6 – Planning and Budgeting
	Ch. 7 – Capital Planning and Budgeting
	Ch. 8 – Taking It Back: Reallocation and Budget Cutting
The Implementation Context	Ch. 9 – Managerial Control
	Ch. 10 – Cash Management: In-Year Budget Control and Monitoring
The Accountability Context	Ch. 11 – Confirming Control: Budget Accountability and Reporting

Financial Management People and Organizations

Too often financial management in any organization has been presented as objective and not affected by such matters as politics, power or culture. The reality is that it is very much about all of these things. Resources are managed within the operating culture of the organization. They are subject to all kinds of pressures. In the public sector, pressures include the general public wanting to know about how their taxes are being spent, the client with a program entitlement, the legislative auditor, the senior managers and political leadership of the organization, and the employees within a single unit who want to know if the budget will keep them in work and doing what they feel they are there to do. All have agendas. All interact. All want to affect outcomes.

Similarly, the interpretation of so-called objective information, (e.g., are we under or over our budget projections at the end of the second quarter?) is always open to question and nuance. Within this framework of financial management in the public sector, therefore, lies a recognition that games get played, that interpretations of financial events and decisions vary, and that many tensions are at play. This is a healthy part of financial management, and one that deserves recognition. That is why this text contains sections with such headings as **"The Budget Games that People Play"** as a frank recognition that financial management operates in a rich and human culture.

The internal management of approved budgets receives considerable attention in this text for several reasons. First, little attention has been given to the managerial and organizational skills often needed to manage budgets within the fiscal year. Second, the process of managing a budget effectively is an important managerial skill, involving not just cash projections, but also judgements about how the organization will behave within the year. Third, cash management is where financial and performance information meets organizational culture. Finally, the effective management of the budget plays a large role in ensuring that budget targets are met in terms of being spent effectively for the public good but are not overspent.

It would be impossible to cover fully all forms of financial management practice in all parts of the public sector in Canada. The objective of this text is to develop a broad understanding of the basic assumptions that come into play in managing public resources for both the student and the practitioner. Their applicability in specific circumstances will vary across the spectrum of public-sector organizations, so the examples are chosen to apply to different kinds of organizations.

For those who are not involved in the complexity of accounting processes or whose heads begin to spin when they see a report with charts and numbers, financial management can be frightening. But, as many students have recognized in considering whether or not to take a course in financial management, "This is something I know I have to understand." Indeed, this is true. One of the principal purposes of this text is to demystify financial management for students and public-sector managers. To that end, they do not have to become accountants or other types of financial experts. Rather, they need to understand the framework, see the principles at play, to develop some awareness of them, and in the end, use financial management as another tool of good governance.

Financial management is the application of wisdom, experience, and sound judgement using tools that you often do not fully understand but that, in the end, deliver what you need as a good public servant: the money you need to get the job done and the ability to use that money effectively while keeping yourself and your political masters out of jail, or worse, out of too many appearances before public accounts committees, or the excessive and never (let's be honest here) happy attentions of your external auditors.

To that end, this Introduction will end with a discussion of just what is financial literacy, both in individual and organizational terms.

What is Financial Literacy for the Public Manager? The Answer is a Two-Way Street[5]

"They Just Don't Get It"

In my teaching, as well as my interaction with senior government officials and commentators, I hear that there is a dearth of what they describe as financial literacy when it comes to sound public administration. This manifests itself in a number of ways, often reflecting the biases of the observer. For the senior government executive, there is a frustration that bright policy or operational public servants arrive in positions of responsibility poorly equipped to effectively manage their financial accountabilities. They rely too often on the school of hard knocks to pick up their financial skills. In addition, they fail to take cost and related financial implications into account when they make proposals. Most tellingly in today's focus on budget deficits, they do not focus enough on cost reduction or cost avoidance.

When I teach public servants in our professional program, they often feel uncertain about their financial roles. Many times, they have no clear sense of where their roles begin and those of financial advisors end – not an easy question. They are uncertain about what level of financial expertise they need to get the job done. I can almost hear some of them asking "Am I there yet?" when it comes to understanding their financial role and executing it effectively. The reality, of course, is that they are never fully there as the demands of the work evolve and respond to the changing environment of public-sector financial management.

Too many times has the phrase, "They just don't get it" been applied by senior executives or financial experts to public-sector managers in general. What don't they get? The need for effective financial control. The need to reduce budgets. The need for good costing. The need to find new ways to finance projects. Often these deficiencies in individual managers are identified by the very people responsible for the strategic management of their department or agency.

There certainly is an underlying theme that financial literacy, however defined, is one quality that needs work in many governments. Financial literacy among public servants is vitally important for the effective and efficient delivery of public goods. Why? Because very few policy pronouncements mean much until we know what resources are going to go into making them happen. Further, as governments strive to reduce their overall expenditures, the impacts of changes in policy, delivery and finances become even more linked. We are also seeing a worthy focus on the intergenerational impact of policy decisions. The introduction of full accrual accounting and budgeting has reduced the capacity of government to make announcements today without taking into account the costs in the future.

Finally, public reaction to financial missteps in government creates the notion that public managers cannot manage the funds effectively – to get the work done, efficiently – best bang for the buck and properly – by the rules and with probity. The truth, seldom finding itself onto the headlines page of media websites, is that most government officials do all three quite effectively. However, we cannot be naïve. These scandals raise again, in a different way, the question of what is enough financial literacy and "Are we there yet?"

But, is there a "there"? I am not sure that we could collectively agree on what financial literacy actually is and, even more daunting, when we have it. What I would like to do is offer some ideas about what financial literacy actually

is for the public manager. My conclusion, however, is that financial literacy will only be achieved when we realize that it is a two-way street. To have a financially literate manager, you need a financially literate organization. This is more than just a matter of personal skills and training. In fact, it takes leadership and good governance too. So, for those top managers complaining about the financial prowess of their managers, tend to your own role in all this. More to follow. It would seem that if financial literacy is missing in some governments, yet abounds in others, the question has to go back to the executives and experts – what are you doing about it, then?

The Financially Literate Manager

However, too much mystery surrounds this question. Financial literacy is not magic, just work. It certainly does not mean that line managers have to become financial experts. But they do have to become informed users of financial information, not just when it arrives as a regular report in their e-mail or on the department's website, but throughout the policy and delivery processes.

Here are some of the characteristics of a financially literate public-sector manager. He or she:

- understands how policy, delivery and costs are linked;
- can identify the key assumptions behind numbers and link them to the policy or to the delivery environment;
- applies a full life-cycle and secondary cost lens to recommendations;
- can identify and, with experience, anticipate the cost impacts of events, changes, or those many small decisions that get made on a daily basis;
- is aware of the financial framework within which his or her unit is working – budget limitations, opportunities, strategic directions;
- understands his or her own budget, the components, the anticipated outputs it should produce, and how those numbers relate to the public policy good they are working to achieve;
- can read and interpret well presented financial reports and recognize badly produced reports;
- can identify the kind of financial information he or she may need on a regular basis – generally built up over time and with inevitable trial and error – to do his or her job; and
- understands the necessary limitations and process requirements of financial practice, be it in procurement, in delegations, and in that very important area: financial probity.

At a practical level, an effective public manager needs to be able to:

- **Understand the lingo:** Some core terminology is essential. However, much of this terminology may have nuanced meaning in the particular operating culture of one organization.
- **Understand costs:** Managers have to spend time developing an understanding of cost factors in their operations. They have to understand the implications on their costs of changes to policy or practice. Even a tweak in procedure can have an impact on virtually any cost element. A minor policy shift seldom comes free of cost. A financially literate manager or policy advisor will understand this and try to determine the cost implications
- **Read the reports:** This is best translated as being an intelligent user of financial information, be it costing for policy design or cash forecasts for the first quarter of the fiscal year.
- **Get clarity:** This may mean asking dumb questions. It may also mean pushing the point of understanding so that everyone is actually talking about the same thing. Financial advisors play a key role in developing this understanding and ensuring that there is, in reality, no such thing as a dumb question.
- **Marry up numbers on a page with what happens at the mission end of the organization:** A financially literate manager can see the link – or insist that it be clearly stated – between what may be for some just a bunch of numbers and the policy and operational impact.

What About the Financially Literate Organization?

There is a simple reality that only seems to present itself when things go wrong. You can have all the most financially literate people working for you but your organization itself does not act in a way that is financially literate. I do not mean corrupt, although that is a possible outcome of this deficiency. More often, it translates itself into managers saying: "Why bother? No one takes this financial stuff into account at the top. They are all policy wonks." Or "Who cares? It's all arbitrary and no amount of good control at our level will make any difference."

As I noted at the outset, I have heard too many senior managers bemoan the poor quality of financial savvy they see in their reports without also talking about their own behaviour. Financial literacy is both personal and organizational. One depends on the other. Go back to the "they just don't get it" mentality, which blames others for failing to appreciate the importance of public finances in policy and operational decisions. People pay attention to what their bosses pay attention to. Therefore, an organization without a culture that respects the financial side of the public good process – policy and execution – will never get it. Further, it is incumbent upon those organizations to set up elements of their governance that do the same. The organization must become financially literate.

Therefore, a financially literate organization is one that:

- works hard to ensure integrated approaches to policy and delivery that takes into account costs and related financial implications;
- establishes decision-making bodies that regularly review financial performance;
- develops means to communicate financial information widely throughout the organization;
- makes financial literacy a core competency in developing its staff;
- links financial performance to overall performance on objectives;
- ensures that financial advisors are on the team, that their work is integrated, and that they too are held to account for achieving the organization's mission; and
- works hard to train managers and upcoming staff on financial issues.

Financial Literacy is a Systemic Quality

Perhaps the final point with respect to the search for financial literacy is that it is not a matter of having finance for non-financial managers training. The reality is that financial literacy means that financial matters are integrated into policy design and delivery. This is everyone's responsibility. This is not to denigrate such training, but the issue is a bit bigger than that. Well-trained line managers need to be supported by financial advisors who also get it with respect to the link between policy and finances, and the need for useful and relevant financial information. These same managers need to know that being financially literate also means there is governance in place that actually uses the financial information and makes decisions based on it.

In the end, financial literacy is both personal and organizational. It is also both technique and art. Very few line managers aspire to be financial managers. But the reality is that they all are in modern terms. However, it is only through time and practice that an individual can be said to be financially literate.

I am offering a small checklist of questions that managers and their organizations can ask themselves. It may not fully answer the question "Are we there yet?" but might help with the trip.

Financial Literacy Checklist

For the Public Servant

- Do I understand the basis for our financial statements: accrual accounting, our external financial statements, funding sources, financing options?
- Do I understand what things cost? Can I apply adequate cost sensitivity analysis to possible changes in costs and predict their outcome?
- Do I understand how budgets are formulated where I work?
- Do I receive timely information on my financial performance in-year so that I can make adjustments and reallocate resources?
- Do I understand what resources I rely upon to get my job done but do not control?
- Am I aware of, and capable of, effectively using our procurement processes?
- Do I regularly include costs in proposals for change?
- Am I engaging with my financial advisor and is that person meeting my needs?
- Are the financial statements I see clear to me? Do they relate to what I do?
- If I have delegated authority, do I understand how I am to exercise it?
- Do I know the main operational and financial risks we are facing?
- Do I understand key financial concepts such as control, materiality?

- Do I link my responsibilities to the government's fiscal situation?

For the Public Organization

- Is there an effective integration of the financial functions into the policy, operations and decision-making activities of the organization?
- Do we as an organization generally understand the financial impact of the policy and execution decisions we make or recommend?
- Are costs well integrated into policy proposals that we consider?
- Do we provide good financial advice to the minister/council/board?
- Does the finance function contribute effective expertise and support to these activities?
- Do we do a good job of full costing of policy ideas?
- Do we have a good understanding of the costs of our operations and where there are cost sensitivities?
- Do we produce high quality financial information?
- Do we regularly review financial performance?
- Does our top management demonstrably lead this review process?
- Is the way we make decisions about budgets, cost proposals and in-year budget variance clearly understood within the organization?
- Do we reward good financial management? Is it part of the suite of key performance indicators for our managers?
- Do we assess our organizational financial performance?
- Do we link our financial information with our performance information?
- Is there a common financial management training package in place for our staff?

Chapter 1
Financial Management in the Public Sector

Chapter Objectives:

- Defining and describing the public sector in Canada
- Understanding the complexity of delivery of public-sector services and programs
- Understanding the scope of public-sector financial activity
- Outlining the unique characteristics of financial management in the public sector

Scope and Nature of the Public Sector

The public sector in Canada plays many roles in our lives. While the appropriate overall size of government is always the subject of political debate, it has remained relatively stable in Canada over a long period of time, even with fluctuations in roles and responsibilities of different levels of government. As various waves of reform have passed through public administration, new forms of agencies, commissions, and public corporations have arisen, all different to some extent, but all under this large umbrella we call the public sector. Financial management has had to keep up to ensure that public funds remain just that and are accounted for in a transparent way.

For the purposes of this text, the term public sector is used in a broad sense. It encompasses:

- **Government:** federal, provincial, territorial, and municipal;
- **Government Enterprises:** Crown corporations, legislative agencies, special operating arrangements, usually with a line of accountability to a political leader, be it a minister or mayor; and
- **Broader Public Sector:** hospitals, schools and universities that derive most of their revenue from government, serve broad public objectives, and are supervised by law, regulation and active oversight by government.

While this definition describes the *scope* of the public sector, we also have to focus on the *nature* of the public sector. One approach is to say that it is not the private sector, i.e., businesses and privately owned firms, which has the unfortunate tendency of leading to a description of what the public sector does not have: profit motive, shareholders, etc. This can make the public sector look somewhat deficient in how it is structured and, in particular, how it approaches the management of its financial resources. One off-hand and generally inaccurate criticism of public-sector organizations is that the public sector has no regard for the bottom line. The bottom line referred to here is the net profit or loss that drives most private-sector firms. This is expressed in purely financial terms: who is making money, and who is not?

The simple truth is that the public sector does not indeed have a single bottom line.[1] It has several, all being pursued at once. **Figure 1.1** outlines the multiple bottom lines of government. Government does have to manage funds within budget constraints and be measured against such criteria as probity in expenditures, adherence to budgetary discipline, and compliance with financial laws. It is measured also on the results it achieves in non-financial terms. Often these are expressed as policy outcomes. At times, they are process outcomes (e.g., how many applications were reviewed and cleared?). There are also equity outcomes (e.g., did all those eligible receive their due?). There are also broader, social outcomes (e.g., was poverty reduced in this segment of society?).

FIGURE 1.1
Public-Sector Bottom Lines

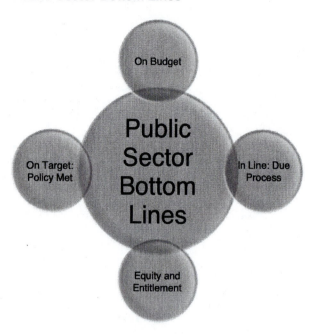

Simplistic comparisons between the private and public sector are dangerous. Contrary to news headlines and clichéd perspectives, the public sector is far more complicated and difficult to manage than the private sector. The end result of public-sector activities can be varied and, at times, conflicting. Results are not always clearly articulated as governments pursue public policy goals in attempts to achieve a measure of consensus, thereby leaving open or vague the actual results to be aimed for. These goals are subject to continuous scrutiny and debate. Attributing responsibility for results can be difficult because it is often shared among many players. So, too, is blame when things go wrong.

How important is it to make a distinction between the public and private sectors? In terms of financial management, this distinction is very important. There are unique features in the public sector that will affect how resources are accounted for and managed, and how accountability is ultimately discharged. It is erroneous to think that these distinctions are starkly drawn or that financial-management experience in the private sector has no relevance in the public sector. For instance, many volunteer organizations operate as if they were profit-and-loss entities, with cash flows (from fundraising, endowments, or fees charged for services) that dictate the scope of their activities in a similar way to firms that

are fully revenue-dependent. While their objectives are public in a broad sense, they can act like private organizations from a money-management perspective. They simply do not have a profit motive.

Similarly, many Crown corporations or special agencies of provincial governments are deliberately created by their governments to act on a commercial basis, even though ownership is retained by the government that created them. In many cases, they receive no direct funding from public sources. Their sources of funds are referred to as off-budget (that is, they are not provided in appropriations voted by the authorized legislature). They rely entirely on their own revenues arising from their operations. Their accounting systems therefore closely resemble those in the private sector.

The areas in which the public and private sectors are similar, and the public sector draws on private practices, are accounting systems (notably large computerized financial systems), planning and budgetary tools, increasingly sophisticated financial management, and enterprise management systems (EMS).[2] The public sector is becoming more sophisticated in its financial management, generally following private-sector practices. Similarly, in accounting and budgeting systems, the public sector has now adopted for the most part the accrual basis for accounting (see Chapter 4), a practice that has been common in the private sector for more than a century.

Size of Canada's Public Sector

There is no single number that adequately quantifies the public sector in Canada, especially in view of the considerable debate about what is considered public sector.

One significant methodological issue is where to position the health and education sectors. For its purposes, Statistics Canada lists health and social service institutions, as well as universities, colleges, and vocational and trade institutions as part of government.[3] This is described as the broader public sector. This is valid because most of the funding for these functions comes from government. In addition, most health and educational facilities are undoubtedly publicly owned and governed. On the other hand, figures for the health and education sectors are also listed in Statistics Canada's information on the voluntary sector.[4] For our purposes, sorting out these methodological problems is not as important as an understanding of its relative extent and scope.

Employment: The Government Side of the Public Sector

Figure 1.2 shows data from Statistics Canada on employment in the public sector across Canada at the federal, provincial, and local levels.

The number employed is considerable. So, too, is the income earned by public servants. In itself, public service employment represents a major economic and distributional reality in this country. See **Figure 1.3** below.

The Real Extent of Public-Sector Employment

It has already been noted how difficult it is to arrive at a full picture of public-sector employment in Canada. The information outlined above speaks only to direct government employment. By that, we mean the employment of individuals by governments, hospitals, educational facilities, and government enterprises within the normal definition of government. The reality is that many jobs in the voluntary and private sectors depend entirely on government funds.

FIGURE 1.2
Public-Sector Employment, Wages, and Salaries

	2007	2008	2009	2010	2011
	Employment (persons)				
Public sector	**3,383,821**	**3,493,580**	**3,563,406**	**3,609,274**	**3,631,837**
Government	3,090,234	3,183,310	3,248,253	3,294,159	3,313,320
Federal general government*	387,121	400,196	415,397	420,685	427,093
Provincial and territorial general government	352,931	361,988	358,461	358,237	356,709
Health and social service institutions, provincial and territorial	783,142	800,200	822,904	844,762	859,350
Universities, colleges, vocational and trade institutions, provincial and territorial	358,138	365,137	374,745	387,056	382,245
Local general government	548,298	581,221	596,144	605,562	608,094
Local school boards	660,603	674,568	680,603	677,857	679,828
Government business enterprises	293,587	310,270	315,154	315,114	318,519
Federal government business enterprises	99,121	104,864	104,692	104,042	102,319
Provincial and territorial government business enterprises	135,876	144,779	147,616	145,616	147,914
Local government business enterprises	58,589	60,627	62,845	65,456	68,286

Notes:

Employment data are not in full-time equivalent and do not distinguish between full-time and part-time employees. Includes employees both in and outside of Canada.

As at December 31.

*Federal general government data includes reservists and full-time military personnel.

Source: Statistics Canada, CANSIM, table 183-0002.

Last modified: 2012-05-30.

Highlights to Note:

- The federal government, although the single largest employer, is small in relation to other levels of government.
- The health and education sectors are huge – and growing.

FIGURE 1.3
Public-Sector Earnings, 2011

	Employment	Wages and salaries
	persons	$ thousands
Public sector	**3,631,837**	**194,193,338**
Government	3,313,320	174,195,018
Federal general government	427,093	31,103,207
Provincial and territorial general government	356,709	23,198,296
Health and social service institutions, provincial and territorial	859,350	45,172,690
Universities, colleges, vocational and trade institutions, provincial and territorial	382,245	19,846,260
Local general government	608,094	21,161,298
Local school boards	679,828	33,713,366
Government business enterprises	318,519	19,998,322
Federal government business enterprises	102,319	5,349,386
Provincial and territorial government business enterprises	147,914	10,667,874
Local government business enterprises	68,286	3,981,059

Governments contract for many services, supplies and infrastructure. Many Canadians who see themselves as working for a business are actually dependent on public funds through such contracts.

This is also true for most other countries. As Paul C. Light pointed out in a 1999 paper for the Brookings Institution,[5] there exists, in the American context, a shadow government – employees working in private firms under government contracts or through grants to non-governmental voluntary agencies. The same is true for Canada.

Light's study, which has been updated regularly, most recently in August 2006, estimated that, while the federal government of the United States would report the number of employees as 1.9 million, the actual number employed in other federal organizations such as the armed forces and the postal service as well as those employed by third-party contractors was actually more than 16 million. This estimate was based on Professor Light's research, not official calculations. In fact, it would be nearly impossible to gather the information to arrive at a firm figure. In Canadian terms, no research of this kind has been undertaken, although some interesting extrapolations are possible. A good example of the extent of this scope is the relative dependence of the voluntary sector on government

FIGURE 1.4
Voluntary-Sector Dependence on Government Funding

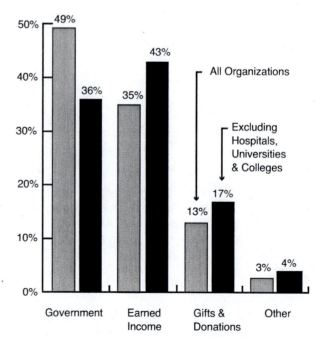

Source: Imagine Canada, available at http://library.imaginecanada.ca/sector_research/statistics/nsnvo.

funding, be it through direct contribution or, as is more often the case these days, through conditional contracts. **Imagine Canada,** a national advocacy group for the volunteer sector, published information (**Figure 1.4**) showing sources of funds for the sector.

Implications of Contracting in the Public Sector

All modern governments use contracts extensively to obtain goods and services, a practice that creates employment in both the private and nonprofit sectors. Although information about the extent of that employment is not gathered in a systematic fashion in this country, some governments do report on their contracting activities. For instance, the **Public Accounts of Canada**, an annual report of the Government of Canada of all its financial transactions, including the consolidated financial statement, summarized the federal government's buying activity in **Figure 1.5**.

The expenditure of over $17 billion in any budget is considerable. In many instances, the contracts involve the employment of people doing work for the government. They may not be public servants, but they are doing public work. Similarly, this contracted work does not mean that the regular public service is relieved of all work associated with these services. Taken in the context of an operating budget for the federal government during that period of approximately $60 billion, this is a significant portion of government expenditure.

The employment impact of public-sector expenditures goes well beyond the employment of public servants. Governments use contracting as a means of acquiring expertise, outsourcing work, or extending their workforces while appearing to contain the growth of the public service. In doing so, governments gain many advantages. They obtain expertise that it would be difficult to develop or pay for within traditional bureaucratic structures. They also obtain goods that the private sector is better equipped to build and provide to government. In addition, they avoid long-term employment commitments when their need is for shorter-term delivery of specialized services.

On the other hand, governments also have to manage and account for contracts. They must be able to financially monitor and account for the costs of contracts, their effectiveness, and their compliance with requirements. Governments must also manage and operate a publicly accessible bidding system, fairly weigh competing bids, and then administer contracts, often managing complex contractual relationships for large projects with high risk. This generally is done in-house as part of the cost of doing

FIGURE 1.5
Federal Government Purchases of Service, Lands, and Equipment for 2010–2011

Professional and Legal Services

Business services	1,848,244,748
Engineering and architectural	2,409,207,413
Health and welfare	1,179,680,479
Informatics	1,066,736,206
Interpretation services	260,701,763
Legal services	486,893,818
Management consulting	526,026,061
Protection services	390,509,263
Scientific and research	373,459,032
Special fees and services	92,211,764
Temporary help	229818,,599
Training and education	441,311,892
Other services	1,443,724,525
Total professional services	**10,694,525,523**

Acquisition of Buildings, Lands and Services

Land purchases	52,382,459
Engineering works	2,185,688,877
Buildings – non residential	1,018,416,081
Buildings – residential	30,055,713
Total land and buildings	**1,319,543,130**

Acquisition of Machinery and Equipment

Transportation	2,017.631,025
Weapons	569,747,120
Communications	242,052,503
Computers and related	1,024,193,459
Specialized equipment	542,437,467
Furniture	176,076,660
Industrial machinery	35,785,178
Other office (non computer)	26,017,840
Other equipment	454,571,397
Total machinery and equipment	**5,088,512,649**

Total purchases of services, property and equipment	**17,102,581,302**

Note: These figures, available in the Public Accounts of Canada, 2011–12, report only purchases above $10,000.

Source: Public Accounts of Canada, 2012, available at http://www.pwgsc .gc.ca/recgen/pdf/v3pa05-e.pdf.

Highlights to Note:

- The high level of use of engineering and architectural services reflects the difficulties governments have in maintaining "in-house" expertise.

- These are not figures for "outsourcing" of government services to the private sector. While they represent contracting for only one year, there has been a long history of governments buying services, in particular, highly specialized ones that they cannot create themselves in an economic or efficient way.

business. Ensuring a full accounting for the legitimate use of the funds expended is of major importance. So, too, is the need for effective cost controls and risk containment, especially for major capital projects such as new information systems, which tend to demand considerable funding. This is why the use of the term contracting out is so ill advised. Governments, when they administer contracts, assume an array of responsibilities as outlined above. They do, in that process, relieve themselves of any responsibility for the final outcome.

Contracting for goods and services is but one example of how financial management within the public sector is becoming more complex. As Lester Salamon, in *The Tools of Government,* points out when speaking of the various tools for delivering government programs:

> Indirect tools paradoxically require advance planning of far more operational details than is the case with more direct tools … all of this requires new processes and new skills that differ considerably from those of traditional government management.[6]

That is, the various tools of public goods delivery in no way reduce the demand for effective financial management. In fact, they increase it.

Salamon[7] has identified a series of tools of public policy and service delivery. He defines a tool of public action as "an identifiable method through which collective action is structured to address a public problem."[8] Using his tools approach, he identifies a range of common tools and then, through the collaborative efforts of an impressive range of contributors, subjects each to a structured and detailed analysis. The tools examined are the following:

- Direct government
- Social regulation
- Economic regulation
- Contracting
- Grant
- Direct loan
- Loan guarantee
- Insurance
- Tax expenditure
- Fees, charges
- Liability law
- Government corporations
- Vouchers.

He concludes that, while discretion and flexibility in delivering services are important elements in a shift towards indirect government, government remains accountable for both the policy and delivery of such services:

How to square these new approaches with the more traditional procedural safeguards of administrative law, however, is still far from settled, leaving administrators and courts alike significantly adrift.[9]

It can be argued, however, that administrators are not adrift or without guidance, especially when it comes to their financial responsibilities in an era that emphasizes delivery options. In circumstances where delivery is distributed, the potential for fraud and misuse of funds increases. Greater scrutiny is therefore prudent. Similarly, administrators have to understand the financial records and statements of the various delivery agents in order to assure themselves that they are receiving fair representation in financial reporting. What this era is creating is the need for public managers with financial responsibilities to be more nimble and possess what has been called financial savvy, a topic that we will address later in this book. Therefore, as a review of financial management in the public sector proceeds, it must do so in a fully modern context. It cannot focus strictly on traditional budgetary, financial-management, and accountability models associated with direct government action. Even though the *form* of the public service may differ, the essential *requirements and characteristics* – which demand close scrutiny of public funds, probity in their use, and the capacity to account for the funds, to trace their use, and to assess the impact of that use – remain the same.

Expenditures and Revenues: Government Sector

Measuring the amount of money that governments spend is fairly straightforward. The public accounts and summary financial statements of virtually all governments are readily available, and Statistics Canada provides this material in both graphic and tabular form. The full impact is only fully understood when we look at all governments, their agencies and the broader public sector. The provinces, territorial and local governments combined actually spend more money than the federal government. The health care sector is huge. In addition, in Canada, one has to take into account the impact of intergovernmental fiscal transfers. These are funds, in the form of either general grants or program-specific grants, that are transferred from one level of government to another.

Figure 1.6 outlines the scope and sources of governmental expenditures and revenues from fiscal years 2005–2009. Since this chart covers all governmental activities at all levels of government, it is difficult at times to determine from it which level is spending what amounts. Charts that

FIGURE 1.6
The Scope of All Government Expenditures and Revenues in Canada

Consolidated government revenue and expenditures
(Expenditures and surplus or deficit)

	2005	2006	2007	2008	2009
	\$ millions				
Total expenditures	**516,576**	**547,465**	**578,174**	**616,090**	**631,251**
General government services	18,792	20,074	20,857	21,505	22,822
Protection of persons and property	41,096	43,299	46,396	50,689	50,790
Transportation and communication	21,172	24,838	26,280	29,966	32,197
Health	94,497	99,531	107,497	114,245	121,577
Social services	156,762	164,568	174,290	187,734	190,276
Education	77,140	84,760	87,455	92,722	95,732
Resource conservation and industrial development	18,652	19,760	21,078	21,360	19,975
Environment	11,903	13,158	14,420	15,516	16,933
Recreation and culture	13,476	14,268	15,008	15,809	16,306
Labour, employment and immigration	2,328	2,480	2,619	2,917	2,395
Housing	3,880	4,527	4,942	5,544	6,120
Foreign affairs and international assistance	5,556	5,585	6,500	6,211	6,508
Regional planning and development	2,057	2,235	2,338	2,524	2,775
Research establishments	1,823	1,859	2,023	2,332	2,268
General purpose transfers	0	..	..	..	..
Debt charges	45,506	44,784	45,578	45,715	43,634
Other expenditures	1,935	1,738	894	1,303	945
Surplus	**21,689**	**26,107**	**26,418**	**31,461**	**2,421**

Consolidated government revenue and expenditures
(Revenue)

	2005	2006	2007	2008	2009
Total revenue	**538,265**	**573,572**	**604,592**	**647,552**	**633,672**
Own source revenue	538,265	573,572	604,592	647,552	633,672
Income taxes	207,415	225,158	245,867	269,467	248,655
Consumption taxes	104,495	107,857	105,809	111,684	107,150
Property and related taxes	46,721	49,509	51,277	53,882	54,862
Other taxes	18,018	18,917	20,489	21,129	21,807
Health and drug insurance premiums	3,206	3,258	3,268	3,457	3,390
Contributions to social security plans	69,039	71,532	74,697	77,740	80,010
Sales of goods and services	40,822	42,966	44,913	49,685	53,168
Investment income	40,525	47,544	50,122	52,436	57,793
Other revenue from own sources	8,022	6,830	8,151	8,070	6,836
General purpose transfers	0	0	0	0	0
Specific purpose transfers	0	0	0	..	..

Note: Data for the consolidated, federal, provincial and territorial governments are as at March 31 and the local government data are at December 31.

.. : not available for a specific period of time.

Source: Statistics Canada, CANSIM, table 385-0001.

Last modified: 2009-08-31.

break this down to provide such information are available through Statistics Canada's website, although some overall factors relevant to financial management bear consideration. The point here is to look at the cumulative impact.

In Canada there is a poor match between actual spending responsibilities and the ability to raise funds within a specific level of government, and between governments as well. While the federal government has certain spending requirements, it has taxation capacity well beyond those requirements. At the other extreme, local governments generally have very limited and inflexible taxation powers, using mainly property taxation, while growth of their costs has been much the same as in other levels of government. In Canada, this is referred to as the fiscal imbalance.[10] Governments dispute the extent of this imbalance, and some even suggest it does not exist. It is not surprising that it is the government with the greatest revenue flexibility – the federal government – that minimizes this issue. The ones with the least flexibility, notably the provinces and local governments, are most likely to advance such claims.

In reality, while taxation jurisdictions may be shared, the federal government has control over the most profitable taxes. Provinces are loath to raise personal and corporate taxes because of the potential political consequences even though they can. On the other hand, provinces have access to natural resource royalties that can, in robust economic times, bring high yields. As one way to meet some of the shortfalls in provincial needs, but still retain the power to tax, the federal government uses its taxation ability to effect policy objectives through specific grants to provinces for program purposes. It also has established a system of equalization payments for provinces to create a level playing field for basic services across the country.

The result of a complex series of policy negotiations involving both equalization and program-specific transfers is that a significant portion of the federal government's budget involves the movement of monies to the provinces. The trend in this movement is shown in **Figure 1.7**.

A federal tax transfer involves the federal government ceding some of its tax room to provincial governments. Specifically, a tax transfer occurs when the federal government reduces its tax rates to allow provinces to raise their tax rates by an equivalent amount. With a tax transfer, the changes in federal and provincial tax rates offset one another and there is no net financial impact on the taxpayer.

The distribution of federal government transfers in **Figure 1.8** also shows how policy direction and priorities can be set by means of such transfers.

From a financial management perspective, this movement represents interesting accounting challenges. For every transfer from one level of government, the financial statements record an expenditure. For the same transfer at the receiving end, the financial statements of the other government must record a revenue. How this is done will reflect the conditions associated with such transfers and the need to be able to follow the movement of that money. In some cases – equalization, for instance – provinces receive funds into general revenue and are not required to distinguish its use from any other revenue source, i.e., the money goes into the consolidated revenue fund of the province. In others, where program-specific conditions apply, a more detailed accounting to ensure that the funds were spent for the purposes agreed upon may be necessary.

A Closer Look at Government Expenditures

Figure 1.8 presents the distribution of expenditures at each level of government in chart form. For more detailed information, one has to go to each government for either its budget or its public accounts.

What Makes Financial Management Different and Important in the Public Sector?

This brief survey of the extent of financial activity in the public sector shows how complex and varied it can be. It also shows the importance of managing these funds well. Public services range from national defence to disaster management to sustaining historical locations to providing meals on wheels to senior citizens. Similarly, the organizational structures to deliver those services also vary dramatically. It would be a mistake to think of the traditional government sector with specialized departments or ministries as the sole image of the public sector.

This section sets out in this context what is unique about the public sector and, for the purposes of this text, what impact that will have on the management of financial resources. The Canadian Institute of Chartered Accountants (CICA) *Public Sector Accounting Handbook*, created and maintained by Canada's premier accounting standard-setting body, the Public Service Accounting Board, provides some useful ways of looking at financial management in the public sector. So, too, does its international equivalent, the IFAC, the International Federation of Accountants. They each have set out what they feel are the key characteristics of public sector entities. What follow is a distillation of their work, with some discussion of their implications, strictly from the perspective of the author.[11]

FIGURE 1.7
Federal Support to Provinces and Territories

	2005–06	2006–07	2007–08	2008–09	2009–10	2010–11	2011–12	2012–13
				(millions of dollars)				
Major Transfers								
Canada Health Transfer[a]	*20,310*	20,140	21,729	22,768	23,987	25,426	26,952	28,569
Canada Social Transfer[a]	*8,415*	8,500	9,857	10,560	10,865	11,186	11,522	11,861
Children			*1,100*	*1,100*	*1,133*	*1,167*	*1,202*	*1,238*
Post-Secondary Education			*2,435*	*3,235*	*3,332*	*3,432*	*3,535*	*3,641*
Social Programs			*6,202*	*6,202*	*6,388*	*6,579*	*6,777*	*6,980*
Equalization[b]	*10,907*	11,535	12,925	13,462	14,185	14,372	14,659	15,423
Offshore Accords[c]	*219*	386	563	663	645	869	787	458
Territorial Formula Financing[d]	*2,058*	2,118	2,279	2,313	2,498	2,664	2,876	3,111
Other Payments[e]					563	668	952	680
Subtotal	*41,909*	42,680	47,352	49,765	52,743	55,185	57,747	60,101
Change from 2005–06		+771	+5,443	+7,856	+10,835	+13,276	+15,838	+18,192
Direct Targeted Support								
Labour Market Training Funding				500	500	500	500	500
Wait Times Reduction	625	1,200	1,200	600	250	250	250	250
Subtotal	**625**	**1,200**	**1,200**	**1,100**	**750**	**750**	**750**	**750**
Total – Federal Support	**42,534**	**43,880**	**48,552**	**50,865**	**53,494**	**55,935**	**58,497**	**60,851**
Per Capita Allocation (dollars)	*1,321*	*1,348*	*1,476*	*1,529*	*1,588*	*1,641*	*1,698*	*1,747*

See explanatory notes.

[a] CHT/CST include transition protection payments as of 2007–08. CST also includes $31.9 million from Budget 2008 transition protection payments to Saskatchewan and Nunavut notionally allocated over five and three years respectively beginning in 2008–09.

[b] Includes payments and additional amounts. Also includes 2009–10 transitional Equalization protection to Nova Scotia and Manitoba. From 2007–08 onward, reflects the 2007 formula for all provinces except Newfoundland and Labrador (NL) which remained under the previous Equalization formula until 2010–11, when NL made the election to enter into the 2007 Equalization formula.

[c] Includes cash amounts from the 1985 and 1986 Accords and cash and notional amounts from the 2005 Accords. Also includes $83 million in 2011–12 and $312 million in 2012–13 in cumulative best-of payments to Nova Scotia.

[d] Includes payments, additional amounts and data revisions.

[e] Other payments include the 2009–10 transition adjustment payment to Nova Scotia ($74 million), the separate payments to Ontario for 2009–10 ($489 million) and for 2010–11 ($142 million) to ensure it receives the same per capita CHT cash support as other Equalization-receiving provinces.

Other payments also include Total Transfer Protection (TTP) provided in 2010–11 ($525 million), 2011–12 ($952 million) and 2012–13 ($680 million) ensuring that a province's total major transfers in one of these years are no lower than in the prior year. For the purpose of calculating TTP, total major transfers comprise Equalization, CHT, CST and prior year TTP. One-time recoverable payments to Ontario ($150 million) and Prince Edward Island ($1 million) for 2011–12 not included.

FIGURE 1.8
Expenditure Distribution by Government

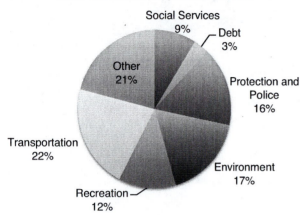

Local Government Expenditures: 2009

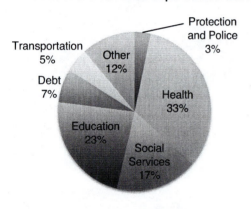

Provincial and Territorial Expenditures: 2009

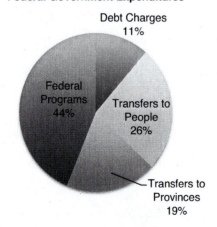

Federal Government Expenditures

*Governments Serve Multiple Objectives and
Not Only the Profit Motive*

The first element is the explicit absence of a profit motive and the attribution of the public good motive. There is a distinction to be drawn between making a profit and earning money to fund programs. The essence of this distinction is that the profit, while readily defined as the excess of earnings over costs and therefore applicable in many public sector organizations, goes to shareholders or owners of the organizations for their private purposes. Whatever a private enterprise does, its first objective is to be profitable. Public-sector profits (often called margin) are returned to the consolidated revenue fund of the government or held in specialized reserves, to be used strictly for some public purpose, not personal gain. Just occasionally, they are returned to the taxpayers by way of reductions in taxes or fees.

This defining element sets out the purpose of the organization itself. While it is difficult to generalize, most public sector organizations exist to meet one or all of the following objectives:

- **To achieve a public good.** A public good is one that applies to all citizens or those included in the mandate of the entity. Further, it is often indivisible among individuals as consumers but applicable to society as a whole, e.g., public safety, fairness, defence. The concept of what should be considered a public good is legitimately open to political debate, but the key point here is that the raison d'être of many public entities is to provide such things as policies and regulations designed to achieve a public good.
- **Broadly speaking, public-sector organizations are measured by the achievement of their goals, not the profit they make.** In fact, many public-sector organizations that failed to spend their budgets have faced criticism from some part of society that felt that needs were left unmet or the organization was deficient in delivering on its objectives.
- **To provide goods and services to the public or to special categories of the public.** The range of these within the public sector is impressive. Which goods and services are delivered in the private sector, and which are provided in the public sector, is a matter of political ideology. Health care, for example, is treated by Canada as a public good, while the United States sees it as a mixed good with both public and private elements. More careful examination will show that this distinction is really a matter of degree, not an absolute one. For instance, in Canada, many health-

related services, such as most dental services, are not public at all. Similarly, most family doctors are private operators who happen to derive most of their income from public insurance.

- **To redistribute wealth.** There are different ways of doing so, from social assistance to intergovernmental transfers based on equalization formulae. The degree of redistribution is subject to political decisions deriving from varying views of the state and its role. However, redistribution is not simply a matter of transferring from the rich to the poor. It can also be regional and collective in its nature. For instance, major economic stimulus packages have an important element of redistribution.

Governments Bear a Wide Range of Risk

It can be argued that governments are the holders of a vast array of residual risks that cannot be assumed by others or insured against. This would include natural disasters, economic swings and, increasingly, acts of terrorism of an unforeseen nature. Therefore, even with the best of plans and budgets, governments may have to intervene with resources in short order, drawing upon their vast capacity to do so, but remaining answerable for the use of those resources after their mobilization.

With Great Power Comes Higher Levels of Accountability

All government entities derive their power to act as well as responsibility to do so from an elected authority. Even government agencies, often created to operate at arm's length from normal government operations and possibly in a quasi-commercial manner, have a line that goes back to the act, regulation or order that created it. However, with that power and responsibility comes great accountability. Public resources are being used. These come from the citizens. A myriad of legislated requirements, financial and operational reporting standards, openness to scrutiny by the public and elected officials, ensure that there is a high standard of accountability in the public sector. This highlights the importance of sound financial reporting as part of that infrastructure.

It is also one of those elements of financial management in the public sector that moulds the character and nature of that management. Accountability, as will be discussed in Chapter 10, is diverse and multi-layered. On the financial side there are a number of types of accountability for funds:

- **Public Policy:** Are they spent for an appropriate use?

- **Allocation:** Are funds allocated for the stated purpose?
- **Process:** Are the funds spent according to the rules that apply?
- **Equity:** Are funds distributed fairly and equitably?
- **Outputs or Outcomes:** Did the funds achieve the intended results?
- **Accounting:** Can the funds be traced and identified?
- **Efficiency:** Were the funds spent in the lowest-cost way?
- **External Review or Audit:** Can others assess the financial information of the organization?

Government Financial Management Operations Are Governed by Legislation

This means much more than the fact that all organizations must obey the law. For the most part, at all levels of government and well extended into what is known as the broader public sector (hospitals, school boards, government agencies), the form and substance of how all elements of financial management will be carried are governed by legislated and regulated formatting, reporting and standards requirements. Compliance must be not only to the objectives of the public expenditure, but to requirements of form designed to assure transparency and fairness.

The Importance of the Budget

As we will see in subsequent chapters, a budget is a plan for expenditure and revenues in a future period. However, in the public sector, it takes on a much higher level of significance than in the private sector. It is a key tool for financial management and control. Its approval by the legislature or council represents the authority by public organizations to spend. It also represents a firm limit on what can be spent. It serves as the first point of accountability. Did the entity remain within its budget? Did it spend the money for the purposes voted? These are simple but key questions of public-sector accountability.

Lack of Equity Ownership/Reality of Collective Ownership

Public-sector organizations do not act in a way to render profit to individual owners or to grow their enterprises for the benefit of individuals. Rather, they manage their resources, received either from such collective revenue sources as taxation or through legislative authority to charge rates or collect fees. In turn, they use them for the public good, not the individual benefit of a shareholder.

Most Governments' Tangible Capital Assets Are Different in Nature than Those Held by a Business

In general, public-sector organizations do not build or acquire capital assets to improve their income flow at some later date or to convert to cash in the future. They own capital assets, which can be considerable, in order to deliver services or to meet the public-good objectives that they want to achieve.

Government Capital Spending Will Focus on a Range of Policy Benefits Rather than Only the Efficiency of the Operation or Lowest Cost

The *CICA Handbook* makes the simple point that the end product of most capital expenditure in the public sector is not financial; that is, it is not to increase earnings and, hopefully, profits. This means, for instance, that the return-on-investment model of assessing capital projects can be a limited tool in the public sector. That does not mean that such models cannot and should not be used, especially in the project-planning phase and where an income flow may derive from the building of the asset. But, as with many ways of assessing government spending, it is very seldom that a single measure applies.

Many capital projects and investments made by governments have both redistributional and social purposes. One Canadian example is regional economic development. Various governments over the past fifty years have tried a range of capital construction and infrastructure programs to ensure that poorer, often rural, parts of the country received additional economic benefits, usually in the form of investments in capital infrastructure.

From a financial-management perspective, achieving these goals must also go hand in hand with sound project design, sound financial management of the project, and a capacity to evaluate it afterwards. In other words, the financial-management considerations must also be an important aspect of the goals that are to be achieved.

The Principal Source of Revenue for Governments Is Taxation, but This Is a Non-Exchange Transaction

Governments have the power to compel people to pay taxes, pay fees for services, and impose charges and special payments. In some cases, the fee is for a service rendered to an individual. However, in general, taxation does not create a situation of equal exchange of goods and services for payment.

While the public sector acquires funds to achieve a known set of goals, that income is not tied to any one specific goal. Rather, funds are combined into a consolidated revenue fund and subjected to a decision-making process that distributes them across a range of activities. This is what we know as the budgetary process, which is dealt with in chapters 5 and 7.

Consolidation of revenues removes the capacity of the individual taxpayer to act like a consumer when it comes to paying for public goods. An important principle is that public goods are equally available to all citizens and are not for private purchase. This changes somewhat when fees and charges are applied to government programs and services. In such instances, there is certainly an element of consumer choice, but the basic principle stands: the ultimate distribution of funds is based on policy and political choice, not consumer choice.

Governments sometimes choose to deviate from this concept of consolidation of funds. Government can create special funds or enable public-sector organizations to receive and use funds on an exclusive basis. For example, all revenues that Canada Post receives from the sale of its services are held and managed by that organization and accounted for in a separate manner. They never enter the federal government's consolidated revenue fund, which is the central fund that receives general taxation and then disburses it among various activities within the government.

Nonetheless, the general principle stands and is an important one. Taxation applies to the entire population. The capacity of the public-sector organization to distribute its funds according to its policy requirements is important. One of the challenges in public-sector financial accounting is to ensure that all funds are accounted for and that taxpayers know their money was spent wisely.

Governments Hold Assets Acquired in the Right of the Crown

This principle applies to the government side of the public sector but can extend into such nonprofit sectors as health and education. For all, the public-good value of the assets may far outweigh a market-based valuation or resale value of the assets. In some cases of such assets, the purposes for holding such an asset render its market value marginal in calculating its future uses. Similarly, the public sector often holds assets that have lost their value for their original public-policy purposes. Perhaps one the best examples of this would be railway lands in urban areas. After many years of abandoning rail lines as a result of operational and economic changes, governments realized that they held valuable landholdings that were no longer needed. Because they had lost their original public-good objectives, these could, then, be readily sold.

Governments Operate in a Non-Competitive Environment

This CICA principle seems to contrast the monopolistic powers of government with the free-market nature of the private sector. The reality is certainly less clear. In general, market mechanisms cannot apply to most public-sector goods. Hence, competition based solely on price, supply, and demand do not work effectively in this much more complex environment. In fact, they distort many of the redistribution and equity objectives that public-sector organizations have. Financial managers therefore cannot rely solely on market-pricing mechanisms to determine value.

For the most part, the public goods that the public sector produces are not ones that the private sector would normally produce in a price-driven competitive market. That does not mean that the private and nonprofit sectors cannot deliver these goods. In such instances, the public sector or government becomes a buyer of such products and services. As already noted, the use of contracting for the provision of services is growing in the public sector. A distinction has to be made between the delivery of public goods on the one hand and the accountability and ownership of the good itself on the other. In that sense, the public sector remains accountable and responsible for the services it buys.

In addition, as part of the many changes in government management over the past twenty-five years,[12] some governments have introduced internal competition for the delivery of services, introducing private-sector pricing and permitting both private- and public-sector delivery organizations to compete with each other for the public good that they seek to purchase.

Governments Have Debt Capacities Unparalleled by Most Other Organizations

While both the federal government and the provinces have borrowing powers, provincial legislation generally limits municipalities and the health and education sectors in the extent to which they can borrow. Both the senior levels have rich and diverse tax bases. As such, they can alter their tax structures, i.e., raise taxes to pay for debt and the cost of debt. Municipalities have limited tax bases, centred

mostly on property taxes, and so their capacity to carry debt loads is severely limited. For the health and education sector, the constraints are even greater.

The principal contrast here, however, is between the broader public sector and the private sector. The constraints on borrowing for a business are limited to its ability to pay for the debt and the reliance that it would remain a going concern, from the perspective of the lender, not the borrower. Here the larger governments in the public sector are considerably less constrained in formal, legal terms. However, as we have seen over the past decade, the accumulation of debt loads by government and the cost of carrying those loads can become matters of urgent public-policy concern.

Other Factors that Affect Public-Sector Financial Management

The characteristics listed above, based on the PSAB and IFAC frameworks, provide a fairly complete picture of the public-sector financial landscape. Added to this framework are a series of further characteristics that, taken together, provide a full picture of financial management in the public sector.

The following are some of these characteristics to consider.

- **A Mix of Criteria:** As noted, governments tend to have multiple goals, but also multiple stakeholders with different views of what the desired public good is. For instance, in the area of public safety and policing, a variety of interests are at play at any time: victims, neighbourhoods, offenders, the courts, other police services, and interest groups, to name just a few. While many factors also come into play when decisions are made in the private sector, it is how the action will ultimately affect the bottom line of financial profit, in both the short and the long term, that is the criterion that must be met. In contrast, a government organization may debate a course of action that must balance a number of objectives: impact on clients, impact on staff and staffing, potential for funding sources, priority of one area over another, etc. For government and many nonprofits, the use of resources in one area will mean ignoring the need in another. For example, often it is the case that municipalities are weighing the potential for more books in their libraries or more fire fighters. The resources operate on a zero-sum basis, but the needs and priorities do not.
- **Difficulty of Relating Costs and Benefits:** Because of what they do and what they focus on, governments

are often challenged to determine the direct benefit of a specific action. Further, the line connecting resource expenditure and outcomes is often a very tenuous one. A series of causes and effects, some under the control of the organization but many not, can affect the final outcome. Further, outcomes can occur over an extended period of time and in an unpredictable fashion. Certainly, in the case of social and health services, the number of variables is immense. Human beings often exercise their free will, even with help to guide them to the desired improvement. This reality is hardly a reason not to pursue a better understanding of the outcome of public-sector programs. Rather, it is a caution that an excess of zeal in this area, which ignores the nuanced character of many public-sector goods, will lead to some very clear but very stupid conclusions.

- **Performance Measurement Is Elusive:** Public-sector organizations often have a number of objectives that are difficult to measure. Measuring *ultimate* outcomes is one thing, but a very difficult one. Measuring *interim* outcomes or outputs is often a substitute, but at times equally difficult. For instance, is the objective of an educational institution to ensure employability of its graduates or to ensure a high-quality, engaged citizenry? The former might be measured more easily than the latter. In some instances, the focus of concern for members of the public is the inputs. For instance, citizens may ask if every part of the country got its fair share of the capital investment budget this year. This is a preoccupation with distributional and equity issues, a very important and legitimate concern in the public sector. For this reason, financial information and performance often serve as surrogates for actual performance data. Money spent, regardless of whether or not it is the best use of that money, can be traced and examined in a variety of ways where good public-sector financial reporting exists. Detailed program measures often cannot.

- **Apples and Oranges:** Often the distribution of resources takes place across programs that do not readily compare with each other. Similarly, some programs that may, at first glance, look alike are actually aimed at different goals. Comparing them would, therefore, distort the conclusions.

- **Service Orientation of Many Public-Sector Organizations:** The focus of many public-sector organizations is serving the client. They measure success in terms of how they are achieving that end, rather than how well they manage the funds. Often, this service orientation is dominated by a culture that can be hostile to effective financial management, seeing it as inhibiting effective client service through excessive controls, inadequate funding, or a preoccupation with paperwork over *peoplework*.

- **Constraints on Goals and Objectives:** The reason that a public-sector organization exists is defined either by the laws and policies that government establishes, or by the objectives of the nonprofit voluntary agency. In neither case is the raison d'être defined by profitability. The consequence is that public-sector organizations do not change their mandates for financial reasons, but they do for policy ones. The interaction between policy and funds available is, of course, a different story. Here, policy intentions have to take into account funds available and costs. That is the heart of the budgeting process for any public-sector organization.

- **Varying Forms of Governance:** In government, it is a straightforward process to determine the legal authority that governs a public-sector organization. How decisions are made, however, is quite a different matter. Legislation creating public-sector organizations may be very broad with respect to the level of legislative control that is exerted as the organization goes about its day-to-day business. In fact, legislatures seldom engage in the actual management of public-sector organizations. Rather, they serve other key roles: creating the organization, setting out the policies that it will carry out, providing the funding to carry out the policies, and holding the organization to account for how it carried out the policies.

- **Political Realities and Necessities:** In government, all policy is created within a political context. Therefore, it is important to focus on some of the characteristics of politics that can affect financial management.

  - *Short-term orientation – from one election to the next:* The need to get re-elected will often produce a short-term focus that drives out long-term considerations. Short-term results may be seen as more important than long-term effects This can have a serious impact on the budgetary cycles of governments. There is also a tendency to give less weight to such matters as maintenance of equipment than to direct services, even though these matters are essential to the long-term health of the organization.

  - *Need for visibility – show me the ribbon to cut:* The desire to achieve high personal or governmental visibility will create an inclination to focus on new initiatives in government rather than on continuing operations. Since funds are limited, there will be a tendency to move funds towards the new and attractive and highly visible priorities.

○ *Multiple external pressures:* The public sector, be it government or the voluntary sector, is all about multiple stakeholders. This can create pressures and counter-pressures within an organization to use funds in erratic or inconsistent ways to please various stakeholders.

○ *In a fish bowl:* Financial management in the public sector is becoming an ever more transparent process. This is fed in part by the number of external stakeholders and their increasingly sophisticated understanding that the management of public funds drives some of the results that they want. It is also fuelled by the presence in most jurisdictions of some legislation relating to freedom of information. None of the key elements of financial management – budgeting, resource allocation, cash management, and accountability – takes place behind walls of privacy. Such transparency affects financial management in many ways, most of them positive. For instance, it forces those managing the processes to use clear language, to adhere to approved accounting standards, and to link financial information to the organization's goals. It also forces the financial professional community to better understand the impact of their work and the language they use in a broader context.

○ *Legislative restrictions:* Public-sector organizations are governed by many different pieces of legislation, all of which impose requirements for the organization to behave in certain specified ways. Mention has already been made of freedom-of-information legislation; in addition, in most complex governments, legislation will set out various financial rules. Some legislation is difficult to change, thereby entrenching certain practices that could benefit from change.

• **Managerial Constraints:** Public-sector management has many unique characteristics that will affect the way in which financial management can be practised. These characteristics go well beyond the considerations of operating in a political context:

○ *Management cultures:* Leaders of public-sector organizations often do not see themselves as managers of resources, but rather as policy managers, operational managers, client-focused managers of highly specialized functions such as scientific research. Because of the complexity of these organizations, the finance function will have its own

senior managers, who are often separate from these line or operating managers. Tensions often develop between these two cultures. The abilities to obtain resources to achieve program objectives (budgeting), maximize program benefits within the budget (allocation), effectively manage the budget to achieve full benefit (cash management), and demonstrate results and adherence to process (accountability) are important management skills. In many cases, they are incorrectly identified as finance functions. Finance plays a supportive role but can often acquire an inappropriate dominance in the absence of effective core management.

○ *Bureaucratic rules and regulations:* Financial rules often are seen as bureaucratic impediments to getting things done. The complexity of government, the dual focus on process and product, the high level of transparency, and the multiplicity of stakeholders guarantee that the public sector will have rules and a dominance of regulation to guide decision making.

Summing Up

Financial management is a key element in delivering public goods. To effectively understand financial management requires an understanding of the role of policy within the public sector. Resources are not managed in a vacuum, and the ways in which funds are managed are matters of policy themselves. This applies to the means of management, to the distribution of the public good or service, to the way in which it is distributed, and to the mechanisms of the accounting for the way in which the public funds are managed. A great deal of public policy is as much about means as it is about ends.

Financial management is an integral part of public management. A public servant cannot be effective in his or her role without a robust understanding of the key elements of financial management. That does not mean that all public servants need to be accountants or experts in finance. Nevertheless, they must be concerned with public resources from the start of their work in the public sector, be it in a policy role or in a front-line service role. As they become managers, their responsibilities as financial managers grow. They are, in fact, financial managers. It is for this reason that the need for an effective measure of financial literacy is an important personal – and organizational – asset. That is not a specialized role. It is, in fact, a general one shared by all managers. Indeed, financial experts are an essential part of any functioning public-sector organization. They, too, play a variety of roles, some of them in apparent tension with line managers, some in complement. In order to have accountability, though, it is the line manager who must be seen as managing the finances of the organization. The financial specialist is needed to advise and guide in a variety of ways. Further, the financial specialist makes sure that the underlying financial systems of the organization function in the intended manner. The financial specialist also serves at times as controller, a concept that will be explored in Chapter 9. The financial specialist brings to the organization a unique set of skills without which it cannot function. Unless those skills are integrated with those of the line manager – the reasons for the organization's existence – they are of not much use.

The focus of this text is the financial manager, not the financial specialist. Built into that focus is the expectation that public-sector managers will develop an understanding of how finance works, how their legal framework guides their financial responsibilities, how to rely on and use financial experts in all phases of financial management. Hence, the need to pursue financial literacy. Financial experts, on the other hand, need to develop an understanding of the policies and directions of the organizations in which they work. They also must develop ways to translate legal financial requirements into sound managerial practice. Because of the complexity of public-sector environments, the one does not trump the other.

Another important implication for financial management in the public sector is the need in large organizations for countervailing checks and balances. While the line manager is the financial manager, that does not mean that he or she can unilaterally create rules. In fact, complex organizations need what might be called internal transparencies or approvals that enable senior managers to obtain advice about financial performance and trends. Further, the risk of some financial transactions (due to their level, complexity, or visibility) may involve complex approval authorities. Such is the kind of dynamic that often places line managers in conflict with financial experts. Some of that is absolutely essential to keeping organizations honest with themselves and with their creators.

Chapter 2
Public-Sector Accounting Principles

Chapter Objectives:

- Understanding why accounting is part of management
- Defining accounting
- Understanding the uses and users of accounting information
- Understanding how accounting standards are created and used

You are Not an Accountant

The purpose of this chapter and the following one is to develop an understanding of what accounting in the public sector entails, what governs it, and the fundamental underpinnings of the accounting process. Effective management of public-sector organizations depends on a variety of factors, some of them related to finance and some not. Effective public management works within an interdependent framework of public-sector values and good management practices, but also having the people, infrastructure and resources in place, in use and, ultimately, accounting for the wise and purposeful use of those resources. In the middle of all this framework is the day-to-day need to know what is going on, adjust those resources to accommodate changes and still have, at the end of the day, a credible and reliable means of accounting for it. Underpinning all this is the need to know what is going on, to identify resources, to use them and explain what happened; the result is a solid accounting system. Managers of programs seldom will concern themselves with the mechanics of this system. They will, however, be very dependent on its reliability and relevance to their operational needs. An effective public manager benefits from understanding what accounting can and cannot do. Normally, they do not need to do it. Therefore, it is helpful to understand how one can use accountancy without necessarily being an accountant. In fact, it can be argued that simply leaving this specialized field to the experts without a robust and sympathetic understanding of what it can and cannot do for the user of the information is a grave error. It can lead to any number of misunderstandings about the meaning of financial information and to poor managerial decision making.

In addition to these internal management reasons for understanding basic accounting principles, there are external reasons as well. Governments are moving quickly to improving their core financial statements, publishing more often and providing more financial performance information. Users of such information are increasing. Transparency is increasing. Therefore, public-sector managers, who deal with a range of stakeholders who have an interest in such reports, have to understand these external reports and how they come together. This is the financial management side of accounting.

At the heart of the financial management of the public-sector organization will be a sound accounting framework. It is essential for managers within the organization to have confidence in the financial information because they need it to plan, control operations, and account for their activities. It is also central to establishing public confidence in the organization, whether we are speaking of taxpayers or potential donors. The accounting framework has two elements, a framework of **accounting principles** (addressed in this chapter) and a set of **standardized financial statements** (addressed in the next chapter).

From the financial management framework shown in **Figure 0.2**, it can be seen that sound accounting forms the basis for credible and reliable information, not only for financial purposes but also for managerial information.

Defining Accounting

To understand how accounting contributes to effective financial management one must know something about its nature. The following characteristics may surprise some, since they fly in the face of the view that accountancy is a clear set of concise rules intended to apply to all circumstances. In fact, the following is more likely the case:

- Accountancy and its boundaries are *dynamic* in nature, always responding to new needs as they arise.
- The *boundaries of accounting are blurred and changeable* as a result.
- Accounting is both an *art and a science*. It involves making judgements and moulding information to the demands of the situation while being able to claim objectivity and independence.

Accounting involves a number of characteristics that help with understanding its role in financial management. The process

- creates a credible basis for capturing, measuring, and having confidence in the financial framework of an organization;
- focuses on economic entities;
- identifies, measures, and communicates financial information;
- provides this information to the users of financial information;
- enhances understanding of what is being measured, and
- provides this information for the purpose of helping the organization reach its stated goals.

Inherent in this set of activities is a tension between flexibility to accommodate variable organizational needs and the need for consistent application of the rules of accounting. One key feature of accounting is that it has to be sufficiently inflexible to permit economic events and the information that flows from them to be compared in a consistent fashion. These events need to be treated in the same way, to allow comparisons to be made over different time periods. Similarly, the rules of accounting have to be understandable to a variety of outside parties if they are to examine the information in a useful and comprehensible way. Because the needs of internal and external users are divergent and varied, some degree of flexibility in reporting formats and uses of information is necessary. This will mean that producers of financial reports will often have to clarify how they are using terms that may be in common use, but whose application in specific circumstances is unique. Hence, one good piece of advice about financial statements: read the notes. Always read the notes.

Accounting is not an end in itself but a tool for an organization, and users of information about that organization, to control its internal activities. It allows users to compare performance against plans, to determine the probity and propriety of the uses of finances that have been entrusted to the organization, and to evaluate overall performance. But, perhaps, more than anything, it establishes confidence and trust in the numbers and what they mean.

Accounting seeks to translate all transactions into monetized terms. That, as we will see when looking at the generally accepted accounting principles (GAAP) in this chapter, speaks to both its strength and its weakness. It provides a common language for comparison and understanding: money. This common language keeps track of transactions that occur within an organization and among other organizations. A weakness is that simply stating what has been spent does not necessarily define what has been achieved.

A principal characteristic of accounting is that it is retrospective, in that it records information related to an organization's past financial behaviour. While such information is invaluable in making projections about future behaviour, it is not the only information needed to do so.

The role of the financial expert in producing accounting information is to observe, screen, and recognize events and transactions, to measure and process them, and to compile organizational reports with accounting information in accepted formats. These are then interpreted, decoded, and used by management and other user groups. But, based on these internal and external users, accounting breaks down into two core roles:

- **Management accounting:** This provides support systems, information and analysis to people within the organization to help them manage, and
- **Financial accounting:** This provides information in the form of standardized reports to stakeholders outside the organization that establish credibility for the organization, determine compliance with legal requirements, and report on financial and programmatic results.

These are not two isolated functions, but rather part of a continuum; one that reflects the interaction between formal external reporting and the internal use of financial information. Therefore, there is considerable interest by external stakeholders in what internal managers know and understand, which is often more detailed and certainly more current, than the formal, more retrospective, reporting found in financial statements. The interaction is reflected in the diagram in **Figure 2.1**.

FIGURE 2.1
The Relationship Between Financial and Managerial Accounting

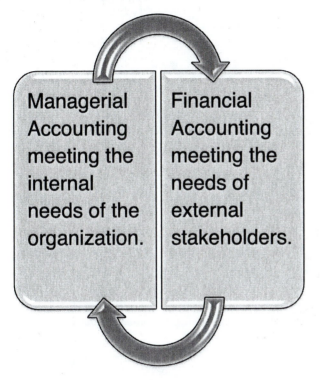

The major objectives of financial and management reporting are:

- to provide useful information to all potential users in a form and time frame that are relevant to their needs;
- to provide information to minimize uncertainty about the validity of the financial information and to enable users to make their own assessment of the risks, accuracy, and implications of the information for the program, outcome, or performance of the organization;
- to ensure adherence to standards of reporting within the reporting environment, but allow sufficient capacity for them to change to meet emerging needs; and
- to be directed towards the needs of users who are capable of comprehending a complete set of financial statements.[1]

Users of Accounting Information: Who Cares? Who Needs to Care?

It's not the economy anymore, stupid. It's the accounting."[2] The evidence from near, and not so near, disasters in both public- and private-sector accounting would seem to support an elevated level of interest, and for good reason. This means an expansion of interest, not just in financial information, but in the accounting practices and assumptions behind it. This is fair and requires governments to respond, which they are doing through increased reporting and greater standardization of practice. Good financial management depends on good accounting practice. A principal challenge in sorting out accounting practice and reporting is the number of users of it. The other reality is that there are more users, using different ways to access information with more sophisticated tools. While we can see how the Internet might affect this in terms of expanding understanding, public managers and leaders are also confronted by those who may have the information but do not understand it fully. The range and scope of users is growing, but not necessarily getting better informed. Some basic realities with respect to users of accounting information, be they internal or external are:

- There are a large number of users.
- Their needs and interests will conflict.
- Levels of expertise in understanding terminology and numbers will vary.
- Users are not necessarily rational and seldom compliant with what one party may want them to understand.
- Some users will not trust the information or its source.
- One person's transparency is another's opacity.
- Users' needs will change over time.

Internal Users

Internal users of accounting information include managers who need financial information to control activities and monitor performance. Even within a management group, needs will vary. Large government organizations have many levels of management, whose needs will be dictated by the roles they play within the organization. Since public-sector managers can be stationed in various regions within the province or the country, their interests in financial information will also vary. Some will be focused on the performance of a unit and the use of the information for control of activities within it. Management at a higher level will be interested in the unit but will want the information aggregated to broader levels of analysis. They will also want to be able to compare units doing similar work. Central offices of an organization or central agencies,

FIGURE 2.2
Potential Users of Public-Sector Financial Information

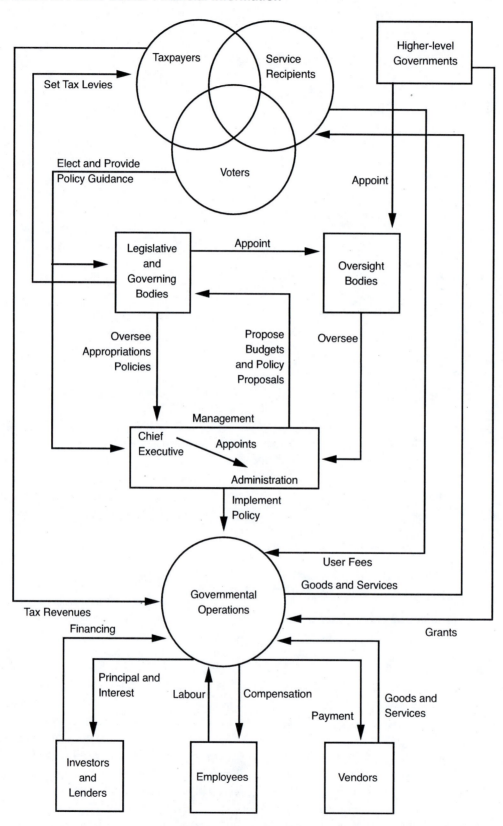

Source: Allan R. Drebin, James L. Chan, and Lorna C. Ferguson, editors, *Objectives of Accounting and Financial Reporting for Governmental Units: A Research Study* (National Council on Government Accounting: Chicago, 1981).

such as a management board, will have a strong interest in the financial performance of the unit in question. This interest will not be as immediate as that of line managers, but it is very real. The information needed here will be complex and situation dependent. However, there may be a concern that the organization is staying within budget in a current year, especially if there had been problems in previous years. There may a concern that specially designated funds are being spent for the purpose intended, e.g., special recession-fighting funds used for the employment programs they were designed for.

Employees other than managers are also internal users of financial information. For example, in a revenue-dependent voluntary organization, all employees will have an active interest in the continued viability of the organization in terms of their own employment. In other instances, they will be interested in the availability of resources for program purposes. This would enable them to make administrative decisions, such as buying more supplies should funds be available.

External Users

In the public sector, there is no shortage of external users of accounting information. The following is a representative list:

- The legislative authority that provided the appropriations wants information to ensure that the funds were spent for the purposes intended. There is also a concern that the funds achieved their objectives.
- In some cases, specialized committees such as the Public Accounts Committee will scrutinize financial reports in detail.
- In the case of government, legislative auditors – that is, those appointed under law by the legislature and reporting directly to it – will have a very strong interest in the financial information because this is at the heart of their mandates. They will also have an interest in the accounting rules and procedures that produced this information.
- Taxpayers, whose money, after all, is used to deliver government services, wish to see how that money is spent.
- Interest groups advocate for and critically analyze the activities of the public-sector organization.
- Clients of the organization have a direct interest in the performance of the organization as it pertains to the benefits they receive.
- Suppliers and vendors have an interest in the economic viability of public-sector organizations or in their capacity to meet their financial obligations.

Internal and external users of the accounting information that is generated for an organization differ in their use of it in several respects: access, frequency, detail, timing, required expertise and understanding, and response.

Access

Internal users generally have direct and unlimited access to financial information in the organization. This information is available to management on demand to support strategic, tactical, and operational decisions, as well as for monitoring and control. In contrast, the external users of financial information have limited and indirect access to that information. These users usually rely on the information contained in the formal financial statements of the organization as well as their own audit processes (if they have legislative authority to conduct such investigations). Such is the case with legislative auditors. These distinctions will obviously be confused in government where freedom-of-information legislation may permit individuals to access internal reports. External users, however, do not generally need the detailed financial information that an internal user would. Nevertheless, for all parts of the public sector, there is a need to assure the public that the externally available financial information is an accurate reflection of the financial situation of the organization. Hence, there is a need for external audit processes.

Frequency

Probably, external users will not need as frequent access to financial information as internal users do. Generally, external users rely on annual reporting or special reports when significant changes occur. As a norm, internal managers can demand such information as frequently as their needs for it dictate, even daily. Their needs are immediate. They need information as soon as they can get it to make program adjustments.

Detail

Internal users of financial information can demand reports to be as detailed or as summarized as their needs dictate. External users will receive higher-level, more general information, generally provided in standardized formats such as the Statement of Financial Position (Balance Sheet). This can be supplemented by additional reporting should it be required, but, for the most part, summary financial statements are at a very high level.

Information for internal users tends to be more current because it is often needed for immediate decision making within the organization. Hence, it is deemed to be more timely and predictive in nature, e.g., specific unit costs changes with a trend analysis. For external users, the information tends to be more retrospective, reporting on the past year's revenues and expenditures through the Statement of Financial Operations. Such information will also be focused on statements of the organization's objectives or results that were published well in the past, so as to permit a comparison of the financial information with the anticipated results.

Expertise and Understanding

Internal users are involved with financial information on a near-daily basis. Their understanding of the nuances or details of the information will necessarily be more complete. So, too, will their appreciation of the background details that explain or condition financial reports.

External users, on the other hand, will rely on information provided by that same organization, but at a more general level. Many stakeholders in public-sector organizations are long-time observers of those organizations, and they develop their own understanding and expertise. Further, public-sector organizations have complex and continuous relationships with those stakeholders who have an interest in the organization. These relationships add context, colour, and depth to their understanding of the financial information. This can result in effective public consultation and long-term relationship building that is vital to a successful working relationship with public-sector organizations.

Response

The responses of internal and external users of accounting information vary. Internal users react to the information they receive to operate the organization and to make strategic decisions. They also use it to assess performance at both the organizational and individual levels.

External users apply the information to determine if the organization is economically viable, worthy of investment through donations, or viable as a partner in joint ventures, or if it is complying with the law or meeting its objectives, providing value for money, to name just a few. The question of who uses accounting information is discussed further in Chapter 10.

What Management and Financial Accounting Do

We can see that meeting the various objectives of the users of accounting information is a complex business. It is for that reason that accounting has developed into the

two streams: financial accounting, to meet the needs of external users, and management accounting, to meet the requirements of internal users.

External users tend to receive the more dated and historical information supplied in annual financial reports. That is why accounting for external users is called financial accounting. Financial information provided to internal users is often more current and timely to meet their needs. As such, it is useful for internal users in predicting or anticipating behaviours such as a budget overrun or the impact on immediate operations of a cost increase. This is why their information is called management accounting. Of course, nothing is simple. We also apply the term financial accounting to a bundle of tasks that set accounting standards, development systems for tracking revenues and expenses, and make it possible to follow the money through the process.

Management accounting can be broken down into the following categories, as shown in **Figure 2.3**, reflecting the fact that there is a significant temporal element to it:

FIGURE 2.3
Accounting for Management

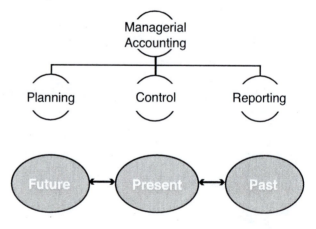

The aim of management accounting is to meet the dynamic information needs of management and employees of the organization so that they can respond to changes in the environment and control performance. Such information will form only one part of the control package that managers must use to achieve their ends. They will also require plans, targets, non-financial performance indicators, and intuitive awareness of the situation. Management accounting will use financial information as part of an overall package of managerial information.

FIGURE 2.4
Examples of Management Accounting Information

- Budget performance: actual against plan
- Variance analysis: comparisons and identification of anomalies
- Cash or budget forecasts
- Costing information
- Income/loss statements
- Activity-based costing reports
- Performance against targets (financial and non-financial)
- Identification of financial and non-financial risk reports
- Forecasts: cash flow, costing, budget projections
- Cost allocation reports

FIGURE 2.5
Terminology for Financial Statements

Government	Private Sector
Statement of Financial Position	Balance Sheet
Statement of Operations	Statement of Operations
Statement of Cash Flows	Income Statement
Statement of Net Change in Financial Assets (Debt)	N/A

Source: Public Sector Accounting Board.

The objective of financial accounting is the preparation of financial statements for public or broad use. It is retrospective in nature and tends to cover past financial activities for the required reporting period. Financial accounting reports in large public-sector organizations will generally conform to an approved chart of accounts.

A Chart of Accounts is an accounting document that defines the structure of the financial recording and reporting system of the organization. It would define the elements into which the budget is divided for the organization; it would further assign an identifying number for each possible element of a financial transaction. Transactions are coded and reports generated in a manner consistent with this chart.

Flowing from these reporting requirements will be a number of well-defined financial reports. As the next section describes, these reports will have to conform to the accepted standards set for public-sector accounting purposes. Because the focus of financial reporting in the public sector is different from that of the private sector, basic financial accounting reports will also be different, as shown in **Figure 2.5**. These statements will be discussed in detail in the Chapter 3.

Internal and external users of financial information have differing needs that are valid and necessary, which has led to diverse characteristics being sought for each. It can also create what are essentially two parallel information systems within organizations, each to serve a different set of clients. Management accounting must meet the current, short-term and changing information needs of management and employees of the public-sector organization. While comparative information is very important, the emphasis on what needs to be closely measured will change

as priorities change. Financial accounts have tended to concentrate on ensuring that the interests of external users are met through reporting at clearly defined frequencies, with high-level information oriented toward meeting their general information needs. This information has to follow well-established formats to permit comparisons not only from year to year within an organization, but among similar organizations. Changes in how information is presented are made carefully and always with explanations and even retrospective changes in reporting for past years to permit these comparisons. It also has to be well enough presented to inspire confidence in the reported outcomes and a belief that the information is accurate and legally reported.

Management accounting, therefore, will be highly flexible in format, designed to meet needs as they emerge within the organization. Financial accounting will be considerably less flexible in format, often conforming to government-wide reporting formats.

This does not mean that organizations are "keeping two sets of books." Both forms of accounting information have to derive from the same basic financial information, the same Chart of Accounts, and the same financial accounting standards that apply to the organization. By law, any public-sector organization will have to meet its external financial-reporting obligations and must have the capacity to assemble that information as required. It is highly unlikely that such information will be used actively within the organization, but at senior levels of management, and also at the political level, the organization has to be able to explain and defend financial reports as they are made public. What links the two uses, and ensures that the accounting basis for both managerial and financial accounting information is sound, is the application of common accounting standards, known as generally accepted accounting principles (GAAP).

GAAP: The Accounting Framework

You often hear or see a statement such as "These statements were developed using GAAP standards." What the person using this phrase is trying to say is that they meet the commonly accepted standards for good accounting. Effective financial management depends upon the ability of those preparing financial information to understand the general form and intent of that information and to meet the many needs of users as outlined above. Similarly, while all organizations will prepare their financial information in different ways, a set of basic principles exists for both government and the nonprofit sector in Canada that guides how financial information will be created, reported, audited, and generally understood. That is the essence of the concept of the **generally accepted accounting principles** (GAAP).

This section outlines the history of GAAP in general terms, the Canadian framework for applying it to the public sector, the core principles themselves, and some discussion of how their application takes on meaning in the use and creation of accounting practices. Note that GAAP is a general set of prescriptions, often supported with more detail for specific sectors. It does not provide an easy formula of reports and forms that, once used, will mean that the financial performance information is accurate or even reliable to the fullest extent possible. Simply adhering to GAAP does not mean the organization is totally honest or straightforward in its reporting. GAAP is simply a basic set of principles for accountancy backed up by detailed interpretations provided by standard-setting bodies. These organizations spend a good deal of time trying to offer interpretations and guidance about how GAAP is to be applied in specific situations. Even with that, accountants and financial professionals often use considerable professional judgement in applying them in specific circumstances. Further, the needs of users of public-sector financial information are varied enough that they will take different views of interpretations of both the data and the way in which they are presented.

Knowing what the GAAP are is invaluable in understanding some of the financial management challenges that managers often confront. This is because they do form one of the key bridges between getting the funds to operate a program and being able to control and account for those funds. They are also the basis for the fundamental financial reports that will be examined in Chapter 3.

Who Sets These Standards?

Accounting standards are not law. They are set not by legislature but by recognized accounting standards

bodies. Accounting standards specify how transactions and other events are to be recognized, measured, presented, and disclosed in financial statements. The objective of such standards is to meet the needs of users of financial statements by providing the information needed for accountability and decision making.

Around the world, a number of boards or organizations are involved in setting accounting standards and in defining exactly what GAAP means and how it applies in a variety of circumstances. In Canada, the standard-setting body for all levels of government and the voluntary sector is the Public Sector Accounting Board, which is part of the Canadian Institute of Chartered Accountants (CICA), the governance structure for all accounting standards in the public, private, and voluntary sectors. The CICA has the responsibility for issuing accounting standards based on GAAP. The mission of the PSAB is:

The Public Sector Accounting Board serves the public interest and that of the profession by recommending accounting standards that will improve the financial and performance information reported by governments and other public sector entities for the benefit of decision makers and other users of the information.[3]

The Board's objectives are as follows:

- to issue recommendations and guidance that enhance the usefulness of public-sector financial statement information;
- to issue recommendations that enhance the usefulness of public-sector financial and non-financial performance information;
- to engage interest and debate by improving stakeholders' understanding of public finances;
- to effectively coordinate activities with other accounting standard setters and other public-sector-related organizations; and
- to provide PSAB's program of standard setting and communications effectively, efficiently and economically.

Each new accounting recommendation issued by the PSAB becomes part of the Canadian version of GAAP, which depends on general acceptance by the community that uses it and the bodies that govern it. In that regard, these principles are one important test of public-sector financial probity.[4]

Generally Accepted Accounting Principles

The quotation from the Auditor General of Canada in **Figure 2.6** indicates the importance of these principles in the public sector. They form the basis for the credibility of financial statements published by government. What follows is a detailed outline of the principles.

1. The Entity Principle

In creating financial reports, the first task is to define the unit, or entity that is being reported. Very simply, the user has to know what these reports refer to and exclude anything that is not related to that entity. For example, in reviewing a balance sheet or statement of operations from the Town of Tillsonburg, we must be able to assume that the information deals exclusively and completely with that entity we know as the Town of Tillsonburg. This may be a simple task, or potentially complex. In the case of Tillsonburg, the parking authority, which is expected to operate as a business, may or may not be included in the town's financial statements. This may seem like a minor issue, but the user has to know. Therefore, financial statements will always explain how the entity is defined – what is in and what is out. Financial statements report only the activities, resources and obligations of the entity as defined.

This can become controversial. For some time, there has been a debate as to whether the financial activities of entities such as schools and health care that are at arm's length should be included in provincial financial statements of provinces. These governments have resisted this, as it increases the overall size of the reporting entity, tends to distort an understanding of how much control governments have over these funds once they transfer them, and buries important activities of what is known as the broader public sector in these larger reports. The PSAB has argued that these arm's-length entities are part of the public sector and part of the overall responsibilities of the provincial government, funded by it and directed, through policy and oversight, by it. As these monies flow from the province, they are part of the overall entity we call the provincial government. Over the past decade, the PSAB has gained the upper hand and financial statements of provinces increasingly reflect this notion of the proper definition of the entity. We have to remember that, in such instances, these arm's-length agencies will also produce their own financial statements to meet their own reporting requirements.

The practical element of the entity principle is quite simple: you have to be able to determine what is in and what is out of the unit for which you are preparing reports. Defining the entity permits the organization to create a budget for it, measure and monitor its use, and report retrospectively with confidence that it is providing full information on the behaviour of the budget, its managers, and the objectives for which it was set in place.

FIGURE 2.6
Why Having Accounting Standards Is Important to the Auditor General of Canada

---

Quotation from the Auditor General on GAAP

9.16 The consequences of not complying with GAAP could be very serious for a business firm. The reason is that the firm's auditors would be obliged to state in their opinion that GAAP had not been followed, which would send a clear signal to readers of the financial statements that the reported results were not credible. Further, Canadian securities regulatory authorities take a very dim view of qualified opinions.* As a result, in the private sector one rarely sees financial statements departing from GAAP. Management cannot tolerate the negative consequences of a qualified opinion and will generally comply with GAAP to avoid it.

9.17 Parliamentarians and the Canadian public should expect no less from the federal government. And yet results frequently were inappropriately reported in the government's financial statements from the late 1970s through the end of the 1980s... This unfortunate situation occurred because there were no arm's-length standards of recommended accounting to which both the government and our Office could refer. It was therefore difficult for readers of the government's financial statements to have confidence that a consistent and fair presentation was being given to them. During debates in the House of Commons at the time, the government described the situation as an "honest division of opinion" between two experts on technical accounting matters, and said that it could "list a number of accountants who will argue one side of this issue and a number who will argue the other side."

9.18 Fortunately, since that time, objective accounting standards for Canadian governments have substantially been developed and published by the Public Sector Accounting and Auditing Board (PSAAB) of the Canadian Institute of Chartered Accountants. Additional information on the activities and outputs of PSAAB is provided in Appendix A to this chapter. As also noted in Appendix A, the government has substantially brought its accounting policies in line with PSAAB standards, as encouraged by the Public Accounts Committee.

* A qualified opinion is the auditor's opinion accompanying a financial statement that calls attention to limitations in the audit or exceptions the auditor has taken with the audit of the statements.

Source: *Auditor-General of Canada, 1998 Report*: http://www.oag-bvg.gc.ca/domino/reports.nsf/html/9809ce.html.

2. The Cost Principle: Money as a Measure

All information in financial statements must be monetized. Accounting recognizes only those activities that can be expressed in monetary terms. Accountants seek objective evidence to value the transactions that they record in the financial reports.

The advantage of this principle is that it is able to pull together heterogeneous information, such as staff, supplies, and rentals, and express it in a single language, that of cost. Additionally, once definitions are set and the entity adequately defined, several different accountants or auditors can produce nearly identical financial statements. The ability to subject them to external review without depending upon subjective interpretations of the cost information is vital in making public scrutiny of financial statements possible.

The monetization or cost principle also permits an organization to develop an understanding of the value of its assets, using the common language of cost. This principle is used whether or not actual money changed hands in a transaction. For instance, a voluntary organization that received gifts in kind, such as computer equipment, will assign a value to those goods for the purposes of its financial accounting. Another interesting challenge that voluntary organizations face is placing a value on the time of unpaid volunteers. The degree to which the organization wants to integrate volunteer time into its financial statements will reflect how it records it, but in the end, it will have to be monetized to be usable in financial-performance information.

This last example also shows some of the restrictive nature of the monetization principle. It reflects only the quantitative nature of many assets. While it is possible, for instance, to assign a replacement value (a tool often used in trying to place a cost figure on large assets) to the War Memorial in Ottawa, that hardly reflects its overall value to the country or the issues that might arise in its replacement. This is a challenge in the public sector, which often holds valuable cultural and historical assets to which a monetized value cannot be readily assigned. Placing a value on assets of this nature is largely subjective, which makes it difficult to recognize them properly in financial statements. Often governments do not even try as doing so stretches credulity and serves no purpose as governments intend to retain such assets in perpetuity.

The tool most commonly used in placing a monetized value on an asset is the historic cost – if that information exists. In other words, you record what was paid for the asset originally. For the most part, this is the accepted accounting standard. If a piece of equipment was bought ten years ago for $100,000, accounting standards will report it at this value, even if a known replacement cost is $200,000. This also reflects the conservatism principle.

The notion of historical cost is at the heart of the problems that the monetization principle creates in financial reporting. Many users of these reports criticize this use of historical data. Further, historical data are unrealistic as a full picture of assets that appear on the balance sheet, since they reflect neither the replacement cost, nor potential market value, of the asset. Hence, historical asset information is presented in balance sheets, but it is not really used in decision making because, first, the asset is costed unrealistically, and, second, it is not really available for consumption in the normal sense of assets. In recent years, accounting standards setters around the world have pushed for the great use of fair market value for publicly owned assets such as land and buildings. Successfully done, this provides a more realistic assessment of the value of the asset held. However, arriving at a valuation is a matter of some difficulty. Once again, governments have to weigh the cost of such efforts relative to the benefits of accuracy and transparency.

3. The Going Concern Principle

This principle states that the organization will continue to operate for the foreseeable future in the absence of evidence to the contrary. Assets are then treated according to what is expected to happen over the normal course of operations and over their anticipated useful lifetime. Thus, they will be expected to depreciate in value or be amortized according to reasonable expectations, e.g., at the rate of 20 percent of this historical value each year for five years, and that the organization will continue to operate over that period of time.

This principle makes it possible to establish reasonable expectations for behaviour and to avoid factoring in unknowns, until they are known. It also avoids the pitfall of valuing assets as if they would be sold off under bankruptcy at lower costs, a possibility for a failing company, but hardly one that would apply to most public entities.

The heart of this principle remains that only what is known can be used in financial statements and that, unless some information is available that indicates otherwise, the organization will carry on.

The opposite of going concern is liquidation, the process by which an organization sells (liquidates) all its assets, pays off its liabilities, and closes down. If a company were planning to do this, we would record all the assets at the prices we would expect to receive for them: their liquidation value.

Some indicators that would cause an auditor or financial advisor to cast doubt on the going concern of an organization are

- significant recurring operating losses or working capital deficiencies;
- inability of the organization to pay its obligations as they come due;
- violation of a debt agreement;
- loss of major customers; and
- legal proceedings or legislation that might jeopardize the entity's ability to operate.

For example, fundamental concerns are arising for a number of Canada's churches as a result of the financial implications of making settlements relating to native schools.[5] The viability or going concern of some churches as organizations has come into question as a result. For a government, this is less of an issue, but remains a valid principle. For example, amortization policies are only justifiable and appropriate if we assume continuity of the department within the reporting entity.

4. The Conservatism and Cost Principle

Like the monetization principle, this concept is contentious and aptly named. This principle requires that accountants value assets at the lower of their historical cost or market value. GAAP holds that the accountant – and, by extension, the organization – will accept the least optimistic financial position. This has been described as a principle by which accountants recognize no gains until they happen, but record all possible losses even before they take place. That is, when in doubt, it is better to overstate expense and understate revenue.

Here we see the application of the concept of risk and the approach that financial advisors generally take with respect to it. Risk is, of course, a diverse and complex area. Under this principle, risk is treated from a pessimistic perspective, unless information is available to move from that orientation.

For instance, an organization may have considerable accounts receivable arising out of short-term program loans that it provides to its client groups. All accounts receivable appear on the balance sheet as if they will all be collected. The conservatism principle holds that some degree of risk is involved in the collection of these receivables. There may even be historical data to confirm this. Hence, treating these receivables as fully collectible probably overstates the asset base of the organization. Historical data may well confirm the fact that, over the past several years, the organization had been successful in recouping only 80 percent of the outstanding receivables arising from these loans. An application of the conservatism principle in this case would be to state probable receipts based on this objective information. In general, accountants want to avoid the use of subjective judgements in making estimates for financial statements. In this situation, however, there is some support both for using historical trends and for taking a more conservative view. The organization's managers may want to improve their performance in recouping loans. The financial advisor, in this case, would have to take a "show me the money" approach rather than accept the highly optimistic and subjective view that they will try harder. Until the organization can show that it is doing better at collecting loans, the truest representation of its financial position will be accomplished by using the historical, conservative view that only 80 percent will be collected.

The application of the conservatism principle can become a battlefield as managers try to project their cash flows and manage their resources. Organizations that are highly dependent on revenue – voluntary organizations that depend on the success of fundraising campaigns and donations, for instance – may want to base their planning on optimistic outcomes. While such projections may be well-founded in terms of good intentions and better planning and management, they can also distort financial projections and discredit the organization should its optimistic plans fall through.

5. The Matching Principle

The matching principle states that all expenses must be recorded in the same accounting period as the revenue that they helped to generate. When expenses are matched with the revenue they helped to produce, then external and internal users of financial statements can make better judgements about the financial position and operating performance of the organization. In general accounting literature, the matching principle normally refers to the matching of revenue and expenses. However, with exceptions, government entities do not generate major amounts of non-tax revenue but are funded through appropriations. As such, the matching principle must take on a slightly different interpretation. Consequently, revenues should be recognized when the goods and/or services have been rendered and expenses should be matched to program delivery outputs of services to the public. For example, in the case of tangible capital assets, an allocation policy may be used to approximate the matching principle. This type of expense recognition involves making assumptions about the benefits that are being received as well as the costs associated with those benefits. The cost of a long-lived asset is allocated over the accounting periods during which the asset is used because it is assumed that the asset contributes to the generation of program outputs throughout its useful life.

6. The Consistency Principle

This principle holds that, once an organization has adopted a set of standards for accounting and financial reporting, it will continue to use them, so as to allow for consistent comparisons between time periods. Organizations have options with respect to how they value assets and report expenses. Once they have decided how to do this, they should continue to use the same methods. When they change them, they have to provide what is a called a "cross walk" to explain where changes have been made in the financial information in order to permit comparisons.

Users of the financial information should be comfortable that the figures they are looking at mean similar things if they are presented in such a way that they invite comparison. Further, they should be confident that, should there be a change in the accounting rules, this will be fully disclosed and information that enables comparisons will be presented. This means that the organization can be consistent but still change to meet new circumstances or new rules as they emerge. Disclosure is the key. As well, the organization should, where possible, recalculate previous financial information under the new rules so that the readers and users of the financial reports can interpret the changes in terms of past performance and information.

In the financial statements of any organization, the notes attached to summary statements need to state the basis of accounting used and also any changes made in that basis since the last reporting period. This permits the user, usually an external user, to compare one year's report with another and understand the shift in information.

7. The Materiality Principle

In the context of financial reporting, materiality may be judged or measured in relation to whether the information being reported is significant to users of the financial statements in making decisions or arriving at an understanding of the organization's financial position. In broader terms, an amount would be considered material if it were substantial enough that an error of that magnitude in the financial statements would cause users of the statements to make a different decision than they would have made if they had known the information.

Here, the accountant has to be concerned about how and when financial events are recorded if they will materially or significantly affect organizational performance. This is often a matter of judgement or precedent. In the public sector, it is also a matter of political judgement and, at times, of legal parameters.

For example, the early estimates documents of the federal government listed every position employed in each department. Eventually, this was not seen as material to Parliament's needs. For a considerable time, the estimates simply reported total salary dollars and total numbers of employees. Even though the number of employees is a highly distorting figure, because departments can use part-time and contracted workers and not report them as such, the total number remains an item of great public interest which makes it material. Similarly, some governments choose to make the salaries of those earning over a certain threshold a matter of public record, the so-called *Sunshine Law*. This practice was initiated because such information was seen as material. It was probably also intended as a way of inhibiting the growth of high-paying jobs in the public sector. As salaries grew, the *Sunshine* threshold level stayed the same, thereby guaranteeing the government an annual stream of embarrassing questions about the ever-increasing number of public servants above the threshold. Some wounds are self-inflicted.

Organizations in the public sector will apply the principle of materiality differently, depending on the facts and circumstances as well as the degree of risk involved and the amount of money being spent. For instance, a small organization may want detailed information on staff travel on an individual basis for its financial reports. Travel may be unusual for some staff, and there may be a wish to ensure that it is monitored closely. On the other hand, a town may ask that its financial report roll up all staff travel into a single reporting item and note only those travel events with a total cost of more that $500. A provincial department may also want its travel information rolled up, but on the basis of categories such as operational travel for front-line workers, supervisors' travel, or travel by senior staff. As well, because of the visibility of such trips, all foreign travel might have to be reported on a case-by-case basis. The materiality must match the circumstances and is highly dependent on the type of organization.

Materiality is also linked to the financial risks that the organization sees as important. For instance, many government organizations will ask for detailed information and reporting on contracts with private providers, usually setting a threshold below which these reports are not needed. This threshold, say $10,000, is seen as a risk factor above which more information and control are needed. This is a form of materiality.

Materiality is important to establishing credible financial accounting. It is also pertinent to overall financial management. Managers are constantly making materiality decisions with respect to financial risks, to what they need to be informed about and what may require either a level of what is termed tight control and what merits loose control, i.e., regular monitoring and review. The materiality wheel in **Figure 2.7** shows the factors that come into play in reaching a view on materiality.

FIGURE 2.7
The Materiality Wheel

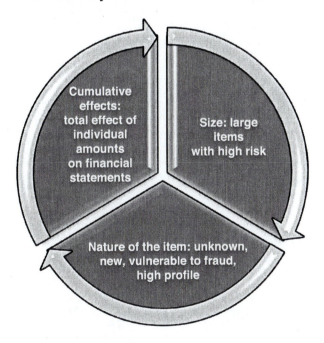

8. The Accrual Principle

Since 2005, the PSAB has set the need for accrual accounting as part of the GAAP for all governments. The concept of accrual accounting and budgeting, which is dealt with extensively in Chapter 4, is one of the underlying principles of GAAP. The elements of the accrual basis that are significant to this principle are that

- revenue is recognized when goods and services are provided, even if payment has not occurred;

- expenses are recorded on consumption of the assets; and
- a full set of financial statements are used to support the accrual basis.

Accrual is seen as providing a much more complete picture of the financial condition of an organization.

The Quality of Accounting Information

Given the concern for accurate and useful accounting information and the need for standards to be used in presenting and using it, there is a continuing preoccupation with not only its conformity to standards but also the quality of information. Faulty and inaccurate financial performance data can greatly distort internal management control. On the external side they can mislead key stakeholders who have constitutional rights to accurate information. In each case, the credibility of the accounting system and the organization itself comes into question.

The CICA's *Public Sector Accounting Handbook* makes a number of recommendations for ensuring the quality of financial reporting. It rightly points out that the function of financial statements is the communication of information to users. The *Handbook* suggests that the information should have the following qualities:[6]

- **Relevance:** It can be used for managerial purposes and understood for accountability purposes, and it applies to the matters at hand.
- **Predictive value and feedback value:** It helps predict future financial results and cash flows. In doing so, it also provides feedback about past performance.
- **Accountability value:** It helps the user assess the public-sector organization's performance.
- **Timeliness:** For either the internal or external user, it arrives within a time suited to the needs of the user.
- **Reliability:** It possesses the following characteristics that, taken together, mark it as reliable:
  - *Representational faithfulness:* Transactions and events affecting the entity are presented in financial statements in a manner that is consistent with the actual underlying transaction and events.
  - *Completeness:* None of the data necessary to achieve representational faithfulness are missing.
  - *Neutrality:* Information is free from bias that would lead users towards making decisions that are influenced by the way the information is measured or presented. While bias always exists to some extent in most human communications, the point here is that the presentation of information

should be devoid of one-sided commentary that advocates or distorts a position.

○ *Conservatism:* Where uncertainty exists about the information, estimates are evidently conservative.

○ *Verifiability:* Knowledgeable and independent observers would discern that the information is in agreement with the actual underlying transaction or event with a reasonable degree of precision.

○ *Comparability:* The report enables users to identify similarities in and differences between the information provided by two sets of financial statements.

○ *Understandability and clear presentation:* Information is clear and simple but with enough detail to make it comprehensible.

Summing Up

For managers, the world of accounting may seem arcane, more a thing to be obeyed than something of use to them. As noted throughout this text, though, the simple reality is that without financial resources not much gets done in any public-sector organization. Finding, using, controlling, and accounting for those resources demand that organizations have a reliable and credible financial- and management-accounting capacity. It is the underlying foundation of the management cycle within public-sector organizations.

Accountancy serves many purposes within organizations. Its outputs, be they formal financial reporting or a plethora of managerial information, are examined by many users with many different interests. The need for standards that protect the integrity of the accounting system is great, especially in the public sector where users' interests are varied and where credibility is absolutely necessary and always under challenge.

A manager uses financial data constantly. Understanding how they are derived is useful for a better understanding of them. As consumers of financial information and creators of financial events for which there can be considerable accountability, managers must also play a role in ensuring that the accounting systems they work with are the appropriate ones to ensure meeting the goals of the organization. Executives in public-sector organizations have a responsibility to see that the line side of the organization and the financial specialists communicate effectively to achieve this result. That is part of their role in creating an effective culture that can achieve all of the organization's goals, including its accountability and reporting ones.

Figures **2.8** and **2.9** provide a list of sample questions that users of accounting information might ask. These are just the beginning of the development of many more in this text and in real life.

FIGURE 2.8
Questions an Internal User of Financial Information Might Ask

Am I on budget? (Line manager?)

How does this unit/region compare to that one? (Mid manager?)

How is the organization performing? (Senior manager)

What are the risks in our spending patterns? (All managers, financial advisor)

Does this confirm that our budget assumptions were correct? (Financial advisor?)

Do we have any flexibility to reallocate? (All managers from their perspectives)

Are there funds to meet emerging needs? (Financial advisors)

Does this suggest any changes in our cost assumptions and in our cash projections for this year and coming years (budget implications)? (All)

FIGURE 2.9
Questions an External User of Financial Information Might Ask

Are the funds being spent for the purposes intended? (Client, auditor, legislator)

Are the funds being spent in the manner intended and permitted? (Auditor, legislator)

Are funds linked to achieve the program objectives? (Auditor, client, public, legislator)

Are funds being equitably distributed? (Provinces, client groups)

Are there enough funds for the program and will they all be spent? (Clients, central agencies)

How does this compare to past years as well as future years? (All)

What does this tell us about program sustainability? (All)

Can I trust these numbers? (Clients, legislators)

Chapter 3
Financial Statements

Chapter Objectives:
- Understanding the accounting cycle and associated functions
- Understanding the terminology of accounting
- Recognizing the uses and forms of financial statements

The generation of financial statements is a key function of the financial accounting side of financial management in the public sector. These reports are needed to communicate financial information about the organization in a manner acceptable to outside users. Line managers are not always involved in the technical aspects of preparing these reports, nor do they use them in day-to-day management. Since their actions in managing their responsibilities generate much of the information that is contained in them, however, that information is directly linked to their accountabilities. They use it in the course of their overall control responsibilities and in communicating with external stakeholders and oversight bodies. In addition, it is the senior managers, with support from financial experts, who must be able to explain the statements when questioned by parliamentarians, auditors, or stakeholders. Thus, this chapter is important because it introduces the background knowledge that line managers need in order to understand the relationship between formal financial statements and effective discharge of their financial duties.

In addition, it will look at public sector reforms in accounting practice and their impact on how governments and public entities have developed their financial statements to be more useful and a better reflection of public sector financial considerations. The next chapter will address one of the fundamental shifts to accrual accounting and budgeting, and its implications.

The Accounting Cycle

At the heart of these reports is the accounting cycle. This cycle is a set of behaviours that any organization, be it public or private, would be expected to carry out in arriving at a set of accounts for the organization. As we proceed through various issues, it is useful to keep this cycle in mind. It is presented graphically in **Figure 3.1**. In simplest terms, the accounting cycle is made up of the steps repeated each reporting period for the purpose of preparing financial statements for users. The net result of these steps is that the organization then has a set of procedures for analyzing, recording, classifying, summarizing, and reporting its financial transactions. Such procedures, being common to most accounting systems, are recognized and accepted, thereby laying the foundation for the legitimacy of the financial statements

Some of the terms used in this description may not be very meaningful at this stage, but they will be discussed fully in this and later chapters. You may wish to return to this section at intervals, and you will find it becomes increasingly clear.

The accounting process is a series of activities that begins with a transaction and ends with the closing of the books, figuratively speaking. This actually means the closing of the records for the reporting period and the expression of the opinion that all these statements are accurate. This is known as the representational statement. Because this process is repeated for each reporting period, it is referred to as the accounting cycle. It includes these major steps as outlined graphically in **Figure 3.1**:

1. Identify the transaction or other recognizable event, and prepare the transaction's source document, such as a purchase order or invoice.
2. Analyze and classify the transaction. This step involves quantifying the transaction in monetary terms (e.g., dollars and cents), identifying the accounts that

are affected, and determining whether those accounts are to be debited or credited.

3. Record the transaction by making entries in the appropriate journal, such as the sales journal, purchase journal, cash receipt or disbursement journal, or general journal. All entries are made in chronological order. Having a chronological record of financial events enables auditing and verification later on.

4. Post general-journal entries to the ledger accounts. This is normally done by means of an automated ledger system.

These four steps are performed throughout the accounting period as individual transactions occur or in periodic batch processes (e.g., at the end of the day or once weekly), depending on volume and the need to capture the information in a timely fashion.

The following steps are performed at the end of the accounting period:

5. Prepare the trial balance to make sure that the total of debits equals total credits. The trial balance is a listing of all of the ledger accounts, with debits in the left column and credits in the right column. The actual sum of each column is not meaningful; what is important is that the sums be equal. While out-of-balance columns indicate a recording error, balanced columns do not guarantee that there are no errors in the figures within the columns. For example, not recording a transaction, or recording it in the wrong account, would not cause an imbalance.

6. Correct any discrepancies in the trial balance. If the columns are not in balance, look for math errors, posting errors, and recording errors. Posting errors include:
   • posting the wrong amount,
   • omitting a posting,
   • posting in the wrong column, or
   • posting more than once.

7. Prepare adjusting entries to record accrued, deferred, and estimated amounts.

8. Post adjusting entries to the ledger accounts.

9. Prepare the adjusted trial balance. This step is similar to the preparation of the unadjusted trial balance, but this time the adjusting entries are included. Correct any errors that may be found.

10. Prepare the financial statements. These generally include the following:
    • Income statement: prepared from the revenue, expenses, gains, and losses.
    • Balance sheet: prepared from the assets, liabilities, and equity accounts.

• Cash flow statement: derived from the other financial statements using either the direct or indirect method.

11. Prepare closing journal entries that close temporary accounts such as revenues, expenses, gains, and losses. These accounts are closed to a temporary income summary account, from which the balance is transferred to the retained earnings account (capital).[1] Any dividend or withdrawal accounts are also closed to the capital account.

12. Post closing entries to the ledger accounts.

13. Prepare the after-closing trial balance to make sure that debits equal credits. At this point, only the permanent accounts appear because the temporary ones have been closed. Correct any errors.

14. Prepare reversing journal entries (optional). Such entries may be used when there has been an accrual or deferral that was recorded as an adjusting entry on the last day of the accounting period. By reversing the adjusting entry, one avoids double-counting the amount when the transaction occurs in the next period. A reversing journal entry is recorded on the first day of the new period.[2]

This cycle and the creation of financial reports are built upon some very simple concepts: double-entry bookkeeping and the Fundamental Accounting Equation. From these, a range of reports can be created to meet the organization's needs. As has already been discussed, in public-sector organizations, these reports differ from those in the private sector, although their general form is similar. The following section reviews some of the basic underpinnings of financial reports and their application to the public sector.

Accounting Technologies

The accounting cycle itself is, as will be seen, part of the larger financial management picture. The work that it entails, however, has moved from the era of the finance clerk making and verifying entries to sophisticated computer systems. Such systems have been introduced in governments around the world. Some have been adapted from private sector use. However, one characteristic is common to all. They provide more information, greater integration of financial with non-financial information (read performance information) and they do this more quickly. Generally the mundane accounting functions that are described here are integrated into cosmically titled enterprise management systems. They provide a higher level of technical efficiency. They also serve to increase the impact of systems of control, which will be discussed

FIGURE 3.1
The Accounting Cycle

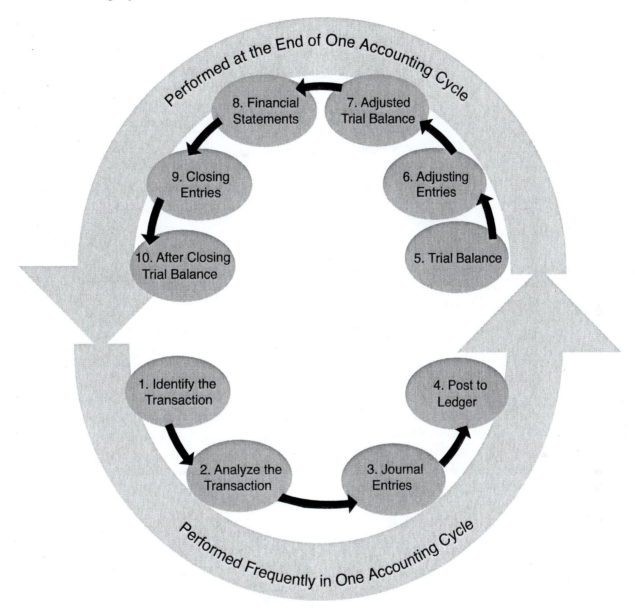

in chapters 8 and 10. Such systems have also been introduced as governments move into the accrual accounting system, which means that the cycle itself is more complex.

New accounting technologies have also increased the capacity to generate internal management reports, which will consist of a mix of the formally defined financial statements that are discussed in this chapter and the additional financial and performance information that managers need to monitor progress, detect variance and risk, and take action. Once the inevitable challenges of implementation have been met, commercial software applications have the added benefit of reducing work on reconciliations within

the accounting cycle and also automatically generating reports that serve both internal management and external reporting requirements.

As such technologies develop into integrated management systems, information becomes readily available to all workers within the organization. This enables them to monitor their own progress, see what their overseers are seeing and be more of a player in the financial management cycle. It also imposes an expectation that they will review such information and act on it well before they are asked to do so. Such technologies therefore increase the visibility and accessibility of financial information.

Double-Entry Bookkeeping and the Fundamental Accounting Equation

The accounting cycle takes place within the framework of rules that lead eventually to the production of credible financial reports. Key to these are double-entry bookkeeping that then leads to the fundamental accounting equation.

Double Entry Bookkeeping: A financial transaction always involves an impact on at least two accounts within the organization's system of organizing its various financial activities and holdings, known as the **Chart of Accounts**. For example, for every asset there exists a claim on that asset, either by those who own the firm or operate the organization or by those who lend money to the organization. Similarly, the sale of a product affects the amount of cash on hand or accounts receivable that are recorded in the financial reports of the organization. The core concept is that any increase in either assets or liabilities will result in a similar decrease in the other.

Recognizing that the dual nature of financial transactions provided a much more accurate picture of the financial position of the firm, merchants in medieval Venice began using a double-entry bookkeeping system that records each transaction in the two accounts affected by the exchange. In the late 1400s, the Franciscan monk and mathematician Luca Pacioli documented the procedure for double-entry bookkeeping as part of his famous *Summa de Arithmetica*. His work earned him the title "Father of Accounting." By the 18th century, most leading governments of Europe had adopted double-entry booking in their financial records, following the earlier adoption by business and local governments.

Two notable characteristics of double-entry systems are that

- Each financial transaction must balance each side of the fundamental accounting equation, and
- Each financial transaction will result in both the crediting and debiting of at least two accounts so as to balance.

Fundamental Accounting Equation: The basic accounting equation is a powerful framework for collecting, organizing and reporting financial information. With this one conceptual tool we can simultaneously:

- Measure how the organization has been doing (*income statement*).
- Show where it stands financially at the end of the period (*balance sheet*).

- Summarize transactions with its funders (*statement of retained earnings, net debt or fund balance*).
- One further extension allows us to summarize balance sheet changes (*statement of cash flows*).

The fundamental accounting equation establishes the rule that: for every action there is an opposite and equal reaction. In more concrete terms, for every increase in the value of one component, there is a decrease in another. Put in non-accounting terms, the equation translates as

What You Have = What You Owe + Your Net Worth

The two accounting entries of double booking keep the Fundamental Accounting Equation in balance so that:

Assets = Liabilities + Equity

Put another way, the assets an organization has will always equal the claims on those assets for the purposes of accounting. This equation, however formatted, is the basis of financial statements, as well as the way in which accounts are structured and accounting practice is set. It is a fundamental equation because it establishes a fundamental principle in financial accounting: that for every action there is an opposite and equal reaction. In more concrete terms, for every increase in the value of one component, there is an equivalent decrease in another. The creation of double-entry bookkeeping was a way to record this in a standardized way that permitted both companies and government entities to produce comprehensible financial statements for the first time.

The same basic principles apply to the public sector, both for governments and voluntary organizations. In the case of government:

Assets = Liabilities + Net Assets (Net Debt)

The rule of the accounting equation is that both sides of the equation must balance. This balance reflects the belief that all funds have been invested in assets of various types, and the total amount invested cannot be less or greater than the amount of funds supplied (through liabilities) to the organization. Alternatively, all assets are claimed by someone, either in terms of liabilities held by outsiders, or as equity or assets (or debts) held by the owners. This is reflected in an organization's Balance Sheet or Statement of Financial Condition, as it is often called in the public sector.

Although understanding how this equation works requires a fuller understanding of basic accounting than this text can provide, it will be useful to explore some basic principles. This begins with an understanding of debits and credits and how they apply to the equation.

> ***Does double bookkeeping mean that you have to make entries on both sides of the equation?*** No, not at all. Double bookkeeping means that every financial transaction will have an impact on two accounts, balancing them out. An **account** is a set of resources defined to meet the organization's accounting needs. Most Charts of Accounts will have a cash account and probably an inventory account as well. If the organization makes a purchase of supplies and puts them in inventory, it is really just moving an asset from cash to inventory, with both these accounts on the assets side of the equation. However, because they balance, there is no change in the overall equation.

Debits and Credits: The Tools to Balance the Equation

The accounting tool for ensuring that the accounting equation is in balance is the use of debits and credits in each account. When there is a financial transaction, at least two accounts are always affected, with a debit entry being recorded against one account and a credit against another. However, in accounting terms, neither debit nor credit means, in and of itself, a decrease or increase, Rather, whether the amount within the account increases or decreases depends more on the location of the account. The rules that apply seem arbitrary but in the end produce what users of financial information want – accurate financial statements. The convention for the use of the terms is more complex than that and, at times, counterintuitive because it depends on the circumstances and one's perspective on the transaction. The terminology may seem arbitrary, but its use is the bedrock of accounting.

For every account affected by a financial transaction that is recorded by an organization, there must be two components, a debit and a credit, as shown below:

Relating the Concept of Debits and Credits to the Fundamental Equation

All categories in the fundamental equation can be positively or negatively affected because double entries record both sides of each financial transaction. **Figure 3.2** offers examples of how this works.

Whether a debit or a credit increases or decreases an account balance depends on the type of account. Asset and expense accounts are increased on the debit side, and liability, equity, and revenue accounts are increased on the credit side. The following chart links the accounting equation to examples of three accounts and how debits and credits apply:

FIGURE 3.2
Linking Debits and Credits to the Fundamental Accounting Equation

Assets		=	Liabilities		+	Equity	
Cash			Accounts/Payable			Retained Earnings	
Debit	Credit		Debit	Credit		Debit	Credit
+	–		–	+		–	+

Account X

Debit	Credit
A debit is an increase in an asset account; a decrease in a liability or equity account.	A credit is an increase in a liability account; a decrease in an asset or revenue account.
All debits are entered on the left side of the General Ledger	All credits are entered on right side of the General Ledger

Debits increase assets or decrease claims on assets (liabilities and owner's equity). Credits increase claims on assets or decrease assets. Here are some examples of typical transactions and the debits and credits and accounts used to record them:

- Cash Purchase: An office pays a supplier of office supplies at the time of purchase: debit the Inventory account (under Assets) and credit the Cash account (also under Assets). Value of Inventory goes up and value of cash decreases.
- Goods received, bill to follow: debit the Inventory Account and credit the Accounts Payable (under Liabilities). Value of Inventory goes up and value of Accounts Payable goes up.
- Pay a Bill: pay for services you have already received: Debit Accounts Payable and Credit Cash. Value of Accounts Payable goes down and value of cash goes down.
- Pay Wages: Debit the Wages Account and credit Cash. Value of Wages goes up and Cash goes down.

To appreciate the importance of double-entry bookkeeping, it is interesting to note its influence on the Industrial Revolution. At that time, businesses increased in size and complexity. Accurate bookkeeping was required for managers to understand the financial status of their businesses in order to keep them solvent and offer a degree of transparency to investors. While a single-entry system can be adapted by a skilled bookkeeper to meet some of these needs, only a double-entry system provides the required detail systematically and by design.

Journal and Ledger Functions: Building Towards Financial Statements

Using the tools of double-entry bookkeeping and debits and credits, the basis of all financial reports is the journal and ledger functions of accounting. The vast majority of managers will never see or use either of these tools, but they will depend on them.

The general journal is a chronological listing of all financial events that affect the organization. The general ledger is a summary of this information, organized according to the types of accounts used in the organization's financial reports. These two basic documents or computerized databases interact to give both historical and analytical perspectives on the impact of financial events as they occur. For the most part, they are a single database.

An account is a category of financial event that the organization deems sufficiently important to list as a separate

category that can be captured in reports. For instance, most organizations will want to have a cash account because cash is their most liquid asset. We have already seen how accounts are organized above.

The primary rule for journal entries – the individual transactions that make up a general journal – is that they must fully respect the fundamental accounting equation. For example, the Hope for Street Kids (HSK) organization buys a $1,200 printer for its office. It has not paid for the purchase but intends to do so when the bill arrives from its regular supplier, within the month. Here is how the transaction will be recorded in the journal:

Assets	=	Liabilities	+	Equity
Account: Equipment		Account: Accounts Payable		
Debit: +$1,200		Credit: = $1,200		

The effect on the overall equation is balance but it has also effectively recorded the full scope of the financial activity. To have simply recorded that a new piece of equipment worth $1,200 had been received would have distorted the financial situation of the organization because it also incurred an outstanding liability. Similarly, the changes in financial condition can take place on one side of the equation only. Suppose that HSK buys supplies for the office, using its debit card. The value of the goods is $750. The financial events are as follows:

Assets	=	Liabilities	+	Equity
Account: Cash				
Credit: –$750				
Account: Inventory				
Debit: = $750				

Both cash and inventory are on the same side of the equation because they are both assets.

Matters can be more complex. Sometimes, more than two accounts are affected. Suppose HSK wants to buy emergency clothing. It will take full delivery and pay half the cost on the delivery date. It will pay the final bill when it receives the goods, to permit adjustments if any are necessary. Based on the supplier's estimate, the overall cost is $5,000. HSK is reasonably certain there will be no adjustments when it gets the bill, so it can enter the transaction into the journal. Three accounts are affected:

Assets	=	Liabilities	+	Equity
Account: Cash		Account: Accounts Payable		
Credit: –$2,500		Debit: +$2,500		
Account: Inventory				
Debit: = $5,000				

In this instance, both sides of the equation rise by $2,500 and the equation is balanced.

General ledgers take the individual journal-entry information, such as that found in the examples above, and turn it on its side. The value of a general journal is the traceability of the information. It is based on time-sequencing and ensures that all transactions are entered in a timely fashion. Once inside the general-journal database, the information then moves into many reports, based on the kind of information system that is supporting the organization and the way the information is coded. It is essential that it be organized into the desired accounts in the general ledger in a timely way. Organizations often have sub-ledgers that are rolled up into the general ledger when needed. The timing depends on the needs and requirements of the organization. For instance, for a special project, a sub-ledger may be created to capture all the costs of that project.

As noted at the beginning of this section, it is highly unlikely that most line managers will ever be engaged in journal entry or in reviewing general ledgers. That is the work of the financial specialists who support the organization. In most organizations, millions of such entries are involved in the basic functions of the organization. For instance, an organization with a staff of 1,500 people who are paid every two weeks would require journal entries to cover each and every pay transaction. Of course, these are now automated and are generally made on a scheduled basis, subject only to changes in status. Feeding those changes to the financial people requires work from the human resources support staff. Once again, there are hundreds of such transactions. These transactions will also be affected by the line manager's needs and behaviours in terms of hiring, approving upgrades, and reclassifications. If money is involved, there is going to be a journal entry at the end of a decision or action.

Reference has been made to the timing of financial reports. This can be very important when managers are eager to know their financial status. Ensuring that these underpinnings are sound and working properly is key to having a good cash-forecasting system, which in turn maximizes the manager's resource flexibility.

Building Blocks of Financial Statements

Further on in this chapter, there will be detailed discussions of the main financial statements that governments must produce. As a summary, and to link the following detailed discussion, those statements are:

1. **The Balance Sheet or Statement of Financial Condition:** This is a snapshot of the financial condition of the government or part of it at one point in time. This provides a picture of the assets, liabilities and net worth/debt of the government.
2. **The Statement of Operations:** This is a report on the financial transactions, both cash and accrued, for a specific period of time. This offers a complete picture of all financial transactions.
3. **The Statement of Cash Flow:** This is a report of all cash changes for the government for a specific period of time.
4. **Statement of Changes in Net Debt or Net Financial Assets:** Because governments hold long term debt and its management is a matter of economic and political concern, some governments will offer a separate report indicating the changes in net debt for a specific period of time. However, some governments are in a surplus position with no debt. The status of their surplus is also an important matter of public concern.

As will be discussed further on, all statements will be accompanied by **Notes**, which provide information on the basis of accounting and explanations for key financial events. These are an integral part of the financial statements. What follows now is a description of the fundamental elements of these reports. Afterwards, they will be shown in their application.

The fundamental accounting equation has already introduced the principal concepts that form the basis of most financial reports: assets, liabilities, and equity or net assets.

Assets

Assets are resources owned, or in some cases controlled, by an individual or organization as a result of transactions or events from which future economic benefits are expected to flow to that individual or organization. The formal definition under International Financial Reporting Standards (IRRS) is "An asset is a resource controlled by the enterprise as a result of past events and from which future economic benefits are expected to flow to the enterprise."[3]

Assets are organized according to their availability, that is, the liquidity or speed with which they can be converted to cash. **Figure 3.3** outlines the various categories for defining assets, and the following section describes them. This does not mean that all assets are in physical form. The test for how they are classified is their availability and their usefulness to the organization in attaining its goals.

FIGURE 3.3
Asset Categories

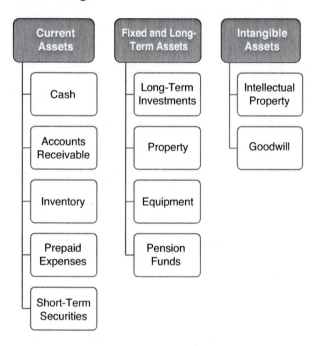

Current Assets

Current assets are those assets that can be reasonably expected to be consumed within the fiscal year of the organization in order to meet its needs. They are available for use and are considered part of the resources needed to carry out the activities of the organization within a given period. There are no restrictions on the number of current asset categories, but those in **Figure 3.3** are the common ones. In some cases, inventories may have a life cycle that extends beyond one year, and how they are reported then becomes a matter of relevance and

materiality. For instance, a road-maintenance unit of a city may have three emergency generators in its inventory. These are, by their very nature, contingent items that may or may not be used in a given time period. For the purposes of financial reporting on balance sheets or income statements, these would generally be treated more as fixed assets rather than as inventory. How they are recorded would be a matter of accounting policy for the city in question. Such policies are reported in the annual reports of the city. Although sometimes difficult to classify, current assets generally fit within the five categories described below.

Cash is money in any form, held either on hand or in financial institutions, that is ready for disbursement at any time.

Accounts receivable is money owed to the organization or individual in exchange for goods and services it has provided, or for obligations such as taxes, fines, and duties. Receivables can take many forms and are often reported in ways that reflect those forms. For instance, a municipality may mail out tax bills that, taken together, have a value of $3,780,000. That figure could be reported by the city as an accounts receivable item or, to provide greater clarity, as a tax receivable (which is another form of the same thing).

Nonprofit organizations may treat pledges as accounts receivable on their balance sheets. Under the general category of accounts receivable, they may have several sub-categories that their managers and overseers want to have in place to provide clarity in reporting. A YMCA, for example, may have pledges receivable, members' dues receivable, and a general category for receivables such as consulting services and day-care fees. This allows the organization to separate receivables that it is confident that it will fully collect from those where some form of discounting will have to take place, based on the likelihood of actually collecting the receivable. In the case of pledges, these are just promises offered or solicited in fundraising campaigns to pay some money at a future date. If the solicitor got a credit card number, then the pledge is a fair bet to be received. If not, then the chances of finally collecting the receivable declines. If the process involves sending out a paper notification and waiting to receive a cheque, the gap between the good intentions on the solicitation and actual receipt of the money is often a wide one, with the organization left holding a receivable but no legal obligation to pay on the part of the donor. Most organizations will treat pledge receivables with some caution and will often subtract long-standing pledges (in essence, treat them as a bad debt) before reporting on the receivable amount.

Inventories are materials and supplies held for use in providing services or making a product. Inventories have at least two different meanings:

1. supplies not for sale but for use in the delivery of goods and services (e.g., kitchen utensils for meal preparation in a long-term-care home);
2. a detailed list showing quantities, descriptions, and values of owned property needed to carry out the operations of the organization (e.g., desks, electronic equipment, and other items typically found in the fixed-asset group).

Some organizations have very large inventories, often with highly cost-sensitive items that are of high value. Matters of inventory management can be important to many public-sector organizations; some of these, especially with respect to valuation, are dealt with later in this text.

Prepaid expenses include assets that have been paid for and have not yet been used but that will be used within the fiscal year. These include such items as rent paid in advance and fire insurance premiums paid in full at the beginning of a year to cover the whole year. For instance, if the organization has paid for its directors' liability insurance for a three-year period and reports are being prepared for the first year of this policy, the insurance is an asset that is listed as a prepaid expense and, in fact, is being used by the organization to achieve its goals over a three-year period.

The prepaid expense is an asset that cannot be liquidated, but it is consumed within the fiscal year. In the case of prepaid insurance, premiums for the other two years are generally treated not as short-term but rather as long-term and are called deferred charges. They would appear in the long-term or fixed-asset section of the balance sheet.

Short-term marketable securities are, after cash, the most liquid of the assets that appear on a balance sheet. Marketable securities are any form of short-term investment, such as stocks, bonds, readily convertible mutual funds, investments, or treasury certificates that can be converted to cash. Their liquidity will vary, depending on the type of investment. For accounting purposes, money held in a cash or savings account in a financial institution is treated as cash, even if it earns some form of interest. It is instantly liquid.

Many public-sector organizations hold securities for a number of purposes:

1. as a source of operating income from an endowment, which is a restricted fund created to produce such income;

2. as a means of deriving some additional benefit from cash held that is not needed in the short term and can be invested;
3. increasingly, voluntary organizations receive stock holdings as donations and can choose either to manage them as long-term portfolios or simply to expedite their sales and realize the cash.

Reporting the value of these holdings on the balance sheet requires that they be valued fairly. In many instances, this is simply the purchasing value of the certificate, stock, or bond. In the cases of funds such as endowment funds, they will have their own reporting requirements and may not necessarily appear on the general balance sheet of the organization.

Fixed and Long-Term Assets

Fixed assets, those assets that will not be used up or converted to cash within a fiscal year, are also referred to as long-term assets. As seen in **Figure 3.3** these assets include categories such as land, buildings, and equipment as well as long-term investments or funds reserved to cover future liabilities. In assigning values to fixed assets, it is useful to go back to the GAAP on cost conservatism. Hence, all accounting begins with the cost of the asset not its current value. For example, the purchase of land is recorded at cost. Although the market value of the land may fluctuate over the years, from an accounting perspective this asset is fixed. Therefore, the organization will list the value of the land as the cost at the time of purchase. This principle is in considerable flux in that there is a concerted drive to replace cost as a basis of valuation with fair market value as a truer representation of the value of the asset.

This rule of valuation may represent a challenge for some public-sector organizations that are responsible for lands that have never been purchased or other assets that are so old that their original value is meaningless. The move from cash to accrual accounting in the public sector, which will be examined in detail in the next chapter, has brought this issue to light. In general, public entities have to weigh the relevance of placing a cost value on these kinds of assets against the cost and difficulty of doing so. There is also the relevance argument in the valuation of certain public-sector assets: for the purposes of accurate financial reporting, it may be useful to place a value on the legislature buildings in Saskatoon, but these are highly valued buildings of great historical significance to the people of Saskatchewan. Their purchase value will seldom figure into decisions to maintain or upgrade them.

Depreciation

More will be said about depreciation in further chapters. For the purposes of the construction of financial statements, depreciation of assets is an important element in reflecting the changing value of those assets for both the Statement of Financial Condition and Statement of Operations. Some have argued that the public sector's past failures at applying cost values and then applying depreciation rates to see where their value terminates have led to a certain disregard for both maintenance and replacement budgeting for public infrastructure. Accrual accounting and budgeting have gone a long way to reducing this problem, but not necessarily instilling the will or resources to replace fully depreciated assets.

The principle of depreciation is that all equipment and plant are used up over a period of time defined by the owners and that, at the end, replacement or refurbishment of some kind would be necessary. The accrual system plays an important role in recognizing depreciation expenses in the period in which they are used. Both plant and equipment are used up over their lives, not all at once. Therefore, the value of the asset at a given time from a financial reporting point of view is the original cost minus depreciation at the rate that is applied to the particular item. Depreciation, then, will equal the annual use of the item in a monetized fashion. Each year, this is recognized in the balance sheet and other reports dealing with equipment.

Depreciation plays a second role, that of distributing the value of the asset over the years in which it is used, not simply up front, when the purchase is made. For example, a department buys a vehicle at a cost of $35,000 to add to an existing fleet. In listing this expense in its journal, it will report the full amount of $35,000 as a reduction in cash. $35,000 will be added to the fixed assets. In this way,

the overall accounting equation is not changed, but the transaction takes place on only one side of the equation.

Current Assets + Fixed Assets = Liabilities + Equity/Net Assets

$$-\$35,000 \quad + \quad \$35,000 \quad = \quad \text{No Change}$$

The department will also make a decision about the usable life of the vehicle, assuming appropriate maintenance is factored in. Let us say that this is five years. The department can also assume, on the basis of either experience or an accounting convention developed within the organization, that at the end of its life, $5,000 will be recouped through the sale of the used vehicle. Therefore, to attribute full value from the asset, $30,000 will be distributed evenly over the life of the vehicle. **Figure 3.4** illustrates how this translates into the following depreciation rate and value assigned to the asset at the end of each year.

The amount of depreciation reported each year is a depreciation expense of $6,000, which is accompanied by a reduction in the net value of the asset. This is known as the net book value of the asset. In order to avoid overly complicated reports, the balance sheet often uses the term "Equipment, net of depreciation." It bundles together all the equipment with their different depreciation rates and provides a sum for them all. Depreciation charges for the current year are reported in the Statement of Operations. Explanations for this figure would have to appear in the explanatory notes accompanying the financial statements.

There are several methods for calculating depreciation, generally based on either the passage of time or the level of activity (or use) of the asset. The simplest and most often used technique, as described above, is straight-line depreciation.

FIGURE 3.4
Depreciation Schedule for Vehicle

Year of Purchase	Year 1	Year 2	Year 3	Year 4	Year 5
Expense reported in Statement of Operations: 35,000	Depreciation expense reported on Statement of Operations: 6,000	6,000	6,000	6,000	6,000
Value reported on Statement of Financial Position: 35,000	29,000	23,000	17,000	11,000	5,000

Liabilities

Liabilities are legal financial obligations the organization has arising from past transactions or events. They are claims against the assets of the organization. Alternatively stated in the IFRS, "A liability is a present obligation of the enterprise arising from past events, the settlement of which is expected to result in an outflow from the enterprise of resources embodying economic benefits."[4]

Current Liabilities

Current liabilities are those obligations that will come due in a relatively short period of time, usually within the fiscal year for which the reports are being prepared. Generally, they are presented in order of liquidity, demanding cash to discharge the obligation. **Figure 3.5** presents some typical categories, but each organization will define those most pertinent to it.

FIGURE 3.5
Array of Liability Categories

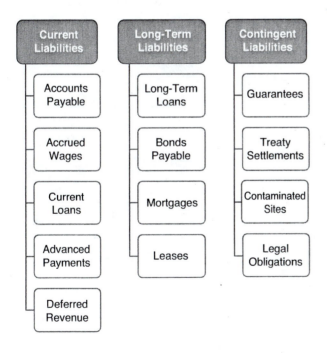

One category of current costs, accounts payable, represents the amounts that the organization owes its suppliers, creditors, service agents, etc. Wages accrued is the amount of obligation that has been accumulated to discharge staff salaries that have already been earned. This, too, is usually a current account, to be cleared shortly. Current loans

are loans that will be paid within one year. Included in this category, or put in its own if it is material, will be the amount to be paid on long-term liabilities such as mortgages within the current fiscal year. Advance payments are payments for services that have not yet been provided by the organization. This is seen as a liability because the asset has not yet been discharged.

Deferred revenues are funds set aside for specific purposes as laid out in legislation, regulation or through a specific agreement. In essence, the government has received money for goods or services not yet provided. This will be eliminated when the funds are used for the agreed purpose, recognized as revenue and the deferred charge eliminated. An example of this would be a government receiving a sum for brownfield restoration per a development agreement, but not undertaking the work immediately. Once it begins the work, the money can be recognized as revenue, an asset.

Long-Term Liabilities

Long-term liabilities are obligations that are not required to be discharged within the current fiscal year. They include the following:

- Long-term loans are funds borrowed with a multi-year repayment schedule.
- Mortgages are actually loans, generally secured by capital assets, for a longer period of time. As the amount of principal owed decreases each year, this will be reflected in the financial position of the organization.
- A bond is simply an IOU, an agreement under which a sum is repaid to an investor after an agreed period of time at an agreed-upon rate of interest. By purchasing a bond you are lending money to the institution, company, or government issuing the bond. Such loans normally pay a fixed rate of interest over a specified time and then repay the original sum in full after a fixed period, when the bond matures. They are treated in a similar manner to loans. The net present value of a bond reflects the current cost of future cash flows that are anticipated in meeting its obligations.
- Leases are long-term rental agreements for property and equipment. Often they extend for many years or for the useful life of the piece of equipment.

Contingent Liabilities

A contingent liability is one that may become an actual liability when anticipated future events occur or fail to occur. As such there is a degree of both certainty and uncertainty to them. However, for governments, there has to exist a probable expectation that the liability will occur and will be sufficiently material to record on the financial statements. Governments may choose to recognize such contingent liabilities as loan guarantees, clean-up costs of identified contaminated sites, treaty settlements (First Nations) and future legal claims. The last item is certainly subject to judgement both with respect to the probability of it occurring and the wisdom of booking a liability in a case that the government will contest its lack of responsibility.

Contingent liabilities have to have some reasonable probability or legal contractual obligations associated with them that would justify posting them in financial statements. Unknown costs or risks associated with a purchase or obligation are not contingent liabilities. Amounts owed for services received but for which no billing has occurred are not contingent liabilities. In this instance, the service has been received – a past event – and the only uncertainty is the timing of the bill.

Governments book contingent liabilities with care. There is a line between such actions and the identification of risks in financial statements. The latter are identified in the notes without being booked or monetized in the financial statements. The line is the degree of certainty and the ability to actually produce a credible dollar cost of the liability.

Net Worth

Equity/Net Assets/Fund Balance/Municipal Position shows assets held but not needed to discharge liabilities. **Figure 3.6** sets out typical categories in Equity or Net Assets or Fund Balance for the private, public, and voluntary sectors. It can be argued therefore that the determination of Net Worth provides important information about the fiscal sustainability of a government, department or agency. It also provides information on the amount of intergenerational debt or asset transfer that is occurring. High debt means the transfer of that debt to future generations, thereby reducing intergenerational equity.

In the private-sector model, equity represents the amount of funds that should be available for shareholders, or shareholder wealth. When a company is privately owned, it represents the worth of the company to the owner. The other category is income that is earned by the company when it operates profitably but is not distributed to shareholders. This is retained earnings or capital and is treated as part of equity or net assets. These represent the portion of the profits of a for-profit corporation that have been earned over the years and have not been distributed to the owners in the form of dividends. For a government, these are the funds that are held for future use in the form of a reserve or used to discharge debt. Retained earnings arise either from

FIGURE 3.6
Array of Net Worth Categories

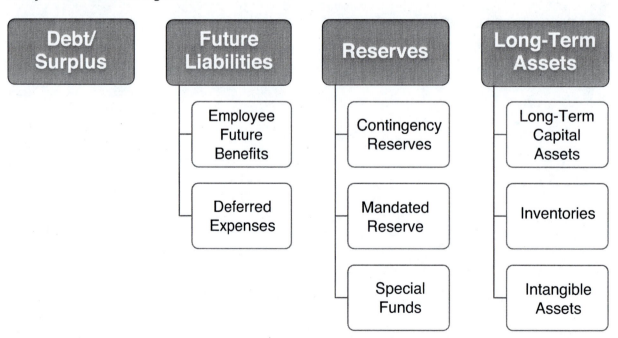

profits or from operating surpluses. Reserves derive their worth from such earnings, from previously held funds or from direct infusions of cash as is often required by law to reduce fiscal risk.

For the public sector, therefore, the equity portion of the financial equation has some different elements than the private sector. The key elements that may be included are:

- reserves, held under varying degrees of restricted use;
- funds – special accounts held for specific purposes;
- net debt or surplus;
- tangible capital assets.

According to the CICA *Not-for-profit Reporting Guide*:

> Net assets, which are also referred to as fund balances or accumulated surplus, represent the organization's residual interest in its assets after deducting its liabilities. In other words, net assets are the net resource available to the organization in carrying out its service delivery activities. Most not-for-profit organizations have some restrictions on their net assets.[5]

In public-sector organizations, the equity section can be divided in many ways to meet the reporting needs of each organization. For example, some municipalities use the term "Municipal Position" for the equity section of the Statement of Financial Position or Balance Sheet.

Financial Statements – A General Overview

In determining where financial statements fit into the overall picture of management and accountability within the public sector, the CICA offers the useful outline in **Figure 3.7**. What is important about this diagram is how central financial reports are to both financial and managerial reporting. Further, since they are used in many different ways, their validity becomes a touchstone for governmental performance as a whole.

A complete set of financial statements for any public entity, based on the *Public Sector Accounting Standards*, includes all of the following components:

1. Management Report, which outlines managerial responsibilities for the preparation of the report as well as the signatures of those designated responsible for them;
2. Independent Auditor's Report, which provides an attestation that the information conforms with established accounting practices;
3. Consolidated Statement of Financial Position;
4. Consolidated Statement of Operations;
5. Consolidated Statement of Changes in Net Assets/Debt;
6. Consolidated Statement of Cash Flows; and
7. Notes to the statements.[6]

These components are referred to by a variety of names both within and across jurisdictions. A good description of such statements can be found, for the Government of Canada for example, in **Figure 3.8**. The Statement of Financial Position may also be referred to as a Balance Sheet or Statement of Assets and Liabilities. The Statement of Operations may also be referred to as a Statement of Revenues and Expenses, an Income Statement, an Operating Statement, or a Profit and Loss Statement. The notes to the financial statements may include items referred to as "schedules" in some jurisdictions. One cannot fully understand financial statements without the explanatory notes. In fact, these notes are an integral part of the financial statements.

The term "consolidated" deserves some notice. The list above focuses on high-level financial statements, often at a government or departmental level. These will bring together all the entities within their reporting universe. Many of these units will produce their own financial reports. All of these various reports have to reconcile and cross-check which keeps financial people busy. However, if the user wants what is called a whole-of-government view, then the consolidated report is what is needed. However, if the user needs to drill down into more detail, then the specific individual reports are beneficial. One thing is certain: consolidated financial statements must, in the MDA/Notes, be very clear about how the entity they report upon is defined, i.e., what is in and what is out.

Balance Sheet

Regardless of the terminology used, the Balance Sheet is one of the basic financial reports. It reports on the resources controlled by the organization and the ways in which they are financed, providing a snapshot of the financial position of the organization at a specific point in time. The Balance Sheet does not record flows of cash and resources, merely the results of those flows. It is recorded at one point in time and may change the next day. It includes all resources, regardless of how accessible they are for current use. This report focuses on the worth of the organization.

A typical Balance Sheet for a small organization is shown in **Figure 3.9**. Hope for Street Kids is an urban nonprofit organization that helps homeless kids through

FIGURE 3.7
Structure of Government Financial Reporting

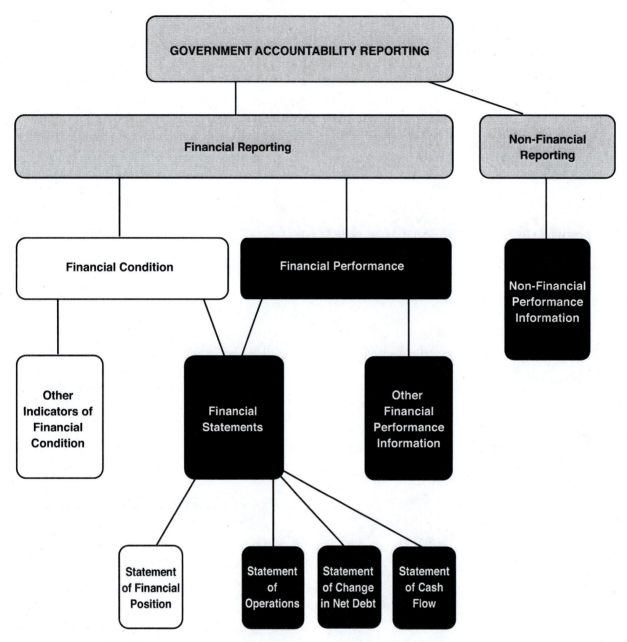

Source: Canadian Institute of Chartered Accountants, *Twenty Questions about Government Financial Reporting*, available at http://www.cica.ca/multimedia/Download_Library/Standards/PSAB/English/e_PSAB20QuestionsGRE.pdf.

counselling and liaison with schools and social agencies. It operates for the most part with volunteers and one staff member but has good financial support from the community. The period ending November 30, 2005, has been chosen because it is the end of the first quarter of this organization, which began its fiscal year on September 1, 2005.

The first point to remember about balance sheets is that they are, as noted, simply snapshots. They do not report flows of cash, etc. Further, a table like this would normally be accompanied by notes explaining the various elements. For instance, to understand the Net Assets portion, it is necessary first to understand what makes up the Restricted Fund and the relative liquidity of the Unrestricted Fund.

FIGURE 3.8
Government of Canada Financial Statements

The first is the Statement of Operations and Accumulated Deficit, which presents the Government's revenues, expenses and surplus for the year, and the net accumulation of the annual surpluses and deficits since Confederation.

The second is the **Statement of Financial Position**, which discloses the Government's cash balances and investments, amounts owing to and by the Government at the end of the year, and the Government's non-financial assets such as its tangible capital assets and inventories. It also presents both the accumulated deficit of the Government and its net debt, which is the difference between the Government's total liabilities and its financial assets.

The third is the **Statement of Change in Net Debt**, which explains the difference between the Government's annual surplus and the change in the net debt for the year. It reports the extent to which revenues recognized in the year were sufficient to offset expenditures, as opposed to the expenses recognized in the annual surplus. In that regard, it is an important flow financial statement, one that shows changes over a specified period. This is seen as important as the part of the Statement of Operations called Net Worth is actually a stock statement, one that reflects the state of overall worth at one point in time.

The fourth is the **Statement of Cash Flow**, which provides information on the Government's cash provided by or used for operating, capital, investing and financing activities.

Source: *Public Accounts of the Government of Canada.*

FIGURE 3.9
Balance Sheet Example

Hope for Street Kids
Statement of Financial Position
November 30, 2005

Assets		Liabilities	
Current Assets		**Current Liabilities**	
Cash	10,000	Accounts Payable	40,000
Accounts Receivable	20,000	Accrued Wages	10,000
Inventory	50,000	**Total Current Liabilities**	50,000
Total Current Assets	80,000		
		Long Term Liabilities	
Fixed Assets		Bonds Payable	200,000
Equipment	250,000	Mortgage Payable	150,000
Building	150,000	**Total Long-Term Liabilities**	350,000
Land	110,000		
Total Fixed Assets	510,000	**Net Assets**	
		Restricted Fund (Permanent)	100,000
		Unrestricted Fund	40,000
		Reserve	50,000
		Total Net Assets	190,000
Total Assets	590,000	**Total Liabilities**	590,000

"Reading the Balance Sheet"

There is an element of reading all financial reports that is strictly intuitive. That is what is called being able to "read a balance sheet," a common way of describing the skill of analyzing numbers, setting them in context, and identifying elements of importance. For instance, HSK appears from **Figure 3.9** to be fairly well-resourced in terms of having built up retained earnings over the years. At least, it is holding reserves and funds in Net Assets that are disproportionate to the staff levels (which can be deduced from the amount of Wages Accrued). It might also be assumed that there are very few paid staff but

many volunteers. Otherwise, the physical plant would not be necessary. There is very little to tell us what HSK does in terms of helping street kids and very little program information. That is normal. Financial reports would generally be incorporated into external reporting with program information. It is of interest to note when combining this with the Statement of Operations (**Figure 3.13**) that its rate of spending is at a deficit level, which it can cover, but not forever.

A much more complex balance sheet, but one that also informs the public of its financial position, can be found in the example of the City of Windsor in **Figure 3.10**.

FIGURE 3.10
Consolidated Statement of Financial Position

THE CORPORATION OF THE CITY OF WINDSOR Consolidated Statement of Financial Position December 31, 2001, with comparative figures for 2000 ($000's)		
	2001 $	2000 $
		(Restated) (see note 15)
Financial assets		
Cash and temporary investments	52,299	23,411
Taxes and grants-in-lieu receivable	27,879	28,063
Trade and other receivables	38,441	43,274
Prepaid expenses	4,970	1,840
Promissory note receivable [note 4 (b)]	21,520	71,718
Total financial assets	145,109	168,306
Investment in government business enterprises [note 4 (a)]	179,799	177,621
Total assets	324,908	345,927
Liabilities		
Temporary borrowings [note 5]	–	41,204
Accounts payable	50,895	42,866
Deferred revenue [note 8 (d)]	9,898	10,124
Accrued interest on long term debt	3,354	2,266
Long term debt [note 6 (a) and (f)]	139,210	116,434
Employee future benefit obligations [note 7 (b)]	157,614	148,609
Total liabilities	360,971	361,503
Municipal position		
Operating fund [note 8 (a)]	20	(1,785)
Capital fund [note 8 (b)]	(54,105)	(69,423)
Reserves and reserve funds [note 8 (c)]	121,706	78,471
Fund balances	67,621	7,263
Equity in government business enterprises [note 4 (c)]	179,799	225,821
Amounts to be recovered in future years [note 8 (e)]	(283,483)	(248,660)
Net municipal position	(36,063)	(15,576)
Total liabilities and municipal position	324,908	345,927

Here we see the fairly common practice of providing year-to-year comparisons in the balance sheet. Note how the Net Assets portion is entitled "Municipal Position."

The city's financial statements are accompanied by 27 pages of notes. Such notes are normal – in fact, absolutely vital to a full understanding of the financial statements. This balance sheet represents a fairly complex yet rich source of information. Often larger governments will aggregate their balance sheets to such a level that specific information will be hard to find. Municipalities, on the other hand, generally provide a mix of high-level, i.e., highly summarized, information and detail.

Some of the elements to be taken into account in preparing notes for balance sheets are:

- any changes in accounting policies;
- any adjustments to previous year calculations;
- detail that would assist in understanding the balance sheet figures;
- areas of material concern, such as amounts so large as to require some delineation, or so different from the previous reporting period that an explanation is required.

A good source of information lies in the Municipal Position Section and, more specifically, in the Reserves section, shown in **Figure 3.11**. It is difficult to understand fully the assets sections without understanding that the Reserves listed here in the notes are actually part of the spending plans of the city, just held for a different time. Reading the notes, though, one sees the richness of the information that is available.

One aspect that somewhat differentiates how voluntary organizations deal with the balance sheet is their treatment of funds, as shown in **Figure 3.12**. Most voluntary organizations use fund accounting as a way to display their financial position. This comprises the collective accounting procedures that result in a self-balancing set of accounts for each fund established by legal, contractual, or voluntary actions of an organization. Fund accounting involves an accounting segregation, although not necessarily a physical segregation, of resources. Movement of resources between funds is often restricted by specific rules or requiring specific authority, perhaps even legislation or changes to budget provisions. This is done to provide clarity in the use of funds and also to ensure that specially designated funds are used for their intended purposes. Their financial position using such funds must be reported.

The fund system provides a useful means of segregating monies that come from specific sources and that are designated for specific uses from more general funds. Also, as already noted, special restrictions may limit their

application to the purposes of the fund. The basis of a fund is that it is a self-balancing accounting entity. Like nonprofits, governments often employ funds to protect designated program monies from other uses within a department. Municipal governments use funds in order to clearly designate the purposes for which funds are voted.

FIGURE 3.11
Explanation of Reserves and Reserve Funds: Notes Attached to the Financial Statements of the City of Windsor

The consolidated statement of financial position reflects a balance of reserves and funds of $121,706 ($78,471 in 2000) and are detailed as follows:

	2001 $
Reserves set aside for specific purpose by Council:	
Enwin recapitalization	47,310
Working funds	1,098
Encumbrances	1,322
Future planning	188
Post-retirement death benefit	22
Recreation services	467
Police services	241
Fire services	115
Transit services	154
Winter control	78
Environmental services	3,084
Total reserves	**54,079**
Reserve funds set aside for specific purpose by Council:	
Replacement of equipment	14,948
Capital expenditures	16,318
Tunnel improvements	18,659
Insurance	434
Health benefits rate stabilization	374
Sanitary sewer expenditures	2,642
Tunnel debt repayment	6,710
Airport capital expediutres	198
Budget stabilization	1,848
Children's fund	248
Environmental services	325
Social housing	2,022
Long-term disability	2,901
Total reserve funds	**67,627**
Total reserves and reserve funds	**121,706**

City Council has approved the use of the Enwin recapitalization funds, largely to transition traditional debt and lease financing to a pay-as-you-go funding approach.

Source: *City of Windsor, Consolidated Financial Statements, Year ending December 31, 2001.*

FIGURE 3.12
Statement of Financial Position – Nonprofit Organization

			NFP A Statement of Financial Position as at December 31, 19x2			
	Operating Fund	Research Fund	Capital Asset Fund	Endowment Fund	Total 19x2	Total 19x1
CURRENT ASSETS						
Cash and term deposits	$118,000	$ 4,000	$ –	$ –	$ 122,000	$160,000
Accounts receivable	20,000	–	–	–	20,000	10,000
Grant receivable	–	30,000	–	–	30,000	25,000
	138,000	34,000	–	–	172,000	195,000
Investments (market 244,000 – 19x1, 102,000)	–	–	80,000	160,000	240,000	100,000
Capital assets, net	–	–	627,000	–	627,000	135,000
	$138,000	$34,000	$707,000	$160,000	$1,039,000	$430,000
CURRENT LIABILITIES						
Accounts payable & accrued liabilities	$ 24,000	$ 1,000	$ –	$–	$25,000	$ 20,000
Mortgage payable – current	–	–	6,000	–	6,000	–
	24,000	1,000	6,000	–	31,000	20,000
Mortgage payable – long-term	–	–	441,000	–	441,000	–
Deferred contributions	110,000	8,000	147,000	–	265,000	175,000
FUND BALANCES						
Invested in capital assets	–	–	113,000	–	113,000	65,000
Externally restricted	–	–	–	150,000	150,000	100,000
Internally restricted	–	25,000	–	10,000	35,000	–
Unrestricted	4,000	–	–	–	4,000	70,000
	4,000	25,000	113,000	160,000	302,000	235,000
	$138,000	$34,000	$707,000	$160,000	$1,039,000	$430,000

Source: CICA *Not-for-profit Reporting Guide*, 101.

Management Discussion and Analysis

Before turning to the Income Statement, it is useful to discuss the Management Discussion and Analysis (MDA). Our examination of the Statement of Financial Position included some discussion of the notes that were attached to the City of Windsor's full Financial Statement for 2002 – 27 pages in all. These notes form part of the MDA. They are an essential part of financial documentation and should be studied when coming to an understanding of the full meaning of financial statements.

The purpose of the Management Discussion and Analysis is to provide a means for government management officials to discuss what the financial statement numbers mean (financial information), what was accomplished during the reporting periods (performance information), and the organization's systems, controls and legal compliance (governance information).[7]

The point of adding a textual portion to the overall financial and performance data is that such information tells the story about what happened to the organization in a given period. The role of the MDA is to explain why the results or changes came about as they did. Without this, a full understanding of the financial data is not possible.

The CICA, in its guidance to public-sector organizations, outlines the following principles for MDA material accompanying financial statements. This material should:

- enable readers to view the organization through the eyes of management;
- complement as well as supplement financial statements;
- be reliable, complete, fair, and balanced, and provide material information;
- have a forward-looking orientation;
- focus on management's strategy for generating value over time;
- be written in plain language, with candour and without exaggeration, and embody the qualities of understandability, relevance, comparability, and consistency over reporting periods.[8]

One should not confuse the MDA with narrative performance reports or annual reports of organizations. The focus of the MDA is an adjunct to the financial statements. While it may have many similarities to such reports, it must link back to the financial information.

The following general categories would be part of an MDA:

- Mission and organizational structure information
  - mission
  - major programs, functions, and activities
  - organization structure
  - operating environment
- Financial information
  - financial highlights
  - financial condition
  - sources of financing – taxes and other receipts
  - financing provided by debt and debt management
- Performance information
  - results and achievements
  - expectations
  - costs versus results
- Governance information
  - systems and controls
  - changes in accounting procedures
  - compliance with legal requirements
  - comparison of budget to actual
- Forward-looking information
  - major changes in policy
  - risk factors taken into consideration

The Statement of Operations

This financial statement has many names:

- Income Statement
- Operating Statement
- Activity Statement
- Statement of Revenues and Expenditures
- Profit and Loss Statement

Unlike the Balance Sheet, which is a snapshot on a given day, the Statement of Operations covers the financial transactions of the organization for a given period of time – a month, a quarter, a year. This report sets out the details of the organization's revenues and expenses for the period. It also gives information about the changes in its economic resources and obligations as a result of its activities. The focus for public-sector organizations is that the report should accurately describe the delivery costs for the organization and the extent to which those costs were covered by the approved budget, inflowing fees or contributions, or other revenue. As these reports are now based on accrual accounting, they will also take into account the depreciation incurred during the period being reported upon.

Organizations may use a number of different ways to group together or categorize their revenues and expenses in the Statement of Operations:

- by object: salaries, benefits, rentals, cost of services;
- by function: research, client service, inspection, support, or administrative services, etc.;
- by program: operations unit, administration unit, etc.

Where organizations operate different programs that they want to distinguish, it is possible for the statement to be organized along functional or program lines with a further breakdown using common objects. This will provide greater detail. **Figure 3.13** offers a simple Activity Statement for HSK.

FIGURE 3.13
Statement of Operations

Hope for Street Kids Statement of Operations For the period ending November 30, 2005 (First Quarter)		
	2005	2004
Revenues		
Total	29,800	38,300
Expenses		
Total	36,000	41,200
Increase (Decrease) in Net Assets	(6,200)	(2,900)

This is about as basic as it can get. Even for a small operation such as this, it is hardly adequate. A more complex version of this statement would provide more information. The organization of this information, and what is included in it, are matters of discretion for the reporting entity. A statement for HSK that provides further detail would look like this.

FIGURE 3.14
Detailed Statement of Operations

Hope for Street Kids
Statement of Operations
For the period ending November 30, 2005 (First Quarter)

	2005	2004
Revenues		
Government grants – program specific	17,500	15,000
Grants – general	0	2,000
Non-governmental contributions – specific/restricted	4,000	7,500
Unrestricted contributions	6,000	10,000
Fees	0	1,000
Interest	2,300	2,800
Total	**29,800**	**38,300**
Expenses		
Salaries and benefits	10,000	10,000
Rentals, equipment	2,000	2,200
Supplies	5,000	6,000
Aid to Kinds: program, financial assistance, travel home	19,000	23,000
Total	**36,000**	**41,200**
Increase (Decrease) in Net Assets	**(6,200)**	**(2,900)**

Reading the Statement: The most notable feature of this report is that HSK is currently operating in a deficit position, and it is persistent. This does not mean that it does not have the resources to cover a deficit or that it is operating inappropriately. From the Statement of Financial Position (or Balance Sheet) in **Figure 3.12**, it is clear that this organization has a good supply of net assets in all forms. The Statement of Financial Position indicates that it has been successful in raising money and could readily dip into its Reserve fund of $50,000 to cover its deficit. Notes to the statement should indicate that this is happening, if that is the course of action the organization has chosen to pursue.

While HSK is a small organization, it appears to have a number of funding sources: government funds for specific purposes (restricted), government funds with no restriction, contributions for specific purposes (restricted), and general donations with no restriction on their use. In fact, aside from some standard expenses like salaries and supplies, all other expenses are for one program object: aid to kids. This report, while accurate, does not help certain users sort out if the funds are being spent for the intended purposes or exactly how needs are being met. For instance, from **Figure 3.15**, it would appear that HSK has three lines of activity:[9]

- program grants to organizations and individuals to provide counselling services to street kids,
- short-term financial aid given directly to kids, and
- funds to help kids return to their home towns.

An additional table, such as **Figure 3.15**, would provide greater clarity as to the distribution of resources. Organizations will often put such more detailed information in the Notes. Similarly, given the relatively uncomplicated chart of accounts, this information could readily be in the financial statements themselves.

FIGURE 3.15
Line Item Distribution

Hope for Street Kids
Statement of Operations – Supplement in Notes
Line Item Distribution of Aid to Kids
For the period ending November 30, 2005 (First Quarter)

	2005	2004
Program activities: grants to counselling services	11,000	13,000
Short-term financial assistance	6,000	5,500
Travel assistance – kids to their homes	2,000	4,500
Total	**19,000**	**23,000**

Looking at the City of Windsor, a much larger public-sector organization, one finds many more matters of interest. In the Statement of Operations (**Figure 3.16**), we see the treatment of debt, both acquired and discharged, as part of the statement. Expenditures are divided between Operating and Capital, once again reflecting the importance of capital items in municipal governments. Under these two broad categories, expenditures are then reported on a program basis. This is a useful way to inform the public where their

FIGURE 3.16
Statement of Operations, City of Windsor

THE CORPORATION OF THE CITY OF WINDSOR
Consolidated Statement of Financial Activities
Year ended December 31, 2001, with comparative figures for 2000
($000's)

	Budget $	2001 $	2000 $
Revenues			
Property taxes and grants-in-lieu	223,949	223,834	210,204
User charges	140,467	139,331	119,756
Provincial and federal transfers	82,619	82,915	81,204
Revenue from other municipalities	17,765	17,836	18,256
Other	24,185	46,818	34,669
Change in equity in government business enterprises [note 4(a)]	–	2,178	2,443
Total revenues	488,985	512,912	466,532
Expenditures			
Operating			
General government	43,010	51,694	45,532
Protection to persons and property	84,853	89,554	83,208
Transportation services	40,726	45,517	48,512
Environmental services	33,806	36,013	30,688
Health services	9,417	9,054	7,153
Social and family services	159,653	155,922	140,085
Recreation and culture	36,016	37,010	36,371
Planning and development	5,917	5,697	5,043
Total operating	413,398	430,461	396,592
Capital [note 10(a)]			
General government	3,764	6,429	3,341
Protection to persons and property	1,857	1,465	12,090
Transportation services	31,606	37,798	26,276
Environmental services	18,107	25,450	15,519
Health services	6	6	144
Social and family services	917	323	582
Recreation and culture	7,277	8,373	14,872
Planning and development	3,651	23,094	11,224
Total capital	67,185	102,938	84,048
Total expenditures	480,583	533,399	480,640
Acquisition of ownership interest in electric utility [note 4]	–	–	131,141
Transfer of assets of newly defined government business enterprise [note 4]	–	–	88,360
Net revenues (expenditures)	8,402	(20,487)	205,393
New debt issued	23,200	44,017	22,550
Debt principal repayments [note 6(f)]	(21,980)	(21,911)	(17,900)
Change in employee future benefit obligations	–	9,005	8,506
Other items affecting amounts to be recovered	–	3,712	(210)
Increase in amounts to be recovered in future years	1,220	34,823	12,946
Transfer of revenue from government business enterprises	–	(1,288)	(221,944)
Transfer of GBE Equity to reserve [note 8]	–	47,310	–
Change in fund balances	9,622	60,358	(3,605)

The accompanying notes are an integral part of these financial statements.

FIGURE 3.16
(Continued)

To fully explain this Statement, certain notes are reproduced from the Report:

4(a) Investment in GBE:

The City of Windsor has investments in GBE totalling $179,799 (2000, $177,621) which is comprised of the following:

	2001 $	2000 $
		(Restated) (see note 15)
WCUL	82,417	83,590
WUC	93,748	90,305
CWHCL	3,634	3,726
	179,799	177,621

A continuity of the investment in GBE is as follows:

	WCUL $	WUC $	CWHCL $	2001 Total $	2000 Total $
					(Restated) (see note 15)
Opening investment	83,590	90,305	3,726	177,621	3,877
Acquisition of ownership interest of electric utility	–	–	–	–	82,941
Transfer of net assets of new defined GBE	–	–	–	–	88,360
Capital contribution	–	1,354	–	1,354	2,011
Current income (loss)	(1,173)	2,089	(92)	824	432
Closing investment	82,417	93,748	3,634	179,799	177,621

10(a) Capital Expenditures:

During the year, the Windsor Tunnel Commission funded a $3,010 capital expenditure investment in a public-private limited partnership between MDC Madison Developments Ltd. (general partner) and the City (limited partner). The parties agreed to form a limited partnership for the purpose of erecting a parking facility ("Park 'N' Go") which would be managed by the general partner with the intention of earning a profit. Windsor Tunnel Commission's additional parking requirements and the need for additional public parking within the downtown area resulted in the City entering into this arrangement whereby the City receives an 80% equity interest in the partnership. All partnership profits will be shared on an 80/20 bais and the City's pro-rata portion wll be recorded in Windsor Tunnel Commission's Capital Rehabilitation and Improvement Reserve Fund at the time of receipt.

6(f) Debt Principal Repayments:

Included in the debt principal repayments of $21,911 on the Consolidated Statement of Financial Activities is an amount of $670 relating to principal repayments of debentures held as own investments for which no long term debt is reflected on the Consolidated Statement of Financial Position. Therefore, a continuity of long term debt would require exclusion of the amount of principal repayments relating to debenttures held as own investments.

Source: Financial Statements, City of Windsor, sourced at www.citywindsor.ca.

money is being spent. It focuses not on the inputs but rather on the purpose of the expenditures. Notes are included to provide more detailed explanations.

For many public-sector and voluntary organizations – and increasingly for governments that establish special-purpose funds outside of the general accounting framework – the statement should treat the funds as self-reporting entities, even if they are on the same sheet. The CICA's *Not-for-profit Financial Reporting Guide* offers an example of such a fund-based report, reproduced in **Figure 3.17**.

Neither of these examples lists elements that may appear on the expenditure side of the equation: bad debts

and depreciation. Bad debts are amounts owed to the organization but are never collected, or amounts that the organization realizes it will never collect or that will cost more to collect than the total amount of the debt. In general, organizations will set a time limit on how long an accounts receivable item can be left on the books before it is declared a bad debt and written off as a charge. That is assuming that the organization is taking reasonable measures to collect its receivables in the meantime. Organizations want to remove these bad debts from their books of accounts receivable, so they write them off and take a charge in the expenditures under the category of bad debts.

FIGURE 3.17
Statement of Operations and Changes in Fund Balances

NFP A						
Statement of Operations and Changes in Fund Balances						
for the year ended December 31, 19x2						
	Operating Fund	Research Fund	Capital Asset Fund	Endowment Fund	Total 19x2	Total 19x1
REVENUES						
Federal government grants	$105,000	$30,000	$ –	$ –	$135,000	$125,000
General contributions	55,000	–	–	–	55,000	50,000
Contribution from XYZ Foundation	25,000	–	–	–	25,000	–
Amortization of deferred contributions	–	–	8,000	–	8,000	7,000
Seminar fees	80,000	–	–	–	80,000	75,000
Investment income	8,000	2,000	–	–	10,000	15,000
	273,000	32,000	8,000	–	313,000	272,000
EXPENSES						
Salaries & benefits	200,000	30,000	–	–	230,000	195,000
Purchased materials and services	23,000	2,000	–	–	25,000	30,000
Amortization of capital assets	–	–	23,000	–	23,000	12,000
Mortage interest	–	–	18,000	–	18,000	–
	223,000	32,000	41,000	–	296,000	237,000
Excess (deficiency) of revenues over expenses	50.000	–	(33,000)	–	17,000	35,000
Fund balances, beginning	70,000	–	65,000	100,000	235,000	200,000
Endowment contributions	–	–	–	50,000	50,000	–
Interfund transfers	(116,000)	25,000	81,000*	10,000	–	–
Fund balances, ending	$ 4,000	$25,000	$113,000	$160,000	$302,000	$235,000

*Consists of	Down payment for new land and building	$50,000
	Purchase of equipment	10,000
	Mortgage principal and interest repayments	21,000
	Total transfer from General Fund	$81,000

Source: CICA, *Not-for-profit Financial Reporting Guide*, accessible at www.cica.ca/focus-on-practice-areas/.../not...profit.../item65428.pdf.

Another element that will be found in the Statement of Operations is depreciation. This is treated as an expense. For organizations using full accrual accounting (see the next chapter), all assets must be depreciated and listed as an expense. This represents the amount of the asset that has been consumed in the reporting period.

As discussed earlier in this chapter, the two most common ways of calculating depreciation are the straight-line method (recall **Figure 3.4** as an example of this type of calculation) and accelerated or declining-balance depreciation (which assumes a preference to charge more depreciation in the early years of the use of the item and less in the later years when there will be more maintenance costs to offset the lower depreciation costs).

Statement of Changes in Net Assets or Net Debt

This statement is used by some public-sector organizations, but not all. That decision depends on the size of the organization and the materiality of the concern for net assets that have not already been adequately addressed in the Statement of Financial Position. Also called the Statement of Change in Net Debt, the Statement of Changes in Financial Position, or a Funds Flow Statement, it describes the details of the changes in the organization's net assets during the reporting period, usually a year. It shows the degree to which the organization's operations have added to, or depleted, its net assets or net debt. This statement identifies the sources from which additional funds or cash were derived and the uses to which these funds were allocated.

The Statement of Changes in Net Assets reconciles the organization's net assets position as reported in the Statement of Financial Position at the beginning and end of the reporting period. This clearly identifies the resources available to the organization for future activities. Alternatively, as we see in **Figure 3.18** for the Government of Canada, the question of providing a separate report has been decided in favour of doing so. This is probably one of the most sought after reports in the government's package.

FIGURE 3.18
Government of Canada Condensed Consolidated Statement of Change in Net Debt

Government of Canada
Condensed Consolidated Statement of Change in Net Debt
for the Year Ended March 31, 2012
$ millions

	2012 Budget	2012 Actual	2011 Actual
Net debt at beginning of year	616,908	616,908	582,472
Transition adjustment (Note 3)		3,337	
Change in net debt during the year			
Annual deficit	32,259	26,220	33,372
Acquisition of tangible capital assets	8,130	6,976	8,061
Amortization of tangible capital assets	−4,930	−4,859	−4,756
Other	−260	−739	−99
Net increase in net debt due to operations	35,199	27,598	36,578
Other comprehensive loss or income (−)		2,292	−2,142
Net increase in net debt	35,199	29,890	34,436
Net debt at end of year	652,107	650,135	616,908

Source: *Annual Financial Report of the Government of Canada Fiscal Year 2011–2012* (Table 11), available at http://www.fin.gc.ca/afr-rfa/2012/report-rapport-eng.asp.

Cash Flows Statement

Even though most public-sector organizations use accrual accounting to better reflect the actual financial position of the organization, there remains a need to display changes in cash and cash equivalents resulting from the organization's activities during the period. Very simply, an entity needs to know if it has the cash to operate. For them, the old rubric that "Cash is King" is a reality. While most of a public organization's cash inflows will come from appropriated funds (voted by the legislative authority or transfers from another government, or part of government), with respect to agencies – unlike the private sector where sales and financing are the main sources – knowing the cash viability is important. This is particularly the case with agencies or public entities such as hospitals that are highly dependent on the efficient movement of funds from other governments through transfers. While the Statement of Cash Flows cannot tell the user how the entity is performing against budget, it does provide useful information about viability and the presence of cash as needed.

Thus, this statement focuses on cash transactions as opposed to such non-cash items as depreciation and amortization, which can be reported in this report, but as non-cash information. This statement gives information about the current financial viability of the operation. The cash flow statement reports on:

- cash inflows and their source,
- individual and material cash expenditures over the reporting period, and
- cash balance at the end of the period.

Cash flow statements typically report on the following categories of financial information:

- **Cash flows from operations:** This will include all cash receipts – taxes, fees, pledges, and contributions – and disbursements resulting from the main service-delivery activities of the organization.
- **Cash flows from investing activities:** This includes cash outflows related to the purchase of capital assets and the purchase of investments and cash received from the disposal of assets of a similar kind.
- **Cash flows from financing activities:** This includes cash used to pay for prior financial obligations and the acquisition of debt through bonds, loans, treasury bills, etc.
- **Non-cash financing and investing activities:** Certain financing and investing activities do not involve the receipt and use of cash; for example, contributions of capital assets or an investment portfolio to be held for an endowment fund.

The Auditor General of British Columbia has provided guidance on how all financial statements should be prepared in the document, **Public Sector Accounting Standards.**

In the Model Financial Statements for Government Organizations, the sample Statement of Cash Flows is copied here in **Figure 3.19**.

Having information on cash flows is very useful in assessing the financial health of a government or reporting entity within it. Generally, this report will enable the user to:

- determine future cash requirements,
- assess the ability to generate necessary cash flows in the current fiscal year, and
- determine the ability of the entity to fund future activities or changes.

Financial Condition Analysis and the Application of Financial Ratios in Determining the Solvency and Sustainability of an Organization

Beyond just being able to read meaning into financial statements to better understand what they can tell you about the financial health of an organization, Financial Condition Analysis (FCA) is a formal element of how stakeholders and organizations view all financial statements in order to determine from them some key understandings, which centre on such questions as:

- Can the organization meet its overall financial obligations?
- Does the organization have the cash solvency to meet it obligations in a specified period?
- Do the financial statements show that the organization – or government – has the revenue capacity to meet its budget plans, i.e., budget solvency?
- Is the organization solvent over the long-term, i.e., is it sustainable?
- Does the organization have program solvency, i.e., do the funds committed and available provide resources to sustain the current level of program delivery?

Why FCA is of Importance to Government Financial Managers

Financial managers in government can ask these questions of their own budgets and use FCA tools to help point to issues. However, increasingly, as governments deliver through arm's-length entities and through transfer payment or contribution agreement tools, they have to ask similar questions of the organizations delivering services on their

FIGURE 3.19

Sample Statement of Cash Flows, For the Year Ended March 31, 20x2

Statement of Cash Flows Organization X For Year ended March 31, 20X2	20X2 000s	20X1 000s
Operating Transactions: Cash received from:		
Transfers	47,000	45,000
Operating	1,822	1,478
Fees, permits, licences, fines	37,709	32,676
Interest	2,651	3,296
Business enterprises	2,145	2,542
Other	2,261	2,599
	93,588	87,591
Operating Transaction: Cash paid for:		
Salaries and benefits	47,685	47,540
Material supplies	8,035	7,856
Services	2,473	2,432
Interest	264	510
Rent	0	0
General administration	26,887	26,458
Other	5,941	5,538
	91,285	**90,334**
Cash provided by (applied to) operating transaction	**2,303**	**(2,743)**
Capital Transactions		
Proceeds on sale of tangible capital assets	0	0
Cash used to acquire tangible capital assets	(2,231)	(826)
Cash provided by capital transactions	**(2,231)**	**(826)**
Investing Transactions		
Proceeds from disposal of investments	2,675	2,750
Repayment of loans and advances	50	(47)
Temporary investments	(1,618)	1,007
Portfolio investments	(3,673)	636
Loans and advances	0	0
Investments in government enterprises	209	87
Cash provided by investing transactions	**(2,357)**	**4,433**
Financing transactions		
Debt issues	2,000	(500)
Debt retirement	0	0
Cash provided by financing transactions	**(2,000)**	**(500)**
Change in cash and cash equivalents	**(285)**	**364**
Cash and cash equivalents: beginning of year	**9,418**	**9,054**
Cash and cash equivalents: end of year	**9,133**	**9,418**

Source: *PSAB Model Financial Statements and Comparison of PSAB with the CICA Handbook*, available from the Office of the Auditor General of British Columbia at http://www.bcauditor.com/online/pubs/675, accessed February 2013.

behalf. Included in this growing range is the oversight function that governments have over the broad public sector such as school boards and healthcare organizations. In high-risk situations, including such major investments as capital projects involving public-private partnerships, governments have to keep a close eye on the financial viability of their partners. Further, governments providing international assistance have legitimate duties to question the financial condition of the recipient country in terms of the use of funds through budget instruments and the capacity to actually deliver on aid commitments.

Using FCA tools, such as financial ratios and attendant analysis, assists in this process. The key objective is to come to a conclusion about the financial condition as reported through its financial statements. As we shall see, however, this entails a mix of numeric analysis combined with contextual understanding. Some of the consequences flowing from this analysis involve important political policy, as well as financial and operational consequences. For example:

- Change in the credit rating for the organization or government.
- Requirement for the organization to change its activities to come within budget if budget solvency is not convincingly determined after FCA.
- Changes in program structure to establish sustainability. (Think here of the continuing struggle to bring pension plan costing down to a sustainable level.)
- Increases in oversight, or even a form of direct supervision, where FCA reveals poor management of resources.
- Reconfiguration or renegotiation of third-party agreements to mitigate risk.

Key Tools of FCA

As noted, a full FCA involves more than just numbers. However, a series of financial ratios have been developed that provide key bits of insight into an organization's financial condition. As we will note at the end of this section, these ratios are only as good as the soundness of the accounting information. They seldom provide a good picture on their own. They are signals. However, when used in a consistent manner with a good understanding of the context, they can be powerful first levels of analysis. Further, there are many financial ratios and they can be expanded, depending on the user's thirst for information and level of detail. Some of the ratios presented here are the most commonly used and most applicable to public sector use. Certainly, when government managers are

dealing with complex arrangements with private sector firms whose financial condition is an important factor, they are wise to seek advice from those competent in private-sector analysis.

Some of the most commonly used financial ratios are:

Current Ratio: This is the simplest and most commonly used measure of an organization's liquidity, i.e., the availability of funds to pay the bills in the short term.

$$\text{Current Ratio} = \frac{\text{Current Assets}}{\text{Current Liabilities}}$$

While this is a popular ratio, it can also be misleading if left on its own. For example, a high Current Ratio is not necessarily a positive thing as the organization may be sitting on a great deal of cash and not executing its program. Similarly, the idea that all assets, even if they are liquid, can be dispensed immediately violates the ongoing concern principle.

Quick Ratio: Also known as the Acid Test Ratio is a liquidity indicator that adds further to the Current Ratio to include inventory and other current assets. A higher ratio means a more liquid current position.

$$\text{Quick Ratio} = \frac{\text{Cash \& Equivalents \& Short-Term Investments \& Receivables}}{\text{Current Liabilities}}$$

Operating Ratio: This is one of two ratios that address issues of budgetary viability or solvency. The question here is: has this government or organization sufficient sources of revenue to pay for its planned expenditures?

$$\text{Operating Ratio} = \frac{\text{Total Revenues}}{\text{Total Expenditures (Expenses)}}$$

A higher value of the ratio indicates a more desirable level of budgetary solvency.

Own-Source Revenue Ratio: This is a very important ratio when assessing the degree of dependence that an organization or government may have on revenues over which it has less control. We see many parts of the broader public sector dealing with transfer payments from other levels of government. This movement of these funds, the clarity about the amounts, and the timeliness of their arrival affect the ability of these entities to project revenues accurately. The first question to ask is: to what extent is the entity dependent on revenues generated from its own sources, rather than intergovernmental transfers, which increases uncertainty and risk.

Own-Source Revenue Ratio = Own Source Revenues

Total Revenues

We now turn to two sample ratios that move off the financial statements alone and start to look at program sustainability and debt.

Net Assets per Capital: This is one way in which, over time, program solvency can be tracked.

Net Assets per Capita = Total Net Assets

Population

Long-Term Debt per Capital: This ratio, manifest in public discussion of debt in a number of ways, is an important element in determining the viability of public entities to take on more debt or to meet their operating and debt commitments. It can point, for instance, to the possibility that a government may default on its bond payments. It would also be a factor in setting the cost of future borrowing. It can be calculated either as below, or by subtracting cash from the overall debt.

Net Debt per Capita = Total Long-Term Debt

Population

The Use and Abuse of Financial Ratios

Financial ratios can be powerful analytical tools. The examples offered here cover the range of public sector financial management concern, but do not exhaust the number of available ratios. However, one ratio does not a conclusion make, although unfortunately it can make a headline. Further, it is a signal not a solution. A number of further elements of FCA have to be in place to make them truly as useful as they can be:

- There needs to be some form of period-to-period comparison.
- It pays to be able compare the ratio with some form of norm, standard or common guide.
- Trend analysis is important.
- Consistency in comparison is vital. Changes in accounting policies, transfer agreements, or scope of jurisdiction have to be explained.

Summing Up

The financial statements of governments and other public-sector organizations have to be read in an integrated way. There are a number of them, not because some groups or individuals necessarily want that many, but because of the general complexity of the activities of most organizations. Multiple reports are needed in order to provide a full picture so that external users can understand the organization's financial situation.

Similarly, some managers will focus on certain elements of the statements and ignore others. Being able to pull useful information out of such statements means being able to "read the balance sheet," a skill that is often referred to when describing financially literate managers. This is a skill bred from experience and from seeking good financial advice. It is also based on the manager's appreciation of the basic truths behind such numbers. That means understanding the nature of the organization in which she works and how it operates. The ability to read a balance sheet is a skill at pulling out financial information, not necessarily operational or future-oriented information, which is built into how the organization works. There is a difference between financial information on its own and financial information in context. Good financial advisors help managers bridge that gap. Poor ones just throw numbers at you.

As already noted, financial reports exist to meet many needs, some internal and some external to the organization, and their structures tend to be similar across organizations, whether they are in the private or public sector. Generally, though, they serve the needs of external accountability and scrutiny first.

Financial information has two main uses: financial and management. These statements are important for both purposes but are most worthwhile from the financial perspective. Financial information for management purposes involves managing the resources in an effective and efficient manner. This encompasses elements of control, effective budgetary and cash management within a budgetary period, and reporting on results, using a combination of financial information such as has just been described and other performance information to provide a full and balanced picture. Thus, a line manager needs financial information that includes, but also goes far beyond, that found in the financial statements we have examined here.

Chapter 4
Accrual Accounting and Budgeting

Chapter Objectives:

- Understanding the difference between the cash and accrual bases of accounting and budgeting
- Understanding the shift towards accrual in the public sector
- Examining the impact of accrual on financial management in the public sector

Accrual Accounting and Public-Sector Reform: It's an Accrual World in Government Now

The previous chapter described how core principles of accounting guided the preparation of both the formal financial statements of an organization as well as the internal financial reports that it uses to exercise control of its activities and resources. Before embarking on a review of budget formats and the budgetary process in the public sector, we will examine the basis for recognition of financial events and how that has changed in the past two decades from cash to accrual. This change is more than a technical one. It is part of the general trend in public sector reforms and modernization. It has important implications for how governments report and view their assets and liabilities. It has enhanced how governments see their future liabilities, such as pension funds, as well as how they manage their capital assets. Accrual budgeting has an impact on how legislators view their role in the approval of budgets, offering both new advantages in terms of fuller costing information and challenges in terms of weakening the closely guarded role of legislative purview over the annual budget allocations of government. For the financial manager in any part of government or its many agencies, understanding the accrual principle is important, not only in terms of that manager's individual responsibilities, but also in providing the best advice on the full cost of any policy or implementation proposal set before decision makers. Simply put, the sticker price of a

fighter aircraft fails to inform those making the decision of the true cost of that weapon. Cash is the sticker price; accrual is the full life cost.

Whether the organization used the cash or accrual basis was once seen as the great divide between the public and private sectors, with the public sector practicing cash acounting and budgeting, and the private sector using accrual methods. That is changing around the world, with the encouragement of the accounting profession and its standard-setters. An impetus for this shift has been the need to have more transparent financial information and to provide that information in a more generally accepted way to a variety of stakeholders, most of whom want more complete financial information than a purely cash system will provide.

In particular, a key attribute of accrual accounting and budgeting is that both provide information that matches costs to the period in which they are incurred. That change is significant to public financial management for a number of reasons:

- The adoption of the accrual basis represents an effort to bring to both accounting and budgeting a totally inclusive approach to identifying costs and revenues, thereby providing a fuller picture.
- Accrual budgeting represents a major challenge to the concept of annualized budgets approved by legislatures, although it in no way reduces the authority of those legislatures.

- Accrual accounting forces a better integration of finance, operations, and strategic direction because of its inclusive nature.
- Accrual accounting demands a higher level of sophistication on the part of public-sector managers and their overseers, be they legislatures or boards of directors.

The shift to both accrual accounting and accrual budgeting is a major change process for any organization, creating more work, often accompanied by the adoption of new financial information systems to support it. Adopting the accrual basis makes good sense as it achieves a number of important outcomes:

- increased transparency of costs at the right time,
- a full cost picture for programs,
- valuation of public-sector assets, and
- better accountability derived from providing oversight bodies with more complete information.

The adoption of the accrual basis has been closely associated with reform in the public sector around the world. Perhaps the leader in this context was New Zealand,[1] but many countries have followed suit.[2]

Over the past three decades, the collections of public-sector management trends known as New Public Management (NPM),[3] have increased the pressure on governments to modernize their accounting systems. Beyond simply being more business-like, NPM focused on different means to deliver public services, often involving the outsourcing of services, delivery through contracted third-part providers, or through specialized agencies within government that had greater flexibility to carry out their missions. In addition, various governments have pursued different ways to finance large government investments, often involving some form of private-sector financing, thereby complicating how assets and liabilities are accounted for.[4] However, in order for government to fully assess the costs of these various instruments to implement public policy, great clarity was needed with respect to costs so that comparisons would be on a level playing field for decision makers. Accrual accounting is central to developing those full costs.

Consistent, as well with NPM thinking, the adoption of accrual accounting offers a different way of thinking about public resources. The traditional cash basis in the public sector focuses on the annualized approval of funds, their appropriation by the legislature, and the spending of the funds within the same time period accompanied by the necessary financial statements detailing how the funds were spent. Accrual accounting offers a fuller view of costs, thereby encouraging full-cost thinking, as well as longer-term consideration of how resources will be used up, when they have to be replaced, and how to reflect full costing. This is a shift in mentality as much as technique.

The final shift arising from NPM thinking is that governments had to consider all the assets used to achieve public policy ends and reflect that thinking in their financial statements. The inclusion, therefore, of capital assets, most notably assets held over the long term, is a reform arising from the adoption of accrual. The inclusion of hitherto ignored long-term liabilities such as public servant pension liabilities, and bringing those liabilities into the calculation of the net debt of governments, has affected the transparency of such obligations. It has also forced governments in some instances to change pension benefits to reduce future costs. On a cash basis, governments could easily commit to future benefits without having to actually register them in the financial statements until payment was required, thereby passing on the more negative aspects to future generations.

Already, the impact of accrual accounting is being felt in many areas of public management. Here are some examples:

- Various governments in Canada and the United States have become engaged in discussions of the sustainability of under-funded entitlement programs, most notably pensions. While experience varies and debate is often tinged with ideological preoccupations, there are genuine issues that only the application of accrual accounting, which provides full funding, would reveal.
- Capital infrastructure is increasingly being seen as a long-term asset that demands attention, rather than one to be depleted and not renewed. The sudden – and surprisingly surprising – collapse of highway overpasses after years of neglect has forced the government responsible to build replacement and repair costs into the life cycle of those assets. Accrual would have made this deterioration more transparent. Only political will can take action on that information.
- Given the application of accrual accounting to procurement of major assets, the true cost of weapons acquisition, including maintenance and future upgrades, as well as training has brought into focus the scope of such investment. As the embattled minister of defense said when challenged on the costing, "It's just accounting." He was right about that, but so wrong to dismiss it.

So What Does Accrual Mean for the Line Manager?

Managers responsible for public funds and the programs they support are well aware of how accountable they are to spend the money both efficiently and effectively. Accrual accounting is designed to provide the user with fuller financial information about a decision. It will, when done well, project full costs over the life of the decision, rather than deal with it in terms of acquiring the good or service in a single year. This approach therefore helps both planning and transparency. For a public manager, this will also mean that he or she will have to explain the full costing of projects and programs, or the lack thereof. Matters such as depreciation, maintenance and replacement costs can no longer be ignored.

The other reality, however, is that for the day-to-day life of most program managers in government, cash remains king. The budget at hand and its management within the current fiscal year is an important preoccupation in terms of getting the work done and monitoring performance against a planned budget. As we shall see in chapters 9, 10 and 11, understanding cash flows in the here and now remains vital. Public managers must straddle both worlds today.

It is also true that, in the end, no amount of better accounting information will get around bad decisions once a manager or organization is determined to make them for reasons of ideology, expediency or convenience. What accrual does is to set the stage to do a better job.

Moving from Cash to Accrual in the Public Sector

There has been a long tradition in Westminster-type democracies that the legislature must approve monies for the executive on an annual basis. This right was fought for and secured in 1644 in Great Britain and has formed an important tradition in democratic societies around the world, including Canada.

Thus, legislatures jealously guard their right to review government expenditure plans on a detailed basis every year. As a result, there is a strong tendency to focus on how much cash is needed in a public-sector budget. This has led to the common practice of annual approval of cash expenditures, otherwise known as appropriations, which are generally made for a one-year period only, with some exceptions for capital projects. Reinforcing this culture is the strong desire to see who gets what in terms of the distribution of resources within the framework of an election

cycle, rather than the long-term overall costs, as accrual forces one to do.

To forestall any sense that the accrual basis excludes legislative intervention or flies in the face of this democratic tradition, both systems require approval by the legislature, on an annual basis, of these appropriations of actual cash requirements. Under the accrual system, the full costing is better displayed and is not restricted to a single year. Still, the authority for the approval to actually spend and, by implication, to raise funds through taxation and fees, remains with the legislature.

A purely cash approach to both budgeting and accounting practice has flaws that limit the capacity of oversight bodies such as legislatures and boards of directors to get full financial information. The restriction of budgetary approvals to one year at a time can distort, or fail to reveal, the true cost over time of a particular program or purchase. Cash accounting satisfies the annual budget-based interests of legislators and is simple in its presentation but has a number of serious drawbacks:

- *Failure to accurately represent the amount of resource usage*; for instance, a large capital acquisition will distort expenditure upward in the first year, but usage of that asset will not be recognized in following years.
- *Failure to take account of future commitments, guarantees, or other contingent liabilities*. A liability will not be recognized until the cash is paid to settle the debt.
- *Concentration on cash payments alone*, sometimes resulting in an unnoticed deterioration in fixed assets.
- *Focus on control of the inputs* purchased, rather than on the outputs produced.
- *Distortion of incentives* by encouraging managers to underestimate the costs of programs and to spend their full annual appropriations.

Recognition

When organizations manage their funds on a cash basis, they recognize an expenditure or revenue event only when cash is actually received or expended. The term recognition has a specific meaning: it refers to the timing of entering a financial event into the accounting system. Recognition is a formal means of reporting and recording financial events. Rules of recognition take on significance when organizations try to establish their exact financial position or provide stakeholders with full information on revenue and expenditures. In general, recognition of costs and expenses will be based on rules created by the organization, rules found in its accounting practices as stated in the Notes of its financial statements. An example of a recognition policy that might be found in a public-sector organization is that a liability will be recognized only once a contract is signed and approved by both parties. Recognition needs specific events or acts to make it clear.

In practical terms, the transition of a traditional cash-based government department into an accrual-based one does not mean the wholesale adoption of a private-sector practice. As previously discussed, unique standards exist in government for accounting in Canada, based on the guidelines set out by the Canadian Institute of Chartered Accountants and the Public Sector Accounting Standards Board. Further, the accrual model has been modified to reflect the products, services, and outcomes of public-sector organizations. As Professor Allan Barton of the Australian National University noted in discussing the relatively early adoption of the accrual basis in New South Wales:

> The business model of accrual accounting did not fit easily into departments which do not sell their services to the public and retain the proceeds but whose activities are funded from budget appropriations, do not pursue profits, own assets or have their own liabilities. So, rather than adopting an accrual accounting system to suit the unique environment of government, the reverse process was adopted of converting departments into pseudo business enterprises.[5]

For that reason, many governments have moved very cautiously in adopting the accrual basis, generally in step with the development of accounting standards by the standard-setting body for their jurisdiction.

Just What is Cash-Basis Accounting: An Overview

An organization that operates on a cash basis recognizes income when it is received, and expenses when they are actually paid. Suppose that organization provides a service for a fee to one of its clients on December 31st. The client does not pay until January 31st. If the entity operates on a cash basis, it does not count the sale as income until it collects the money – in this case, January. Likewise, if the organization bought office supplies on account at the local office-supply store on December 31st but did not pay for them until January 31st, then it does not count the purchase as an expense until it actually writes the cheque to pay for it in January. The first example relates to recognizing revenue: on a cash basis it is recognized when the actual money is received. The second deals with the recognition of expenses: on a purely cash basis, this is done when the bill is paid.

Example of Cash Accounting

A new computer system budgeted for $8.0 million is being installed in two phases in the 20x1 and 20x2 fiscal years. The computers are bought on account, and $6.0 million will be paid at the beginning of the fiscal year. The balance will be paid at the beginning of the next fiscal year. A cash-based accounting system would display these items as shown in **Figure 4.1**.

FIGURE 4.1
Example of Cash Accounting

Fiscal Year	20x1-x2	20x2-x3
Expenditure: New computer system	6,000,000	2,000,000

Accrual Basis Accounting: An Overview

Accrual accounting recognizes the effects of accounting events when such events occur regardless of the time cash is exchanged. Therefore, the expense is recognized in the financial records when it has an economic effect on the organization. When an organization using an accrual basis for accounting sells a good, it recognizes that sale when the sale is made, not when the payment is received. In doing so, it creates an accounts receivable item as part of its asset base. Similarly, when it obtains goods and takes them from a supplier into inventory, it recognizes two things: it has created a liability in the form of accounts payable, and it has also increased its asset base by adding to its inventory. This gives the organization a better picture of its actual financial position.

Using the same computer system as in the previous example, to reflect when the asset would actually be used, we can assume that it has a five-year life cycle. Even though the actual cash outlay is the same as shown in the cash example, the accrual system recognizes the expense when it occurs, not when the money is paid. Hence, an accrual financial report would show the costs of $8.0 million as in **Figure 4.2**.

FIGURE 4.2
Example of Accrual Accounting

Fiscal Year	20x1–x2	20x2–x3	20x3–x4	20x4–x5	20x5–x6
Expenditure: New computer system	1,600,000	1,600,000	1,600,000	1,600,000	1,600,000

Expense or Expenditure in Accounting

These terms are often used interchangeably in everyday language. However, in accounting, they have specific meanings, ones that often involve whether the basis of the accounting system is cash or accrual.

In general, the term expenditure refers to the actual outlay of money for a service, salary, or article. It is used extensively but not exclusively in the cash system to reflect that the event recorded is the actual expenditure. For example, an expenditure can be made to purchase an expense item (e.g., payment of salary owed to an employee) or a capital item (e.g., purchase of a building). It is not a measure of the consumption of the goods or service.

In contrast, expenses represent the cost of goods and services consumed in the process of fulfilling the organization's objectives. They are measured by the amount of an asset used (e.g., depreciation) or the amount of a liability incurred (e.g., an amount owed to a creditor).

Under the cash basis, the expenditure is recognized in the accounts once the cash is paid out. Under the accrual basis, the expense is recognized when the benefit arising from the goods or services is received. Examples of expenses include:

- salary owed to staff for time worked as an employee of the university,
- payroll tax owed to the government as a result of employing staff, and
- purchase cost of stationery.

Expense, a term used both as a noun and as a verb, refers to the identification in the accounting system of an obligation to pay, a liability, or an unpaid obligation. It does not necessarily mean that actual payment has been made but that assets of the organization have been used up. A contrast between expenditures and expenses can be seen in the case of assets that are used up over time: as noted above in the example of the computers, an expense would reflect the decrease in the asset as it is used up, and an expenditure

would reflect the outlay of funds to pay for them. A cash-accounting system would treat this as a single event, while an accrual system would expense the decrease in assets over their useful life while also recording the expenditure upon payment of the monetary obligation. Thus, in the example in **Figure 4.1**, the payments would be recorded as expenditures under the cash system.

Key Differences Between Cash and Accrual Accounting

Cash accounting does not record many of the impacts on assets and liabilities that will result from the consequences or events associated with a transaction. For instance, with cash accounting, money borrowed with a long-term loan is recorded as a cash inflow. The long-term liability is not brought into the financial statements again until it is due and payable.

Accrual accounting recognizes events and transactions when they occur, regardless of when cash changes hands. By recording accounts payable and receivable, and thus the changes in the values of the assets and liabilities, it keeps a running tally of what an organization owns and owes in economic terms. It also depletes the value of those assets as it uses them up. If a government promises pension benefits in the current period, and must pay retirement claims in future periods, the liability and expense are recorded when the event occurred. When the cash is actually paid, the liability is removed.

Figure 4.3 illustrates how the different systems operate. This table also illustrates the relative capacity of the systems to capture information. For instance, even though the manager operating in a cash system may have created an encumbrance in her cash-forecasting system because she plans to spend money on a purchase not yet made, the cash accounting system does not pick up this information until payment is made. As a result, there is no recognition, and transparency is diminished. In the accrual system, the accounting system creates two important pieces of

FIGURE 4.3

Comparison of Economic Events: Cash Versus Accrual

Event	Cash Treatment	Accrual Treatment
Asset ordered from a supplier	No effect	No effect
Article received and taken into inventory	No effect	Increase inventory Increase accounts payable
Article is used (completely)	No effect	Decrease inventory
Article is used but only partially	No effect	Increase depreciation Decrease inventory
Article is paid for	Decrease cash	Decrease cash Decrease accounts payable
Organization bills service recipient	No effect	Increase accounts receivable
Payment is received	Increase cash	Increase cash Decrease accounts receivable

information upon receipt of the good: the creation of a liability or obligation to pay, and information about the level of inventory. Because inventory is an asset, the accrual system ties it directly to the accounting system.

A detailed comparison of the treatment of an asset by the federal government is offered in **Figure 4.4**.

FIGURE 4.4

Cash and Accrual Treatment of an Asset

> **The Canadian Coast Guard Buys a New Icebreaker**
>
> Under modified cash accounting:
>
> - The ship is not included as part of the government's assets. Other things being equal, the federal debt (accumulated deficit) increases by the amount of cash used to pay for the ship, in the year in which the Canadian Coast Guard takes ownership, without any recognition that this cash has purchased a long-lived asset.
> - The only part of the annual cost of owning the ship that is recorded is the annual cash outlay for operations and maintenance.
>
> Under full accrual:
>
> - The ship is included as part of the government's assets, offsetting the reduction in cash needed to pay for the ship.
> - The annual cost of owning the ship is reported as the depreciation in the value of the ship, plus the cash outlays for operations and maintenance.

Source: *Finance Canada, 2003 Budget Statement,* available at http://www.fin.gc.ca/budget03/bp/bpa6-eng.asp.

Treatment of Non-Cash Transactions

In addition to recording cash transactions, accrual accounting entails recording non-cash transactions, such as depreciation, provisions, or bad debts. Non-cash transactions have a monetary value and contribute to the organization's financial position, but they do not involve the receipt or expenditure of cash.

For example, a photocopier has a life span greater than a year. In accrual accounting terms, it is a long-term asset. The initial cost of the copier is recorded as an asset in the Statement of Financial Position to recognize the ongoing benefit the copier provides to the organization. The capital cost of using up the photocopier is allocated across the years to the unit or department that uses it. This cost allocation is called depreciation and is recorded as an expense in the organization's Statement of Operations. Note that this does not include the costs of operation: supplies, ink, electricity, maintenance, etc. These costs are recorded elsewhere. When the photocopier is replaced, the depreciation covers the cost of the asset, and the value of the asset reduces to zero over time unless there is a salvage or resale value, if there is any.

In summary, recording transactions in the correct time period and recording non-cash transactions is designed to allow the true cost of operating activities for a specific time period to be monitored. That is the heart of accrual accounting. The cost of using assets and providing for accumulated leave or outstanding debts is identified and recorded. **Figure 4.5** describes how the Canadian federal government would handle disability benefits for veterans,

FIGURE 4.5
Cash and Accrual Treatment of a Liability

Disability Benefits for Veterans

Under modified accrual accounting:

- The government's liability for veterans' disability benefits is not recognized on its balance sheet.
- Expenditures for veterans' disability benefits are recognized in the fiscal years in which the payments are made.

Under full accrual accounting:

- The government's liability for veterans' disability benefits is recorded on its balance sheet. This is the present value of all expected future payments for these veterans' future benefits as a result of past services provided by veterans.
- Payments for veterans' disability benefits are no longer reported as expenditures in the years in which payments are made, but instead reduce the liability that has already been recognized on the government's books.
- For currently serving members, the annual expense cost reflects the net present value of all future payments expected as a result of new disabilities arising during the year.
- Each year, as the liability is adjusted to reflect its current actuarial value, an interest component is added and charged to public debt charges, similar to the recording of the liability for federal employees' pensions.
- Thus one result of moving to accrual accounting is an increase in recorded public debt charges. However, the increase will have no impact on cash outflows.

Source: *Finance Canada, 2003 Budget Statement,* available at http://www.fin.gc.ca/budget03/bp/bpa6-eng.asp.

which are both a current liability and a non-cash transaction, under accrual, as they create a future obligation.

Implications of the Accrual Basis for Public-Sector Financial Reporting

The following illustration of **A Week in the Life of One Government**, shown in **Figure 4.6**, shows how a public-sector organization would record a number of financial events. It demonstrates the differences between cash and accrual means of handling accounts.

Two important points emerge from this comparison. First, the accrual approach provides much more information about the impact of each financial event on the government. The second is that the actual financial condition of the government is better displayed through accrual accounting. On a cash basis, the government is in surplus. On an accrual basis, it faces a deficit. This deficit does not mean the government needs to immediately raise cash to pay down the deficit. Rather, it means that the actual financial resources of the government are displayed, so that its full liabilities over time are shown. That is, the government is not currently in a position to increase spending, as the cash report might suggest.

An example of this is the way in which pension obligations are managed. On a cash-accounting basis, the $30-million pension obligation is ignored until the pension payments are actually made, usually years later. On the other hand, accrual accounting immediately recognizes the obligation. Such recognition has both positive and negative implications. As already noted, it provides a more accurate picture of the full financial obligations of the small government in question. It also forces the government to take this obligation into account as it makes policy and program decisions. On the other hand, such information, especially expenses that will not be discharged for a considerable amount of time and whose value will change over time, may not be relevant to short-term decision making. They may have the perverse effect of dampening the capacity of a government to meet short-term needs. Psychologically, public debate over government expenditures may be conditioned by the presence of long-term obligations clearly booked and taken into account in the calculation of bottom lines. To overcome this problem, such obligations may be managed so that strategies such as special-purpose charges are used or taxes are levied to cover those costs, hence separating them from overall government budgeting. The creation of special funds is often a way to ensure that long-term obligations are addressed without being a drag on regular financial reporting.

A focus on cash only can distort the true cost of government. It also ignores what are called downstream costs of specific decisions made on an annualized basis. It also tends to create spikes in costs, especially capital costs because it costs the product as the cash flows out for construction or purchases at one time, rather than distributing the costing over the use of the item.

FIGURE 4.6
A Week in the Life of a Small Government

A series of financial events...

The following examples take place during one week in the life of a small government. The effects of the following five transactions are shown in the financial statements.

1. Corporate taxpayers are required to make tax payments of $100 million to the government, but only $90 million is received. At the end of the week, $10 million is outstanding.
2. The government sells fixed assets for $100 million. The assets had been valued at $100 million.
3. Government salary payments are made during the week. In addition to paying employees $60 million, the government is obligated to provide for their pensions when they retire; employees earned $30 million in future pension rights during the period.
4. The government settles a long-running legal dispute. It agrees to pay $30 million to the plaintiff in two months' time.
5. All the government's borrowings are held in foreign exchange. The exchange rate declined by 2% during the week.

Reporting These Events by Two Accounting Methods

Accrual Accounting Information
(in millions of dollars)

Cash Accounting Information

Cash Flow Statement		Operating Statement		Balance Sheet			
					Opening	Changes	Closing
Receipts		**Revenues**		**Assets**			
Taxation	90	Taxation	100	Bank	50	130	180
Asset Sales	100			Receivables	20	10	30
				Fixed Assets	700	(100)	600
Subtotal	190	Subtotal	100	Subtotal	770	40	810
Payments		**Expenses**		**Liabilities**			
Salaries	(60)	Personnel Costs	90	Litigation	–	30	30
		Foreign Exchange	10	Pension Liability	–	30	30
		Litigation Expense	30	Borrowing	500	10	510
Cash Surplus	130	Subtotal	130	Subtotal	500	70	570
Bank Balance				**Net Assets**	270	(30)	240
Opening	50						
Closing	180	**Accrual Deficit**	(30)	**Equity and Reserves**	270	(30)	240

Note: Cash accounting would report a $130-million surplus, while the accrual operating statement shows a $30-million deficit. The $160-million difference arises from the following:

*   cash accounting ignores the pension liability of $30 million because it is a future cash outlay;
*   the asset had a value equal to its sale price of $100 million, which would reduce fixed-assets inventory;
*   the change in exchange rate increased the value of the foreign exchange borrowings by $10 million;
*   the judgement created a liability of $30 million that the cash system would not capture until two months later, when the payment would be made; and
*   outstanding taxes of $10 million remained payable to the government even though they had not been received.

Source: S. Lakshman Athukorala and Barry Reid, "Accrual Budgeting and Accounting in Government and its Relevance for Developing Member Countries," Asian Development Bank, 2003.

Accrual accounting is certainly more complex and difficult. It does, however, have a number of advantages:

- it provides more useful financial information;
- accrual is more complete than cash accounting, and provides a full balance sheet approach;
- the scope for manipulation of cash is removed (although it must be understood that accounting or budgeting systems are never fully immune to manipulation);
- accrual facilitates better-quality financial management;
- accrual forces full recording of assets and their use, including their depreciation and replacement – something that governments in particular have been remiss in systematically programming into their spending plans;
- accrual provides the opportunity to change organizational behaviour through anticipating ways to either manage future liabilities, or fully assess the cost of replacing depreciating assets in a systematic way; and
- accrual provides better assessment of financial health and can be linked more easily with organizational performance data.

Risks of Accrual

The risks associated with accrual accounting are that:

- It can be seen as a technocratic exercise and not driven by management needs, especially when it is left to the financial experts.
- A lack of adequate accounting standards may mean that the interpretation of the financial information from accrual accounting will have different meanings for different users.
- Standards are open to manipulation.
- There may be a poor linkage to budget information when the budgets are still on a cash basis, making financial reporting difficult to understand and creating the need for "cross-over" reports that can lead to confusion.
- Politicians may not impose fiscal discipline. For example, committing funds over the long term for intergenerational liabilities such as pensions, in order to reflect their full cost implications, is a matter of leadership or will that no system will rectify or replace.
- Management may be unwilling or unable to use accrual information to improve control of resources, impose effective oversight, or make necessary changes.

The introduction of accrual budgeting, as it becomes more common around the world, has also raised two primary concerns. First, an accrual budget might be said[6] to risk budget discipline as it has been practised through legislative oversight. The view here is that the political decision to spend money should be matched with the time it is reported in the budget. Only cash provides for that because the flow of cash within a specified time period is seen as the ultimate control on budgetary expenditures. There is a fear that if, for example, major capital projects could be voted on with only the depreciation expense being reported, then expenditures for such projects would increase. Legislatures would have to approve, in the accrual budget, the full cost of the project, including depreciation of assets over time. The decision has two features that are of note: it is long-term, thereby apparently relinquishing the annual control offered by cash appropriations, and it is more complex. The second, and somewhat contradictory, concern is that legislatures have often shown resistance to the adoption of accrual budgeting, due to its complexity.

Just as the accrual system can provide much more information about the actual financial condition of the organization, it can also be distorted through manipulation of some of its key elements. Many of the major private-sector accounting scandals have centred on this very issue. This can happen in two ways:

- Revenue is recognized on the basis of very flimsy evidence. For example, a sale is recorded as income on the company's books even though the actual transaction was only an intent-to-buy agreement that was subject to a series of highly risky conditions.
- The write-off of bad debts or deferral of the timing of certain cost flows is manipulated to make the organization's performance look better in a specified period.

Such practices show the potential for distortion and abuse of an accounting system. They have not proven one way or the other than the system itself is flawed. They have merely established, as if that were needed, the capacity of those who would act unethically or illegally to find the means to do so. The lesson for public-sector organizations is that they need internal audit practices, accounting policies that are public, and oversight by the legislature and its officers, such as an auditor general. As the Auditor General of Canada indicated in her comments on the government's 2001–02 financial statements:

> I remain convinced that accrual accounting is superior to the Government's current accounting policies. It provides a more complete measure of the overall size of the Government, which should enhance account-

ability to Parliament; it eliminates the distortion of reported financial results caused by altering the timing of cash receipts and disbursements; and it is an essential component of management reform initiatives underway in the Government.[7]

Accrual Budgeting

Accrual accounting and accrual budgeting do not necessarily go hand in hand. In fact, most public sector entities and governments have followed the course of full adoption of accrual accounting, but a continued reliance on cash budgets in terms of legislative approvals and presentation of actual spending plans. For the purposes of this text, the budget process and budget design will be treated on a cash basis. The reason for this is that accrual budgeting is still contentious among governments and there remains a lot of learning and adaptation to take place before it can be regarded as fully compatible with how democratic institutions treat budgets. There is also considerable controversy about how accrual budgeting actually works. The benefits of accrual accounting have already been outlined. The experience to date in countries such as Australia and the United Kingdom is that securing the benefits of accrual budgeting are not entirely clear, especially with respect to overall fiscal policy and how to manage debt over any given fiscal year.[8]

For the financial manager, the benefits of accrual have already been outlined. So much of what she has to manage will, however, be in cash terms, especially when we discuss managerial control in future chapters.

Summing Up

The movement towards full accrual bases of accounting in the public sector is part of a larger trend towards public-sector reform. However, it has not been an easy change. Arguments have been made that introducing accrual accounting and budgeting systems muddies the waters of legislative oversight.[9] The tradition of an annual voting of appropriations – that is, the actual funds needed to run programs – is inherent in the parliamentary systems of most countries. While there has been strong political support for improving financial information and reporting, the accrual basis does require a political framework that demands a longer-term perspective and understanding of slightly more complex accounting notions than have been used to date. The New Zealand and Australian experiences have shown that there is a steep learning curve for both politicians and senior officials who must make sense of

and communicate the meaning of information provided on an accrual basis.

Because the adoption of the accrual basis is a major public-sector reform, the proper conditions for success must be present. Noel Hepworth suggests the following.

- Consultation and acceptance are indispensable to the introduction of accrual accounting.
- There is no point in a central agency command-and-control type of approach.
- The organization needs to be prepared culturally for its introduction.
- It must be willing to recognize and accept the benefits that the changes will bring about and the costs of implementation in their widest sense.
- Acceptance has to go beyond a relatively narrow group of technocrats.
- The accountancy profession must have the capacity and the willingness to work effectively with managers to advise them.
- The reform probably requires an increase in the number of financial managers (who may be qualified accountants) employed by government and an acceptance of their contribution to the efficient and effective management of the public services.[10]

In the end, there are also managerial consequences to accrual accounting, some positive and some negative:

- Complexity of information rises exponentially, thereby requiring more accounting skills and personnel to both manage and interpret the data but also providing that information in a better form.
- Depth of organizational knowledge about its assets and liabilities rises significantly, but the actual use of that knowledge depends on factors well beyond the accounting system.
- Cost of accounting rises, but returns do as well.
- Costs are better understood, but over a timeframe inimical to political direction.
- Non-financial strategic goals may prevent the realization of the benefits of full depreciation and market valuation of assets, and that may be a good thing.
- Managers still have to manage the cash side of the work, most notably having information relevant to in-year budget management as shall be seen in Chapter 10.

Some preconditions also exist:

- There must also be a willingness to meet the financial-management education and training requirements of the public sector.

- Another essential element is co-operation by the accountancy profession (which, in the case of Canada, would be the CICA) in the development of accounting standards for the public sector.
- The accountancy profession must have a capacity to both understand the nature of the public sector and recognize that circumstances are different from those in the private sector.
- Equally, the public sector needs to have the capacity and capability to influence the public-sector standard-setters.
- Successful implementation depends heavily upon the government's external auditor's understanding and being willing to support the system. Therefore, the external auditor should be involved in the process from the outset.
- It is essential to have a comprehensive management-training program for line managers in how to use an accrual accounting system, so they can derive benefits from its operation.
- There must be no systemic corruption, and there should exist no informal parallel processes that are allowed to complement the formal processes.[11]

From the perspective of financial management, accrual accounting provides valuable information. It is a trend that is rapidly becoming the norm in public-sector accounting.

Chapter 5
Budgets: What They Are and What They Do

Chapter Objectives:

- Understanding the meaning and uses of budgets in the public sector
- Discovering the different types of budgets
- Reviewing different structures for budgets
- Identifying trends in public-sector budgets and budgeting

Dr. Evert Linquist of the University of Victoria has said, "Unveiling a budget is a most important occasion for any government; it is an event of great drama, a public spectacle."[1] Dr. Linquist is referring here to the budget announcements of a government as a whole, the much publicized budget speech of a minister of finance, new shoes and all. Similarly, Aron Wildavsky has clearly situated the link of policy to budgets: "If politics is regarded in part as conflict as to whose preferences shall prevail in the determination of policy, then the budget records the outcome of this struggle."[2] However, as we shall see, the very word budget has a variety of applications, even within the context of this text. For governments, creating a budget is an important way to make policy a reality. This is when the rubber hits the road. The exact dimensions of a policy will really become clear only when, in the budget process, resources are allocated to implement that policy. It is then that the amount of money to be spent, the number of staff to be hired to deliver the program, or the proposed investment in infrastructure gives flesh to a policy pronouncement. Our attention, however, will focus on how public managers create and use budgets, on the hands-on work of developing budgets, matching money to policy intent and reallocating budgets when needed.

The focus of this and the next chapter is how budgets are designed and then built so that public organizations can deliver public policy. There is a rich line of enquiry on budgeting as a public policy process itself. We will touch

on such matters where they are relevant to our ends. We then turn to an increasing preoccupation of governments around the world that have impacts at both the macro and micro level of public management: budgetary reallocations and cutbacks. Finally, we end this cycle on budgets with a closer look at capital budgeting. The budgeting game is an important one for public managers. It is a serious one, but not without its sardonic elements. For a somewhat tongue-in-cheek look at the behavioural dynamics of budgeting, see **Appendix 1, Budget Games People Play.**

What Is a Budget?

A budget is a plan that puts resources in place to implement the goals of the organization. In the public sector, this is the link to policy, legislation, and organizational objectives and strategic plans. For much of the public sector, a budget is a monetized plan that establishes spending limits for programs. Finally, a budget is generally time limited, usually for one year, but with the introduction of multiyear budget forecasting and accrual budgeting, timeframes may vary.

A budget is the basis for financial control within the public-sector organization because, as a planning and policy statement, it articulates expectations about the results of the expenditures and begins the control cycle for the responsibility centre manager.[3] As such, it is a useful benchmark for controlling the operations of departments, agencies, hospitals, schools, or voluntary organizations.

No examination of public-sector budgets would be complete without contributions from Aaron Wildavsky, who opened up discussions of budgets through an analysis that combines cultural studies, political science, economics, and street smarts. Wildavsky's definition of budgeting contains as clear an understanding of the logic of budgeting as is found anywhere:

> In the most literal sense a budget is a document containing words and figures which propose expenditures for certain items and purposes. The words describe items of expenditure (salaries, equipment, travel) or purpose (preventing war, improving mental health, providing low income housing), and the figures are attached to each item. A good budget document should include a detailed specification of how its objectives are to be achieved. In the most general definition, budgeting is concerned with the translation of financial resources into human purposes.[4]

Wildavsky's "financial resources" are translated into his "human purposes" by means of his "plan of work." It is through these processes that the public-sector organization accomplishes a number of important objectives:

- A budget translates policy intention into specific activities through the allocation of resources to that goal or to one or more objectives. As we have already noted, this will define just how much is actually done, how many clients are serviced, and precisely what entitlements will look like.[5]
- A budget is a key outcome of the organization's planning processes, once again translating goals and objectives into action.
- A budget sets limits on expenditures to guide managers within the organization. In government, it is dangerous and often illegal to surpass those limits.
- A budget is an economic document that allocates resources.
- Through the budgetary processes, voluntary-sector organizations can define money-raising targets or set fees for services.
- Budgetary decisions will set the stage for internal financial controls and effective budget (or cash) management to come into action.

The budget can also be regarded or used as an instrument of public policy and management, as described by Jerome B. McKinney and Lawrence C. Howard:

- **Planning Instrument:** Sets goals, priorities, and strategies and coordinates the government/agency resources into an expenditure plan identifying what program or activities will take place and at what levels.
- **Political Instrument:** Involves competing interests attempting to influence a government or agency to form policy favourable to them.
- **Social Instrument:** Provides a vehicle to grant and deny privileges and disburse burdens and benefits to individuals and businesses.
- **Economic Instrument:** Offers powerful potential for affecting the growth and productive capacity of the community and its citizens.
- **Legal Instrument:** Grants authoritatively the rights, responsibilities, power, and guidelines that regulate the budget format, timing and process.[6]

A budget performs four functions:

- **Authorization function:** All money spent from the public treasury is subject to legislative authorization or approval from the governing body of the organization.
- **Allocative/distributive function:** The budget determines how much is spent for each program or department.
- **Macro-economic function:** Public-sector budgets affect economic instruments, such as tax rates, and allocate monies to specific programs to improve employment or redistribute wealth.
- **Administrative function:** The budget is a tool to distribute and control resources within the organization according to a specific structure and assignment of responsibilities.

Finally, any budget is the result of a series of decisions and compromises. There are winners and losers. Governments have to make choices. Perhaps it can best be described as the result of a process that takes the needs or wants of its citizens and agencies, grinds these to see what it can do – and wants to do – and offers up the end result.

Cultural Dynamics of Budget Formulation

Budgets, their formulation, and their management take place within the culture and context of the organization for which they are designed. Any understanding of formal budgeting must also be accompanied by awareness that the informal processes within bureaucracies have an important role to play in the ultimate outcomes. For that reason, some emphasis is given to the informal dynamics of budget creation and budget management in **Appendix 1**. This is a somewhat humorous review of bureaucratic ploys that managers can and do use to maximize their resources, and includes some suggestions as to how their superiors might counter such moves. It is a reminder that these formal processes take place in the rich milieu of organizational culture.

Similarly, this chapter and the next describe budgetary planning cycles and systems. It is useful to know what these are and how they work within the organization. It is also prudent to remember that they take place in the same arena, where power and influence are important. Getting the resources you want to meet your objectives through the budget process is an important aspect of the power relationships in an organization. Holding and controlling resources are key instruments in that game.

As we will see in the next chapter's discussion of budgeting process styles, how a budget is formulated – be it top down or bottom up or a variant of both, also reflects the organizational culture. There are clearly advantages and disadvantages to any style. Certainly, there is no right one. Key to success in financial management is understanding how the budget is formulated within your organization.

A Budget is a Budget … Well, That Depends: Many Uses of the Term Budget

The term budget is used at many levels and for somewhat different purposes even within the same organization. It is important to recognize these distinctions because they may lead to confusion. Budgets, whether at a government level or a unit level, are the result of an iterative process coming from both levels.

Whole-of-Government Budget: The annual budget address of the minister of finance announcing the budget for the whole government is a high-profile event. This event is often how most people think of public-sector budgets. In the case of federal and provincial governments, the budget is a high-level document in which the minister focuses on the specific issues that are important to the government, those seen as the most deserving of attention: increases to programs, cutbacks, tax and fee changes, new programs, and debt repayment, for instance.

These budgets, while documenting and seeking authorization for annual spending plans, deal with government-wide revenue expectations, marry those income projections to expenditures across a full range of government programming and tax policy and place the government either in surplus or deficit. They are also important economic statements, affecting the country's debt and investment levels, even to the point of affecting the value of its currency.

One useful way to look at this kind of budget is as the legislative budget,[7] the one that, along with specific changes in laws, demands the approval of the highest governance authority. It is also closely linked to confidence in the government: in the Westminster system of parliamentary democracy, all financial votes can be taken as a measure of confidence in the government. As such, in the Canadian parliamentary tradition, the defeat of a money bill such as the budget constitutes a vote of no confidence and the government falls. Students of public administration will also realize that a government's budget is the result of an amalgam of policy decisions and directions. Budget making, therefore, is policy making.

Agency or Department[8] Budget: Government budget documents signal major changes in policy and taxes. However, they also break down government expenditures by departments. Once the broad direction is set in the overall budget, the details begin to flow out for various departments and agencies. These are the detailed spending plans of government, broken down by department, program or results area. These estimates documents, as they are called, flesh out exactly where government will spend and not. But they will hardly be a surprise to the agencies whose plans are outlined there. If the budgetary process is working, and it does in most governments quite well, budget targets, spending authorizations and changes are known in advance of the minister's speech. It is not, however, fully guaranteed that individual units will have full budget breakdowns from within their departments. More worrisome, as well, is the realm of transfer payments to delivery agencies such as regional health authorities and boards of education. Often the details are not worked out, just the global figures. Moving the funds into the right area can involve serious inefficiencies, often leaving individual managers without a formal budget figure at the beginning of their fiscal year. That is when, as one seasoned hospital manager paraphrased the wartime slogan, "You stay calm and carry on."

For instance, a department's budget, contained in the Estimates documents that accompany the Budget Statement of the minister of finance, begins to turn the process inwards. The documents define the exact spending plans of an identifiable entity within the public-sector organization, generally a department or agency. The level of detail provided will vary but will certainly be greater than in the overall government budget. Departmental budgets are often broken down into various forms of expenditures, such as staff, capital, and operational costs for the department. They are also budgeted on the basis of the programs that they manage or the results that they will achieve. More about this later in this chapter.

It is through a vote of the legislature, referred to as a vote of supply, that funds are appropriated for the department's use. It is only after appropriation is authorized that funds can legally be spent.

Unit or Branch Budget: We now move into the organizational units of a department or agency, where the land of the responsibility centre manager lies. As noted earlier, the responsibility centre is a part of the organization, such as a department or a unit, of which the manager is the individual who is accountable for its budget and its performance. At this level of budget operation, greater levels of specificity are needed.

It is here that the cash to spend within a given timeframe, usually a year, is defined and that the responsibility centre manager gets the authority to spend funds within a specific year.

This can be seen as a management budget, usually the subject of allocations that take place within the department or unit and not necessarily reflected in budgetary spending plans. The concept of a management budget is a useful translation of larger policy and planning processes into resources available to a responsible manager. It is also the focus of this text.

Distinguishing Public- and Private-Sector Budgets

Companies do not really have to draw up a budget the way that governments do. For them, budgets are targets that have to be flexible in responding to changing market conditions and input cost variation. They are a plan, subject to market fluctuations and adaptation. For governments, a budget is necessary to allocate resources and get the authority to spend.

Planning and programming are very important to both the public and private sectors, but their use differs. In the private sector, a budget is generally a flexible set of planning parameters that can change as market conditions change. For instance, a firm may project annual growth of 15 percent in sales of a specific product, with the budgetary plan to spend an additional 10 percent on labour to meet that anticipated demand. Should demand vary up or down, the firm would respond as quickly as it could to adapt to the change by increasing or reducing its workforce. It could immediately decide to find funds through borrowing or using retained earnings to fund additional hiring. The budget, then, is responsive to the market's behaviour, and

a financial manager would face intensive career vulnerability if he or she failed to respond to such opportunities, as long as they positively affect the firm's profitability. To simply say that a response was outside the budget would not make any logical sense in this context.

In the vast majority of public-sector organizations, however, such a statement would be the essence of good sense. There are several reasons for this. First and foremost, the budget is a spending limit, the fullest extent of the legislature's authority to spend funds. It defines the limits of a government's commitment to a specific policy. But governments are not insensitive to change or unprepared to adapt to changing circumstances. We see this most notably with disasters, both natural and man-made. As we will see, that authority can be altered, even within a fiscal year, to accommodate changes, but this is not a frequent event.

Conditions within the public sector tend to be more stable and less subject to change. That is because demands for services or resources are controlled at the outset. For instance, a college will set a limit on the number of students it will take into a particular program, thereby controlling costs and making them more predictable. While governments and other public-sector organizations may have some form of contingency funding, it is not intended to respond to changes in established program demand, but rather to unforeseen circumstances, such as natural disasters for which emergency funds may be required.

Another point of contrast is in the area of accountability. In the private sector, the bottom line of accountability lies with profitability, share value, and the economic sustainability of the firm. Compliance with a budget is more a form of short-term internal control, subject to fairly rapid fluctuations as outlined above. For the public sector, working within an approved budget is a distinct measure of sound management. This works in two ways: on one side, a public-sector manager who overspends the assigned budget is open to very strong criticism and censure but would also face criticism for failing to spend all the funds available for the programmatic purposes intended. Recipients of such programs, with either a legislative or personal sense of entitlement, expect funds to be spent for the purposes intended, not left on the table at the end of the year.

Another fundamental difference between private-sector and public-sector budgets is the complexity of objectives that a public-sector budget may wish to achieve. A public-sector budget is a major instrument of policy articulation and delivery. Kenneth Kernaghan and David Siegel make this point very well:

One of the great difficulties in preparing a government budget is that the budget typically has many objectives, not all of which are consistent with one another. In preparing a personal budget, one usually thinks in terms of the fairly one-dimensional problems of adjusting expenditures to fit a relatively fixed income. The complicating factor in the preparation of government budgets is that they must address at least three objectives.[9]

To paraphrase, these objectives are:

- to set macro-economic policy,
- to use micro-economic powers to affect people's behaviour, and
- to raise resources needed to fund expenditures.

Unlike a private-sector budget, a government's budget statement may have so many different objectives and uses that it does not paint a clear picture of the government's financial position, or one that is easily disaggregated into specific objectives. Of course, in the public sector, this is often the case.

Cyclical Nature of the Managerial Budgets Past, Present, and Future

As in the Dickens' Christmas tale, the spirits of budgets look back, at the present, and forward, often with reminders of past errors, present challenges and risks that await. For public-sector managers, these three budget realities are in play at all times, as outlined graphically in **Figure 5.1**. The manager has an immediate concern for the management of funds within the current fiscal year. That means the use and control of funds, cash management, and program management. The manger also has to continuously participate as part of the planning process to secure, reallocate or reduce funds for coming years. This involves the organization's expenditure-planning process – the policy-planning cycle or the strategic exercise for development of the future budget. Finally, the manager must account for the past use of funds. This is based on the past budget and the way it was spent. Managers must be able to answer such technical questions as:

- Are supportable financial statements prepared?
- Are they valid? Were legally required reports prepared?
- Were funds properly spent?
- Were there over-expenditures?
- Were funds left unused at the end of the year?
- Do all transactions reconcile so that year-end financial statements can be signed off?

A manager is also accountable for performance, which is results-oriented. In that context, questions such as the following arise:

- Did the funds accomplish the predetermined goals?
- Were the estimates correct?
- Were the funds spent according to plan?

This third budget life – the past – is critically important in the public sector because so much of the budgeting process is *incremental* in nature, with changes made in small adjustments based on levels of resources in prior years (e.g., an increase of 2 percent per annum with no change in program fund distribution). Many organizations make the majority of their budget decisions on the basis of past performance and allocations. How much was actually used in the past is an important factor. Similarly, except in the event of a major policy shift or program change or major budget cuts, public-sector budgets generally tend to rise in small amounts based on past use

FIGURE 5.1
Three Budget Realities

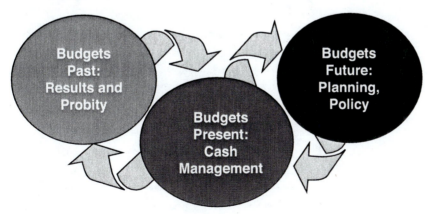

Performance	Control of Funds	Planning
Reporting and	Cash Management	Policy Cycle
Accountability	Program	Reallocation
Auditing	Management	Enhancements
Year-end Reports	Adjustments	

and general increases permitted by the central finance authorities.

The past-oriented budget phase focuses on the need to account to legislative authorities, be they the public accounts committee of a legislature, the board of a voluntary organization, or a city council. Increasingly, public-sector organizations provide annual performance reports of some kind. These will contain financial performance information that will be of great interest to the stakeholders and granting authorities. In general, such performance information uses comparative data, such as performance against budget, change from year to year, or possible use of projections.

Types of Budgets

Budgets can be structured in different ways to meet the needs of the organization for which they are created. In the public sector, these needs are varied, so budgets can be as complex or simple as the situation demands. Therefore, a smaller voluntary organization might well be served with a straightforward cash budget that shows only revenues and expenditures and is managed by a flexible budget, using only the cash basis of accounting. Larger, multidepartmental governments will require a master budget with both operating and capital budgets linked both to a policy framework and to organizational planning documents, using the accrual basis of accounting and budgeting.

In order to understand the structure of complex budgets, it is necessary to break them down into simpler forms. Often, the more complex budget will be an amalgam of different types of budgets. As already noted, budgets in the public sector serve a number of different purposes: policy, planning, resource allocation, and communication. They also operate at different levels within the organization: strategic, departmental, and unit. To meet the various needs of the public, stakeholders, decision makers, budget managers, and staff, budgets can be configured differently. Generally, the forms are not mutually exclusive. Examples will demonstrate how they can be created in layers that meet multiple needs.

One point bears keeping in mind in this regard. Because budgets serve different purposes, they cannot simply focus on just outcomes or results, as is so often the buzz in management for the past decade. Of course, a great focus on results is important. However, in order to get to results, resources need to be lined up and understood in fairly concrete ways. Therefore, inputs such as staff, capital investment and operating money, are key components of getting those results. Similarly, the link between results at a

societal level and an individual departmental budget is not always clear. There are many factors, many of them well outside of the department's control, that lead to specific results. Just a word of warning: do not be afraid, especially if you are the actual budget manager, to take a deep interest in the input or supply end of the budget process. That is where results begin.

Relationship of Revenue Budgets to Expenditure or Operating Budgets

Because the focus of this text is on the financial management of public-sector organizations, the emphasis will be on the expenditure side of the budget in terms of management. As in the private sector, there is a very close relationship between the revenue side and the expenditure side, but generally at the aggregate or whole-of-government level. Therefore, the relationship between revenues and expenditures is often detached from the day-to-day activities of responsibility centre managers in the public sector. For the most part, governments manage their revenue strategies at the whole-of-government level and then distribute money to departments or units through the budgetary and appropriations process, thus making expenses the primary focus of the financial manager, especially in larger public-sector organizations such as a provincial or federal government. There are exceptions to such rules. For instance, governments can create revolving funds within departments or for unique agencies. These are funds that are intended to be self-financing, and organizations that use them are generally permitted to retain all or part of their revenue. Similarly, municipalities can tie specific charges or levies to fund particular programs, e.g., road improvements.

In general, government expenditures are not as closely connected with revenues because revenues of government are usually put into a consolidated revenue fund and those funds distributed among the departments or units. The consolidated revenue fund is a centrally managed revenue account common to Canadian federal and provincial governments, and one which describes the principal operating fund of the government. In principle, all revenues from all government activities are to be placed in this fund. Exceptions abound, but governments generally want to draw as much of their revenue into one central source as possible to ensure that the expenditures it approves are fundable and under a central control.

Knowing the overall revenue situation is vital for governments to make good on their policy and program goals. Their entire expenditure plan is built on a set of revenue assumptions. The revenue budget serves a number of purposes for the whole of government:

- to assure an accurate match of revenues to expenditures plans,
- to adjust basic taxes both for revenue purposes and for the expenditure budget,
- to interpret and project current economic behaviour and patterns as a whole to provide an estimate of revenue expectation,
- to adjust other taxes in order to implement policy changes where tax expenditures are used as instruments of such policy (e.g., child tax credits in the federal government),
- to make changes in fiscal policies (e.g., borrowing levels), and
- to determine if alternate revenue sources – borrowing, reserves – are needed for current operations or capital investments.

Governments continue to improve how they relate revenue to expenditure. Ontario's introduction of quarterly financial reports offers an example of this match, but, as we will see, at the whole-of-government level. **Figure 5.2** shows the third quarter revenue of expenditure projections for the 2012–13 fiscal year.

For smaller public-sector organizations, the relationship between revenue and expenditure is clearer and more direct. For small voluntary agencies, the level of expenditure is dictated by funds raised (revenue). It is highly unlikely that this type of organization would have a separate revenue budget, let alone see it prepared and managed separately from the expenditure side by a distant central office. Rather, there would be a single budget, subject to short-term revenue variations unless the organization secured, on the basis of its overall expectations for the period, some form of interim funding, such as a line of credit.

Budget Architecture

The general or master budget of an organization has two main components: the operating budget and the capital budget. With the introduction of accrual budgeting, this distinction is becoming less relevant. In Canada, higher level governments – federal, the provinces and territories – merge the two as capital is expensed when consumed over the life of the asset. For most municipalities, which hold a large portion of Canada's public capital assets, separate capital budgets remain the norm. However, for purposes of understanding how each is planned and organized, we are presenting them separately. Because capital budget planning has such unique elements, **Chapter 8, Capital Planning and Budgeting,** will focus on them.

Operating Budgets

Operating budgets describe the programs and resources used to carry them out within a specified period of time. The operating budget contains the plan for revenues and

---

FIGURE 5.2
Ontario Finances: Quarterly Update, December 2012

Fiscal Summary			2012–13	
($ Millions)	Actual 2011–12	Budget Plan[a]	Current Outlook	In-Year Change
Revenue	**109,773**	**112,573**	**113,823**	**1,250**
Expense				
Programs	112,660	115,774	114,722	(1,052)
Interest on debt[b]	10,082	10,619	10,461	(158)
Total expense	**122,742**	**126,393**	**125,183**	**(1,210)**
Reserve	–	1,000	500	(500)
SURPLUS / (DEFICIT)	**(12,969)**	**(14,820)**	**(11,859)**	**2,960**

Note: Numbers may not add due to rounding.

[a] Reflects the 2012 Budget plan as outlined in the April 25, 2012 fiscal update.
[b] Interest on debt expense is net of interest capitalized during construction of tangible capital assets of $234 million in 2011–12 and $248 million in 2012–13.

Source: http://www.fin.gov.on.ca/en/budget/finances/2012/ofin12_3.html.

expenditures for the period, usually referred to as a fiscal year. In governmental terms, the expenditure plan represents the authorized limit of expenditures for the operating unit or responsibility centre. As we shall see, for nongovernment public-sector organizations, the potential variations of revenues and expenditures will mean that the budget can be more flexible than in government.

For the most part, the operating budget is for one year, but most public-sector organizations now offer information either about the previous year or about future-year plans that have not yet been approved or appropriated but that appear in public-planning reports. Doing so is important as it signals the government's spending intentions in future years, thereby providing greater stability or, in the case of reductions, certainty about the need for adjustment.

The operating budget is also called the **recurrent budget**. This reflects the fact that most operating budgets provide funds for such elements as staff, benefits, supplies, and operating expenses as well as for grants and disbursements on a continuing basis. These expenses are expected to carry on in the same manner from year to year, with adjustments for funds available and for policy and program changes. The term recurrent budget also reflects the generally incremental nature of operating budgets.

The operating budget is the main focus of this chapter and will be explored further after a brief examination of the other forms of budgets.

Cash Budgets

The terms cash budget and operating budget are often used interchangeably, depending on the form and amount of program information contained in the operating budget and whether the budget is organized on a cash or accrual basis. It is best to think of a cash budget as a stripped-down version of the operating budget. It contains information on planning cash receipts and disbursements or expenditures only. It may break the information down according to line items that refer to the uses to which the money will be put (e.g., staff costs) but goes a little further in providing information about the use of the funds in terms of programs or geographic distribution. It will not contain depreciation or accrual charges such as pensions or accumulated sick credits.

A cash budget is often prepared for a period shorter than a fiscal year. (This forms the basis of cash management as described in later chapters. Cash management can best be understood as that part of financial management involved in the management of budget funds within the fiscal year to ensure maximum use and control of those funds.)

The following are some of the elements of a cash budget that distinguish it from operating and capital budgets.

- The principles of accrual accounting are disregarded in development of a cash budget, often necessitating the conversion of an accrual-based budget to a cash format.
- Instead of matching expenses with revenues where this is relevant to the organization in the period in which they are incurred, a cash budget is concerned with matching cash inflows and cash outflows in the periods in which they are incurred.
- All cash items are accounted for in a cash budget.
- Non-cash items (such as amortization) never appear.

Although cash budgets are important for planning within a budget year (and are referenced extensively in **Chapter 10, Cash Management**), most public-sector organizations provide operating and capital budget information in the master budget for purposes of external reporting and use cash budget for internal-control purposes. However, where the organization's concern is on liquidity, the cash budget is very important.

Capital Budgets

Capital budgets contain the plans and resource allocations for capital acquisitions to support the program of the organization. Capital acquisitions cover a variety of goods. They receive treatment different from operating funds because their use is typically a more complex and longer-term proposition than the one-year operating budget process can accommodate. They often involve complex planning processes with considerable financial risk and cash outlay, and are governed by laws and regulations for the purchasing of such goods. Capital budgets involve multi-year expenditure projections with approval for current-year expenditures. Increasingly, governments are providing multi-year approvals to facilitate implementation. And, with the introduction of accrual budgeting, we are seeing the disappearance of separate operating and capital budgets at senior levels of government, although this is still much the practice in municipal governments and parts of the broader public sector such as hospitals and schools boards. That is because an accrual budget will recognize the use of the capital asset in the year in which it is consumed. Therefore, the cost of a building with a 10-year life will be distributed in the budgets over the life of that building. In cash budgeting, it would be budgeted as a one-time cost. This does detract, however, from the fundamentally different nature of the capital budget planning process, which is discussed in **Chapter 7: Capital Planning and Budgeting.**

Unlike operating budgets, capital budgets focus on non-recurring goods. Buildings are built on a one-time basis, and the capital budget would not automatically contain a plan for another building once one was built. Hence, the capital budget is non-recurring. **The *Ontario Government Municipal Capital Budgeting Handbook*** defines capital budgets in the following terms:

> Capital expenditure refers to any significant expenditure to acquire or improve land, buildings, engineering structures, machinery, equipment and related services used in providing municipal services. These normally confer benefits lasting beyond one year.[10]

Land and buildings are well-known capital goods. Increasingly, information technology infrastructure is a part of capital budgets. Determining what is and what is not treated as a capital item is a matter of policy within public-sector organizations. Often cost thresholds are set such that the purchase of a good is treated as a supply item if it costs less than, say, $500. Governments will treat computer peripherals of lower cost, such as printers, as a supply item to be purchased from operating funds and not a capital item, but will require that the computer itself and the infrastructure (services, networks, etc.) be treated as capital goods. The point is that not all physical purchases by a government are treated as capital. The key features for deciding are:

- Is the good to be used over more than one year?
- Is there a higher level of risk given the nature of the investment?
- Is the good material enough to be treated as capital?

At times, the nature of the good being acquired determines if it is to be treated as a capital good or simply as a supply item. Goods that are highly visible, with high potential for abuse, are often recorded as separate capital items rather than simply as supplies. For example, an organization may choose to highlight certain relatively inexpensive capital items, such as GPS units, because they may be subject to abuse and the organization wants to exercise greater control over them. Putting them into capital also makes them part of the organization's inventory and subject to greater scrutiny. On the other hand, a potentially higher-cost item, such as paper for computers, may be treated as a supply item and not taken into inventory.

What You Can't Budget For

It is great to hear that a budget is a plan. The reality is that once a plan hits the real world, it has to adapt to change, to the unexpected and the complex reality of adaptation. As well, you cannot budget for the unexpected such as natural disasters or major shifts in economic conditions. In some areas, governments simply cannot set money aside for such change. In others, most notably for disasters and emergencies, they need to build in flexibility to adapt. It is seldom the case that they will successfully budget for emergencies. That does not mean they do nothing. For it is certain that emergencies will occur. Being resilient in operational and technical terms means that some resources actually do have to be set aside for planning, training, equipment and monitoring. Further, governments can and do budget for certain events, based on a projection of probability and severity. This risk-based approach is often informed by experience. Therefore, municipalities will budget for a certain anticipated level of snow removal based on their experience. However, they are hard-pressed to budget for extreme weather occurrences such as floods or hurricanes. Reasonable budgeting for emergency planning is a normal government activity. However, responding to the severity of events means governments have to have a way to replan their plan, to reallocate funds in an emergency.

There are a number of measures that governments can take to budget for disasters. These include:

- budgeting for planning and monitoring to improve response capability and reduce response costs;
- budgeting for stockpiling of equipment and vitally needed items, such as vaccines, creation of special restricted reserve funds for disaster response that can accrue over the years, managed as a separate fund and replenished after use; and
- creation of general-use contingency funds.

Who controls these funds and how transparent they are is a matter of budgetary and cash management dynamics within a government or agency. For federal systems, such as Canada and the United States, there is also a legislated system of emergency support for extreme events. In the end, especially when a new form of disaster arises for which there is no anticipated response, governments will also have to retrospectively fund the response. Seldom do governments hold back when public safety is severely threatened. They then have to go back and find funds or approve new ones through their regular budget management or through special means. As we shall see, most governments have ways of approving funds outside the annual cycle. This is a good thing, especially when the unexpected happens.

Structure of Operating Budgets

The next part of this chapter deals primarily with operating budgets. Capital budgeting receives separate treatment in **Chapter 7**: **Capital Planning and Budgeting.**

Budgets can be structured in a number of ways, depending on how the information is to be presented and the purposes for which the budget is created. Similarly, elements of each budgetary form can be used in conjunction with each other. It is common, then, to see that program budgets, centred on the programs offered, also have elements of line-item budgets, which are designed around the functional uses of the funds. These are not mutually exclusive, but help users understand the budget, its use and impact, in a number of different ways.

Line-Item Budgets

The line-item budget is one of the easiest to prepare and one of the most useful within the confines of a specific program, project, or small organization. The financial information is organized according to types of expenses or cost categories. These are often referred to as inputs. These generally focus on staff, supplies, rentals, and contracts, all of which can be characterized as costs of operations. In more complex governments, these line items are standardized into what are called object codes so that they are used in a similar way across the organization. An object code is a numeric code, part of the overall budget code structure of the statement of accounts used to identify the nature, purpose, or object of each financial transaction. These codes are used in all budgeting and accounting systems for consistent reporting purposes. They also form the basis for the structure of journal entries in the accounting process, as discussed in Chapter 3. To illustrate, **Figure 5.3** shows a simple line-item budget for the Killaloe General Hospital for fiscal year 2005.

FIGURE 5.3
Simple Line-Item Budget

Object Code	Budget
100. Salaries	$ 8,000,000
200. Supplies	2,000,000
300. Rentals	250,000
400. Professional fees	750,000
Total	$11,000,000

Highlight to Note: This is a budget that outlines expenses only. The hospital would have both revenues set by the provincial government and other revenue sources.

Line-item budgets are good for control of inputs and accounting for how funds were spent. This budget will tell the manager or stakeholders how much is being spent on what

item of expenditure. These amounts are known as inputs in that they identify the categories of resources (staff, supplies, etc.) needed to do the work. Since it uses common objects or object codes, it also permits inter-budget cost comparisons between programs or organizations with similar functions. As a good example, if all hospitals used the same object codes or line items, an interested observer would be able to determine if the Killaloe Hospital had a higher ratio of staff cost to overall budget than another similar hospital.

The line-item budget is also simple to prepare. Since most line-item definitions are commonly used, there is little ambiguity with respect to their meaning. The accountability in these budgets is focused on the money approved for the individual items and how it is spent. This is known as dollar or input accountability. In the public sector, the line-item budget is often subject to great scrutiny. There is heavy reliance on conformity with the limits set by each item and how monies may or may not move from one item to another.

Line budgets are often criticized for their focus on inputs and not on the results or outputs of the organization. This is fair criticism, up to a point. While it is vogue to say that managers should focus only on results, it is a considerable challenge to achieve any results without proper management of the necessary inputs. Hence, getting the funds straight with respect to such elements as how many people you can hire is essential in accomplishing the results desired. No level of great results will be acceptable to the public, the external auditors, or the authorizing governing bodies if the inputs are poorly managed.

As important as it is, the line-item budget contains very little information about what the money is being spent for in terms of the program or public goods that are being delivered. It does not offer any information regarding the activities and functions of the program. For example, even though we know what is being spent on staff costs at the hospital, we have no idea what results those costs achieve relative to health outcomes. They could be providing mental health services, cancer care, or administrative services. We will see that there are better and more informative ways to link budget information to what is being done (program) and what is being achieved (performance). It starts with the responsibility centre budget.

Program or Responsibility Centre Budgets

This type of budget assigns resources to the operating unit, zone, area, or specialized program within which it is being spent. This is often identified as a responsibility centre.

These centres are often set out in a hierarchical fashion within an organization, with varying degrees of delegated authority to spend and approve expenditures.

In a program budget, the focus is on the programs and program elements that represent the activities for which the funds are to be spent. In **Figure 5.4**, we see the 2012 budget of the Killaloe General Hospital, which has been realigned along the lines of how it defines its main programs or services:

FIGURE 5.4
Program Budget of the Killaloe General Hospital for Fiscal Year 2012

Responsibility Centre	Budget
01. Operating room	$ 4,000,000
02. Laboratory	1,000,000
03. Radiology	1,000,000
04. Patient care	2,500,000
05. Outpatient care	1,500,000
06. Administration	1,000,000
Total	$11,000,000

This budget display offers useful information about what the funds are being spent for – that is, the programs – but very little information about how they are being spent in terms of inputs – the line items. It also provides no information about what is being achieved with the funds. That reflects in a small way the major challenge of all budget formats. They have to provide useful information, but there is a limit to just how much information can be provided in a given document. In addition, different users want different information. For example, the responsibility centre manager for Radiology will find this useful, to a limited extent, as it shows the overall budget figure for her unit. However, she will want to know more than that. What are the component parts that make up this figure? In this instance, as we will see below, this can be reconciled through a functional budget, which combines both.

From the perspective of decision making, it is vital to know how the funds are to be distributed across programs, some competing and some complementary. Much budget decision making is concerned with the allocation of limited resources among competing program demands. This format of budgeting enables both the decision makers and the public to identify the relative program priorities within this hospital.

Functional Budgets

A functional budget is a format that combines the line-item budget with the responsibility centre budget to provide a more complete picture of the distribution of budget resources within an organization. It has the benefit of providing a better basis for comparison among responsibility centres within the organization. Of course, one has to be sure that oranges are being compared to oranges. For instance, a responsibility centre, e.g., Operating Rooms, may have high salary costs, while another, e.g., Administration, may be lower. That may reflect the labour intensity of the work or the size of the unit, as well as the different costs of the professional and support staff in each unit.

The functional budget delivers a better understanding of what funds are to be spent for. It combines information about inputs and responsibility centres or programs that are being funded. It also permits a certain amount of cross-program comparison within the overall budget of the organization. **Figure 5.5** displays the functional budget of Killaloe General Hospital for 2012.

FIGURE 5.5
Functional Budget of the Killaloe General Hospital for Fiscal Year 2012

Responsibility Centre	100. Salaries	200. Supplies	300. Rentals	400. Professional Fees	Total
01. Operating room	3,250,000	250,000	50,000	450,000	4,000,000
02. Laboratory	550,000	350,000	25,000	75,000	1,000,000
03. Radiology	450,000	450,000	0	100,000	1,000,000
04. Patient care	2,000,000	400,000	0	100,000	2,500,000
05. Outpatient care	1,200,000	175,000	25,000	100,000	1,500,000
06. Administration	475,000	325,000	50,000	100,000	1,000,000
Total	7,925,000	2,000,000	150,000	925,000	11,000,000

Flexible or Rolling Budgets

Budgets are put together on the basis of assumptions about the future. For the most part, especially in government, they are treated as fixed for the period that they cover. This is important in order to establish effective cash control within the period, to assign responsibilities and authorities to spend with some certainty for individual managers, and to use the budget as a tool for assessing organizational and personal performance at the end of the period.

Such certainty is not always possible, especially for organizations with highly variable demands or those with a stronger market orientation. For instance, a local museum in a small community that is run on a volunteer basis and depends on its program for visitor income may have volatile income flows. This also holds true for those that are totally revenue-dependent in highly volatile markets, such as those that depend on community fundraising. Often there are too many variables to permit the certainty of a locked-in budget with both secure funding and a certain level of service. These organizations are likely to have no really solid indicator of demand, or else their mission directs them to take in all those who demand their services without the kind of program controls that government can use to restrict access.[11]

Two types of factors can change budget assumptions and may require the use of the flexible budgeting approach:

Shifts in demand or workload: In many instances, public-sector organizations structure their services so that they are open-ended, available to anyone or to all who meet some form of needs test. Such is the case with many entitlement programs. As noted, for some larger organizations funded with some certainty by a central government, these fluctuations can be accommodated; in others, contingencies can be built in. For a smaller public-sector organization, such fluctuations can have a major impact: either by seriously encumbering its ability to meet its mission and objectives or by forcing it into a new round of fundraising.

Shifts in revenue flows: Smaller voluntary organizations are much more sensitive to sudden shifts in revenue, especially organizations that lack secure funding or cannot manage sudden changes through credit. Major fundraising efforts may fail: often, fundraising is sensitive to economic fluctuations, and resources may fall just as a sudden downturn in the economy creates greater demand for the organization's services.

For these reasons, the flexible budget may be the most reasonable way to hedge against such uncertainties. The flexible budget is built around a series of "what if" scenarios. These are hypothetical situations, usually involving either changes in demand or sudden fluctuations in revenue. For the most part, however, a flexible budget, when used as a formal management tool, will focus on the impact of demand or workload changes. The organization will want to have some sense of certainty with respect to funding before committing any funds for the coming period.

Fixed and Variable Costs in Determining Budget Fluctuations

To fully understand the basis of flexible budgeting and the application of "what if" scenario building, one has to understand that not all costs or inputs respond to change in demand in the same way. The concepts of fixed costs and variable costs have roles to play in several parts of this text, so introducing them at this stage is a useful way of discussing how to build flexible budgets.

Fixed costs are costs that do not change as volume changes within the relevant or normal program range. An example of a fixed cost is the rental of a building or use of an information system. It is assumed that these will generally accommodate normal fluctuations in activity. In extreme cases, such as a natural disaster, this may not be the case, but for budget purposes, the normal range would apply. Therefore, for an organization whose mission is providing breakfast meals to pre-school and school-age children in a certain neighbourhood, the rent for the hall and kitchen facility will not change with volume of service.

Variable costs are costs that vary in direct proportion with volume. For the breakfast program, each meal provided is a variable cost item in that feeding each additional child will add to the costs. That is, the larger the number of children who come for breakfast, the higher the costs of such items as food, milk, and supplies to prepare the food.

The organization used in this example, **Hot Meals for School (HMS),** has to budget very carefully at the best of times. It has to think through the implications of changes in demand. It will take in any child who comes through the door for a breakfast because this is its mission. It gets only a small grant from the municipality and raises funds through a variety of means well known to volunteer groups: holding bake sales and yard sales, selling raffle tickets, and seeking donations constantly. As a relatively new organization, it has only a couple of years of experience. These two years have been up-and-down years for the local economy, so the first year saw an average of 300 children getting a breakfast every school day; in the second year, when a major factory suddenly closed, 450 were arriving each day. The board of HMS went to work and found more donations on the fly to meet the higher demand. Now it wants to become more systematic in its budgeting so that it can make a good business case for help. It turned to flexible budgeting (see **Figure 5.6**) as a tool.

FIGURE 5.6
Hot Meals for School Flexible Operating Budget

	Number of Breakfasts Provided Daily[a]		
	300	**450**	**600**
Expenses			
Salaries	$ 50,000	$ 50,000	$ 50,000
Supplies[b]	180,000	270,000	360,000
Rent	14,400	14,400	14,400
Other	5,000	5,000	5,000
Total expenses	249,400	339,400	429,400
Revenues			
Municipal grants	200,000	200,000	200,000
Fundraising	75,000	125,000	125,000
Total revenue	275,000	325,000	325,000
Surplus (deficit)	**$ 25,600**	**$(14,400)**	**$(104,400)**

Assumptions:

[a] The service is provided 200 days a year.
[b] The cost per meal is $3.00 with little flexibility for economies of scale. In this sense, an economy of scale would be getting a lower price for buying more supplies, perhaps a bulk buy, but with the small scale of the operation the price per meal does not get cheaper as you buy more.

As the cost of meals changes – the only real variable cost in this scenario – costs rise and the potential for a deficit arises. At this stage, this kind of what-if scenario building helps organizations realize their vulnerabilities. Conversely, they can also establish a sense of the normal range, in terms of both demand that can be accommodated and the need to seek more revenues.

Flexible budgets force organizations to deal with both sides of the equation – revenues and expenditures – and to determine where they might try to cut costs or develop contingencies should the more extreme cases come to pass. They are also a signal to an organization that it may want to launch new fundraising efforts to shore up support for

its program. Finally, they may suggest that there is a real need for an organization facing these fluctuations to develop contingency funds to reduce the impact of changes. For instance, in this case, it can be readily assumed that the surplus that would build up when intake is low would be held or invested and available to manage the demand when it is high.

Funds in Budget Structure

Generally, it would be assumed that a budget is a single entity created by a government or other organization. In that sense, all monies would go into a single account, perhaps a single bank account from which all expenses would be paid, and a single set of accounts would suffice to disclose transactions and details of financial conditions. Such is not the case in most governments. For a variety of reasons, they will frequently create special funds. A fund is an accounting entity with its own separate set of financial records for recording and reporting assets, liabilities, fund balance, and changes in fund balance.

Although we have already explored the use of funds and fund accounting in the accounting side of financial management, the concept is relevant to budget formulation for all levels of government and the broader public sector. Fund accounting comprises the collective accounting procedures that produce a self-balancing set of accounts for each fund established by legal, contractual, or voluntary actions of an organization. Fund accounting involves an accounting segregation, although not necessarily a physical segregation, of resources. How such segregation takes place is a question of budget construction. Movement of resources among funds often is restricted by specific rules, or requires specific authority – perhaps legislation or donor permission – to make changes.

Funds are created for a restricted purpose. There may be legal restrictions on the use of the funds. Similarly, organizations may want to ensure that each program or expenditure is isolated, and to an extent, protected from others and that there is adequate reporting on each fund at the end of the period, for a variety of reasons. Creating a special fund also serves some useful public accountability purposes:

- A special fund creates greater transparency for the designated purpose, so that stakeholders can identify the funds allotted and track their use.
- Funds protect and segregate special purpose spending from reallocation as part of the general fund or consolidated revenue fund of a government.

- Funds may also direct a specific source of revenue to pay for the activity being funded.
- Funds can provide some level of risk mitigation in the case of funds such as legislated reserves or contingency funds. This is an application of prudence in budgeting, a principle which holds that some degree of contingency is needed to deal with unexpected events.

For example, the Expenditure Budget, 2013–2014 of the Government of Quebec identifies 35 different funds within its overall budget. They are found in many of the ministries. They total over $9 billion in spending, ranging from the Green Fund of $448 million to the Natural Disaster Assistance fund of $12 million.[12]

Types of Funds

Funds are created for different purposes and governed by different rules. The great distinction is whether funds are restricted or unrestricted. An unrestricted fund is one whose assets may be used for any normal purpose. It is usual for only the general operating fund to be completely unrestricted. Organizations that structure their budgets entirely on the basis of funds must have a general or operating fund for all expenditures that do not fit into clearly defined categories. Further, funds tend to limit flexibility within a budget, so having a general fund creates some scope for moving funds to meet emerging demands. These general funds are also used for the day-to-day operation of the organization.

A restricted fund is one whose assets are limited in their use. Restrictions vary across organizations. Some exist because of the nature of the activity or program. For example, the commercial operations of a municipality, e.g., its parking authority, may be managed within a restricted fund. Other funds may be restricted because their creator, through a donation, restricted the use of the funds by the organization; for example, an endowment may be intended only for scholarships. **Figure 5.7** shows some of the different kinds of funds that public-sector organizations can use.

Off-Budget Funds and Expenditures

Off budget expenditures refer to financial transactions that are not accounted for in the budget plan. While taking public expenditures and revenues off budget connotes dishonesty and lack of transparency, there are many legitimate forms of government resource commitment that do not appear on what would be seen as a traditional budget. That is changing as the impact of accrual accounting and budgeting is being increasingly felt. Similarly, governments can create a range of entitlements and enterprises that do not draw funds from general revenues, but are either contingent liabilities or self-funded enterprises that populate what is called the broader public sector.

Examples of off-budget expenditures include:

- activities of government enterprises, especially those that do not draw appropriations for their activities;

FIGURE 5.7
Different Types of Funds

Fund	Definition
General fund	Consists of general revenue sources such as taxes, fines, licences, and fees.
Special revenue fund	Consists of resources that are restricted for special purposes. Examples would be special funds from other governments or organizations for special program funding, e.g., infrastructure improvement.
Debt-service fund	Consists of resources used to repay long-term general obligation debt.
Capital project fund	Consists of resources restricted for construction and acquisition of capital facilities.
Fiduciary or trust fund	Account for assets held by the organization in a trustee capacity.
Endowment fund	Usually a donation for specific purposes that is intended to earn income for the organization or university. Often governed by a separate governing board.
Program-specific fund	Special-purpose program, e.g., Millennium Fund, which manages its own resources and does not have to return those funds at the end of the fiscal period. To be used for intended purpose only.

- specialized self-financing entitlement programs such as pension plans, which would also mean that governments cannot access the accumulated surplus of such plans, a matter of contention over the past decades;
- loan guarantees or credit provided by a government, which can take the form of direct government loans or guaranteeing private loans;
- tax expenditures, such as special allowances for individuals or companies, which reduce revenues to the government; and
- public-private partnerships in which a government assumes risk but uses private financing arrangements, thereby not drawing down appropriations.

To an extent, some entitlement programs can be considered off budget in the sense that the level of expenditure for the entitlement is determined by the legislation which creates it and is, therefore, less subject to the discipline of the budgetary process. However, for the most part, such entitlements and the estimated costs are displayed in budget documents.

Being off budget does not mean being out of sight. Governments, especially as they seek to deliver services in different, more cost-effective ways, will look to third party entities as well as public-private partnerships to get the work done. The challenge is understanding where the boundaries are and what has to be kept on-budget and what can be off. Accrual budgeting challenges that ability to conceal, deliberately or otherwise, major contingent liabilities such as pension fund shortfalls in future years. Therefore, the exact cost of this contingent liability should appear in forward budget documents.

The challenge of off-budget expenditures is one of control. Political control, the ability to direct the public purpose of the expenditure, is less direct than for the budget. This may or may not be a problem, as, in some instances, entities are taken off budget to reduce political control of their operations. That being said, political control is essential in a democracy. It has to be achieved through other means. Accountability for expenditures is often weaker when expenditures are off budget. This is due to the relatively lower transparency of those expenditures.

There is a strong movement for governments to budget and exercise budget control for as much of the array of its activities as possible. Where this is not possible, such as with the case of commercially based government entities, there is a strong movement for more standardized financial reporting. As governments move in a variety of public-private delivery tools, this will be a challenge.

More Complex Forms of Budgets: Linking Money to Results

As we have seen, public-sector budgets can take many forms, and some budgetary concepts have emerged in the past decades that direct them into areas of greater and greater complexity. These try to link the concept of the budget as a financial statement with the business plan of the organization marrying the top line of strategy with the bottom line of the budget. Some of these concepts have succeeded, and some have not. Some continue to evolve. In the public sector, however, one sees a greater trend towards attempting to link financial data to results. The challenge in the public sector, quite unlike the private sector, is that these results are seldom financial themselves.

Two types of budgets that attempt to build better links between budgeted funds and the results they are intended to achieve are zero-based budgeting and performance or results-based budgeting.

Zero-Based Budgeting

Most budgets are incremental in nature. Put simply, this year's budget is based on adjustments to items in the previous year's budget along with the additions and subtractions arising from program or funding changes. Using the example of the Killaloe General Hospital, it can generally be assumed that, policy changes aside, its program will continue from one year to the next with relatively little change. Creating a budget thus becomes a matter of making small adjustments to salaries, supplies, etc. Often this is done within the context of some overall budgetary cap that will govern the overall bottom line.

Of course, it is possible, and at times, absolutely necessary to start from scratch in creating a budget. This is known as zero-based budgeting. This form of budgeting is a harsh reality for some small public-sector organizations where funding is so uncertain that they are often forced each year to reassess all of their spending and justify their needs to either a skeptical funding source, a board, or a public that will have to find the funds. For other organizations, that form of budgeting is a management trend that has seen better days. A conceptual approach to budgeting that emerged in the 1970s, it achieved its moment of fame as the new solution to all budgeting problems and then went on to become just another set of letters in the pantheon of failed quick fixes – ZBB.

This form of budgeting assumes that all expenditures will be thoroughly reviewed on an annual basis and subjected to intense scrutiny. Decisions about their desirability will be made afresh. With ZBB, no assumptions about carrying on can be made. A formal system is put in place to scrutinize existing programs, which must be approved before they can carry on. In theory, the decision makers are operating with a starting budget of zero and building a new spending plan on an annual basis.

The heart of the ZBB budget is that managers must defend their current resources before they can argue for more. This involves putting in place a budget-planning process that carefully examines all expenditures on a line-by-line basis. It also assumes that the organization can create a challenge function, with people in the organization and in consulting firms, to advise the decision makers about the validity of the assumptions made by those asking for the funds. Often this will pit the finance function against the operational or line function in the organization. However this comes about, ZBB assumes that there is ample analytical capacity and time to determine if each expenditure is valid.

The table in **Figure 5.8** compares the characteristics of ZBB and incremental budgeting with respect to concept and process.

ZBB can be a very time-consuming process for an organization. When attempted on a large scale in the United States government in the late 1970s, the process quickly ground to a halt. The problem was not so much with the concept as with the scope of the effort needed to implement ZBB across the board.

The zero-based approach has considerable theoretical merits, but the organization requires certain capabilities to do so. The first is that it needs to assess all its spending on an annual basis. For small volunteer organizations, this is exactly what they must do. Many municipalities face considerable pressure to do this as well. The second is that, for many other organizations, with established programs fixed in legislation, such efforts are simply a waste of time because neither the political nor organizational will exists to alter the programs. The third is that the ZBB approach often fails to identify potential savings and benefits that could result.

A ZBB approach to budgeting can be very effective during a time of drastic reduction that requires the organization to undertake a thorough review of its programs in order to determine how to make fundamental adjustments. We will see in the discussion of reallocation and cutbacks that the inherent elements of ZBB can be useful, when applied on a selective and focused basis. What is key for any kind of base review to work is that:

- Nothing was held sacred.
- Assessment criteria are given.
- All programs were subject to initial or cyclical scrutiny.

FIGURE 5.8
Comparing Incremental Budgeting with Zero-Based Budgeting

Zero-Based Budgeting	Incremental Budgeting
1. Evaluation of current activities and examination of alternatives leads to operational budget.	1. Operating budget is subject to a series of incremental changes (increases or decreases) on a line-item basis, often with an overall budget increase set.
2. Ignores past behaviour and assumes a clean slate of activities.	2. Accepts the existing programs and estimates costs of new activities or changes, including decreases.
3. Creates cost/benefit analyses of all alternatives for all programs including the status quo.	3. Focuses analysis and alternatives on changes to programs and on new activities.
4. Focus is on the program architecture and need, which ensures the continuation of activities.	4. Focus is on costs and money, rather than program continuity, and generally assumes that existing programs will continue.
5. Examines new means of delivery for existing programs.	5. Budget process not used to re-evaluate existing programming.
6. Decision makers faced with options, alternatives and different levels of services decisions within the budget package.	6. Little scope for examining alternatives.

Source: Adapted from Jerome B. McKinney, *Effective Financial Management in Public and Nonprofit Agencies*, 3rd edition (Westport, CT: Praeger, 2003).

- A formal governance process was created at the Cabinet level to ensure that decisions are made.
- Decisions were based on this process.

Governments and other public-sector organizations have struggled with many forms of budgeting in order to get at the problem that ZBB was trying to address: how to deal with entrenched programming costs that had become virtually immutable. Where this form of budgeting floundered was in trying to do too much within the budgetary process itself. As a result, it has been dropped in the United States, which is now trying various forms of performance budgets. Where it shows continued applicability is in the current trend toward reallocation and program review type activities to be discussed in Chapter 8, **Reallocation and Budget Cutting**.

Performance or Results-Based Budgets

Performance or results-based budgets are intended to draw a link between the resources being dedicated and the results desired from the program. While a line-item budget is focused entirely on inputs and a zero-based budget goes back to basics and reinvents itself each year, the performance budget has certain features that move it more into the realm of public-sector accountability with a greater emphasis on outcomes and results:

- Budgets are closely linked to the results, objectives, outputs or outcomes desired.
- The desired results – based on public policy decisions – would justify the budget levels.
- Performance measures, targets, and anticipated outcomes would be stated in the budgetary process.
- Results are reported in retrospect as a means of increasing this link between money and what it buys, and improving accountability.

Performance-based budgets have a number of essential elements.

- Services are defined and measures are created for them.
- Disaggregating services permits individual costing and the development of workload measurements.
- Service standards are developed.
- Costing methodology is standardized.
- Unlike other budget formats, they contain a considerable amount of narrative to explain service levels, the basis on which they are costed, and how costs are distributed.
- They involve some form of benchmarking, to provide comparative data for costs and workload levels in

similar circumstances (e.g., comparing the cost of garbage collection between one town and another).

In a sense, a performance budget is a functional budget that defines both outputs and, to some degree, outcomes. It is a functional budget because most of the line items will be functions to be delivered – public safety in a municipality, counselling services of a family-service organization, etc. In addition, however, the performance budget is designed to provide a clearer picture of what level of service is to be provided for how much money and with what results. An example of this would be adding to the Killaloe Hospital budget documents information that outlines some of the following outcomes:

- number and types of operations,
- waiting times for operations,
- cost per operation, and
- changes in service levels.

It could be argued that some of these items are not results. This is true. That is why the term performance also comes into play. Often results, let us say, a healthier population at reasonable costs, can prove elusive. Attribution can be contentious. Are more operations going to make people healthier? Is cost important or not? Therefore, in developing a linkage between budgets and results, often surrogates or approximate measures are used. The simple reality is that the desired results – a healthy population – has so many mitigating factors that it cannot easily be linked to a budget without making some inherent assumptions about performance.

Often the link between budget data and performance outcomes is not entirely clear and may be difficult to define. For example, a performance budget could readily develop standardized costs for police patrols and show the cost of that activity. This would permit decision makers to see that adding more resources in this area would increase those patrols. There would be an assumption that these added patrols would reduce crime and increase public safety – which is the desired outcome – but even a performance budget could not stretch the linkage that far on its own. It would take other studies and data to establish that patrols actually reduce crime and that this increases public safety, a very amorphous outcome. Rather, the performance budget is a good step towards costing services, clearly identifying service levels of current resources, and helping decision makers make a better link between those two when determining future resources. A direct link to outcomes requires more information or built-in assumptions about policy outcome than even a performance budget can provide. **Figure 5.9** compares performance budgeting with traditional budgeting on a number of dimensions.

FIGURE 5.9
Traditional Budgeting and Performance Budgeting

	Traditional Budgeting	Performance Budgeting
Budget Orientation	Money control	Linking money to program and activities
Appropriation Control Level	Department	Program
Basic Budgeting Unit	Object, object code or line item	Activity
Efficiency Measurement	None	Unit cost, volumes
Result Measurement (Effectiveness/ Quality)	None	Program levels, activity levels
Budget Period	One year	Ongoing – year over year

A performance-budgeting approach takes considerable groundwork and time. In **Figure 5.10**, Jerome McKinney sets out the steps.

Organizations find that the development of costings and workload measures often meets internal resistance. For example, there are very few child counsellors who believe that standardized costing for a counselling session has any meaning whatsoever. They are probably right. The organization has to struggle with measures that have both internal and external meaning. Such measurements may not even be possible or affordable. Often, the development of such measures entails so much work that the organization loses focus on its clients.

Similarly, the public or stakeholders involved with a performance budget have to be convinced that what is being costed is valid. This debate will involve a mix of discussions about both the validity of the metrics and the efficiency of the current service. Suppose a 911 call is

presently costed at $25 per call and the 911 unit is trying to base a case for more resources on a workload increase; it must do two things to meet performance-budget criteria:

- show how it developed the original cost of $25 per call and defend that costing as the most efficient output it can produce for this amount of money (the effectiveness and efficiency arguments);
- show how demand has changed; and
- demonstrate how the resources contribute to the timely emergency response capacity of the city.

Through performance budgeting, the 911 unit would subject itself to a degree of public scrutiny and debate before any decisions on resource increases could be made. If the agency has properly established its costs and services, this can be a powerful tool for arguing for the resources it believes it needs to deliver its service. Getting that understanding and consensus takes considerable effort, but it does serve a greater purpose in that the budget process is better informed.

FIGURE 5.10
Seven Steps in the Development of a Performance Budget

1. Define individual work activities in terms that are measurable and can be related to resource requirements.
2. Inventory the work units and the kind of work that must be performed on each.
3. Develop quantity standards for each activity to permit an estimation of the amount of work required during the year, expressed in terms of annual number of units of work. Quantity standards are used to define the workload to be undertaken and the minimal acceptable quality of work necessary to carry out an activity.
4. Determine the number of work units per activity. This task is made easy after the quantity standards and inventory of the amount of work to be done on each activity have been established.
5. Establish production standards. The efficiency with which work is performed is a function of how the workers are assigned and equipped and the methods used in performing work activities. Responsibility should then be assigned to investigate and evaluate alternative methods for accomplishing each activity.
6. Compute resource requirements by applying production standards to the defined work program.
7. Collect cost data and convert the performance-budget resource requirements into financial terms.

Source: Jerome B. McKinney, *Effective Financial Management in Public and Nonprofit Agencies*, 3rd edition (Westport, CT: Praeger, 2003).

Performance budgeting is similar to ZBB in that it can become mired in process. Perhaps the grandfather of large performance-budgeting systems was Planning, Programming, and Budgeting Systems (PPBS). This complex planning and budgeting process is often associated with Robert J. McNamara, who tried to introduce it into the American Department of Defense during the Vietnam War. Not only was it complex and demanding, but it also led to macabre measures such as body counts of those killed in the war. Such complex systems tend to consume valuable executive and managerial time in internal processes while ignoring the realities of the client base.

Even simple systems of performance budgeting may become too much for the organization to bear in terms of time and attention. Developing applicable costings and unit prices for specific activities demands both technical expertise and considerable bureaucratic clout to come up with measures that make sense for the program. This latter concern can lead to internal debate and conflict.

Notwithstanding the challenge that the use of performance-budgeting presents, it is a wise manager who has good measures of his or her activities, who can establish costs, and who can then use those costs and measures to advise on the implications of program changes. Without these, the manager is often left at the mercy of those who would assign their own measures or leave decision makers with the impression that the program is not using all its resources effectively and so could readily absorb a greater workload.

Governments around the world have adapted various forms of performance or results-based management, often with different names, but all with characteristics similar to what has been discussed above. For instance, in 2012, the Province of Alberta passed the ***Results-based Budgeting Act*** to require that all parts of the broader Alberta public sector budget in this way. This follows the adoption of a results-based budgeting approach in Ontario in 2003, making it an early adopter. At a more global level, the United Nations published its ***Results-based Programming, Management and Monitory (RBM) – Guiding Principles – UNESCO***.

Some Concluding Thoughts and What This Means to Managers

Budgets in the public sector are an important link between those who create public policy and those who implement it. They are, in fact, the principal means of putting those policies in place and assigning the required resources to implement them. By law, they create both a limit on expenditures for the manager and the authority to spend the resources.

Budgets play an important role in the management of public-sector organizations. While they can be organized in a number of different ways, they always serve as valuable instruments of public policy. The structure of a budget will generally reflect the complexity of the organization itself. Managers, however, have to navigate among a variety of objectives in order to fully understand the budgetary process (getting the resources), the allocative and reallocative processes inherent, and the accountabilities built into those budgets.

As to the budget as an internal management tool, once again, issues of clarity and timeliness emerge. The key to holding managers responsible for results is to ensure that they have the resources they need to do the job. They must also have them in a timely fashion, i.e., when they need them. As we will see when we examine the budgetary process, there are tremendous time distortions in Canadian governments, especially when it comes to intergovernmental transfers and transfer payments from funding provinces to hospitals and schools. Such inefficiencies also distort the meaning of budget information.

The budget of a unit or section of a government department further disaggregates the larger departmental or cross-government budget, assigning resources in a very specific way to that unit to carry out its work. It is a fundamental reality that managers must manage their performance targets, not only with the resources they are directly assigned in the budgets (think of their set of line items for staff, supplies, etc.), but also with those resources held centrally for functions that serve all the organization. As a simple example, think here of the dependence of a line manager on computer support provided by another part of the organization. Therefore, it behooves a manager to understand not only her budget and plans, but those of the many parts of the organization upon which she depends to get the job done.

As the next chapter discusses, the budgetary process involves setting goals and expectations about activities to be undertaken with the resources allotted. The assigned budget of a responsibility manager is also a benchmark against which to measure that manager's performance, especially in areas of program and financial control and attention to public funds.

Appendix 1, ***The Budget Games People Play***, gives a sense of the budget as a bureaucratic battlefield. Like any other field of engagement, it invites the use of strategies and tactics so that managers can maximize the benefits for their programs. It is about winning and losing, as resources are scarce. Further, resources equal power and influence as well as a means to get something done. Maximizing resources means having the influence that many seek in organizations.

The companion chapter to this is the next one: ***Planning and Budgeting***. Understanding what a budget is and what it might look like is important, but it also is a vital planning tool within public-sector organizations. How governments plan their budgets reflects the nature of the public sector itself. Budgetary processes can be open or closed. They can be simple or complex. Whatever their form, though, they tend to strongly reflect what the organization does and how it does it. As with most public-sector issues, the public is deeply concerned with the outcomes of budget processes. Very simply, the public pays up front but also expects results at the end of the process. The results are public policy, goods, and services, delivered locally and nationally as well as internationally. These public goods are important to all Canadians, which explains why public-sector budgets – and how we get them – are significant.

Chapter 6
Planning and Budgeting

Chapter Objectives:

- Linking the budget to the planning process of organizations
- Examining simple and complex budget cycles
- Appreciating the dynamic nature of budget decisions
- Relating issues of revenue and cost to budget outcomes
- Examining fundamental tensions in public-sector budgeting

Introduction

Whatever the level of complexity in a public-sector organization, the budgetary process lies at the heart of it achieving its objectives. Learning both the art and the science of budgeting is essential to good financial management in the public sector. Similarly, understanding how the budget-formulation process works within an organization allows the manager seeking funds for program purposes to influence the outcomes to the advantage of that program.

The public also has a strong interest in influencing budgetary outcomes. After all, it is only when funds are allocated that the real policy outcomes become real. The public, be it the general public, special interest groups or lobbyists, has an interest in knowing what is going on. Budget-formation processes have become more transparent and participatory, as the public and interest groups have demanded more engagement before decisions are made. For example, most provincial and federal governments have, in the past, treated the budget as a top-secret document. If any portion were leaked in advance, the finance minister's resignation would be sought. Today, most governments engage in some form of pre-budget consultation process both within their legislatures and directly with interest groups. We see an increase in strategic budget leaks, often made to test out an idea.

Municipal governments in particular are very open in their budget processes, engaging citizens very early in decision making so that there is very little surprise when the budget is formally presented. One other important feature of municipal budgeting is that the budget as presented is seldom the end of the budget process, but rather the beginning. Unlike at provincial and federal levels where the budget is a matter of government policy and subject to a confidence vote, in our towns and cities, the draft budget goes through a very open process of give and take with many alterations along the way before there is a final budget that the Council approves. Increasingly, within public-sector organizations, most of the budget is known in advance – the results of good planning and an adequate level of stakeholder involvement, as well as a recognition of the new world of intense lobbying, complex communications, and technological capacity to move information around.

The budget process is an important management tool, not just for assigning scarce resources, but for purposes of planning, setting direction, internal control and accountability. As we see in so many aspects of financial management in the public sector, not much happens until the money is in place to make it happen. Further, the monetized resources of public-sector organizations are subject to so many controls and scrutiny for the simple reason that they *are* public funds. Effective management of them is a first step of accountability for public-sector managers. Moreover, in the absence of good measures of outcomes or output performance, the budget often serves as a means of measuring performance. Even as governments improve their performance measures, everyone still watches the money. They have a number of concerns that start to move us, as we will see throughout this text, along the continuum of accountability. This gradation in accountability associated with the budget is shown graphically in **Figure 6.1**.

FIGURE 6.1
Budgetary Accountabilities

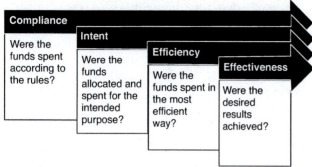

Clearly, the budgeting process is important for both the public and managers within public-sector organizations. For that reason, this chapter links the formation of the budget to the planning and policy process. It examines the role of legislative authorities in terms of both approvals of budgets and scrutiny of them. Because of its unique character, capital budgeting is addressed separately in Chapter 7. Chapter 8, Budget Reduction and Reallocation, looks at how managers often must reverse the process and reduce resources or find other means to fund programs.

Finally, this chapter examines the issues of budget dynamics, both formal and informal. The latter part outlines some of the basic tensions at play as public-sector organizations formulate budgets. Budget decision making is rich in organizational dynamics, be they internal relationships and power, or external strategic direction, values, and influence. While budgeting is often just about getting the money, it is also about power, or influence, and holding one's own in a complex organizational environment with many competing internal and external forces. Hence, the budget games people play in Appendix 1 present just some of the dynamics that can come into play as individuals engage in defending turf, trying to get more or to change the budget.

The budgetary process is central to how public-sector organizations function internally, and how they are seen by the public. In 1986, Aaron Wildavsky wrote:

> The allocation of resources necessarily reflects the distribution of power. Budgeting is so basic it must reveal the norms by which men live in a particular political culture; it is through the choices inherent in limited resources that consensus is established and conflict is generated. The authority of government is made manifest by its ability to not only make a budget but also to make it stick. Public policymaking decides what programs will be enacted, who will benefit from

them, and at what monetary levels they will be supported. Public policymaking is epitomized through the budget. So is implementation, for when push comes to shove, programs will not be carried out as intended (or at all) unless commitment is memorialized by money. If justice delayed is justice denied, then a budget rejected is a program aborted and a fund diverted is a policy perverted. When a process involves power, authority, culture, consensus, and conflict, it captures a great deal of national political life.[1]

Finally, governments have tried many ways over the years to reform budgetary processes to make them more responsive to political control, more or less decentralized, better managed, and more closely linked to the results desired. Some of these efforts have borne fruit and budgeting has become more transparent and comprehensible. Appendix 2 outlines some of these efforts.

Budgets and Planning Cycles

Most governments, departments, or units of organizations establish formalized processes to produce their final budgets. Within operational units, arriving at the final distribution of the operating budget will entail some measure of forecasting, analyzing of options, setting plans in place over the long term, and finally, assigning resource levels. This is the budget cycle.

The Budget Cycle: The Basics

Budget cycles, planning systems, and procedures form key elements of public-sector management. You can call them anything (strategic-planning systems, planning, budgeting systems, etc.); you can flow-chart them, PowerPoint them, and build in all the bells and whistles that the organization needs, wants, and likes. With all that, some basic requirements have to be met, regardless of the size or complexity of the public-sector organization. Organizations will have:

- **a basic framework** with common language, meaning, and reference points for all the players in the process to use;
- **desired outcomes** from the political leadership, be it Cabinet, an executive director, or a board of directors;
- **linkage to the strategic plans** of the organization, especially with respect to increases or reductions in program levels, investments in new programs, and the multi-year implications of the plan;
- **a format used by all units** of the organization that will ultimately roll up into the organization's spending plan for the coming period as defined (usually one year);

FIGURE 6.2
Working Definition of a Budget Process

A good budget process is far more than the preparation of a legal document that appropriates funds for a series of line items. Good budgeting is a broadly defined process that has political, managerial, planning, communication, and financial dimensions. The following definition recognizes the broad scope of the budget process and provides a base for improvement of the budget process.

The budget process consists of activities that encompass the development, implementation, and evaluation of a plan for the provision of services and capital assets.

A good budget process is characterized by several essential features. A good budget process:

- incorporates a long-term perspective,
- establishes linkages to broad organizational goals,
- focuses budget decisions on results and outcomes,
- involves and promotes effective communication with stakeholders, and
- provides incentives to government management and employees.

These key characteristics of good budgeting make clear that the budget process is not simply an exercise in balancing revenues and expenditures one year at a time, but is strategic in nature, encompassing a multi-year financial and operating plan that allocates resources on the basis of identified goals. A good budget process moves beyond the traditional concept of line item expenditure control, providing incentives and flexibility to managers that can lead to improved program efficiency and effectiveness.

Source: Government Financial Officers Association: "Recommended Budget Practices." Available at http://www.gfoa.org/services/nacslb/.

- **an agreed-upon timetable** for preparation and consideration of budgets within the organization;
- **a set of technical directions** that define the objectives of the current process and whatever budgetary and program limits the organization chooses to set in advance, including expenditure limits and instructions on matters that are handled at the corporate level of the organization and not to be addressed in the units (such as collective agreements that are organization-wide), and their implications for salaries and benefits;
- **methodologies for costing and forecasting** current program levels, the implications of changes in service demands or standards, and the cost of new initiatives; and
- **direction** as to the degree to which the unit manager must seek to reallocate current funding, absorb known cost increases, or access additional funds.

In all probability, these requirements would be met only in an ideal world. Real-life processes are less clear and often less logical than described above, but in trying to outline an effective budgetary process for a public-sector organization, it is necessary to establish standard expectations against which it might be judged. Managers trying to operate in whatever budget process exists in their organization should look for these features and, in their absence, attempt to make them happen. Generally, the budget process is managed by a central finance office. If it is effective, it will be trying to make the above happen.

The Simple Budget Cycle shown in **Figure 6.3** is a good starting point for understanding the budgetary process. It is at a very high level and accurate way of thinking about how budgets are formulated and executed.

The logic of diagrams such as this can be deceiving because the reality of budgeting will not follow the steps of this cycle so precisely. Recall the section in the previous chapter on the multi-level and multi-year elements of the budgetary process. As outlined in **Figure 5.1**, there are three elements to financial management in general and to budgeting in particular: the past performance, the present budget, and the future spending plans. While one budget is being implemented, the next one is being planned. As one approval phase ends, the review of results of the previous year may begin. This sequencing is not linear. Rather, it is multi-dimensional. Separating them out for discussion is necessary, but somewhat misleading as the process, even as it marches through the centrally ordained steps, remains a messy one. **Figure 6.4, Saskatchewan's Planning and Budgeting Cycle,** is a good illustration of the kind of complexity that is the reality of the budgetary process.

Strategic Planning Phase

All organizations plan for the future. Making choices about programs and priorities sets a direction, communicates values, distributes resources, and arouses expectations. Some organizations have complex and well-documented

FIGURE 6.3
A Simple Budget Cycle

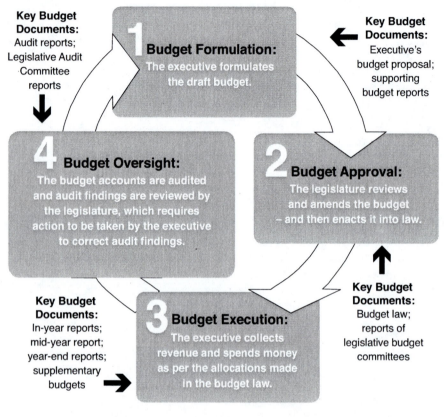

Key Budget Documents: Audit reports; Legislative Audit Committee reports

1 Budget Formulation: The executive formulates the draft budget.

Key Budget Documents: Executive's budget proposal; supporting budget reports

4 Budget Oversight: The budget accounts are audited and audit findings are reviewed by the legislature, which requires action to be taken by the executive to correct audit findings.

2 Budget Approval: The legislature reviews and amends the budget – and then enacts it into law.

Key Budget Documents: In-year reports; mid-year report; year-end reports; supplementary budgets

3 Budget Execution: The executive collects revenue and spends money as per the allocations made in the budget law.

Key Budget Documents: Budget law; reports of legislative budget committees

Source: These materials were developed by the International Budget Partnership. The IBP has given us permission to use the materials solely for noncommercial, educational purposes. Available at http://internationalbudget.org/getting-started/why-are-budgets-important/.

planning processes. These can involve many levels of the organization, often working together in the preparation of documents and the provision of information. For others, planning and budgeting are much simpler because the lines of control and command are shorter and the decision making is more immediate.

The planning and budgeting process of the Government of Saskatchewan as shown in **Figure 6.4** is a good example of a complex budget-planning system. It is designed to ensure that the final budget of the minister of finance is the result of a rigorous planning process.

This process takes into account the relationship of the political leadership – Cabinet and the premier or prime minister with bureaucratic leadership through the Treasury Board, which provides the advice and support needed for decision making. This is both a strategic-planning and a budgetary process.

Strategic planning usually takes place outside the context of direct budget planning alone, drawing on the many

tools of planning beyond simple resource allocation and distribution. At least, that is the theory: that strategic planning should be driven by values and outcomes and that issues of financing the vision should be left to the next iterative phase of planning. The reality is somewhat different. Of course, strategic planning should be long-term and visionary – but based on a realistic assessment of circumstances. Financial information about the past and present naturally feeds thinking about the future, and anticipated revenue flows to public-sector organizations will temper multi-year projections. Otherwise, the political leadership would be accused of creating false expectations. Thus, the strategic-planning process must be conscious of financial realities. Some characteristics of strategic planning differ from the annual budget-preparation phase. For instance, very few strategic plans are for one year. For the most part, they go beyond the budgeting horizon of most governments. More and more, however, governments today are projecting their budget costs into future years to inform public evaluation and decision making. Similarly, the introduction of accrual budgeting will encourage a multi-year and intergenerational understanding of budget decisions. While this trend provides more information in the budget process, it is still the case that legislatures usually approve only a single year at a time, although some governments are moving towards the approval of multiyear budgets or the creation of self-managing funds that exist over several years.

Strategic planning is generally program-oriented. It involves the creation of a hierarchy of strategic tools that permit the organization, in an ideal world, to guide decision making and set priorities for the organization as a whole. It is also important in the establishment of desired end states – say, a certain level of environmental emissions to reduce pollution – as a means of measuring the outputs

FIGURE 6.4
Saskatchewan's Planning and Budgeting Cycle

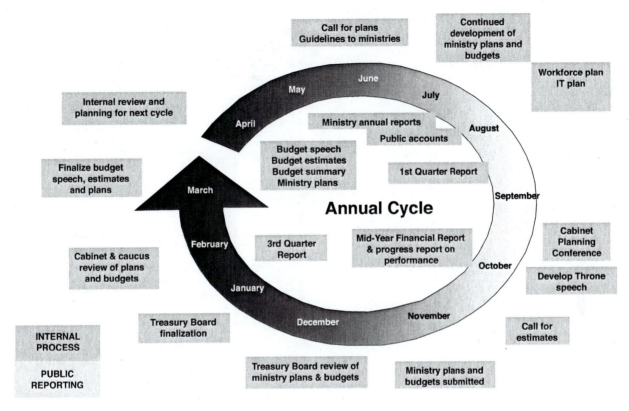

Source: http://www.finance.gov.sk.ca/PlanningAndReporting/GovernmentPlanningAndBudgetingCycle.pdf.

desired for the organization. As such, most strategic planning is mission- or goal-driven, using long-term and broadly based objectives.

The Architecture of a Strategic Plan

Strategic plans usually contain a fundamental set of components that describe the purpose of the organization and its intended direction over a prescribed period, as discussed above. While they may take many formats, they have common elements. The following sections, which have been mandated for American federal government departments by the *Government Performance and Management Act*, 2001, provide good examples:

- **Mission:** comprehensive statement expressing the purpose of the organization.
- **Vision:** statement of the ideal state or end-results pursued by the organization.
- **Guiding Principles:** the philosophy that steers the organization in delivering services and accomplishing its mission. Another phrase used here is **Values.**

- **Situation Analysis:** a description of key internal and external trends that are likely to affect the agency over the time period of the plan. This is also called an **Environmental Scan.** This has to take into account elements such as financial conditions, both internal and external; clients' needs and issues; technology; organizational overlaps; changes to demand levels; character of the clientele; and new issues.
- **Goals:** statements that describe the agency's destination, direction, and intent for the period of the plan.
- **Objectives:** initiatives that implement the goals; that is, precise statements of the desired results of completing a series of action steps.
- **Performance Measures and Targets:** precise milestones for each objective that will help the organization evaluate progress toward its objectives and the goals that it supports.
- **Linkage of General Goals to Annual Performance Plan:** a description of the relationship between annual goals in the performance plan and the general multi-year goals and objectives in the strategic plan.

- **Resources Needed:** a description of the human, capital, information, and other resources, as well as the operational processes, skills, and technology needed to achieve the agency's goals, that highlights where significant change from currently available resources will be needed. Note that this is not the budget for the coming year, but a resource discussion that will certainly affect budget decisions in future years.
- **Program Evaluation:** a description of how the results of programs or policy will be evaluated.

The translation of the goals of strategic planning into results is often a difficult one. A balance must be struck between investing too many resources and too much time in the strategic phase and not enough in the actual implementation phase. Getting the framework right is important, in terms both of getting the right work done but also in convincing stakeholders that the organization deserves support – be that from tax dollars, fees, or contributions – to carry out its role.

Moving to Action and Into the Budget

Many public-sector organizations develop formal strategic-planning processes that include the public and specific stakeholders. Here is how one small community in Utah translates strategic planning into a format that finally arrives at a budget for the city. It formulates its strategic plan in such a way that it can easily move into the budget-preparation phase. **Figure 6.5**, a simple set of contents of the Strategic Plan of the City of Ivers, Utah (taken randomly from many good local government examples), shows this movement from the general, high-level topics we see in such a plan to the specifics of how they apply to the various city functions such as transportation and wastewater. This is the real world of municipal government. It is also where the rubber hits the road for citizens. Great words abound. Assigning the dollars to achieve results is the hard work.

The strategic-planning process of the Government of Alberta shows greater complexity, as did that of Saskatchewan above. It is highly instructive in that it uses that process to guide budget building and to link various departments by means of what are termed cross-government priorities to ensure that the strategic element of the planning is retained. It is outlined in **Figure 6.6**. A cross-government priority is one that involves several government departments in achieving an over-arching objective. Public policy issues seldom align themselves along neat organizational lines. In fact, it is an attribute of 21st century public administration that public policy challenges are complex, multi-dimensional and, increasingly,

FIGURE 6.5
Outline of the Strategic Plan for Ivers City, Utah

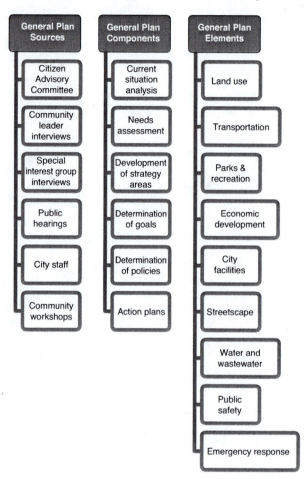

wicked, i.e., a challenge that is not resolved easily in a short period without complex responses.[2] Therefore, a department needs to understand its role in resolving cross-governmental issues.

The strategic-planning format that a public-sector organization develops will suit its needs. Having it well documented and using it in a consistent fashion will ensure greater stability in budget outcomes for the organization.

Budget Preparation Phase

In most cases, budget preparation is the melding of two processes, of which the strategic-planning process is the first. The strategic plan will provide a set of program objectives, overall goals, and proposals for change. Just to complete the picture, let's call this the "wants" of the organization, i.e., its all-out vision.

The second process involves determining what resources a government actually has to meet its many requirements.

FIGURE 6.6
Strategic Plan of the Government of Alberta

The Government of Alberta Strategic Business Plan

Alberta's Vision: Today's Advantage, Tomorrow's Promise: Alberta's Vision for the Future;

20-Year Strategic Plan: Today's Opportunities, Tomorrow's Promise: A Strategic Plan for the Government of Alberta;

Medium-Term Strategies: Cross-Ministry Initiatives and Medium-Term Strategic Plans; and

3-Year Business Plan: 2004-07 Government of Alberta Business Plan.

The **Government of Alberta Strategic Business Plan** consists of the following:

Alberta's Vision for the Future which lays out Alberta's vision of "A vibrant and prosperous province where Albertans enjoy a superior quality of life and are confident about the future for themselves and their children."

It outlines the values that Albertans hold and four key opportunities or "pillars" to realize Alberta's vision: unleashing innovation; leading in learning; competing in a global marketplace, and making Alberta the best place to live, work and visit.

A **Strategic Plan for the Government of Alberta** which is a 20-year strategic plan that flows from the vision document, Today's Advantage, Tomorrow's Promise: Alberta's Vision for the Future. The 20-year plan sketches a picture of Alberta in the year 2025 and contains broad strategies for achieving the four key opportunities outlined in the vision document.

The 20-year strategic plan is based on what the government has heard from Albertans in different forums over the last few years. It provides strategic direction for government planning and policies.

Cross-Ministry Initiatives and Medium-Term Strategic Plans. The Cross-Ministry Initiatives section sets out the objectives and targets for four policy initiatives that bring together various ministries to address corporate government-wide issues. This approach recognizes that many issues are not isolated to a single ministry. The 2004-07 policy initiatives are: the Aboriginal Policy Initiative, the Alberta Children and Youth Initiative, the Economic Development Strategy, and the Health Sustainability Initiative.

The Medium-Term Strategic Plans section provides information on government strategies to address priority issues over a longer period of time.

The **2004-07 Government Business Plan** is an ongoing three-year plan linked to the fiscal plan and aligned with the broader strategies in the 20-year plan. The government business plan is published annually. It lays out the government's goals, strategies, and performance measures to track progress towards goal achievement.

Ministry business plans are also published annually and cover a three-year period. These ministry business plans are required to indicate how they link to the government business plan.

Source: http://www.finance.gov.ab.ca/publications/budget/budget2004/govbp.html#7.

What are the restraints? What are the limits? In short, faced with an endless array of wants, this is what contains the spending to what is possible or the "won't" part of the equation. This is where choices have to be made, and where trade-offs and reallocations come into the equation.

This process will involve direction from the central office of the organization as to budget limits. These are budget guidelines that senior management will issue to all responsibility centres to direct the preparation of their budget plans. Such guidelines will normally contain direction on the technical aspects of budget calculations and may establish spending limits in some or all areas and provide direction on how to incorporate changes – either up or down – in program plans and expectations. Such guidelines would also enforce standardized costing across the government.

The extent of this direction will vary greatly with the organization, with the degree of delegation in place in the organization, and with the extent to which senior management wishes to provide direction. For instance, where collective bargaining is centrally managed, managers will simply be informed of salary increases based on calculations by their staff complements. In some instances, managers may be instructed to absorb additional costs or negotiate them themselves. This can readily translate into a staff reduction if costs of collective agreements rise. It may also mean that managers have varying degrees of flexibility on staffing questions if their staff is formula- or workload-driven, as is often the case in large-scale operational departments.

Once the budget-preparation phase is reached, there is usually very little room for flexibility. This will vary with the size and style of the organization, but a rigorous strategic-planning exercise will certainly reduce the scope for budget negotiations. So, too, will pressures to reduce spending or to limit staff complements. This first phase is typically top-down, usually as part of the organization's planning cycle, under the oversight of a central office, reflecting the directions that the organization's top managers wish to take.

So where does the individual manager fit into this organizational behemoth? Perhaps it would be appropriate to say that the manager is really the third element, one possibly characterized in this tension of want and won't and the maybe. This element of the budget preparation is the influence of the manager who will be controlling the budget through its execution. As noted, the larger and more directive the organization, the less likely that there would be much flexibility in negotiating budget changes in this phase. Some variables and flexibility may still be in the hands of the manager. One example is the calculation or estimation of workload and costs to be used as part of the budget and planning. Another example is the role of the manager in proposing program changes and improvements. In all, this element deals with bottom-up proposals, not just for more money, but for changes to process, efficiency gains, or policy tweaks to reduce or transfer costs. This element of managerial influence suggests that budget preparation can also have bottom-up influences. In fact, any sensible budget process will have a good combination of top-down and bottom-up elements. See **Figure 6.7**,

Comparing Top-Down and Bottom-Up Budgeting. Strong managerial analysis of increased costs or new proposals can sometimes affect the budget-preparation process and financing levels. Timing is everything, however, and managers must understand how to influence these processes. If they wait too long, boundaries will have been set and the organization will have little or no appetite for new funding ideas, especially in the near term.

Role of Revenue and Workload Forecasts in Budget Calculation

Unless a new program is being implemented, most revenue and workload determinants will be based on historical data. Of course, changes in assumptions are possible, and they are often taken into account in the planning process. Similarly, various options exist to alter both revenue and workload through changes in taxes or fees and by altering program eligibilities and availabilities. Managers have to make predictions about anticipated revenues and workloads that will form the basis of the budget. Historical-trend data in both areas make an easily available and useful tool. The challenge in using this information arises when there is a dispute about the meaning of the data. In many instances, a central budget or planning office may see things differently from the line manager. Getting agreement on data, assumptions, and predictions is an important part of budget calculations. One reason that it can be difficult to reach an agreement on the meaning of workload and revenue

FIGURE 6.7
Comparing Top-Down and Bottom-Up Budgeting

Top-Down Budgeting	Bottom-Up Budgeting
Characterized by: • Centralized direction • Global perspective • Focus on program strategy and prioritization • Fiscal constraints • Tendency towards common costing	Characterized by: • Unit-specific view • Client or program end • Exceptionalism • Growth oriented
Tends to treat all budget needs the same	Ignores the strategic nature of government
Fits to global goals	Fits to program goals
Creates one size fits all	Permits adaptation and responsiveness
Enforces budget discipline	Encourages budget proliferation
Directive – organizations need direction	Participative – managers need a voice
Efficient	Potentially time consuming

information is that it combines both the historical and the speculative. For example, a manager must speculate or predict the answer to such questions as:

- Will demand continue as before?
- Will income from fundraising increase or decrease?
- Will unit costs remain as before?

The following are some of the types of cost and volume measures and how they can affect such judgements on revenue and workload.

- **Need Measures:** This is a highly elastic measure that can be the result of applying policy-driven definitions like those found in entitlement legislation, or a pattern of requests that the organization has met in the past or, more debatably, a pattern of unmet needs perceived by the management of the program. While need is often in the eye of the beholder, there are other significant determinants of need. For instance, benchmarks can often identify needs. In terms of how much maintenance needs to be applied to keep public infrastructure safe, many such benchmarks exist.

- **Demand Measures:** Here again, both objectivity and subjectivity come into play. Some can be highly credible measures of demand; for example, a neighbourhood with a certain pattern of break-ins over a number of years has a demand for police services on a regular and measurable basis.

- **Workload Measures:** These should be seen as operational indicators involving units of service to the public. In the example of the incidence of break-ins in one neighbourhood, workload data can be based on the cost of a police call-out and investigation. While these are generally non-financial in nature, combining the results of such measures with costs will generally drive a budgetary process. The disadvantage of such measures is that, being historical, they do not reflect any changes for the future, nor do they necessarily demonstrate the most effective means to achieve the end. The workload data alone cannot provide this information. It may be that less expensive forms of intervention, such as preventive patrols and foot checks of vulnerable buildings, could reduce overall costs and be more effective than current call-out measures. These would be known as process improvements, preventive measures, or alternative delivery options that reduce the impact of the more retrospective workload measure.

- **Productivity Measures:** Often, in the budget formulation, the relationship between costs and outputs will be taken into account to arrive at a per-unit cost. The organization may then seek ways to reduce them. For instance, senior management may direct that budgets be prepared with increases in productivity built in, in which case, workload measures are assumed to be altered a priori, on the assumption that it is possible to reduce costs through process or managerial improvements. Historical data at an eldercare facility may suggest that overtime funds to cover sick and vacation leave would be 12 percent of the total salary budget as has been the case in the past four years. However, senior managers, feeling the pressure of such costs, may ask for improvements to duty rosters, reduction in some nursing stations, and closer leave-management programs to reduce the budget to 6 percent of overall salary dollars.

- **Per Unit Costs:** Standardized costing of procedures is common in organizations that engage in repetitive activities. Such methodology is pervasive and generally useful as long as it is applied with some connection to the real world and with some recognition that there can be significant variation. For instance, it is possible to apply a standardized cost to a paramedic intervention in a particular community. It then becomes possible to look at that cost among communities as long as issues such as distance and traffic congestion are factored into variances that may occur. In another example, the number of medical procedures, costed uniformly, can be predetermined to ensure that excessive or unaffordable demand is controlled.

Revenue Assumptions

For large governments, revenues tend to be separated from the expenditure budget. That does not mean that revenue is not important. However, generally, these governments set their budget targets at a macro level and then expect the central agencies that direct the budget process to work out the internal allocation process. This will certainly mean that restraint, when it is needed, will have to be exercised. However, the budget itself will not address revenue targets. For smaller governments and for nonprofit organizations, the link between revenue and operational capacity is vital; revenue forecasting becomes integral to the planning cycle. Therefore, a clear system has to be in place. The following steps in revenue forecasting are suggested:

- Select the base year to begin gathering information.
- Gather historical data on revenue numbers for a set number of years.
- Assess the revenue growth trend.
- Articulate critical assumptions affecting this trend.

- Evaluate the validity of the assumptions.
- Prioritize and select the best forecasting method consistent with the assumptions.
- Monitor and compare projections with actual collections.
- Update the forecasting model.[3]

Cost Analysis and Forecasting

The costing process in budget formation has both upward and downward dimensions. In the determination of the cost of a particular activity or service, many other organizational issues come into play. The larger and more complex the public-sector organization, the greater will be the tendency for the central budget office to try to assign unit costs for cost-control purposes and to establish uniformity within the organization. From the other end, managers will want to ensure that costing formulae accurately reflect their view of the true cost of the program and that their flexibility is not necessarily limited by the costing formulae. Similarly, in smaller public-sector organizations, the board or council will want to contain costs, whereas the providers will have a tendency to expand them, especially when those organizations offer open-ended services for which demand is hard to limit. Such tensions will play themselves out in any so-called objective process of cost determination. Further, it may take a considerable time for an organization to fully understand or fully agree to the costs of particular programs and services. Finally, and perhaps most contentiously, the distribution of costs to various budget managers in complex organizations becomes a matter of great debate. The following statement sets out the situation nicely:

> As the public services become more competitive and the emphasis of control changes from inputs and cash limits to quality, performance and output measures, an understanding of how costs vary between activities and the volume of output is crucial. Activity or volume can be measured in terms of hours worked, bins emptied, patients seen or some other proxy for output, but without a clear understanding of what is the real cost, sensible resource allocation decisions cannot be made in the short or longer term and may be made inappropriately.[4]

Controllable and Uncontrollable Costs

Most budgets contain a mix of controllable and uncontrollable costs. Determining which is which is important in budget preparation, but when we examine cash forecasting and management control we see how important this is to the continuing management of the budget within the fiscal year of the budget.

A controllable cost is one that responsibility centre managers can change or restrain, or for which they can vary either the level of service or level of administrative support or change other variables. An example of a controllable cost would be one where a manager in a long-term care facility could decide to order locally produced and less expensive apple juice as a substitute for orange juice. Similarly, level of service and controllability of costs are related. For instance, the number of hours an office is open can be varied to control costs. This does not speak to the need for service, but rather to how much the government can afford to give.

An uncontrollable cost is one over which the responsibility centre manager can exercise no discretion. Entitlement programs often create situations of uncontrollable costs: if an individual qualifies for some form of assistance according to the law and regulations, then that entitlement is a right, and budget-level factors have no role in that determination. Another way of looking at this is that these costs are policy-driven, often with legislation to limit the ability to reduce costs without the issue becoming political.

Arguably, within all public-sector organizations, all costs are controllable – at some level of the organization. The example of an entitlement being an uncontrollable cost, then, is valid only for a particular responsibility manager, not for the government that created it and can change it if costs go out of control. Let us say, for example that the responsible manager is in a district social service office, dealing with clients on a regular basis. From her perspective, the calculation of future costs must assume that the entitlement levels are uncontrollable. While other elements, such as anticipated demand due to the economic situation, may be a factor in determining future budget needs, the levels are not negotiable unless the law or policy changes. From the perspective of her more senior managers, the issue is less clear. If they decide, on the basis of the severity of budget restraints or increases in entitlement program use, that perhaps the entitlement levels should be changed to reduce costs, then that becomes a policy matter that they would take to their minister or board. For them, then, these costs are controllable. Of course, the political limitations on that controllability are a factor in such calculations.

Once some determination is made about what costs can be controlled, and at what level within the organization, some responsibility can then be assigned, in order to establish control strategies. Otherwise, there is a tendency within organizations to make implicit assumptions about the controllability of costs or the capability of managers. This often manifests itself in so-called efficiency assumptions that central-budget planners will build into the budgetary process. For example, in organizations with a large staff who work 24 hours a day, seven days a week, absenteeism and the consequent need for overtime are often a problem. Control over these budgets is often a preoccupation both at the responsibility centre level and for the organization as a whole. For purposes of budget formulation, central-budget managers may project a reduction in overtime on the basis of the assumption that improving managerial techniques at the local level can produce greater efficiencies. It is assumed in this process that the operational wing of the organization will put such techniques into play and that individual managerial performance will improve. It is further assumed that the accountability systems are in place both to measure the results and to do something about them. There is often an assumption that such a reduction will have no negative effect on overall organizational performance in terms of meeting its goals. There are many assumptions in this scenario, and we can see that the budget-formulation process is often used to set in place expectations for managerial performance.

Basic Costing Tools and Definitions

From the point of view of both the responsibility centre manager charged with delivering a program and the organizational leadership trying to allocate and make best use of scarce resources, the answer to the question "how much does this cost?" is not so simple. From the perspective of the budget planner, assigning costs is a matter of judgement, compromise, and, usually, some measure of debate. A good example of this kind of complexity takes us back to the district social service office and the responsibility centre manager dealing with her entitlement programs. How much does it cost for her to deliver these programs?

Two definitions begin this process: **cost object** and **cost centre**. A cost object is the unit of service, program, organization, or good for which the cost is desired. In other words, it makes sense for organizations to spend time and energy finding costs that they need to know, either for internal management purposes or to account to their external funders, their legislature or council, or the public. The selection of the cost object can affect the accounting practices within the organization. In turn, it will have an impact on the responsibility centre manager and, potentially, the staff.

Suppose that in the case of the district social service office, the ministry has determined that the cost object of the office is the cost of serving a client, including the benefit received. Alternatively, the ministry could determine that the benefit received, since it is an uncontrollable cost determined by entitlement legislation, would not be one reported by the district and that only staff and administrative costs would be considered. Finally, it could determine, as we will see below, that certain costs not in the district office are relevant to this cost object and are to be included. There is no simple determination of the cost of supporting one assistance recipient. An alternative question, which would redefine the cost object is, "what does it cost for the office to serve a single client?" Another question that would create yet another cost object is, "what does it cost for the ministry to serve a single client at this district office, taking into account not just the costs of that one office but also the other parts of the organization – including headquarters, IT support, common financial and human resources services – that provide some direct or indirect support to the office?"

The cost object tends to centre on the service, process, or program offered. It is often an important consideration in public accountability, in program evaluation, and in explaining budget decisions. As can be seen above, a workable definition that is clear and well understood is important. As with many cost issues, determining where to assign costs and what to do with that information becomes a significant element in the entire managerial accountability cycle. If a cost object for the district office is defined as its costs of delivering services to its clients, then this information can be reduced to a per-unit value. This office, for instance, may have a per-unit cost of $850 per client, the actual benefit not included. In determining this per-unit cost, the ministry will also arrive at other tools for both budgeting and performance management: a province-wide per-unit cost (if it applies a similar methodology to all district offices in the overall budget) and a comparison of district offices to determine variations in cost objects.

The definition of the cost object of the organization affects both external accountabilities and internal management. Generally, however, reliance on cost objects alone can have a distorting effect, especially if they are applied in a rigidly uniform fashion that fails to take into account local variation. It is often the struggle of line managers to get these factors taken into account. One district office may be located in a very large geographical area with many remote communities to service. Travel costs for staff may be disproportionately higher than the provincial average.

Another concept when looking at costs is that of cost centres. A cost centre is a unit or department in an organization for which a manager is assigned responsibility for controlling costs. Implicit in the notion of a cost centre is that it has a manager with some form of responsibility, authority, and accountability for monies assigned to certain objects in the centre. In the case of the district office, which is a distinct cost centre, we can clearly identify the manager responsible for that centre. As we have seen, that manager may not control all the resources needed to deliver the service, often depending on regional and central offices for support services that have been consolidated within the organization for efficiency purposes.

A small organization will not have many cost centres; in fact, the entire operation may be a single cost centre. Organizational distinctions between line and staff are not great. A single responsibility manager will have all the functions needed to deliver the service or program under his or her control. Within larger organizations, however, there tends to be two types of cost centres: line or program centres, and staff or support centres. A line cost centre is responsible for delivering whatever it is that the organization does. (The district social service office is a line centre.) A support centre provides services that support the delivery of the program, provides specialized services internally to the organization, and provides oversight and monitoring capacity to the organization or control elements of the delivery process for accountability and probity purposes. Suppose that the district office manager has financial advisors in the office. These people may not work directly for her but are needed to process the financial documents that are vital to getting the social assistance to her clients. Instead, these financial officers may report to a regional financial officer who supervises staff in a number of district offices.

That officer would then be operating a support-service cost centre. The staff resources for financial officers would be displayed in the regional officer's budget, not in that of the district office manager.

The sorting and resorting of cost centres within organizations tends to reflect the degree to which these organizations are seen as being either centralized or decentralized. Often, highly centralized agencies will use common support centres prominently, with specialized staff in these units reporting through their own management structures. Operational or line managers become more dependent on these support centres to deliver their goals and do not have the resources immediately at their disposal. On the other hand, through separate support centres, the expertise is better concentrated so that specialist support services can improve services to line managers.

Cost centres, then, tend to focus on the responsible manager, not necessarily on the overall program cost. While the examples offered here focus on service delivery, in many public-sector organizations, the line cost centre does not provide direct service to clients; it may be a policy operation or one involved in research or regulation. The criterion for a line cost centre is not whether there is an identifiable client but, rather, if the activity is central to the mission of the organization. In the public sector, especially in government, departments and ministries are often responsible for a range of public-sector activities from policy advice to regulation development, from intergovernmental relations to direct program delivery. Some governments choose to have specialized policy departments in which the line cost centres would be the policy operations. On the other hand, in some agencies and organizations, a small policy-analysis unit may not be seen as mission-central but in support of the operational arm and thus classified as a support centre rather than a line centre. Such distinctions reflect the aims of the organization and its operating culture. They also reflect whether these costs are seen as being direct or indirect costs in the accomplishment of the organization's mission.

Direct and Indirect Costs

Building on the previous discussion, a common way of determining costs is to ask if they are direct or indirect in relationship to the core business of the organization. Direct costs are costs incurred within the organizational unit for which the manager has responsibility and costs of resources used for direct provision of goods or services or activities that relate to the core mission of the organization.[5] They are those costs that are associated with, or have been physically traced to, a specific cost object or cost centre.

Indirect costs are costs assigned to an organizational unit from elsewhere in the organization (e.g., information technology support) and costs within a unit that are not incurred for direct provision of goods or services – that is, are not central to the core business or mission – but are nonetheless needed to provide those services (logistical support, information technology, physical plant, financial services, etc.).[6]

Similarly, indirect costs from support cost centres are often applied to several cost centres. For instance, the cost of providing IT support from the central support office will mean ensuring that the services to the line cost centres are costed in a way that provides a full picture of all the costs of the direct line service. For example, the social workers in the district office are direct costs to the program. So, too, is their supervision, since the manager does case monitoring and direct supervision. A clerk who processes claims in the unit may also be considered a direct cost because he is part of the service procedure. If the office uses a post-audit process of review wherein a financial clerk reviews a number of claims on an audit basis after they have been paid, that clerk may be seen as an indirect program cost. This will depend on how the cost centre is organized financially and on how relevant such distinctions are within a small office or organization. On the other hand, the district office manager is supervised by a regional manager, who in turns reports to an assistant deputy minister (ADM) at headquarters. They have offices, support staff, and costs, but the organization would normally treat such costs as indirect in relation to the district office. With respect to the ministry as whole, on the other hand, this ADM and his organization may be seen as mission-central and, hence, all costs are direct. Where some organizations tie themselves in knots is when they attempt to distribute all indirect costs to cost centres, often dividing up central office services in such a way that defies comprehension. This process is known as cost allocation. It is an important part of budgeting in large organizations.

Often organizations fail to fully take into account all the costs of service delivery. They must identify not only the cost of various line cost centres, but also what indirect, but necessary, services and external support costs are required to ensure that the mission-central cost centres can actually perform. An indirect cost is no less important than a direct cost. Determining the full cost of services and programs requires a full appreciation of both.

The objective of sound budgeting practice is to arrive at a complete understanding of the total cost of providing the mission-critical services of the organization. This is the full-cost principle. Full cost is the total cost associated with the cost object. The full-cost principle can be varied and complex, depending on the organization. There is the added complexity that the service costs are entirely incurred by support cost centres. Increasingly, public-sector organizations, just like their private-sector counterparts, want to know how much big-ticket items like information technology are actually costing the organization. Looking at the IT support cost centres may not tell the full story. In fact, it has been well established that IT costs are highly distributed in large organizations and that direct IT costs are just the tip of the cost iceberg. In some instances, this

is relevant to budget planning and accountability. For example, the district officer manager, using some discretionary funds, may have a contract IT technician ready to meet occasional needs for computer assistance to the staff, in addition to the centrally provided services, which the manager feels are insufficiently funded. This is an IT cost that is incurred directly by the line manager but is not factored into overall IT costs. Other IT costs not factored into the overall calculations comprise the amount of time that staff spend repairing their own machines or doing software upgrades or virus checks. This is a work transfer that is socially and technologically driven. Costing it into the budgeting and accounting system is something very few organizations have done.

Activity-Based Costing and the Distribution of Indirect Costs

Crucial to the budget-formulation process is the way in which organizations take the previous analysis of direct and indirect costs and assigns them to cost objects. This is known as activity-based costing, a process that, as already noted, is important but can demand organizational time and resources. Allocation of costs is the process by which organizations distribute indirect costs for a service to the cost objects of concern to the organization. In turn, it is a means of distributing centrally held service resources to responsibility centres to help them meet their program and organizational objectives. This does not mean that all allocations of costs will result in the resources coming under the spending authority of the responsibility centre manager. Rather, it is an allocation that is retained by the support or staff centre responsibility manager but notionally allocated to show how these support services are distributed across various units. A simple example of activity-based costing would be the assignment of centrally paid cleaning costs to the various units in a building of the organization. Let us say that there is one contract for the building, valued at $300,000 annually. The building is used by three units, Unit A using 40 percent of the of the office floorspace, Unit B using 20 percent, and Unit C uses 10 percent. Note that this does not equal 100 percent. That is because 30 percent of the space is considered common space – washrooms, common meeting rooms, cafeteria, corridors, lobby, etc. We can see how activity-based costing soon gets complicated. So, what to do? An easy solution would be to allocate the common spaces proportionally to the office use. Therefore costs would be distributed as outlined in **Figure 6.8, Distribution of Indirect Costs: Activity-Based Costing.**

FIGURE 6.8
Distribution of Indirect Costs: Activity-Based Costing

Unit and % Office Space Use	Allocation of Cleaning Costs: Office Space	Proportion of Common Space Based on % of Office Space Use	Allocation of Cleaning Costs of Common Spaces
Unit A: 40%	120,100	57%	51,300
Unit B: 20%	60,000	28%	25,200
Unit C: 10%	30,000	14%	12,600
Totals	**210,100**		**89,100**

This simple example is a testimony to the high potential for complexity in arriving at the worthy goals of the full attribution of costs through activity-based costing. Clearly the allocation of the costs of the common spaces is arbitrary. What if one of the units has more employees relative to the space allocated? What if a prime feature of the common space, the lobby, has a service desk run by one unit, which would make it a more demanding user of cleaning services. Finding common ground for allocation of costs is a challenge, but one that is worth the effort if true costs are to be determined.

In terms of external reporting, an accurate display of costs provides the information that funders and budget decision makers want when they review past performance and future funding needs. In addition, the public and stakeholders need a full picture of the costs to avoid either deceptive allocations to reduce program costs, or fail to expose cost risks. Internally, a number of dramas play themselves out over the allocation of costs, some of which are described in more detail in Appendix 1 and may explain, in part, why people think it is important to play these games.

In complex organizations, there is often a struggle to get organizational resources that managers do not directly control although they need the means to get the job done; for example, training for staff may be under the control of the organizational training manager but of great interest to line managers wishing to keep their staff accredited for their work. Getting what they need involves negotiation and persuasion as much as rational need. Often the level of indirectly controlled resources will affect the capacity of the manager to deliver on program needs: the manager who may have some staffing authority cannot move forward with new office space over which he has no control. Meeting his objectives depends on getting these resources.

The distribution of indirect resources may also be seen by managers as a question of fairness and equity. Often indirect resource managers will work hard to develop formulae, so as to be seen to be distributing resources fairly. Major plans for capital and equipment replacement will work on a cyclical basis to ensure that all units are treated fairly over reasonable periods of time. Costs of managing contracted service agreements or the costs of outsourcing have to be taken into account as indirect costs to the organization. While they are indirect, they are real and have to be weighed when considering the use of external services. An example is the overhead charge applied to the direct cost of delivery for educational programs that universities offer to other organizations. The overhead charge can vary but is considerable, often reaching 30 percent of the direct service charges.[7]

Managers will want to avoid the distribution of indirect costs that inflate their cost-object levels to their disadvantage. This relates directly to the treatment of overhead costs that do not affect direct delivery and are therefore not a real concern of managers, either in delivery on accountabilities, or in getting their fair share. Such costs as auditing, various headquarters offices, or communications budgets may not be particularly popular with managers.

The terms overhead and indirect costs are often used interchangeably, with the former more commonly used by the media and public, carrying a connotation of unnecessary waste. One also still hears the term administration used in this way. Public-sector organizations are often faced with the accusation that they waste too many resources on overhead or administration, to the detriment of service delivery. Volunteer organizations have faced considerable scrutiny of their administrative costs over the years. Donors and funders increasingly demand evidence that their funds are going directly to the specific client groups for which they are intended and not towards operations of the office or administrative costs. Similarly, even public-sector funders of volunteer agencies have adopted the same approach, often refusing to support what is generally called sustaining funding, associated with the costs of the office and the executive director as opposed to direct client service. This is short-term thinking that ignores the vital role that legitimate support services provide to service delivery.

For government, the issues of overhead cover a range from minister's vehicles to central offices where people have never seen a client, let alone have any experience of what actually happens on the front lines. However, that does not mean these activities are superfluous. They are part of the operation of large organizations. Overhead, seen from an accounting perspective, refers to expenses such as these that are not part of the direct operations or service delivery of the organization. Taken a bit more positively, overhead costs are incurred for the common goals of the organization. These will benefit, or have an impact on, multiple programs that the organization administers on the organization as a whole. This creates a dynamic within larger organizations in which responsibility centre managers will resist attempts to allocate indirect costs that they see as unnecessary or unhelpful to their direct responsibilities. Still, public accounts committees and auditors general will want to know the actual costs of overhead.

The fact is that there are legitimate reasons to allocate overhead costs, even those costs that managers may not directly find helpful. Some of these have been outlined above. The simple reality is that behind every good program there must be a sound organizational infrastructure supporting its delivery. In other words, programs do not exist on their own. Rather, they depend upon the organizational infrastructures in which they are housed. They are products of governance, management, and complex funding arrangements. An organization's ability to provide services relies on a host of indirect expenditures.

Governments seldom are engaged in just the delivery of a series of services. What counts is not simply a matter of what is being delivered but also of how it is delivered. This requires a degree of accountability, reporting, and record-keeping, none of which is generally regarded as a direct cost. For example, internal audit as a form of control is an indirect cost that responsible public organizations must have. Further, large government departments serve a variety of masters, not the least of whom is the minister. That minister needs logistical support, policy advice, planning, and communications in order to satisfy his accountability and answerability for the department's

activities. These are not glossy add-ons, but part of the workings of the public sector. Unfortunately, there is no magic ratio or formula to establish an appropriate level of overhead for an organization.

The danger is in ignoring overhead or indirect costs in order to sell a program. A good example is the penchant of politicians over the past three decades to support an increase in the number of police officers on front-line service, often characterized as "boots on streets," demanding that all the funds allocated to enhanced public safety be for those officers. This ignores the reality that a frontline police officer depends upon an array of services and infrastructure to get his or her job done. Seldom do officers arrive at a scene or walk a street without communications systems all working. In fact, any officer who did so would be negligent. Further, they depend increasingly on sophisticated information technology and geo-spatial tracking to link the current actions with known patterns and other crimes. These are all indirect costs.

Fixed and Variable Costs

Analyzing fixed and variable costs enables the planner to determine how costs will react when certain variables are changed. It can establish cost sensitivity, i.e., the point at which costs are reduced or increased with changes in activity. Establishing an understanding of cost sensitivities will enable the manager to better understand the impact of program changes. While we have already explored the issue of direct versus indirect costs, it does not follow that all direct costs are fixed and all indirect costs are variable. Fixed and variable costs are the two components of the total cost of an activity. Total, or full-cost, information is important in setting the price or internal cost of a service and in assessing the organization's capacity to absorb increases or decreases in either resources or levels of output. A fixed cost is one that does not vary with the volume of use. A variable cost is one that does vary with volume of use.

Understanding fixed and variable costs is best done with a good example. Here, we have used material published in 1989 by the Physician Payment Review Commission, based on a study done just after the US federal government's program of Medicare started paying for screening mammograms.[8]

To determine fixed and variable costs, information is required. To start, **Figure 6.9** shows the total cost per month of providing different numbers of screening mammograms per day.

FIGURE 6.9
Total Cost of Mammograms per Month (Table Form)

Output Rate – Mammograms per day	Total Cost $
0	6,172
5	9,462
10	10,337
15	13,627
20	14,502
30	18,667
40	20,417
50	22,167

However, this total-cost table is just a summary and provides little understanding of the nature of the costs of providing this service. Seen in chart form in **Figure 6.10,** this same information looks like this:

FIGURE 6.10
Total Cost of Mammograms per Month (Chart Form)

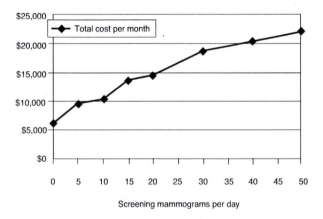

One of the early conclusions that one can reach is that total cost is indeed a function of quantity of service offered. Simply put, as the number of mammograms rises, so do the costs. But, how? Is the increase on a cost-per-service, or is there a mix of costs that change differently, some affected by volume and some not. This is important, especially in cases like this where there is often a heavy investment in capital equipment to service this vital need. Having this equipment will cost so much regardless of use in many cases. This equipment is totally dependent on having qualified staff to run it. That cost will vary.

Fixed costs are those costs whose total does not change as the number of service units changes over a relevant range of activity.[9] It is interesting to note that costs are incurred even at zero delivery of service, principally because of the capital costs involved. As noted in previous chapters, all fixed costs vary eventually, either through wearing out and requiring replacement or by becoming irrelevant to the program. Examples of what is included in fixed costs will be seen as this analysis unfolds.

Figure 6.11 sets out the capital costs of providing screening mammography; that is, the capital outlay required before the first patient is seen.

FIGURE 6.11
Capital Outlay Required

Capital outlay required before the first patient is seen:	
Mammography unit and processor	$ 80,000
Start-up supplies	2,000
Property improvements	15,000
Furniture	5,000
Office equipment	3,500
Miscellaneous	500
Capital outlay — total of above	$106,000

It may be asked why the total cost from **Figure 6.9** for a zero level of service is $6,172 instead of $106,000 to start. This is an application of the accrual principle, which requires that we convert a one-time capital outlay into a cost flow over the time that the equipment is used. We do that by imagining that we borrow the money and then pay back the loan over a period of years at so many dollars per month. Hence, the cost of capital, based on its anticipated depreciation rates, would be reflected as a fixed cost for the period of six years (which is the reasonable life expectancy of this machine). The cost of capital is also calculated to take into account the borrowing of money to pay for the equipment at a 12 percent rate of interest for six years. This calculation indicates that the amortized cost of the equipment each month is $2,072, which represents the monthly fixed cash flow associated with our initial capital outlay.

The overall figure of $6,172 per month includes other fixed costs per month (from **Figure 6.9**). **Figure 6.12** sets out these other costs that recur monthly, independently of how many patients use the machine.

FIGURE 6.12
Other Fixed Costs

Other fixed costs per month:

Maintenance	$ 425
Promotion	250
Accounting	100
Insurance	100
Rent	875
Telephone	100
Taxes	750
Clerk/receptionist salary and benefits	1,500
Total other fixed costs per month	**$4,100**

In chart form, the same information looks like this:

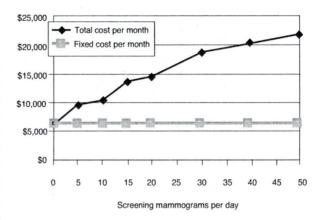

Taken together, the fixed cost of the capital and the other fixed support costs make up the total fixed cost of operating the machine for a month, as seen in **Figure 6.13**.

FIGURE 6.13
Summary of Fixed Costs

Monthly capital cost	$2,072
Other fixed costs	4,100
Total fixed cost per month	$6,172

Adding this fixed cost information to the initial table on total costs begins to show more useful information. Note in **Figure 6.14** that the fixed cost is the same for all output ranges, even if the output is zero.

FIGURE 6.14
Fixed and Total Costs, in Table and Chart Form

Output	Total Cost ($)	Fixed Cost ($)
0	6,172	6,172
5	9,462	6,172
10	10,337	6,172
15	13,627	6,172
20	14,502	6,172
30	18,667	6,172
40	20,417	6,172
50	22,167	6,172

Now we come to variable costs: costs that vary directly with changes in the volume of service units over a relevant range of activity.[10] In the case of the mammogram program, it is assumed that the unit will be functioning 20 days a month. This is an assumption that itself can vary, but it reflects some of the "givens" that may have to come into play before "what if" scenarios on costing can be developed. Theoretically, a mammogram machine can, with minimal changes in fixed costs, operate 24 hours a day, seven days a week, although many factors will mitigate against that happening. Building in that assumption of 20 days of use each month, variable costs work in this scenario as indicated in **Figure 6.15**.

An astute reader will note that the monthly variable costs are equal to the difference between total costs and fixed costs for each output level. With variable costs presented graphically in **Figure 6.16** and combined with the fixed costs, we come to a better explanation of the total cost figure initially offered:

As displayed in **Figure 6.17**, the final element of analysis is to derive, from total cost, the average cost of one mammogram based on the changing cost assumptions.

It is no surprise that average costs go down as volume increases. This assumes that the demand is present, the resources are in place (especially the human resources), and that there is accessibility.

Break-Even Analysis

Of particular importance for nonprofit organizations, or for those in the public sector that have a high degree of revenue dependence, is the analytical tool of break-even cost analysis. In addition, public-sector organizations that

FIGURE 6.15

Variable Costs Broken into Categories

| Cost Category | Unit Cost ($) | Variable Costs (in dollars) per month (20 working days per month) | | | | | | |
| | | Tests per day | | | | | | |
		5	10	15	20	30	40	50
Radiological technologist		2,415	2,415	4,830	4,830	7,245	7,245	7,245
Film	3.00	300	600	900	1,200	1,800	2,400	3,000
Medical records	2.00	200	400	600	800	1,200	1,600	2,000
Supplies and miscellaneous	2.00	200	400	600	800	1,200	1,600	2,000
Postage	1.00	100	200	300	400	600	800	1,000
Forms	0.75	75	150	225	300	450	600	750
Total monthly variable cost		3,290	4,165	7,455	8,330	12,495	14,245	15,995

FIGURE 6.16

Total-Cost Figure with Fixed Costs

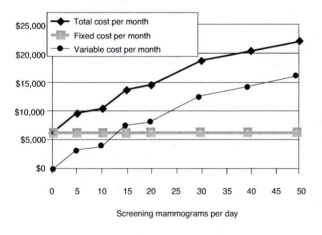

Screening mammograms per day

FIGURE 6.17

Average Costs

Tests per day	Tests per month	Total Cost ($)	Average Cost per service ($)
0	0	6,172	N/A
5	100	9,462	94.62
10	200	10,337	51.69
15	300	13,627	45.42
20	400	14,502	36.26
30	600	18,667	31.11
40	800	20,417	25.52
50	1,000	22,167	22.17

depend on funds based on the volume of services they provide can use this tool. For any of these organizations that are anticipating providing a new service as part of their program, the break-even analysis will provide some indicator of the volume of service provided and the levels of revenues that are needed to make it self-supporting. Knowing this will enable the organization to make a reasonable determination of whether it can actually make this new service happen.

Essentially, break-even analysis costing is a means of determining the level of income based on such variables as rates charged, fees and anticipated volume the organization must the anticipated costs of the service. Calculation of the break-even point is based on the formula:

TR (Total Revenue) = TC (Total Costs)

Costs are made up of fixed and variable costs as described above. **Figure 6.18** graphs these costs for a hypothetical example.

One can readily see how volume represents an important variable, especially when it is possible to generally control other factors through management and allocation. The volume in these cases is often dictated by near-market demand forces beyond the control of the organization or the unit proposing the delivery of the service. It will therefore have to convince its funders that these volumes are attainable if the service is to be worthwhile.

For the manager trying to develop a cost for a service, or inversely the level of service that can be offered with the funds available, break-even analysis is a useful tool. It can

FIGURE 6.18
Break-Even Cost Analysis

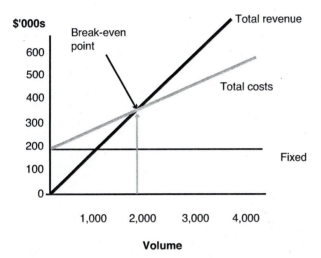

work both ways. The fee for a service will depend on all costs, fixed and variable, along with an anticipated volume calculation. On the other hand, where funds are constrained (which is pretty well all the time) or fees are constricted (government limits on tuition is an example), volume of services, based on the calculation of the individual service is then defined, regardless of demand.

Appropriation Process: Getting Approval to Spend

It should be clear by now that a budget is a plan that builds on a strategic outlook, costed and analyzed for decision making. It is also the way in which these aspirations are finally defined and, in some cases, confined to what is financially possible. It is also a means for setting priorities among all these public goods that are wanted by the public or advocated by public servants or politicians. As the process becomes more institutionalized, as in the Expenditure Management System of the Government of Canada, it engages more players and eventually becomes the formal budget submitted to the authorizing authority that has the power to allocate funds and permit their expenditure. In the case of governments, this will be a city council, a legislative assembly, or Parliament. In the case of a nonprofit organization, it will be the board of directors or governors. In many cases, the formal budget will also be scrutinized, and possibly subject to some form of approval, by a more senior level of government, or by a government funding a nonprofit public-sector organization such as a hospital, or by the principal funders of a program.

The purpose of these submissions is to obtain specific approval to spend money. Such authorization is called an appropriation. In some cases, the terms "voting supply"' and "approval of the estimates" create the authority to spend funds. An appropriation is the approval by a legislative body of an organization's budget. Appropriations create the authorization for spending the amount in the budget. From it flows the important legal authority for individual managers to spend public funds.

The roles of legislatures, however, are not restricted to votes for or against a particular budget plan. They have a number of other functions that will affect the outcome of a particular budget planning cycle, such as:

- engaging in consultation processes, including setting up public hearings on budget priorities for the government;
- detailed scrutiny, at committee level, of individual departmental spending plans, including hearing from the minister and officials as well as interest groups;
- detailed and open decision making (most notably at the municipal level) of budget plans presented by departments in advance of their approval;
- proposing changes to appropriations for individual departments and submitting these to a committee vote and subsequently to a vote in the legislature (this is more likely to happen in minority government situations);
- hearing from the legislative auditor, most notably the auditor general of the jurisdiction, on her views of the financial management of the government, which will have an impact on future budget behaviour;
- holding hearings and investigations into specific aspects of the budget that may cross departmental lines but be of direct relevance to taxpayers; for example, the impact of various user fees by different departments on economic development and small business. Such hearings bring public attention to such issues and often affect future government behaviour; and
- reviewing past financial and program performance by means of departmentally generated performance reports.

Legislatures, then, can be very active participants in the budget cycle. The degree of that participation varies across Canada, but it is clearly increasing as the budgetary process becomes more open as it has been doing for the past twenty years.

Inherent Tensions in the Budgetary Process

The budgetary process is inherently value-laden and rich in conflict. As we describe planning processes, the need to plan and translate policy into resources, various roles of the executive branch and legislative or oversight branch (legislature, council, board of directors) of the public-sector organization, it would be naïve not to realize how many pressures are engaged in the budgeting process. These tensions also have a significant impact on the substantive outcomes of the process itself.

Balancing Revenues and Expenditures: Financial Discipline

For all public-sector organizations, the primary tension in budgeting oscillates between desire and capacity. Of course, the same can be said for any individual or household budget: ideally, expenditures should at least equal revenue. Public-sector organizations have to make that equation work. Often they will do so via a mix of adjustments to both revenue and expenditures, including changes in taxes and fees to increase revenue, and changes in program levels to reduce expenditures as well as incurring debts to cover the difference. This is a complex process because governments, as we have noted, have debt capacities unrivalled in the economy. They have been able to extend program expenditure by increasing debt, often leaving the country or province with large debt burdens. Similarly, they have been able to add fees, secondary taxes, and user charges – all forms of taxation, voluntary or otherwise – to expand their capacity. An example of this is the relatively recent decision in many North American governments to increase their dependency on revenues from publicly licensed casinos.

On the other hand, tremendous pressure exists to restrain the growth of taxation in any form, and of the size of government as a whole. Some of this derives from a strong belief that government is too large and does too much and that the private sector should be used to move so-called public goods into the market. This has manifested itself in legislation in many provinces to cap tax increases and government spending.

Some of the pressure to reduce is a response to debt load: while governments can expand their scope through debt, they have to pay for it. Costs for debt service in the mid-1990s reached crisis proportions in many countries, including Canada. Once again, in response to the Great Recession of 2008, governments took on significant debts to fund stimulus spending. As a consequence, they then had to address means to reduce expenditures to eliminate the operating deficits this created and, eventually, pay down the debt. High debt has two effects: it forces measures to reduce dependence on debt, and it diverts revenues from actual program expenditures into debt servicing.

Chapter 8, Taking It Back: Reallocation and Budget Cutting will address these issues at both the government and individual program level.

The Wants Versus the Won'ts: Central Agency Versus Program Advocates

Very few public-sector organizations are monoliths, acting on the same set of values and impulses to achieve the same set of goals. Large governments are complex entities with central agencies that take a whole-of-government view in their efforts to bring coherence to a myriad of programs, agencies, departments, and available funds. They also have the parts of the whole – program departments – seeking to maximize their own resources to improve their program capacity to achieve the public good for which they were created. As Wildavsky says, "Every agency wants more money; the urge to survive and expand is built in."[11]

There are many motivators behind this desire for more resources: some of these involve genuine assessments of program needs; some involve stakeholder pressures; and some involve power and prestige. Some involve all of the above. It is a rare day when an agency of government offers up funding to a central agency or finance department for the greater good or for another department's use. Generally, most public-sector organizations are dealing with a demand that they cannot meet, so they need more resources in order to try to do so.

Central agencies of government and other large public-sector organizations take a more corporate view. This can translate into trying to enforce limits on the overall budgetary process and its results. It can also result in efforts to find funding in one program area to transfer to another one or to new initiatives, otherwise known as reallocation. This tension plays out at both political and bureaucratic levels. Ministers may be seeking funding for their particular initiatives, while the central agencies may see this as a dangerous drain on scarce funding. They may push back on the ministers to find funds within their own departments. Departmental bureaucrats may argue that no such funding can be found in an already stretched budget. So goes the merry-go-round of dispute that is often resolved through a compromise involving a number of strategies that include new funds, reallocated funds, and program adjustments.[12]

Central agencies also have the demanding role of reconciling overall supply of funds – the revenue side of public expenditures – with overall demand – budgetary requests from departments. One of the underlying strengths of a good budgetary-planning system in complex public-sector entities is that the central assessment of the supply of revenue can condition and restrict the demand for program expansion. It also ensures that debt, one of the default options (along with increased fees and taxes) when all revenues are spent, is avoided.

The New Versus the Old

Budgets are often about announcements, changes, improvements, the state of the economy. Political or bureaucratic leaders find very little appeal in announcing that they are carrying on, paying their bills, or ensuring funding for the programs everyone knows about. There is, therefore, a tension between the cost of current programming and the cost of innovation and change. While most budgets remain incremental at their heart, neither incremental moves up or down ensure that this is sufficient to carry on the level of service that the organization has announced either in its budget or in some other planning document.

Nowhere does this tension between new and existing programs show itself as more problematic than in maintenance and capital reinvestment in existing programming and infrastructure. It is often the case that public-sector organizations will take a cut in maintenance budgets as an easy means of reducing the budget. This creates a deferred maintenance inventory that piles up over time. Similarly, capital upgrades of vital equipment and systems can be underfunded so that program levels decrease or, in one of those twists of long-term costs for short-term savings, maintenance costs rise because of deferred capital replacement. So, too, do risks that the infrastructure will deteriorate and create dangers to the public. Often, as is the case with much of Canada's water infrastructure, such delays only increase costs. In some instances, bridges and overpasses for example, governments have had to scramble to launch massive restoration efforts following tragic collapses of one or two such structures.

Robust planning systems along with accrual accounting and budgeting should incorporate ongoing costs, including maintenance and capital replacement, and factor depreciation into their calculations. That still does not make them exciting or politically appealing. The role that public-sector organizations play in conserving public infrastructure and service levels is, in the end, a political one. The allure of the announceable or the legitimate need to respond to emerging demands will always create tension between the new and the old.

Robbing Peter to Pay Paul: Moving the Money Around

Perhaps one of the greatest sources of tension within budgetary systems is the desire by governments to extract funds from one spending centre and move it to another. While this goes by many names, it is generally known as reallocation of existing funds and is often a matter of funding new programs with existing funds. However, it can serve several purposes, which will be explored in Chapter 8.

Complexity Versus Clarity

Budgets are made up of a stream of decisions, some that involve spending and some that involve limiting spending. It is seldom the case that this stream of decisions is totally clear. Very few decisions are alike, and a variety of political, social, and economic factors come into play in their creation. For many public-sector organizations, achieving the objective of public involvement and transparency can make the budget process a long one, involving many different forums to arrive at a final product. Budget making is complex. Understanding the process itself takes some skill. Managing effectively within it takes another set of skills.

Such complexity can drive out clarity of purpose unless there is a strong, singular force at play. With budget cutting, it is often the force of the simple objective that prevails against the complexity of a planning and budgeting process that, left to its own internal dynamic, would have produced a result quite different from that wanted by the leadership. In other words, regardless of the process design, it is often necessary to cut through all this if there is an urgent need to make changes, especially to reduce budgets.

The tension in the process becomes how to instill clarity into a necessarily complex process. As we shall see, this often means limiting spending options well in advance of the beginning of the process. It can also mean resorting to across-the-board solutions that produce the satisfaction of achieving one result at the cost of vastly distorting program priorities along the way. Regardless, budgetary processes that run on their own dynamic without direction and leadership will land in a very uncomfortable place. It will force leaders to make decisions contrary to the demands presented to them, which takes strong political will and the potential loss of many allies along the way. It can also take strong bureaucratic will when the decision-making process is within the organization. Coalitions also have to be made, rebuilt, and occasionally abandoned to achieve internal budgetary ends.

Summing Up: Trends to Watch

The process of formulating and getting approval for a budget, at any level and in any kind of public-sector organization, is an integral part of how that organization carries out its mission. While it can be complex or simple, depending on the nature of the organization, some common elements for public-sector organizations emerge:

- Budgets bring together needs and capacity, often from different parts of the organizations, be it tax capacity and program demands, or client needs and the fund-raising capacity of the organization.
- Budgets demand a technical command of the key elements of needs measurement, effective costing of programs, and revenue projections.
- Budgets in the public sector are legal documents that define expenditure authority and limit it to those levels once approved by the authorizing legislature.
- Budget making takes place in an organizational culture, rich in nuance, with power playing as much a role as good policy making.
- Budgets are inherently transparent in the public sector, in terms of both how they are formed and how they are executed.
- Budgets are the result of both planning based on past experience and the existing policy or mission framework of the organization and future orientations.
- Budgets in the public sector are subject to intense scrutiny, not only by those who will manage them, but also by those who will benefit from or be subject to them.

Some of the trends that have manifested themselves around the world are starting to take hold in virtually all forms of public sector budgeting. Some of these are:

- Accrual budgeting which will enhance the requirement for full life-cycle costing but also add considerably to the complexity of the budgeting process.
- Integration of capital and operating budgets as a result of accrual budgeting and other demands for a great link of capital and the operational costs and implications of major capital decisions. This will impact the municipal and health sectors, which have tended to separate such budgets.
- The emergence of risk analysis and mitigation in the budget process. This includes applying risk techniques to environmental analysis, costing, program sustainability and infrastructure capacity.
- Increasing commitment to multi-year budgeting and authorization of expenditures.
- Increasing formalized tools to identify budget cuts, opportunities to reallocate, and a priority setting process.
- Better links to results through new measurement tools such as those emerging in American cities and states, using measurement dashboards.

Chapter 7
Capital Planning and Budgeting

Chapter Objectives:
- Identifying the unique features of capital budgeting in the public sector
- Learning to build a capital plan
- Understanding analytical techniques in evaluating capital projects

Capital assets are important to government. A not-so-scientific definition of capital is that it is stuff – the stuff that governments needed to build, buy, operate or install to make public policy goals happen. They can include such varied items as roads, bridges, major equipment, vehicles, land, infrastructure systems such as water and sewage, aircraft, missiles, computer hardware and software systems. Capital assets are treated differently from other assets in financial statements and reporting, in part, because these assets behave differently from most operating assets. Similarly, in budget planning, capital planning takes a special place. There are some good reasons for this:

- Capital assets are expensive, involving both a considerable investment and, very often, complex financing arrangements.
- Capital assets have a long life, generally defined for accounting purposes as being of use for more than one accounting year.
- Capital assets can lock in an organization in terms of reducing alternative approaches (leasing versus building) or emerging technology (yesterday's so-called smart building may not meet today environmental standards).
- Capital assets have longer cost streams that involve the future costs of financing as well as the monies used to build or buy them.

This means that there are risks associated with capital assets that require special treatment and analysis. In terms of budget planning, capital assets and their acquisition represent certain challenges, all of which can be accommodated, but cannot be ignored.

Similarly, the total cost of a capital asset over time may include sizable operating expenses. Its acquisition can distort operational planning if this is not adequately considered at the planning phase. Similarly, capital assets can be subject to **betterments,** which will affect their value, extend their life and adapt the asset to changing operating requirements. However, repairs and maintenance are necessary to ensure the original planned level of service are not betterments. These costs are normally expensed when they occur and their impact not capitalized. For all these reasons, capital requires some special treatment from both the budgeting and accounting perspective. This section addresses some of those issues. It also introduces some important analytical tools and concepts that apply to decision making with respect to capital investment, such as time value of money, net present value, and other considerations of long-term financing.

Characteristics of Capital Assets

From an accounting point of view, outlays incurred on the acquisition or building of an asset, or on a transfer leading to the creation or acquisition of an asset, are included in the capital budget for so long as they meet four criteria:

- **Productivity Criterion:** They are used in the production or supply of goods and services.
- **Longevity Criterion:** Their life extends beyond a fiscal year.
- **Exclusive Use Criterion:** They are not intended for resale in the ordinary course of operations.
- **Materiality Criterion:** Their treatment as a capital asset is of value; that is, many items that would

normally be treated as capital, because they will last more than one year, are not. For example, a stapler usually lasts more than one year, but because of its low cost, it does not merit the special consideration that capital projects merit; it is too costly to report as a capital asset; and no one cares, so it is treated as a supply and is funded out of operating expenditures.

Figure 7.1 sets out the federal government's definition of capital assets as set out in the policies of the Treasury Board of Canada.

Unlike business, governmental capital assets represent service capability or unexpired or undepreciated service potential but not future cash inflows. They seldom provide resources to pay off existing liabilities or finance future operations. As such, they are recorded as non-financial assets along with other such assets as prepaid expenses and inventories held for future use. While public capital assets are not built or bought with an eye to inflows, the disposal of capital items can produce income on the sale of land or a building.

There are a number of reasons to consider and plan for capital acquisition as a unique, but linked exercise:

- Time perspective is long.
- New capital assets require ongoing operations and maintenance costs, which need to be included in the larger budget cycle of the government.
- New capital assets can be debt funded, requiring consideration for governments facing large debt loads.

- Capital spending can vary from year to year, affected by changing priorities and delays in projects.

What does it Cost? What is it Worth?

Because capital assets are consumed slowly, and often, through betterment enhancement, have extended life or are repurposed to meet changing needs in areas such as technology, they are treated with some care in accounting purposes. This means that current value has only a partial relationship with the cost of acquiring the asset in the first place. Similarly, even with the straight-line application of depreciation in accrual accounting, alterations and market shifts, where market value is applied, may mean that these assets have to be valued with caution. Similarly, such valuation has to be material but also feasible. Therefore, government may actually exclude certain capital assets due to the difficulty in valuation. Some examples are Crown lands that the government owns as a matter of historical right, not through acquisition, works of art or historical monuments or treasures and certain intangible assets such as patents and copyrights, although this area is highly contestable.

There are several ways to establish the value of a capital asset for accounting purposes. The first is the application of depreciation to the original cost of the asset. In this case, the asset is amortized over the useful life of the asset, most generally using the straight-line method, which allocates the cost of the capital asset equally over each year of its

FIGURE 7.1
Government of Canada Definition of Capital Assets

Capital Assets are tangible assets that are purchased, constructed, developed or otherwise acquired and:

- Are held for use in the production or supply of goods, the delivery of services or to produce program outputs;
- Have a useful life extending beyond one fiscal year and are intended to be used on a continuing basis; and
- Are not intended for resale in the ordinary course of operations.

For the government, capital assets have the following characteristics:

- Beneficial ownership and control clearly rest with the government; and
- The asset is used to achieve government objectives.

For government accounting purposes, capital assets generally include any asset which has been acquired, constructed or developed with the intention of being used on a continuous basis and is not intended for sale in the ordinary course of business. Capital assets also include betterments. Betterments are expenditures relating to the alteration or modernization of an asset that appreciably prolong the item's period of usefulness or improve its functionality. Departments shall treat as a capital asset any asset that, in addition to meeting the above conditions, has a useful life in excess of one year and a per item cost of greater than $10,000. Departments may establish a lower threshold than $10,000.

Source: http://www.tbs-sct.gc.ca/pubs_pol/dcgpubs/accstd/capasset1_e.asp.

estimated useful value. The second is a variation on this, as described above, depreciation with betterments factored in. A betterment can increase both the value of an asset and its life. Therefore, some form of calculation would have to factor in the relevant variables that would need adjustment to provide the right valuation. Each of these methods establishes the net book value of the assets. A third approach is that of fair market value. Fair market value is the result of an arm's-length determination of the value of an asset as it might be sold in the marketplace. Often this will involve a professional assessor or the use of precedent or similar circumstances in a specific market.

In calculating the value of capital assets and how to apply depreciation, governments generally will set some standards. In this way, some degree of consistency is obtained. **Figure 7.2** shows a sample of the Government of Saskatchewan's policies on valuation of assets, and also when they are to be treated as capital assets through the application of a threshold value.

FIGURE 7.2
Government of Saskatchewan Capital Asset Thresholds and Estimated Useful Lives

Capital Asset Class and Category	Threshold in Dollars	Estimated Useful Life
Land	All purchases	Indefinite
Land improvements	10,000	15 years
Buildings	50,000	25–45 years
Heavy equipment	30,000	20 years
Vehicles	30,000	10 years
IT system development	250,000	10 years
Computer software	10,000	5 years
Bridge construction	All	40 years

Source: *Government of Saskatchewan Financial Administration Manual, Policy on Capital Assets Accounting and Reporting.*

Capital Planning and Budgeting

Effective capital budgeting is made up of several elements:

- **A Plan:** Here we are referring to the capital improvement plan or whatever the government calls it.
- **Risk Oversight:** Knowing the risks, managing them and adapting as circumstances change.
- **Alternative Financing:** Capital projects will increasingly involve different financing and build schemes that will affect the budget.

- **Locking in the Budget:** Capital budgeting has to ultimately be part of the overall government budget, taking into account full accruals, attendant maintenance costs and replacement costs.

Governments face the challenge of marrying up their operating needs and their capital aspirations. In the absence of life-cycle cost analysis and the application of true costing tools such as time-value-of-money- and return-on-investment analysis, capital expenditures are usually seen as an annual expenditure and not as an investment flow. In addition, making choices among capital investments has posed many challenges, especially for those governments with major infrastructure deterioration problems. For that reason, we look at some of the analytical tools needed for capital budgeting.

Capital Improvement Plans

Effective capital budgeting must begin with an effective planning process. This will lead to the creation of a capital-improvement plan or capital plan. Such a plan has a multi-year perspective and is evergreen in that, with good planning over a number of years, it can be renewed and updated rather than re-created each year. This process offers the advantages that major capital-investment depreciation is not forgotten and that maintenance issues remain on the table. It is very easy, especially in a political environment, to forget underground pipes or existing buildings in an effort to focus on more immediate crises or on the desire to create new capital projects. An example of a critical area that is emerging in this regard is the need to upgrade major enterprise computer systems on a regular basis. It may not be the most politically exciting thing, but it is necessary.

Those advantages being cited, it is important to remember that a plan is just that. The budget to fund any plan is subject to the political process, a necessary part of our democracy. Projects can be in a plan for years before funds are appropriated for them to actually be built. This is what could be called the rubber-hits-the-road test. You only know the degree of investment when you know the amount of money locked in to make them. For many governments, there are explicit rules put in place to avoid creating wish-list type plans, ones that have all the desires, aspirations and necessary investments rolled into a largely unfunded and unfundable set of plans. For instance, in many municipalities, staff can only propose a capital plan that is equal to the funds available.

In creating such a plan, a policy has to be set on what will be subject to this kind of intense review. Therefore, governments will make a distinction between a capital asset, which was described above and a capital project. Certainly, risk and complexity may mean that a capital asset acquisition, even if it is below the value and time thresholds set, may be subject to the planning process. In general, however, a government may choose thresholds such as dollar value and anticipated life of the asset before imposing the planning requirements. Similarly, the thresholds will vary with the size of the government. A small township will want to approve any changes to its small fleet of vehicles and have all such acquisitions listed in its capital plan. A large metropolitan government may bundle up such purchases, often with a general policy on replacement and acquisition. The key here is that capital acquisition planning is a form of control over what is seen as high risk, high return assets. Materiality and risk tolerances will be determined by the authorizing bodies in control. In addition, care must be taken to prevent manoeuvers to avoid full exposure of the risk and cost of the acquisition of a capital asset. There are a number of techniques that are used to ensure that full cost exposure is not made public or fully understood:

- **The Salami Method:** Avoid full cost exposure by introducing a capital project in smaller pieces.
- **The Happy Face Method:** Make overly optimistic cost projections.
- **The Blind Eye:** Ignore second costs and return with them as a separate item.

These examples are but a few of many. Governments have to clearly establish their planning requirements. They also have to define what costs must be included in getting to full project cost. They can also require third party evaluation of costs as well as a full risk analysis.

An effective CIP will include the following elements:

- **Strategic Relevance Test:** The capital project has to link to the government's goals.
- **Sound Forecasting Test:** What is the need? Are there projections that justify this investment and, therefore, reduction in future resources for other things?
- **Inventory and Condition Analysis Test:** Is there an inventory of current capital assets? Has full life cycle analysis been applied to determine where reinvestment is needed? Are there agreed upon thresholds and limits for capital replacement?
- **Fit to Relevance Test:** Does the capital project fit with the social and political goals of the government? Are key overall planning lenses applied in the placement, design and functions of the asset: demographic and social, program changes, technology, economic, environmental, access and diversity?
- **The Affordability Test:** Is this well and truly costed – fully and in an agreed-to way? Are there funds available? Have all competing proposals been vetted?
- **The Risk Test:** What are the risks of proceeding? What are the risks of not proceeding? What are the mitigation strategies?
- **The Alternative Means Test:** How else can this asset be acquired? How can it be funded?

Alternative Financing of Capital Projects

Governments increasingly are looking for ways to finance expensive capital projects without the use of appropriated funds, or at least minimizing their use or spreading the high impact of capital funding over many years. For instance, the Private Finance Initiative in the United Kingdom requires government agencies at both the national and local level to seek out private sector financing for major capital projects. Similarly, Infrastructure Ontario is charged with finding new ways to capitalize major projects. These schemes take many forms, often linked to who will ultimately own the asset, and also who will operate it. How these are configured will also have both accounting and budgeting implications. For instance, a purpose-built government facility financed, constructed and operated by a private firm with the government paying an annual fee guaranteed over an extended period, will not appear on the balance sheet of the government. Infrastructure Ontario defines roles depending on the role of the private sector (see **Figure 7.3**).

When looking at different financing and operating schemes, governments have a series of alternatives. Put simply, they are:

- **Traditional:** Governments create the capital asset, finance it through appropriations or special borrowing (bonds) and operate the asset.
- **Commercialization:** Governments create the capital asset as above, but operate it as a separate agency that is on the balance sheet of the government, but operates autonomously or is operated, through a contract, by the private sector.
- **Public Private Partnership (PPPs):** Governments enter into complex arrangements for shared or private financing, building and operation of a facility that remains in the public realm and often reverts to public-sector ownership at the end of the pay-back period.

FIGURE 7.3
Ontario Infrastructure Models for Capital Projects

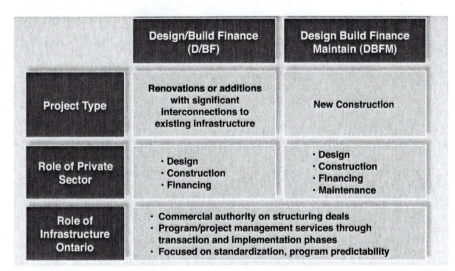

	Design/Build Finance (D/BF)	Design Build Finance Maintain (DBFM)
Project Type	Renovations or additions with significant interconnections to existing infrastructure	New Construction
Role of Private Sector	• Design • Construction • Financing	• Design • Construction • Financing • Maintenance
Role of Infrastructure Ontario	• Commercial authority on structuring deals • Program/project management services through transaction and implementation phases • Focused on standardization, program predictability	

Source: Presentation by David Livingston, CEO, Infrastructure Ontario, available at crgp.stanford. edu/events/presentations/cdnconsul/Livingston.ppt.

• **Privatization:** Governments cease carrying out an activity. Taken up by the private sector or actioned by a part of government that has been privatized, all capital and operating spending is undertaken by the company with no direct government involvement. This does not exclude government creating regulations or rules to govern these enterprises.

It is important to note that PPPs are not privatization. This is a common error. It is also often argued, but contested as well, that involving the private sector in capital schemes increases costs as the private sector cannot access capital at the low rates enjoyed by governments. Much will depend upon the discount rate (cost of capital) being applied to determine the net present value (NPV), which is discussed further in the chapter.

Risk Assessment: "What Can Go Wrong?"

Every capital or infrastructure initiative carries a certain level of risk that must be identified and managed effectively throughout its life. Life-cycle cost is just one of many factors that public-sector organizations need to consider in assessing levels of risk. Other factors include the complexity of the initiative, the organization's experience with similar types of initiative, and the nature of any technology involved. The newer the form of funding arrangement, or the greater the number of partners, the higher the risk. Similarly, organizations with a great deal

of experience in complex construction projects are better equipped to manage new capital-construction projects than those without such a background.

It is critical to understand and assess the risk involved in each initiative. Risks should be identified at the earliest stage of planning because they may affect financing and procurement options.

Once risks have been identified, they must be analyzed and evaluated to determine the likelihood, consequences, and levels of risk. Finally, a strategy must be put in place to manage or mitigate the risk (or both). Risks should also be reviewed and strategies updated as the initiative moves forward.

The table in **Figure 7.4** shows some of the risk categories that should be considered in the planning and management of infrastructure expenditures. It also provides examples of how these types of risks may be treated to reduce the likelihood or consequences of potential losses. It is important to address these categories – and develop targeted treatments to address the specific risks unique to each initiative – to ensure best management practices. The categories listed here are among the more common ones associated with infrastructure investments.

No discussion of risk can end with the identification of risk. Full risk management requires organizations to develop means to mitigate, manage and control risk. This is particularly the case for government. A considerable part of the planning process involves developing such strategies. Just a few of the core mitigation strategies for capital projects are:

• effective project management,
• establishing a risk management policy and practice within the government,
• using third party risk assessment of potential partners,
• requiring fully secured financial arrangements,
• use of modeling techniques to analyze project risks, and
• creation of information systems to monitor performance.

FIGURE 7.4
Types of Risk That Can Affect Capital Planning

Risk Category	Description and Treatment
General Risks	Examples include high-level concerns related to the decision to undertake an initiative. Risk treatment may include documenting how an initiative fits with established strategic objectives; assessing the requirements for a new corporate structure; enhancing the initiative's profile with the public, media and governments; and working collaboratively to enhance labour and industrial relations.
Policy Risks	Examples include the likelihood that an initiative represents, or may be affected by, a major shift in government or agency policy, or change in legislation.
Public Interest Risks	Examples include the initiative's environmental impact and its relation to public health, safety and security issues. Risk treatment may include working with neighbours and the community to address public concerns in the initiative planning phase.
Management or Organizational Risks	Examples include the complexities associated with partnerships, investments and management. Risk treatment may include managing dependencies on linked funding and contingent investments; ensuring the availability of qualified initiative managers; and ensuring the initiative development team has access to appropriate expertise when undertaking a new type of initiative.
Design/ Construction, Commissioning, Partnership or Supplier Risks	Examples include sponsor risk (e.g., the likelihood that a private partner may be unable to deliver) and general supplier/market capacity. Risk treatment may include ensuring the availability of material and equipment supplies; ensuring that experienced designers, contractors and trades are available in the required time frame; anticipating the need for community permits and approvals; and designing construction windows to avoid delays due to adverse weather.
Site Risks	Examples include the risks associated with site selection and acquisition. Risk treatment may include ensuring that the site is available at an affordable price; evaluating site challenges such as soil contamination or potential flooding; and ensuring the desired site is free of potential land-claim issues.
Financing Risks	Examples include an entity's ability to draw the required financial resources and the overall financial viability of the initiative. Risk treatment may include ensuring that financing is available at the appropriate time, anticipating the impact of interest rate increases; and evaluating the creditworthiness of potential partners.
Market Risks	Examples include all possible events that could affect cash flow during initiative development. Risk treatment may include planning for contingencies in the market such as a drop in demand for services; anticipating the potential for labour or material cost escalations; ensuring funding is available to cover operations, maintenance and administration; and assessing the potential for competing facilities.

Source: Based on the BC Capital Asset Management Framework, available at http://www.fin.gov.bc.ca/tbs/camf.htm.

The Financial Outcome: The Capital Budget

A capital budget, when approved, provides the authority for the acquisition and renovation of buildings, equipment, technology, and furnishings that will be used by the organization in one or more years beyond the year of acquisition. How the full project costs, which can extend over a number of years, is reflected in the annual budget, is a matter of the degree to which the budgeting process is fully accrual and whether there is a separately approved capital budget. Practice varies considerably, presenting a challenge in describing this process fairly. How public-sector organizations treat capital in their formal budget processes varies. Some have separate capital budgets, while others integrate them into their master budgets. Much depends on the degree to which the capital program is financed through taxation and other income streams or through debt. In addition, new cost and risk transfer arrangements such as public-private partnerships have complex funding arrangements that should be highlighted separately in the budget decision-making process.

Many organizations do not report capital expenditures separately from operating expenditures in their formal financial statements. Many treat capital expenditures as current expenditures and either ignore or simply report the full costs of the capital investment through their non-budgetary planning documents. Nevertheless, their internal budgeting processes may reflect the use of capital-planning tools and approaches that are outlined here.

Simply treating capital expenditures as current expenditures taken out of operating budgets distorts the true costs of the asset acquisition. Having capital projects dependent on year-to-year approvals restricts the capacity of the organization to commit to the full cost of the project. Approving an investment in the first phase of major construction, and then reviewing it entirely without approving the next phase, can lead to a series of complications ranging from waste of public funds to a reluctance to engage in the high-risk venture in the first place. Finally, it is often the case that capital projects involve long-term debt for the organization. The challenge of long-term financing involves a good understanding of the true costs of the investment, a process of analysis quite different from analyzing operating expenditures.

A distinction that has already been drawn between operating and capital budgets is that of time. Operating budgets are generally appropriated and reported upon for a single fiscal year, although many governments are providing information on future years and some actually provide multi-year approvals. The capital budget, while it involves actual cash disbursements within the course of a fiscal year, more often involves a flow of cash over a number of years to create an asset with a life longer than one year. Both the investment flow and the asset return extend over a considerable period of time.

In addition, as governments move more aggressively into accrual accounting and budgeting, they will be forced to treat capital differently. As an example, adequate budgeting for, and reporting of, capital depreciation will highlight capital costs as never before. So, too, will the reporting of the current costs of debt to finance capital. In the case of voluntary organizations, capital acquisitions are often linked to the organization's debt planning and credit ratings and thus receive particular attention. **Figure 7.5**: Budget of the City of Lethbridge provides a good example of a budget presentation that combines a summary of operating and capital expenditures. Behind that summary document, it has to be remembered, is a 400-page budget statement and a separate **Capital Improvement Plan.**[1]

FIGURE 7.5
Summary Budget of the City of Lethbridge

	City of Lethbridge Total Budget			
	2011	2012	2013	2014
	$(000)	$(000)	$(000)	$(000)
Operating				
General Fund	161,782	172,301	178,455	180,274
Utility Fund				
Utility Services (billing)	3,761	3,693	3,767	3,877
Electric Utility	62,366	72,650	75,750	78,670
Waste Services	5,763	5,706	5,845	5,985
Recycling Services	1,524	1,572	1,619	1,637
Landfill	8,184	8,198	8,425	8,656
Wastewater Utility	14,661	14,725	14,799	14,873
Water Utility	20,135	20,591	21,160	21,742
Total Operating	278,177	299,436	309,820	315,714
Capital				
Transportation	23,605	23,296	15,801	10,398
Community	55,043	39,188	17,747	34,514
Water, Wastewater & Solid Waste	34,775	28,741	8,045	17,222
Electric	19,834	19,492	18,328	20,061
Total Capital	133,257	110,717	59,921	82,195
Total Budget	411,434	410,153	369,741	397,909

Source: Available at http://www.lethbridge.ca/City-Government/Financial-Documents/Pages/Operating-Budget.aspx.

Challenges in Capital Budgeting and Accounting in the Public Sector

In the public sector, the treatment of capital assets has unique features that have inhibited the full use of capital planning, while actually calling attention to the need for more of it.

Social and Public Policy Value Versus Monetized Market Value

Many capital investment projects in the public sector involve more than simply the construction of bridges or buildings and the installation of major computer systems. Along with these physical investments, there is the goal of improving the economic and social well-being of the community in which these investments take place. A challenge then becomes to assess the true value of social capital.[2] Is it simply the value of an asset sold in the market? Will that value reflect the true net present value to society, including the value of the externalities that may exist when it invested in social capital? How should public capital be valued so as to avoid underinvestment in those activities that have large social returns? In addition, should this component be included in public-sector capital budgets?

Depreciation

Measuring the useful lives of public capital assets can be challenging. Some useful lives are notoriously difficult to measure. Many publicly owned buildings are of more historical significance than economic worth. Yet, that historical value can be important to the community. Similarly, an asset may be fully depreciated (for example, a two-hundred-year-old prison that is still being used), but the political and social costs of replacing it will be difficult to calculate and may be prohibitive. Many governments explicitly exclude such properties in their calculation of the value of their assets.

Distinguishing Capital and Operating Costs

Some types of expenditures have both capital and operating components. Education, for example, may be viewed as a consumption good in the year that it is received or as an investment in training that pays off many years down the road. In that sense, the broader definition of capital as being an asset that will be used for more than one year is hardly useful in actual budget planning. The asset, of course, is the educated child who will go on to contribute to society. Very few public-sector organizations have been able to marry some useful research into return on

investment in education to actual budget decision making. Another example is tourism promotion: expenditures on the promotion of tourism may be viewed as current (with immediate effects only) or as capital (lasting more than one year). The issues involved in distinguishing between capital and current expenditures are similar to those in determining the economic life of a particular capital-expenditure program.[3]

Similarly, the purchase of some physical assets is treated as an operating expenditure simply because they are small and disposable or their purchase value is so low that recording them in an inventory of capital assets is a waste of time and effort. Here, the principles of materiality apply.

Asset Measurement

Calculating the true value of capital assets requires a reliable measure of the value of goods and services produced. This type of calculation is very difficult to make when governments invest in capital that does not involve market pricing of net benefits received by the population, as in the case of parks, museums, legislature buildings, and universities. In many cases, the only possible way to value an asset in public-sector organizations is to estimate the replacement costs. This is hardly a comprehensive valuation of the asset, but it is a significant driver of decision making when it comes to replacement or repair.

Third Party Investment Strategies

Governments and other public-sector organizations are increasingly turning to innovative approaches to meet their capital needs, both in terms of financing, as pointed out above, and in the ownership and operation of major capital holdings. Driven partly by a general reluctance to finance many large projects through current tax revenues and partly by an interest in outsourcing either debt management or the management of construction projects, governments have established a number of third-party arrangements. Terms such as public-private partnerships, financial management initiative (UK) and alternative financing have arisen to describe these arrangements.

The Canadian Council on Public Private Partnerships defines such a partnership as "A cooperative venture between the public and private sectors, built on the expertise of each partner, that best meets clearly defined public needs through the appropriate allocation of resources, risks and rewards." One challenge such partnerships pose to governments is how to truly evaluate alternatives and arrive at the best-cost option. While such arrangements may transfer debt and risk to a private provider, the cost of capital and the ongoing costs associated with a future return to the private-sector investor in the partnership must also be calculated.

As these options are explored and developed, risk, as discussed above, also rises because the nature of control over such projects changes from the traditional notion of direct control to a more indirect third-party system of control. One Canadian provincial government shows this risk in the following way (see **Figure 7.6**) as a means of showing a continuum of capital-program delivery.

FIGURE 7.6
Risk Continuum of Capital-Program Delivery

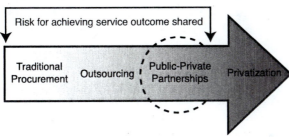

Source: British Columbia, "Capital Asset Management Framework," http://www.fin.gov.bc.ca/TBS/CAMF_Guidelines.pdf.

Tools for Analyzing Capital Costs

Big money, big risk, and a long-term perspective make it important to have good analytical tools available when undertaking capital-asset planning and budgeting. For those involved in budget processes, but not in capital planning itself, it is useful to be aware that these tools exist. The purpose of such tools is to establish the true cost of the capital project over its life as a project and then as a long-lived and used capital asset. This statement points to several elements that will certainly require commonly accepted tools to give assurance that the investment decisions being made are the right ones:

- **Time:** Have the changes in the value of money been factored into the calculations?
- **Value:** Is this the best value for the money?
- **Costs and Benefits:** Do costs and benefits match?
- **Ground Truthing:** Are all the cost assumptions realistic, tending towards restraint, and accompanied by contingencies for unforeseen (some would say inevitable) increases in costs?

Many tools exist. For the purposes of understanding their scope, this text will deal with the following:

- business cases,
- time value of money, and
- cost benefit analysis.

Business Cases

Business cases play in both the creation of a capital plan and in the final project approval process. They set up the argument for a specific project to be included. They argue for its priority, show the benefits that will accrue, and demonstrate that the cost estimates, project plan, and timelines can be trusted. Large governments and public organizations will always have a multitude of challenges for their limited capital resources. Sorting out priorities mean that individual projects – and some of these are very large and complex – have to be compared with other equally (or more so in the eye of the project advocate) deserving proposals. Having a good business plan does not guarantee success of the project proposal. Not having a good business case ensures its failure.

The business case brings together certain key elements that contribute to a decision. First and foremost, the business case provides the argument for change in how the organization is going to spend its scarce resources. A good business case should serve as the foundation for an implementation plan so it deserves considerable work to get it right. It must marry the proposed content to its costs. Therefore, quantitative analysis tools will probably play an important role. As we shall see, multi-year projects with multi-year use and benefits will require calculation of the net present value of the funds being proposed. Further, the business plan must address risks in such a way that the decision maker is confident that, even where they are considerable, there are reasonable proposals for risk mitigation.

For many large government organizations, there will be a standardized business plan format. This certainly helps when a project advocate has to put together a proposal. It does increase the challenge of differentiation among the proposals. Making a business case unique and worthy of inclusion in a plan takes both good analysis and sound linkage to the organization's goals, both in the short and long term. The following format is representative of many examples that are available.

Developing the business case for a specific project in a capital plan is just the beginning of a more complex planning and approval process. However, getting it right provides a firm foundation for moving ahead but also for

FIGURE 7.7
Business Case Format

Executive Summary
- What is being recommended
- Scope and nature of project
- Timelines, costs
- Link to overall plan

Challenge Definition
- What is the problem or opportunity
- Environmental factors
- Strategic alignment

Project Overview
- Goals and objectives
- Description
- Benefits – quantitative and qualitative
- Outcomes – what and when

Alternatives
- Pros and cons

Costing
- Project costing
- Operational implications – impact on budget

Risk Analysis and Mitigation
- Project risks
- Program risks
- Political risks

Implementation Planning
- Project management
- Timelines
- Operational impacts
- Responsibilities for outcomes

---

garnering support along the way. It pays to subject any business case to third party scrutiny so that unforeseen risks or faulty design assumptions can be addressed.

Time Value of Money

Time value of money (TVM) is important in public-sector capital planning for organizations that will have to borrow money for the project or acquisition and, hence, must know the cost of the debt charges they will be paying. Further, as they develop alternate financing schemes, the future costs of money have to be a factor in assessing overall costs. Alternatively, the organization may have other means available for financing capital, such as taxation, but may want to use those funds in other ways. As a consequence,

TVM techniques such as net present value (NPV) can help them determine the opportunity costs associated with funding the acquisition through debt or taxation.

The simplest explanation of time value of money is that a dollar today is worth more than a dollar tomorrow or at any time in the future, and the dollar today is worth less than the dollar you had yesterday or any time in the past. Many attribute this to inflation of the worth of the currency and compounding of interest on funds borrowed. And there is a relationship, but there are other factors to consider in understanding why money has different values at different points in time. Organizations have choices about what to do with the money that they have available to them: they can spend it, they can invest it, or they can hold onto it in some form. This concept of choice is called opportunity cost, the cost being the value of what they do not choose or of what they give up to get something else. Opportunity cost is a term used in economics, to mean the cost of something in terms of an opportunity foregone (and the benefits that could be received from that opportunity), or of the most valuable foregone alternative. For instance, if a city decides to build a hospital on vacant land that it owns, the opportunity cost is some other thing that might have been done with the land and construction funds. Their choices for that dollar closely relate to time value:

- Spending it now means having the things that are needed now.
- Investing it means deferring consumption and earning a return that will increase the value of the dollar, depending on the investment and time it is held.
- Holding it, and making no decision, means deferring any use and foregoing the opportunity to either consume or earn.

Another factor that relates to the time value of money is risk. The dollar in hand today has little risk. It is firmly within the control of the organization, which can dispose of it, save it or invest it as it sees fit. The promise of a dollar tomorrow carries some risk that you won't get it or that you won't get it when you have been promised you will get it. Depending on the source of your promised dollar, there may be almost no risk or the risk may be high. Generally, collection risk increases with distance from today, meaning a dollar owed to you tomorrow has less risk of not being paid than a dollar owed to you next year. More things can happen to prevent the future payment in the intervening time.

Interest-rate risk is also involved in the concept of time value. Market rates fluctuate, and the expectation of whether rates will rise or fall can affect loan and investment decisions. Going back to that dollar in your hand, if you think that rates are going to increase tomorrow, you could wait to invest that dollar at a higher rate than you would receive today (recognizing that you lose one day's interest by waiting). If you think rates will decline, your choice would be to invest the dollar today. Today's dollar, then, has more value than the one you get tomorrow for yet another reason: if rates decline, not having the dollar today means that the opportunity to invest at the higher rate was lost. As with credit risk, the amount of interest-rate risk also increases the farther into the future the payment is expected.

The final factor is inflation. If prices are rising, that dollar in your hand will buy less tomorrow than it will today. Of course, this doesn't mean that you should buy everything now, but it does need to be considered when you are making choices about what to do with the dollar and, if you invest it, what return will be needed to keep ahead of rising prices as well as compensate for not having the use of the money.

Finally we come to interest and its role. Interest is an incentive to put that dollar to work earning money, rather than spending it or putting it back in your pocket. For governments, the real issue may not be investment, but paying down debt to avoid interest charges rather than spending it on projects or programs. Loans are the reverse from the borrower's perspective. The borrower is willing to pay this interest in the future in order to have the money today, for whatever reason. The interest paid is an incentive for the lender to make the funds available as loan funds rather than use the money elsewhere. The interest rate is directly related to each of the risks described above, and is the driving force behind the fact that money has different value at different points in time. It is a variable in the calculation, but it is important to remember that it is not the *cause* of value differences, only a *result*.

Taking all these elements into account, TVM considerations become important in weighing the relative costs and benefits of a long-term capital program. The objective is to bring those costs onto a common field of analysis: present value.

Present and Future Value Calculations

Applying techniques of interest compounding and discounting, it is possible to determine either the present value or future value of a capital investment, using a simple formula that applies interest and time to the amounts that are either available now for investment in capital or the current value of a future payment. The variables used in both calculations are:

PV = present value

FV = future value

i = interest rate per period

n = number of compounding periods

Present value is an amount today that is equivalent to a future payment, or series of payments, that has been discounted by an appropriate interest rate. Since money has time value, the present value of a promised future amount is less the longer you have to wait to receive it. The difference between the two depends on the number of compounding periods involved and the interest (discount) rate.

The relationship between the present value and future value can be expressed as shown:

$$PV = FV \left[1 / (1 + i)^n \right]$$

Example: You want to buy an emergency generator for the fire department five years from now for $150,000. Assuming a 6 percent interest rate compounded annually, how much should you invest today to yield $150,000 in five years?

$$FV = 150,000$$

$$i = 0.06$$

$$n = 5$$

$$PV = 150,000 \left[1 / (1 + .06)^5 \right] = 150,000 \\ (1 / 1.3382255776) = 112,088.73$$

Figure 7.8 shows, year by year, how the calculated initial investment of $112,088.73 will grow to the $150,000 required in the future to buy the equipment. As we can see, future value is the amount of money that an investment made today (the present value) will grow to by some future date. Since money has time value, we naturally expect the future value to be greater than the present value. The difference between the two depends on the number of compounding periods involved and the going interest rate. The relationship between the future value and present value can be expressed as:

$$FV = PV (1+i)^n$$

FIGURE 7.8
Example: Present Value

End of Year	1	2	3	4	5
Principal	112,088.73	118,814.05	125,942.89	133,499.46	141,509.43
Interest	6,725.32	7,128.84	7556.57	8,009.97	8,490.57
Total	118,814.05	125,942.89	133,499.46	141,509.43	150,000.00

Example: In weighing the opportunity costs of replacing a computer now or in five years, what would be the future value of $10,000 in the capital fund if it were left today in a savings account that pays 6 percent interest compounded annually? That is, how much would you have five years from now?

$$PV = 10,000$$

$$i = .06$$

$$n = 5$$

$$FV = 10,000 \, (1 + .06)^5 = 10,000 \, (1.3382255776) = 13,382.26$$

Figure 7.9 breaks down the above calculations, year by year, to show what your initial investment would grow to in five years.

Applying these formulae to capital projects in the public sector is a way of analyzing alternatives. For voluntary organizations that have a direct interest in the cost of money if they plan to borrow to finance a capital project, these calculations are very important. What they accomplish is to portray the real cost of capital and the real potential costs of delaying decisions. In the case of the $10,000 computer, the reality is that it will have to be replaced eventually and that more money will have to be spent to replace it in the future, taking into account its present value. Overhanging all of this is the question of the availability of funds and the relative priority this purchase may have. Generally, an organization would have to decide if it believes the increased cost to replace the computer in the future will be more or less than $13,382.26, and accordingly, whether to replace it now or later. These calculations alone do not give a complete picture of capital-planning issues for government.

Using Present Value Calculations to Compare Options

Figure 7.10 outlines the application of present value to the cost of two office accommodation options. These numbers clearly suggest the renovation option, even with increased operating costs, is the better one. However, several factors need to be brought into the picture:

- Is this really an apples-to-apples comparison in terms of the quality of the accommodations as well as the fit to need?
- Is there a policy or political desire to expand the park adjacent to the existing building by tearing down the building that can be renovated?
- Are there additional benefits that a new building might bring such as easier client access or the potential for shared facility use with other departments?

Such factors will be called externalities by some, but are very real in the world of public administration.

FIGURE 7.9
Example: Calculation of Future Value

End of Year	1	2	3	4	5
Principal	10,000.00	10,600.00	11,236.00	11,910.16	12,624.77
Interest	600.00	636.00	674.16	714.61	757.49
Total	10,600.00	11,236.00	11,910.16	12,624.77	13,382.26

FIGURE 7.10

Present Value Application to Determine Annual Cost of Two Office Accommodation Options

Situation: Environmental Services of Fordville needs to have new offices. Two options exist:
- Renovate and operate, in the current location, land owned by the town and not intended for sale as it is designated for future park use if the building is ever torn down. Given the age of the building, operating costs will remain high.
- Build a new building on town-owned land that is valued at $250,000.

Cost Assumptions
- Renovation costs are $400,000. Land costs in this instance are 0.
- New building costs are $650,000. Land costs are to be factored in as the land is available for sale.
- Additional maintenance costs for the renovated building, compared with the maintenance costs estimated for the new building, are $15,000 per year.
- Both options can be completed in one year.
- Life cycle of the renovated building would be 18 years. For the new building, the life cycle is 25 years.
- Discount rate is 5 percent.

Review of Alternatives				
Renovate Existing Facility			**New Building**	
Capital costs	400,000		Capital costs	650,000
			Land	250,000
Total	400,000			900,000
5% discount rate for 18 years	0.0855		5% discount rate for 25 years	0.0710
Annual cost in present value	34,200		Annual cost in present value	63,900
Additional operating costs	15,000			
Full Annual Cost in PV	**49,200**		**Full Annual Cost in PV**	**63,900**

The Government of Ontario's *Infrastructure Planning, Financing and Procurement Framework* strongly encourages the use of such concepts as TVM in infrastructure or capital planning, but it sets the use of such tools in a broader public-policy context:

> The evaluation process must include a value-for-money assessment of the options. In the broadest sense, the option providing the best value for money is the one that uses the fewest resources to achieve desired service outcomes. Relative value is determined through a rigorous examination of service delivery options and business-case analysis, considering a broad range of factors including service levels; cost; promotion of growth and employment; environmental considerations; and other health, safety and economic issues.

With the introduction of accrual-based accounting for the province's finances, accounting considerations are no longer a driver of the model to be used for delivering infrastructure investments. The choice of model must be driven by economic considerations such as the efficient allocation of construction; financial and technical risks; effective project management; accountability; and financial discipline.

A value-for-money assessment must consider the quantitative factors to which a dollar value can be assigned, such as initial capital costs, operating and maintenance costs over the life of an initiative (adjusted for risks), and ongoing operating costs related to service delivery (including energy costs).

Quantitative factors also include those that can be quantified but are difficult to accurately translate into monetary terms. Examples may include the number of indirect jobs created by an initiative, the potential for broader economic stimulus, the level of measurable environmental benefits or the number of people served within a given timeframe.[4]

Using Net Present Value to Evaluate Investment Decisions

The acquisition of a capital item may set in place a cost flow for staff, maintenance, and upkeep that will add considerably to the net present cost of the decision that is about to be made. Net present value (NPV) is the future stream of benefits and costs converted into equivalent values today. NPV is a way of calculating whether the public-sector organization will be better or worse off if it makes a capital investment. It does so by subtracting the present value of outflows from the present value of inflows:

$$NPV = PV\ Inflows - PV\ Outflows$$

As you can see, calculating present value may involve receipts as well as expenditures. For example, the alternatives may have some salvage value after their useful life has ended. The estimated receipt, discounted to present dollars, from the sale of the item must be incorporated into your analysis as a PV inflow. The difference between the present value of the receipts and the present value of the expenditures (PV outflows) is net present value. The best financial choice is the option with the highest net present value. NPV is not necessarily a measure of profit or economic viability of a project. Rather, it is a measure of the net value of the project, captured, as best it can, as a monetary value. Projects with a positive NPV are considered cost effective, while those with a negative NPV are generally not.

The major factors affecting NPV are the timing of the expenditure and the discount rate. The higher the discount rate, the lower the present value of expenditure at a specified time in the future. Using NPV analysis to aid decision making in capital budgeting, the following factors are key:

- All cash flows, both outflows and returns (if there are any), must be included.
- TVM has to be a consideration and must be factored in because it will affect the value of the flows.
- Risk must be factored in, either quantitatively or qualitatively.
- Some method of ranking competing projects has to be established and aided by these forms of calculation, despite the complex and often subtle world of political trade-offs, compromises, and balanced considerations.

Net present value is a component of cost benefit analysis. It can be used as a criterion for deciding whether a government program can be justified on economic terms, which we realize is only one factor.

Cost Benefit Analysis

Cost benefit analysis (CBA) is a basic and important tool not just for capital projects, but also for many other forms of financial decision making. At its heart it is a calculation,

sometimes made intuitively, many times formally, adhering to prescribed formats, especially for organizations with many decisions to make and the need to use common tools for comparing the options that are available to them. A business case presents many of the elements of a CBA or may well be a CBA in all but form. It would come as no surprise, however, to note that CBA in government does not simply involve the application of tools such as NPV, but have to take into account the public purpose, broad public sector criteria as well as sustainability issues. It is therefore broader, more complex, but potentially less clear than one that relies strictly on return on investment. Many of the benefits and costs are less direct and more difficult to measure in quantitative terms. Nonetheless, its applicability in capital planning is real for the public sector. Many factors, most notably alternative delivery options (make or buy) and alternative financial options (expense, borrow, PPPs) mean that tools such as CBA be applied to establish a relatively common base of comparison. Even then, challenges persist for CBA in the public sector. These will be addressed below.

The steps in creating a cost benefit analysis are:

- Establish full costing of the project, including construction, cost of land, equipment, etc. Project such costs over the life of the project and the life of the asset.
- Establish the life expectancy of the project, e.g., will the building be used for 40 years?
- Project the known operating costs (with contingency) over the life of the asset use, i.e., 40 years.
- Do the same for the status quo or alternate project that could achieve the same purpose, e.g., build or buy options.
- Discount cost flows to determine present value of costs.
- Define measurable benefits, e.g., fees or revenue. Discount over the life of the asset.

The challenges this process poses for the public sector are great. While the tools of determining NPV are indeed important, given the number of soft outcomes and inferred benefits accompanied by the real but vague concept of public good, analytical tools such as this have to be accompanied by two conditioning elements. The first is that measurement in purely economic or quantitative terms is only part of the analysis. Softer benefits need to be taken into account, just as softer costs do. The second is that public administration works in a political environment in which factors well beyond the purview of such analytical tools are at play. For this reason, there is considerable interest in the notion of cost-effectiveness analysis, a form of modified CBA that incorporated as much of the quantitative analytical tools as possible, but also leaves room for consideration of the softer, less tangible factors. The key point here is that in capital planning and budgeting, every effort has to be found to develop analytical tools to permit good cost and benefit comparison and apply them in a consistent fashion in making choices.

Summing Up

While not all public-sector organizations actually use separate capital budgets, they are a common feature, most notably at the municipal level. In others – the federal government, for example – they are integrated into departmental plans and budgets and reported within the master budget. The conceptual tools and planning processes suggested here are important aspects of organizational financial management wherever capital plays an important role in carrying out that organization's mission. Thinking about capital often challenges the line manager to escape the year-to-year operating budget orientation and look at the implications of such elements as the actual cost of an investment in capital for both operating costs and further capital investments.

One of the other important reasons to have a special awareness of capital budgets and how capital behaves over time is that in government, the issue of maintenance and replacement of capital goods often is easily deferred when difficult budget cuts have to be made. What this has led to in Canada is a serious underinvestment in infrastructure that will now cost much more, in present-value terms, to replace. This has been the victory of the short term over the long term. Unseen sewers very seldom attract political attention – until they break down.

One feature of the emerging financial management scene in the public sector is that accrual accounting and budgeting make it much harder to ignore the total costs and value of assets and their depreciation. It is difficult, if not impossible, to apply depreciation to assets that are held for historical or aesthetic reasons well past any accountant's notion of depreciation, but the vast bulk of public-sector assets do depreciate in a normal fashion. Past failures to recognize this show hopeful signs of disappearing. This positive trend will certainly require a better understanding of capital assets.

Chapter 8
Taking It Back: Reallocation and Budget Cutting

Learning Objectives:

- Understanding the dynamic nature of budget allocation and reallocation at the budgetary and in-year management control level
- Learning techniques of budgetary reduction
- Learning techniques on in-year resource allocation to meet emerging needs and achieve maximum budget efficiency

Context: Budget Level and Program Level

Public administrators and politicians are often portrayed as budget maximizers – the more the better. Program advocacy within government and on behalf of it often leads to that one solution: more money. In reality, when looking at budgeting at the governmental or organizational level, the situation is very dynamic. As governments become increasingly concerned with their country's overall debt load and the cost of government, means to reduce budgets are being tried and applied around the world. Similarly, policy priorities shift. When that happens, budgets can also shift. What we have seen in the past decade, and can expect to see for some time, is a combination of variables that will inevitably lead to budget reductions in some areas with growth in others. The key variables are a commitment not to grow overall government combined with a prioritization in certain areas. The best example has been the challenge to provinces to contain health care cost growth while restraining or reducing growth in other government services. This has led to an effective reallocation of the overall budget. When this happens, some have to find ways to reduce their spending. As this text is focused on financial management and not fiscal policy, taxes and the option to increase them will not be fully addressed.

Similarly, governments around the world are looking for ways to achieve expenditure rationalization within their existing budgets. The array of programs that governments offer is often dizzying and each has an advocate, good public purpose or historical presence. As pressure builds, however, governments have to look at questions such as whether a program really should continue, can it be offered in a more efficient and economical way, should governments even be doing this any more, and what can be done within the program to reduce costs. Such questions often translate themselves into such catchphrases as "Doing more with less" or "lean management" or "rightsizing." This list goes on. The experience of some governments in systemic reviews is instructive and useful to understand.

At both the budgetary and program delivery levels, new options exist for delivering public goods, often involving forms of private sector engagement or arm's-length public entities with greater independence from central government controls. Part of the budget reallocation process involves sorting out – and costing in a complete way – such alternatives. It also entails reassigning resources from the traditional departmental model of government to this more complex world.

There are times when governments just have to reduce their budgets. This will often translate into across-the-board cuts for all government services. There are many ways that governments can shrink the size of their budget. All have an impact on the financial manager in some way.

The other side of this examination is how public organizations effectively use the funds that they have in the course of a budget year. When we say organizations, we are speaking of such entities as government departments – often large ones with large budgets. Their capacity to effectively manage their funds means that they must, and generally do, have considerable flexibility to reallocate funds to meet emergency situations, unanticipated short-falls or move surpluses to areas of need. All of this takes place within the approved budget and the delegations the departmental management has to do this. This is an important part of good financial control in any organization. The next chapter, **Cash Management: In-Year Budget Management and Monitoring** will address many of the techniques for doing this. In the context of this chapter, reallocation should be seen as an important tool of sound financial management.

Figure 8.1, Drivers of Reallocation, summarizes the points that have been made above. The first two can be seen as variable, adapting to changing external circumstances, policy shifts and politics. The last three are continual processes in both budgeting and in-year cash management. They are a generally more internal process, driven by the need to adjust to circumstances that do not neatly comply with plans.

FIGURE 8.1
Drivers of Reallocation

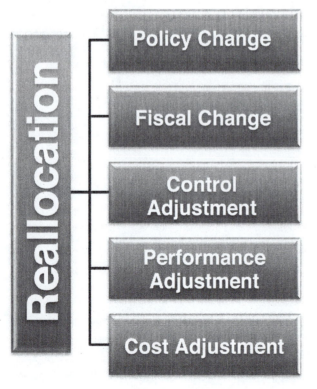

The notions of reallocation and budget cutting seem to attack the concept of incremental budgeting that has been prevalent in the public budgeting process for many decades. To a degree it does, and that is a healthy thing. While, for the most part, budgeting does involve a considerable amount of incrementalism, and budget management often does entail strategies to guard what you have, the reality has always been that these are just some of the ways in which budgets are formed and managed. As governments learn, as some have, that budgets are organic, and dynamic, not static, they have begun to build tools to more effectively achieve their objectives of either greater efficiency in resource use or straightforward reduction in the size of government. Similarly, as public managers have learned that their funds are limited and subject to fluctuations on both the revenue and expenditure side, combined with a seemingly endless array of demands within their established program mandate, they look for ways to squeeze every bit of use from the funds they have. They look as well for ways to find funds for emerging priorities without seeking more funds from outside their unit or organization.

Decremental Budgeting[1]

The phrase decremental budgeting, taken here from Robert Behn's 1985 article, *Cutback Budgeting,* is not new, reflecting the fact that governments have struggled with how best to cut budgets since they had budgets. Cutting budgets is no fun. Someone loses and, in both political and bureaucratic terms, that means some misery will be incurred. It is much easier to add than it is to subtract. As already observed in chapters 6 and 7, the incremental budgetary process appears to be rational, albeit with a few added elements of a bar room brawl as final decisions are made. Cutting is often presented as irrational, reactive and reactionary. That is why some governments, as we shall see, have developed more institutionalized means to review existing budget commitments to free up resources. Results have been promising, but mixed, to date.

Reducing budgets and whatever processes are used have some characteristics that are quite different from the notion of incremental budgeting. Before looking at the techniques that are often applied, or being tried, it would be useful to understand how different the context of budgetary cutbacks can be:

- Historically, budget reductions, especially at the global level, are not routine.
- Cutbacks are often linked to deficit reduction, a universal problem but one that has little appeal at the personal level.

- Conflict – on many fronts – is inherent in the process of budget reduction, whether it is across the board or at a specific program level.
- There are winners and losers, often with loud voices.
- There is nothing automatic about these processes. They must be driven by political and organizational will, often using up political capital in the process.

Robert Behn, in a recent newsletter ably summarized the different worlds of incremental and decremental budgeting, which is outlined in **Figure 8.2**.

Continuous Reallocation: In-Year Cash Management

This is the ying to the budget reallocation yang. As **Figure 8.1** points out, there are many reasons for reallocation, some of which are permanently manifest in the budget process. However, moving funds with authorized allocations to meet emergent short-term needs is an important part of the reallocative process. So, too, is finding funds internally to meet new priorities and needs that can be, or have to be, accommodated within current budget levels. Often surges in demand, sudden requirements or just poor management mean that one part of the organization is in need of a rescue, a temporary funding of what is expected to be a temporary anomaly. Prior to departments going to

externally available emergency or contingency funds, they must do their best to meet these needs internally. The obverse of this circumstance is what to do with unanticipated surpluses. Government organizations will always be for ways to fund initiatives that are within their mandate and within their authority to act on, provided they can find the funds. Similarly, internal improvements, even those that will ultimately yield savings for the organization, may require an internal allocation from within an existing budget.

A key difference between decremental budgeting and reallocation in-year cash management, even though they involve forms of reallocation is that most budgeting decisions are multi-year and permanent, while in-year decisions are meant to be just that, in-year. They are intended to address short-term demands but not, at least at first blush, to have an impact on longer-term budgeting issues.

This area of financial management is a constant preoccupation of the public sector manager. What follows should be read in the context of both **Chapter 9, Managerial Control** and **Chapter 10, Cash Management: In-Year Budget Control and Monitoring**.

General Approaches to Reduce Spending

Whether the reduction is permanent or temporary, governments have a number of means to bring them to effect.

FIGURE 8.2
Qualitative Difference Between Incremental and Decremental Budgeting

Difference Between Incremental and Decremental Budgeting	
Incremental Budgeting...	**Decremental Budgeting...**
is decentralized;	is centralized;
permits substantive decisions to be made in a fragmented way;	requires all substantive decisions to be put into a comprehensive package;
focuses only on the increment; the base need not be examined;	requires a re-examination of the entire budget;
is routine and consensual;	is chaotic and conflict-ridden;
involves negotiations and accommodation, based on mutual respect;	requires confrontation and coercion, and generates mistrust;
can be delegated to specialists and is mostly invisible;	provokes political engagement and is very visible;
appears to be merely distributive;	is clearly redistributive;
is historical, annual, repetitive, and predictable;	is precedent-breaking, multiyear, erratic, and unpredictable;
is rewarding (for there is credit to be shared), creates stable coalitions, and thus is automatic.	is painful (for there is only blame to be absorbed), involves unstable coalitions, and thus requires active leadership.

Source: Robert Behn, *Performance Leadership Report*, Vol. 10., No. 12, August 2013, available at www.ksg.harvard.edu/TheBehnReport.

This section will consider the broader tools that are available. Subsequently, we will look at what resources can be reduced or changed and some of the implications in each case. Finally, we will look at reallocation tools as part of the reduction and cash management efforts that are ongoing in most organizations.

In general, governments are pursuing a mix of four strategies to achieve budget reductions. These are:

1. across-the-board cuts,
2. strategic reviews,
3. efficiency gains, and
4. outsourcing and privatization.

We will look at each in turn. They seldom occur in isolation. Governments will mix and match depending on the urgency of the situation and the availability of opportunities. An across-the-board approach takes less time to bring into effect than a strategic review. Efficiency gains can only be realized if there is an alternative approach developed. Privatization will only occur if there is a willing buyer.

Across-the-Board Cuts

Across-the-board cuts are budget reductions that apply to all budgets in a more or less equal way. They can take the form of a percentage budget cut to the total budget or cuts to budget categories, e.g., a 4 percent reduction in all equipment budgets or a 25 percent reduction in travel. The key feature is that it applies to all such areas within the government's budget. Given the number of criticisms of across-the-board cuts, it is interesting to note how frequently governments use them when confronted with the need to reduce expenditures. Tom Peters, a notable management guru has wryly noted, *"Making across-the-board cuts is like going to the bank and asking for five inches of money."*[2] A recent example, dramatic in scope, of across-the-board cuts is the 2013 budget sequestration legislation in the United States. This imposed dollar reductions on a range of programs, with some exclusions. Congress did not direct what was to be cut, just the amount. For instance, Medicare spending was to be reduced by a fixed 2 percent per year over the next ten years.

In some respects, this form of budget decrement is the easiest, seen from the perspective of the decision maker. Some even argue that it is fairest as it affects all programs in the same way. The fallacies in that argument are threefold. First, cutting evenly fails to reflect program priorities. A cut in one area may affect many people while an equal cut in another area may not be as important or have such a great impact. Second, even distribution of decrements also assumes that the capacity to absorb or manage these decreases is the same. Some parts of government are better off than others. Some organizations can absorb the cuts. Third, this form of budget reduction effectively delegates much of the final decision making to individual units within the government organization being reduced. This will depend on the degree of flexibility that is permitted. However, some organizations may choose the route of reducing client service, while others may simply delay the replacement of infrastructure costs. In each case, the effects of these is unknown. This can lead to unintended consequences or, in the case of infrastructure, future costs and risks.

There remain good reasons for taking the approach. The first is that it is fast, at least from the perspective of making the decision and making the announcements. Rolling out the decision is another matter. That can certainly take time. The second is that it does distribute the burden of the reductions across the entire government or organization. Some perceive this as fair, even with the distortions in priorities and capacities that have already been noted. The third is that it does leave managers to sort out the best way to effect the reduction. This flexibility permits them to be more creative in finding a solution. As well, governments will want to see if such reductions can be absorbed without an actual impact on programs. This hope is built upon the notion that there is slack in the system. Some call it waste. Some call it an opportunity to improve. Often across-the-board cuts will involve proposals for rule changes, regulatory and policy changes, or efficiency gains to enable organizations to absorb the reduction.

One concern about this form of reduction is that, due to the reasons cited above, it has been popular for some time. It has seldom been used once, but has been a key source over several decades in governments. Therefore, it eats away at program capacity over time and in an insidious way. This has been notable in the under-spending on infrastructure renewal. Often, it leaves organizations stripped of all redundancies, a dangerous situation for many public organizations that have to respond to dramatic changes such as emergencies, weather disasters, power failures, etc., and find that they have little spare capacity.

For the individual financial manager in government, the call to cut, yet again, another x percent from travel or training or core staff costs, becomes a reactive crisis. Across-the-board is a top down, often urgency-driven event. While the budget cycle may often prove such a reduction target is necessary in that budget, or directions for the coming year may require such a reduction, for the most part, these announcements are less planned than that.

The manager has to respond, trying to maintain program integrity. It means that she has to have a good understanding of her budget and the capacity for reduction within it.

Strategic Reviews

Strategic reviews provide a more targeted and, in some cases, a more institutionalized approach to finding ways to reduce government expenditure. Canada, Australia, the United Kingdom and the Netherlands have led the way with a variety of approaches to strategic reviews. The objectives of a strategic review process are to identify savings or make funds available for reallocation in a way that examines individual programs to see if they can be eliminated, reformed, reduced or changed to yield the desired savings. Usually these reviews are centrally driven by the Treasury Board of the government. There will normally be a set of targets, a set of guiding principles for the review process, a central oversight provided either by politicians or by senior bureaucrats. Operating with a reduction target, departments are often asked to produce a plan based on the identification of their lowest priority programs or, alternatively, propose policy or delivery changes that will yield savings.

In 2006, the Canadian government launched an annual strategic review process. All direct program spending was reviewed on a cyclical basis. Each year, 25 percent of government spending was reviewed. The government provided a set of terms of reference for the review:

- **Comprehensiveness** – assessment of mandate, departmental objectives, program effectiveness, efficiency and alignment to government priorities.
- **Reallocation proposals** – options for program reductions or eliminations to reallocate to government priorities and support overall spending control.
- **Reinvestment proposals** – options to better support government priorities.

Departments were to review the relevance and performance of their spending. They were to identify the lowest performing or lowest priority 5 percent of programs, seek outside expert advice and report to the Treasury Board.

Departmental strategic reviews were to answer specific questions in key areas:

- government priority, federal role, relevance (i.e., continued program need);
- performance (effectiveness, efficiency, value for money); and
- management performance.

Departmental strategic reviews were to be conducted using the following key elements:

- Analytical Framework: The department's program activity architecture.
- Information Sources: Evaluations, audits, management accountability framework assessments, auditor general reports, and other reports.
- Reporting Requirements: Outlined in the terms of reference.
- Steering Committee: A departmental steering committee to be established with ex officio membership from TBS.
- External Advice: Expert outside advice to be involved on each review to ensure neutrality and credibility.

As can be seen, this is a considerable amount of work. However, it did produce results in many areas, if the targeted result of reduced government spending is the objective. For example, in 2009, twenty federal organizations undertook strategic reviews of 100 percent of their total direct program spending. In total, almost $26 billion, or 23 percent of all government spending was examined. A savings of $287 million was approved. These savings were redirected by the government to other priorities, including deficit reduction.

Reviews of this kind take time, resources and energy. They have proven successful, but only when the process is well formulated, managed with discipline and there is a clear sense of the desired monetary result. Some of the downfalls are that such reviews inevitably lead to political controversy as programs are closed or reduced. Rather than appearing, as across-the-board approaches do, to apply to all, strategic reviews will have the opposite effect: interest or advocacy groups feel singled out (which they are) and take up the challenge of criticizing the government. Strategic reviews really are a kind of injury by a thousand cuts. If they are sustained over many years, the political and bureaucratic will to keep at it is fully challenged. On the other hand, they are targeted and not random. They also involve a deliberative process to get to a result. Finally they open the door to policy and service delivery changes as part of the process that would modernize and improve the service. Experience around the world indicates that review processes of this kind fail when conflict arises that is not resolved. It needs discipline and long-term commitment, qualities often lacking in electoral cycle driven governments. Further, bureaucratic resistance to the amount of work required and to the limited results in some cases often diminished sustained commitment.

Strategic reviews involve the individual financial manager in many ways. As an area under review, the manager will have to provide information on the programs, their performance and input to changes that might be made. For this, he will have to draw on multiple sources of evidence such as evaluations, audits, benchmarking and international comparisons. Similarly, he will have to demonstrate that his program is strategically aligned with the government's direction. He will have to offer up alternative means of delivery. He can also suggest ways to save money and improve the program, such as efficiency gains, which will be discussed in a moment. Should decisions be made to reduce or eliminate a program, the manager then becomes engaged in change management as well as winding down the program.

Efficiency Gains

"Efficiency measures are reductions resulting from minor or major changes in the way existing programs are delivered. The objective is to deliver the same program outputs and outcomes with fewer inputs (resources)."[3] The mantra of making government more efficient will always be with us, even after centuries of making government more efficient. However, governments continue to try to find ways to reduce costs through better practices, finding cheaper means of delivery and reducing waste and duplication. Sagas of failure abound. However, there have been many successes as well. As a form of budget reduction, it remains important. Further, the field is still fertile.

Efficiency gains take a number of forms:

- Integrating points of service to the public among departments to reduce the number of offices and share services in each office.
- Amalgamating support or back-office functions into centralized shared service units.
- Replacing people (a high cost element of the budget) with automated systems (theoretically less expensive).
- Modernizing delivery systems and information systems to identify costs and control them better – this is different than using automated delivery systems in that it is intended to enhance internal management.
- Reducing travel costs through the increased use of videoconferencing.
- Outsourcing elements of program delivery, or of support systems to lower cost, often to private sector providers.
- Changing processing rules, regulations and eligibilities to reduce the number of people eligible or the time needed for review.

- Strategic procurement which would standardize purchasing specifications, limit vendors to increase volume, and buy as a single unit and even with other government units to drive cost reduction in purchasing major items.

The first test of changes like this is whether they actually achieve the budget reduction wanted. For the most part, any savings are longer term, as some form of investment is usually needed to achieve them. This may take the form of investment in new technology. This takes time to implement and, with large risk projects, costs may increase, which reduces the attractiveness of the original business case. Often, as well, this means making capital investments to reduce operating costs. Lining up the two processes becomes key.

Efficiency gains drive at the heart of the productivity element of government. It also is another means of avoiding so-called arbitrary across-the-board cuts. However, unlike the strategic review, they will involve some form of investment, reconstructing the old cliché, "You have to spend money to save money." Of course, strategic reviews can point to efficiency gains as a means of reducing government costs. In that sense, the two can go hand in hand.

Outsourcing and Privatization

Reference has already been made to possible outsourcing for efficiency gains. The link here is a strong one. However, in terms of permanent budget reduction, some definitions are in order. Privatization means that the government divests itself of the ownership of an asset or program and leaves its operation to the private sector. It can do this in a number of ways. As in the case of many national airlines, it can sell the operation outright. It gains the capital from such a sale, but loses the income (or operating loss) stream forever. The asset leaves the balance sheet. The net effect is a reduction in the size of government as well as a lower overall budget figure. Governments may retain a strong public policy interest in, for instance, airline safety and competition. However, they are not owners or operators of airlines. They exercise that interest through other means such as legislation, regulation and the creation of oversight bodies.

Outsourcing simply means to buy goods or services that have been carried out by government staff from an outside of government supplier on a contractual basis. Gilley and Rasheed[4] point out that outsourcing is the procurement of something that was either originally sourced internally or could have been sourced internally but the decision was made to go outside. Therefore, government remains in control of the funds used, the assets created and, ultimately, the quality of the service or good being provided. Outsourcing can take many forms and affect many services. In the context of this text, the objective of outsourcing is to reduce costs of a particular function. In essence, the function is purchased from a supplier. The test is whether, over time, the costs of the service and of managing that outsourced service are less. This is a challenge as governments use outsourcing for many reasons and these are often mixed in with issues of cost savings. For instance, government occasionally needs expertise that they do not normally use. Hence, the use of consultants is a form of outsourcing.

Because outsourcing has developed a panacea-like quality, especially during the era of new public management (NPM), it is not without its detractors. Experience has shown that major efforts to outsource information technology have resulted in escalating costs and, in many cases, failed implementations. Critics will point out that there are considerable risks in outsourcing, ones that can, over time, lead to higher costs, thereby negating the budget reduction intent. Such risks are loss of control of the cost drivers, loss of internal competence in a core or near core area of activity and oversight failures that lead to corruption or the misuse of funds.[5]

General Approaches to Reallocation

Reallocation has two sides, reflecting the budget-based or in-year cash management base of analysis. From a budgetary perspective, reallocation involves a permanent movement of resources from one program or unit to another. It seldom happens in such a direct fashion. Rather, as in the strategic review process, funds are reduced in one area, and returned to the central agency responsible for budget allocation (Treasury, Ministry of Finance, etc.) and then reallocated to another program or unit. In-year reallocations generally take place within a program or units. They are for one year only and the funds do not involve a permanent reallocation. The mechanisms of this process are addressed in **Chapter 10.**

The net effect of reallocation is not to reduce the overall budget level. Rather, it is to make priority adjustments in the budgetary allocation and to resolve temporary changes in demand or cash requirements for in-year management. However, in both instances, some decisions have to be made concerning the continuance of the existing program from which resources are extracted or moved. Further, some accommodations to permit the freeing up of those resources have to be made. It is to these that we now turn.

Strategies and Tools for Reduction and Reallocation

This chapter has already addressed some of the tools available to government should they decide, through any of the broad techniques outlined above, to reduce or reallocate resources. This section will address specific areas of reduction. Each is contentious politically and risky in a number of ways. Even in the face of those risks, these measures have been used by many governments, with varying degrees of effectiveness, around the world. These strategies and tools are not mutually exclusive. In fact, they affect each other. For example, reducing staff in a client service operation will inevitably lead to service reductions, brave claims to the contrary notwithstanding. As well, the service and organizational impact such as morale, institutional memory, and contingent capacity to respond to emergencies are affected by any and all of these steps.

Service Level Changes

Governments can simply reduce the level of service it is providing to the public. Hours that an office is open can be reduced. Eligibilities can be changed. Access can be restricted. In each case, there has to be some reduction in staffing and use of other resources. Alternatively, government can reduce the number of inspections or audits where it operates in a regulatory mode. Finally, government can simply stop a service entirely.

Change the Employment Arrangements to Reduce Salaries

This strategy entails seeking major changes to collective bargaining arrangements that set employee salaries and benefits. It can also involve making such changes unilaterally for non-unionized staff such as the executive. It can also entail changing the way in which pension schemes are funded. This has become an even more contentious issue for budgeting as full accrual accounting now requires that the pension liability of governments be fully reported on its books and integrated into its deficit calculations.

Reduce Staffing – Permanent and Temporary

One of the largest portions of most public-sector budgets is personnel. Staffing level reductions, whether through attrition or outright dismissal, is an essential part of any budgetary cutting scheme. It is also one of the most complex challenges. The public sector remains one of the most unionized in the developed world. As well, the traditional public service has been designed around the notion of permanent employment. In addition, most governments have employment standards that dictate how employees are to be treated when their jobs are declared redundant. Therefore, there are transitional costs associated with staff reductions. If the government decides it has to move quickly, it will go the termination route. This will mean some form of severance cost may be involved. Similarly, the government may provide a transitional period in which the employee can seek another job within government. This means that the savings are delayed. Should the government decide to reduce staffing through attrition, it imposes on itself a much longer process, as it awaits the departure of the employee through job change or retirement, thereby leaving a vacancy, which it then does not fill. Once again, savings are delayed.

For in-year budget control, staffing can be delayed. Positions can be left vacant, thereby realizing a temporary salary saving. Temporary staffing can be used rather than full-time permanent staffing. This should be at a lower cost and also permit management to terminate without the processes outlined above. This is generally characterized as a hiring freeze, one in which the normal staffing delegations will be removed from managers and all staffing reviewed by a more senior person.

Renegotiate Contracts: Governments depend heavily on procurement of goods and services to carry out their business. The scope and level of contracting varies across agencies, but some are very heavy users. Facing overall cutbacks, the agency has to review what it can do, either immediately or at a contract's renewal, to either decrease the contract's cost or gain additional service to displace what is being lost on the staff front. As in the efficiency gains discussion, managers can look to partnering with other agencies to share procurement to reduce costs by gaining leverage to reduce the bid cost and reduce the administration costs as well.

Defer or Cancel Investments

Investments include capital purchases, major systems changes, reclassifications of jobs and other major purchases. Governments can cancel major projects or choose not to invest in them to reduce their budgets on a permanent basis. They can defer maintenance (at some considerable risk) or lengthen the cycle to lower overall costs. Major purchases such as military equipment can be cancelled. In-year, governments or units of them can re-examine their commitments to see if maintenance and purchases can be deferred, thereby punting the cost into future years.

Equipment replacement cycles can be lengthened so that vehicles and computers are replaced less frequently.

Ridden throughout these options are risks and hidden costs. Further, the late 20th century saw governments doing just what was described in the above paragraph in bridge and road maintenance across North America. The tragic outcome of bridges collapsing is well documented. On the other hand, there is ample potential for savings in such practices as well. As in all of these options, the risks have to be acknowledged and managed.

Reduce or Eliminate Discretionary Spending

In addition to staff costs, there are budgetary elements that are frequent targets in reduction processes. Therefore, eliminating travel money or reducing the training budget are easy and frequent targets. Similarly, programs with funds that support voluntary organizations will reduce their support to these groups. Funds to support program-related research activities can be eliminated, as can funds to hire summer students. The list is long.

Amalgamate and Reorganize

Similar to the efficiency gains overriding strategy, this can take the form of bringing services offices together with a specific reduction in the number of staff and scope of service. Back office operations, generally administrative units that support program units through business functions such as finance, information technology and human resources, can be amalgamated or outsourced. The number of offices for a program can be reduced. Smaller offices in the area being served can be closed and a larger office designated to serve the same area. In each of these instances, there are transitional costs and potential service implications.

Increase Fees and User Costs

Even governments that steadfastly resist raising taxes will willingly permit user fees and charges for service to rise. These moves are unpopular but those affected are more isolated than broadly based tax increases. The effect on the Treasury is the same – more money. There are already many user fees built into the provision of government services, from park entry fees to road tolls to license fees. In addition, government can limit access to services that transfer the cost to the user. For example, listing a medication for free access by seniors increases costs to the government. De-listing it reduces those costs and transfers them to the patient.

Internal Transfers – Temporary and Permanent

Governments are complex entities. While the general view is that there is one budget, in reality, there are many. Departments of government have individual budgets. In turn, units within departments are assigned budgets from the departmental funds. In order to make this operate smoothly, reserves are created at various levels to permit governments or their agencies to react to changing situations. Such contingency will vary with the government. In some cases, creating such reserves is legally mandated. In others, it is a matter of managerial practice. Facing pressures to meet gaps in either current spending or in budget planning, these reserves can be brought into play. Certainly, with respect to in-year cash management, having this kind of flexibility relieves the need to take some of the steps listed above. For a permanent move, the risks and consequences are greater in that the reserve is therefore lost forever and, with it, a certain amount of redundancy to meet emergent needs. That is a risk decision that must be considered.

In this complex environment, some units may overspend and some underspend. Therefore, agencies are expected generally to manage such overages and underages by internal reallocation, on a temporary basis, from one budget to another to cover off the problem. What has to also happen, as we will see in detail in **Chapter 10** is that it must also manage the situation that created the variance in the first place. This may well mean making adjustments to the program and its budget to accommodate what the agency identifies as a permanent change. It may also be a question of short-term anomalies, emergency situations that can be accommodated within the budget, or just poor management that will have to change.

Sell Off Assets

Governments won a lot of land, buildings, equipment and related assets known as non-financial assets. However, the scope is larger. It can include intellectual property, valuables such as precious metals, natural resources, contracts, even frequency bandwidth. In the latter case, many governments have made windfall profits in the sale of such bandwidth. Disposing of assets like these that are not mission centric, or that can be acquired differently, is a ready way to make some one-time cash gains. It seldom is relevant to the individual manager as large governments will dispose of these assets centrally.

Cutback Management

Whatever the mix of strategies and tools that are put in place, the management of cutbacks and reallocations is a major challenge for public administrators. As Moore, Baber and Bartlett said in an article in **Public Finance and Management,**

> Much of the politics that make budget cutting difficult have to do with resistance to disruptions in the supply of these [valued] sorts of public goods in the absence of which people must work harder, work longer or work in different ways to achieve their objectives."[6]

First, they are challenged to be ready for such changes. Any public manager who is not aware of budgetary pressures on government and the continuous need to find a way to reduce costs is working in a rather comfortable parallel universe. These pressures are a constant in the life of government. Second, they are challenged to manage their resources, with adequate controls and monitoring, so that they can identify potential deficits or surpluses and deal with them. Third, they are challenged to respond, defend and clarify the nature of the cutbacks. They have to look to the sustainability and adaptability of their programs, making sure that all risks are understood, mitigated or accepted. They also have to find ways to adapt the program to its reduced circumstances. Finally, they are challenged to implement the cuts through whatever set of strategies have been chosen. These are all active roles that will now be examined in more detail.

Framing the Cutback: Risks and Consequences

The careful preparation of any budget change proposal is vital if it is to be successful in terms of program sustainability and also actually realizing the savings. Managers have to understand and advise on the risks inherent in the change. They also have to search for ways to mitigate such risks. For instance, the introduction of a new user fee can be spread out over a number of years, each year rising slightly, until the desired income level is reached. This reduces somewhat the risk of a user revolt. On the other hand, it increases the risk that the desired budget reduction will not be reached if the pressure against the fee increase results in a political decision to halt it. Further, there will be pressure from the central drivers of the budget reductions to achieve the savings as soon as possible. **Figure 8.3** points out some of the risk areas that have to be considered.

Knowing Where to Look: Control Brings Insight

Managers have to have adequate control of their budgets to not only deliver their programs but also understand the pressures on the budget and the potential for variances from plans. That also equips them with a good

FIGURE 8.3
Risk Framework for Cutback Management

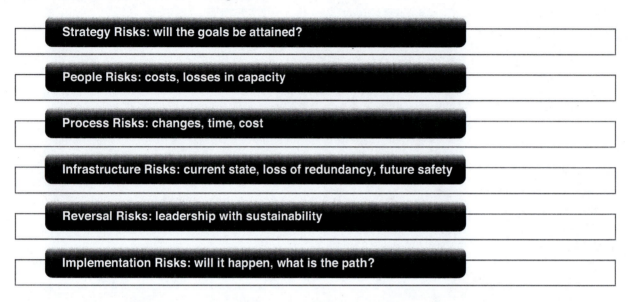

Source: While this is a compendium of risks identified through a variety of research, part is taken from Canadian Parliamentary Budget Office, *Budget and Expenditure Reporting to Parliament: Strengthening Transparency and Oversight in an Era of Fiscal Consolidation*, 25 April 2012, retrieved from www.parl.gc.ca/pbodpb/RedirectDocument.aspx?Url=/Macintosh%20HD/Users/AG/Downloads/Budget_and_Expenditure_Reporting_EN.pdf.

understanding of the impact of a budget reduction or reallocation direction on their capacity to deliver. They will also understand where they can cut and how, often at a level of granularity more refined than those centrally located (be that in the Treasury or the Finance office of the agency) would have about individual programs. For instance, a program may have a large staff component, but a significant number of them are temporary staff. Reducing their numbers is easier and less expensive than indeterminate or permanent staff who would have transitional entitlements such as job priority or severance, all of which adds to the costs of the reduction.

Implementing Cutbacks

The consequences for the public manager of cutbacks are extensive. They include:

- **Personnel:** The impact on personnel can be immediate or, worse still, a slow and lingering threat of job loss. The announcement of cuts has to be accompanied by effective communication within the working unit on the impacts and processes to be followed. Ambiguity creates serious performance and morale problems within the unit. Taking that into consideration, there are a number of short and long ways to reduce staff costs: slow down hires, keep positions vacant, announce outright layoffs, resist replacing staff who retire or leave, shift to less expensive contracted services or less costly short-term employment, modify working hours and work arrangements to cover peak periods. In undertaking any of these, consideration has to be given to the transitional costs such as possible retraining, severance and relocation. With respect to contracted services, full costing is essential, which includes contract management and transitional costs.

- **Programmatic:** Do the cuts represent a fundamental shift or loss of capacity to deliver the program as it is presently construed? If so, what has to change – the law, regulations, policies – to match the new resource state? The greatest danger in all of this is saying that nothing will change as a result of these cuts. Aside from being an odd way of saying that you had too much money, it may also be a lie.

- **Clients:** Should fees be raised, or savings made due to a reduction in personnel leading to reduced service components, clients will be concerned. As Joni Mitchel sang, "Don't it always seem to go that you don't know what you've got till it's gone?" Many public programs are highly valued and have broad client bases. While there are political consequences to be dealt with by politicians in such cuts, there are also programmatic ones.

- **Systems Changes:** As noted, many cuts come in the form of cutting with policy, program or systems changes. The implementational and transitional elements of these have to be managed as the cuts occur.
- **Performance Expectations:** Managers are caught in a dilemma when it comes to cutback management: how much and how long to resist or try to negotiate in defence of the program versus faithfully implementing the decisions once they are made. Bureaucracies are not without their guerrilla warriors. There is a tension here that is well recognized by agency leadership. That is why, generally, cutbacks take on a more centrally controlled element.
- **Hitting the Target:** Calculating and agreeing on the baseline against which savings are measured has proven elusive for many governments. Some have had to go back and recalculate savings once they realized that the baseline was not correct. This is important for the manager, as she will be assessed in terms of performance against the target. However, if the baseline is accurate, reaching that target becomes more difficult. In addition, savings should be reported net of implementation costs.

In Summation

Cutbacks, reallocation, looking for ways to use money more effectively and efficiently are a constant factor in public-sector financial management. Financial managers have to be ready to engage in these activities, whether they are imposed from above or outside or are part of their own needs to gain better control of their in-year budget, find flexibility to fund policy and service shifts, or improve operations in any number of ways. Therefore, they should, as they develop their internal control process, also develop their own process of identifying possible reduction and reallocation. Getting there first puts them in a positive position to assess the impacts of resource reductions or shifts.

Being protective of one's resources is a good thing. Being stupid about being protective is another. Treating all suggestions for reallocation, modification or reduction with full flight guerrilla resistance will eventually put the individual manager on a career spiral driven by gravity not ascension but also leave the organizational unit vulnerable in terms of its adaptability and capacity to manage imposed change. The financial manager therefore has to be the one to ask the tough questions, such as:

- Is the activity designed to operate as efficiently as possible?
- Can we find partners within the agency to share costs?
- Have necessary materials been purchased at the lowest price while maintaining quality?
- Are we locked into contractual arrangements beyond our control?
- Can the process be mechanized or computerized to minimize staff costs?
- Can this be delivered through a third party more cheaply?
- Can processes be standardized within and across units to reduce costs?
- Can units be amalgamated?
- Can IT be better sourced?
- Can you look at fleet reductions or better management?
- Can you increase revenue?

Financial managers need to know their cost structure. For instance, what is your costliest input? For much of government, it is people. Drill down. Is it regular salaries or is it overtime? How does your position classification system, which establishes salary levels, work in this regard? Do you have a top-heavy organization? Do you have a major sick leave issue and is it costing you? Compare and contrast. Find cost comparisons that help you determine if your processes cost more or less to operate than similar ones. This also enables a knowledge transfer that permits the manager to find places where other solutions have been tried and worked.

It pays to know the budgetary and financial performance history of the unit. What has already been done? Have all the low hanging fruit, i.e., the easy solutions, been plucked? On the policy and program side, the manager should be able to link reductions, permanent or temporary, to results. Will this change the results? Will this threaten promised delivery? If so, what can be done to reduce the impact?

Reductions seldom occur in a singular, one-off way. There are generally a series of reductions taking place in an agency at one time. Financial managers should be sensitive to the impact of reductions in other parts of the organization that will affect them. This is most significant in staff functions, which often operate centrally, but provide services that are vital to operating units. For instance, changes in the level and service capacity in Human Resources, Finance, Information Technology or Procurement will affect many operational units. The manager cannot assume that this has been considered or thought through.

Cutbacks and reallocations may involve some give and take in order to bring them to effect. For example, a manager might be able to reduce staff requirements if certain additional flexibilities in making decisions and levels of inspection are provided. This would change operating procedures, delegations, and authorities. These changes could also achieve greater program efficiency and effectiveness. As noted above, keep this process happening today in perspective: this will happen again. Often managers will be able to accommodate the reduction this time, but put in markers about the decreased flexibility in the future. Managers can also seek transitional assistance and money to achieve the cuts. This may sound at odds with the overall objective, but it often does happen. For instance, if a number of staff are affected in one unit, the manager may ask that staffing actions in certain other units be halted until the affected personnel are reviewed for suitability for those positions. Further, they may require some training to be eligible, a cost that the manager has to seek to be covered as a transitional one.

Above all, the financial manager, when faced with cuts or reallocation, should move with deliberate speed. As already noted, ambiguity is the greatest enemy of staff effectiveness and morale. As soon as the word is out that reductions are on the way, the first question each employee asks is, "What about me?" The manager may provide all the communication in the world about the process and give assurances about impact. Until that question is answered, it is all noise.

Chapter 9
Managerial Control

Chapter Objectives:

- Understanding managerial control of finance and operations in the public sector
- Outlining the range of controls available to managers and organizations
- Exploring the role of risk management in developing control systems
- Outlining recent efforts by several Canadian governments to improve their controllership function

Introduction: Control is About Delivering

As this text has moved from public-sector budgetary processes toward effective use of the funds obtained within the legislative or organizational framework, its focus must, of necessity, turn to the effective management or execution of the budget. As noted, the budget is a plan. Now it has to be carried out. The desired outcome of implementing the budget is to achieve the objectives of the program, project, or line of activity in the most efficient and effective way that is reasonable in the situation but with an equal concern for the proper use of public funds. So, results for sure, but in the right way. In any enterprise, this requires a series of controls to be put in place to make sure that the objectives are being met in the context that has just been outlined. Such controls extend beyond the more readily visible ones such as audits and external review. In fact, these comprise but one element of a full control framework. Control begins and ends within the management environment. Increasingly, internal control and new tools for risk management are merging into a single enterprise. This is why we address risk and risk management in this chapter.

A control framework is the set of practices, rules, procedures and policies that provide the agency, its governing body and external stakeholders with the assurance that it is operating in a way to achieve its objectives in the manner laid down in law and sound managerial practice. The objectives of the framework, as set out by COSO (Committee of Sponsoring Organizations of the Treadway Commission),[1] a global standard setter in this area, are:

- achieve operational objectives: do what you are there to do;
- provide financial and non-financial information for internal and external monitoring: is your information reliable and accurate? And
- ensure compliance with relevant policy, laws and procedural rules.

The key tools of control are:

- monitoring,
- information and communications,
- control activities,
- risk assessment, and
- a control focused culture.

Figure 9.1, now a well-known one created by COSO, shows how these objectives and tools have to interact with each other and also within the structure of the organization for which the controls are needed.

This chapter will explore ways that financial managers exercise effective control. It is not simply about following the rules. It is truly about being in control of the resources you have been given to achieve the goals of the program in the desired way. To do that, the manager has to have, and give, reasonable assurances in each of these areas.

Two elements of control receive more detailed discussion in subsequent chapters. The first (in Chapter 10) is the question of cash management: the in-year management of resources so as to make the most effective use of them.

FIGURE 9.1
COSO Control Framework

The second (in Chapter 11) is the issue of accountability in general and its application to financial management.

Who Has an Interest in Control?

An effective control framework delivers more than accountability for results for the budget. As the discussion of financial information has shown, it provides managers with valuable information to let them know what is going on within their operations. Similarly, it gives more senior managers information about how their managers are performing. It also informs stakeholders about the organization's performance. Defining just who the stakeholders are in the public sector is a challenge in itself. It could be the client group, interest groups, or donors.

It could be a bondholder assessing the credit-worthiness of an entire government. Certainly, it supplies those governing the organization – a legislature or a board of directors – with the information to assess how the organization is doing financially. Finally it permits internal and external auditors with information as to conformity with the organization's financial-practice laws or policies as well as the use of funds voted. Agreeing to a control framework for agencies of government that operate at arm's length is an important means for governments to oversee the performance of these organizations. As governments extend their use of contracted and arm's-length operating agencies, such frameworks are key to the continued exercise of their accountabilities.

In like fashion, establishing controls within the management cycle provides many groups and individuals with valuable information. For line managers, it establishes the extent of their discretion and outlines the rules by which to make decisions. While many programs have well-defined parameters and operational guidelines, the pressures of public service always lead to the exception, the situation that demands some flexibility, or the anomaly that no weight of bureaucratic direction will successfully anticipate. As well, for the line manager and many other actors in the public-sector organization, effective controls will address risks to the organization in achieving its goals and the degree of risk acceptance and mitigation within the organization. Finally, for the line manager and all the management hierarchy involved in decision making within the organization, effective controls will ensure that there is a timely understanding of the performance within the organization that would permit adjustments in budgets, behaviour, or program expectations to accommodate unforeseen situations and monitor the impact of managers' decisions.

In some instances, head-office managers (e.g., financial officers, human resource managers, strategic planners) will want controls that will allow them to see if all the funds are needed for a program within a particular year. This is because most public-sector organizations have a plethora of demands and are often seeking to free up unneeded funding to meet them. Equally, managers at the upper levels of an organization will want controls of a nature that will assure central agencies in their government that they are using funds effectively as an organization and complying with process requirements.

For the governing bodies of the organization, effective control means that rules about financial behaviour avoidance of misuse of funds, together with a common platform for understanding financial statements, are in place and are being applied. The basic level of control ensures that no one is absconding with the money. Another dimension of control is seeing that the program meets its objectives in a proper manner and with due regard for efficiency.

For stakeholders, effective controls mean that they have information about how well program managers and their organizations are using either public or donated funds. This information also shows whether they are doing so legally, obeying the laws or policies governing their financial responsibilities, and whether the funds are being spent for their intended purpose and are not being diverted elsewhere.

All the various players described above have an interest in having a reasonable assurance that public funds are spent for the purposes intended, with maximum efficiency and program effectiveness, and in the manner that obeys the law. Their interests vary in both degree and substance. They will also differ in how they interpret performance and control information. Satisfying everyone is a hard task in such a complex field.

Control then becomes a key knowledge function of the organization, the sensory devices needed to give continuing assurance that what is happening is what was intended and someone is in control. Without control, bad things can and do happen and results are not achieved. Here are a few of the things a public servant never wants to hear, all of them pointing ultimately to lack of effective controls:

- Legislative authorities were not obtained to spend the funds.
- Normal financial practice was not followed and authorities exceeded.
- The budget was overspent and no one knew that it was happening.
- Contracting rules were broken and no one knew.
- Contracting rules were broken and someone knew.
- Money disappeared.
- Results and mistakes were deliberately hidden from the public.
- The program failed to achieve its objectives.
- Risks were known and no effort was made to mitigate or avoid them.
- Senior management or governing authorities were not informed of the problems in a timely manner.
- The organization lacks basic information to control its activities and finances.

Public-sector organizations operate on trust. This trust assumes that public funds are being spent for the purposes intended and in the manner intended. From the perspective of individual managers seeking to maximize the potential of their programs, controls provide the information they need to determine if they are on plan, both programmatically and financially. For the public, control frameworks confirm that their interests are being taken care of, not only in getting the desired public-policy outcome but also in the expected manner. Control must not take place simply to enable management; it must also *be seen to take place*, as one of the foundations of that all-important trust factor in public-sector management.

The Control Process: It Never Ends

The need for control has existed as long as organizations have. Every organization, no matter how large or how small, whether public or private, creates and uses some form of control over its activities. Such processes can be formal or informal, depending on the needs of the organization.

Managerial control takes place on a continuous basis. Too often associated with rules *a priori* of making decisions, or reviews *ex post* to reflect on their quality and adherence to rules, control is actually a means of knowing what is happening in an organization to ensure that it meets its objectives. In the public sector, it is not simply a matter of what is to be achieved but also how and by whom. Managerial control involves having in place the means, based on risk, materiality, and political sensitivity, to monitor how an organization is performing against its stated objectives, within the rules set for it to operate, and with due regard to efficiency along the way.

Aside from the COSO elements listed above, a useful way to describe what is meant by management control in the context of financial management is as follows:

> Management control systems consist of all organizational structures, processes and subsystems designed to elicit behavior that achieves the strategic objectives of an organization at the highest level of performance with the least amount of unintended consequences and risk to the organization.[2]

This definition covers many of the key characteristics of management control:

- Control cannot occur unless the organization knows what it has to do, has organized that work accordingly, and can link it to achieving its strategic objectives.
- Control extends beyond control over individual transactions and financial reporting, without excluding them.
- The objectives must be achieved at the highest possible level of performance; that is, they must seek to be as efficient as possible.
- Risk must be minimized so as to avoid any chance of unintended consequences in terms of either outcomes or deviations from the rules governing the work.
- Structure refers to the formal task, authority, and responsibility assignments in an organization.
- Processes are the activities through which control is accomplished.
- Subsystems support the structures and processes by providing the right incentives to guide behaviour.

The architecture of a control framework, presented graphically in **Figure 9.2**, within an organization will involve certain key features:

- organizational goals and objectives;
- assignment of roles and responsibilities;
- delegation of program and financial authorities;
- performance standards, results statements, benchmarks to provide comparison with actuals;
- risk management tools in place and in use;
- risk mitigation and monitoring tools to continually reassess the risks;
- control procedures and policies, both to address the risks identified, and to satisfy legislative or policy-created requirements for adequate control;
- a system of monitoring at both the operational level and the financial level to ensure that the organization fully understands what is happening relative to its goals and the risk environment;
- a system of auditing and evaluation, both internal and external, that provides assurance, from an independent perspective, that there is an adequate control framework, that it is working (and not just on paper), and that the outcomes, both operational and financial, are as the organization claims.

In the public sector, there are many levels of control and that control can often be imposed from outside the agency. For instance, the legislature or council is a control mechanism for the government as a whole, as well as for individual departments and agencies. Its scope of interest is essentially global – the whole government. Nonetheless, it participates in setting the goals of the programs by approving the laws that create them and the appropriations to fund them. Further, through various forms of budgetary reviews, it gets into the details of program delivery. Equally, it reviews the expenditures of the government on a regular basis, often through appearances by ministers and other officials before committees or in general sessions. Finally, in most instances, there is a legislatively appointed external auditor who serves the legislature directly, providing independent assessments of the government's performance. All these activities are functions of public-sector control and accountability. Their existence is a fundamental feature of our democratic system, and its strength.

The focus of this text is primarily on managerial control within a public-sector organization. The reality is that so much of the control framework, whether it is consciously thought out or the accidental outcome of a series of individual decisions and reactions to specific events, is driven by the concerns of the legislature and the legislative auditor.

A management control framework is designed to help the organization achieve the state of being in control. It involves the basic steps outlined above, but inherent in this must be the understanding that there is an active use of the results of these steps. In other words, the framework may be well written, and may involve a multi-coloured chart outlining how the control framework is designed. However, if it is not used by senior management, then it is simply meeting external requirements and is not part of the managerial culture of the organization.

What does this mean? In the first place, it means that all managers must be active users of the information that is produced through the control framework. Second, they must actively participate in contributing to the conclusions of such exercises as risk assessments and receiving and reviewing monitoring reports, be they financial reports such as a statement of operations, reports on variances in operational goals, or reports on specific audits. Third, they must direct mitigation in the context of risk and take accountability for it. Fourth, they must assess the overall financial condition of the organization on a regular basis and be seen to treat seriously the information they receive. They must be seen to be the active consumers of the information. In summary, there

FIGURE 9.2
Management Control Framework

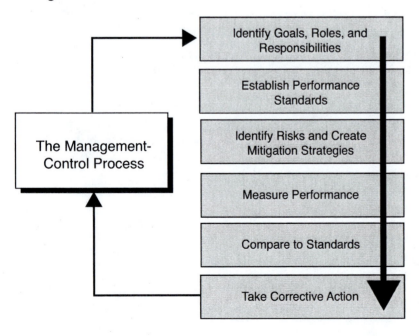

must be active management of the control framework, not simply lip service to the notion or active attention only when something goes wrong. To that end, they must be risk managers.

Risk and Risk Management: Heart of the Control Process

Risk is a principal tool for determining what to control as well as the degree of control. To identify the correct control, you must know what risks have the potential to affect the objectives being sought. However, any discussion of risk management in the public sector is fraught with misunderstanding. Even in financial management, where risk assessment and mitigation are elements of well-known sound managerial practice, an underlying concern always exists that a robust preoccupation with risks is politically unacceptable or an admission that all is not well. This is unfortunate, since the steadiness of the political state of affairs depends greatly on the support of a bureaucracy that has a capacity to mitigate many of the programmatic and political risks that often land politicians in the answerability, if not the accountability, zone to which they have some legitimate aversion. Knowledge of risk leads to one of those states where you are in grave danger without it and in equal danger with it, particularly if you know about a risk and do nothing about it. In spite of views to the contrary, no public organization is actually risk averse. The simple reality is that it delivers its programs with considerable uncertainty about certain outcomes, about factors that can affect their successful realization and about assumptions of cost, probity and predictability. Being risk averse implies not managing risks. That is not being risk averse; that is being risk stupid. An effective system of control is built on the presumption that some level of risk exists within the organization. Identifying and assessing risk but failing to act on it is irresponsible and not particularly helpful.

Rather, risk management that serves the agency and its leadership will involve the identification, assessment, mitigation, communication, and reassessment of risk on a continuing basis. For the purposes of internal control, this is essential. The dynamic of the relationship can be captured with this formula:

Risk – Control = Exposure (Residual Risk)

The controls that an agency puts in place are meant to mitigate risk. What is left is an exposure that can lead to further action should it not be tolerable to acceptance of the risk, as the probability or impact is relatively low or the costs of mitigation too high.

What is Risk and Risk Management?

Risk and risk management are directly associated with financial loss, but increasingly with more comprehensive ones associated with organizational goals and the threats to attaining them. In the public sector, the two go hand in hand. Similarly, the precision and degree of concern for certain risks will vary with the level and outlook of the organizational unit. For example, a unit operating a loan program will be very concerned about the risks of default and what steps have to be put in place either to avoid this risk (applicant clearance procedures designed for high-risk groups) or to recover money when the loan is defaulted (special programs for repayment negotiation).

Accordingly, the manager of that unit would regard the default situation as a risk that must be managed actively in order to achieve the program's objectives. At a corporate level, this may or may not be a material risk of concern to senior managers and, hence, not subject to special control procedures as they are confident that the program risk is being well managed. On the other hand, they may have a focus on the risk posed by the management of large capital projects for which they are responsible. They may want to ensure that the risks are thoroughly understood and that adequate mitigation strategies are put in place, accompanied by special reports and oversight of these projects. Suppose the senior-level management of the organization have chosen to focus on an area where there is the most danger (in their view and understanding of the risk), of the greatest financial loss and potential criticism and political embarrassment for the government. Risk, to them, becomes a matter of scale and judgement. Different levels within the organization can have different risk preoccupations and outlooks.

Definitions of risk have evolved from a focus on hazard and accident to a more strategic view that encompasses these but also looks at risks relative to the goals of the agency. Risk can broadly be defined as follows:

> *A risk is any threat, event, pattern of past or anticipated behaviour, or predicted event that could deter the organization from achieving its goals.*

For financial management, some of the forms of risk are:

- shifts in policy direction or adjustments as policy is implemented;
- changes in the costing of program inputs or parameters;
- managing funds ineffectively or illegally;
- inadequate funding combined with exaggerated objectives;

- fraud or misuse of funds;
- unforeseen circumstances that strain or threaten the financial capacity of the organization; and
- losing the confidence of the public, the legislature, donors, or stakeholders in the organization's capacity to deliver its services as promised.

We can see how readily the notion of risk can become very specific. It is built on the notion of uncertainty. Therefore, while risks may abound in the imagination, they take some work to actually anticipate, and then decide how to deal with them. We can also see how one can become consumed by risks or the fear of uncertainty. As Sir Humphrey (of the 1970s British comedy, *Yes Minister*) would say, "I can foresee all kinds of unforeseen difficulties here, minister." When the minister asked for specifics, the bureaucrat replied: "How should I know? They are unforeseen!" Of course, that is hardly effective risk management, and it is an approach that is not recommended in this text, but it was certainly effective ministerial management if Sir Humphrey's objective were to discourage his minister's desire to do something. The reality is that most political leaders fully expect their public servants to manage most of the risks in their agencies and only involve them when needed.

Risk management is the process that supports the effective treatment of risk and the controls needed for that. It can be defined in the following way:

> *Risk management is the establishment of procedures and management systems to identify, assess, validate, mitigate, and monitor risks to the organization in such a way as to eliminate them, effectively reduce their impact, or be prepared to respond to them.*

Risk management is not about risk identification alone. In fact, in public-sector organizations, just as in the private sector, leaving the process at the identification level actually opens the organization to additional risks. For instance, if a voluntary organization identified the possibility that a major donor would withdraw funding and then did nothing, the leadership of that organization would be open to criticism that it failed to respond to a real threat and placed the organization in jeopardy. Similarly, if information is received at the senior-management level that a particular program is not being effectively managed and it is possible that funds are being misspent, failure to act upon this risk puts the organization in greater peril of criticism.

Risk management operates in a continuous cycle, best demonstrated by the typical risk-management process in **Figure 9.3**. This type of cycle adequately reflects the processes that risk management entails if it is to be successful. Risks should not only be identified, but they should be managed and communicated to the organization. Further, they must be reassessed on a cyclical basis to ensure that the control procedures established to mitigate the risks are really needed.

The development of management plans is the point at which controls are assessed as adequate or not. For controls, many of which will be listed below, are both residual, that is, permanent or responsive, i.e., put in place to address an emergent risk arising from this process.

Not All Risks are Created Equal

Part of this cycle involves the need for managers to make decisions about which risks require action and which ones to do nothing about. This is often entails judgements and consideration of the organization's overall risk tolerance. Risk tolerance involves a mix of qualitative and quantitative measures. In some cases, for example, developing stress tolerances for bridges, and ensuring quantitative measures are available and verifiable. In other cases, it is less clear. In seeking some sort of quantification of risks, one must weigh the potential loss against the costs of mitigation. For instance, in entitlement programs, the cost of miscalculating eligibilities, where the error is a minor amount, may be such that the cost of preventing the error, or even collecting on an overpayment, may not make it worth trying to control for such a risk. However, the public context will

FIGURE 9.3
Risk Management Cycle

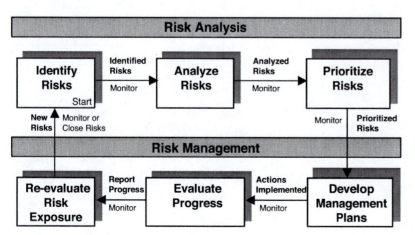

lead to the careful treatment of risks that are qualitatively significant but not necessarily quantitatively material. For example, small financial or program errors can become major political embarrassments. It also explains why many public-sector organizations are reluctant to engage in formal risk-management programs in the first place: the fear of being exposed to criticism or of embarrassing political leadership, should these risks be communicated to the public.[3]

Not all risks are the same. Agencies have to decide which ones are important enough to demand mitigation and which ones are not a significant threat, not pressing, or easily mitigated if they do occur. Key to that decision is the confidence in existing controls. Two key variables – impact and probability – are the core ways to start the risk assessment process. **Figure 9.4** shows how impact, and likelihood or probability, interact in the development of a comparative risks analysis. A variety of tools exist to assist in making defensible placements of risk in this scale. How they are used will reflect the degree of complexity of the risk challenge as well as the way in which it is used in the agency. Certainly, knowing the methodologies used makes it more understandable to a broader set of users. It also makes it more defensible to critics or oversight bodies.

Managers respond to risks in different ways, based on their impact and probability. The higher the risk is in the quadrants, the more focus and immediate the response. In many cases, however, control systems are key to managing in all quadrants. However, the degree of reporting, oversight and frequency of review of risk will be driven by where it is on this grid. It pays to be confident in the risk identification and evaluation process. The dangers are in either minimizing

the risk or in exaggerating it. Agencies take time to learn how to do this. They will have to communicate their assessment of risk within the organization, to their political leadership and to their stakeholders. At the same time, they have to say what they are going to do about them.

General Approaches to Managing Risks

It has already been pointed out that once an agency embarks on risk management, it has to be prepared to say what it did once it identified and categorized a risk. Needless to say, agencies do this all the time. Risk management provides a more systematic and disciplined platform for response. Our concern with it here is to focus on building controls that respond to risk effectively and affordably. However, as it builds the controls it needs, it has a number of broad responses, some of which obviate the need for increased controls. There are a number of approaches agencies or governments as a whole can take to mitigate risk:

- **Avoidance:** This is the "Don't go there" option. For instance, an agency might choose to not enter into what it sees as a risky public-private partnership.
- **Preventive:** Here is where controls begin to be relevant. Measures that reduce both probability and impact are extensive and will be addressed in the Control Tools section of this chapter.
- **Transfer:** For a variety of financial risks, finding or buying a partner to insure or cover losses or assume the risk for a return can reduce risk. Buying insurance, requiring performance bonds in construction projects, and changing pensions schemes from defined benefit to defined contribution schemes are examples.
  - **Share or Spread:** Finding partners to take on part of the risk
  - **Diversify:** Avoiding the tendency to put too much authority in one person, finding new sources of revenue, or having multiple suppliers can spread the risk.
  - **Hedge:** Buy or invest against future cost increases. Buy fuel in anticipation of price increases.
  - **Reduce:** This involves a range of operational, strategic and control options to actively reduce the risk. We will deal with control options below.
  - **Cap:** Limit the degree of financial exposure by capping the funds available, or limiting the amount that the program will pay.

FIGURE 9.4
Four Quadrants of Risk

High Impact/ Low Probability: Significant risks that happen infrequently	High Impact/High Probability: Significant risks that threaten business objectives
Low Impact/Low Probability: Real but non-threatening risks	Low Impact/High Probability: Risks that occur regularly

Impact ↑

Probability →

- **Create Contingency:** Create reserves to respond to risks. Take operational measures in anticipation of high impact events. Develop contingency and emergency response plans.

No agency or government can manage its risks down to zero. The world is too complex and dynamic for that. There are also costs to risk mitigation that have to be taken into account. The principle of ALARP[4] – as low as reasonably practicable – is a useful one to apply to the amount of risk mitigation that is both possible and affordable. This principle suggests using benchmarks, performance standards, or norms in a given field of practice, as well as legislative guidance.

Good risk analysis and management will drive an agency's control framework. Some elements of control are a given, a requirement of legislation, or internal government practice. However, control is not just about complying with external requirements. Risk management fills in the agency's needs.

Control: Who, What and How

Whom to Control, When to Control and Who has Control

The controls that an agency chooses will be directed by its take on its risks, on those things that the laws say it has to do, and on the expectations of its stakeholders. It has a number of choices. The first is whom to control and the second is at what point to do it. These issues are summarized in **Figure 9.5**.

FIGURE 9.5
Some Basic Choices in Setting Up a Control Framework

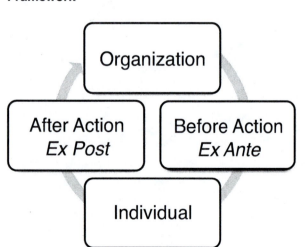

With respect to the question of whom to control, there are two approaches: the organization as a whole or an individual, be it someone working within the organization or the recipient of its services (perhaps a person who receives money from government based on an entitlement such as welfare or tax credits). Controlling at the organizational level means establishing measurements, process checks, and audits to examine the propriety of its overall actions. Applying control at the individual level will mean instituting safeguards to ensure that the individual's actions can be scrutinized either before or after the transactions occur to prevent fraud or miscalculation of benefits, or to ensure compliance with rules or standards. As to the timing, or when to control, the alternatives are to exercise control either before or after the individual or organization takes action. Before-the-fact, or *ex ante*, controls involve subjecting a decision that the organization or individual is about to make to some level of review or approval in advance. An official may not be able to authorize an entitlement of more that $2,500 for any individual claimant without a supervisor's approval. Such controls involve submitting a proposal to a superior officer or to a higher authority. They are usually incorporated into the control framework through a delegation matrix and signing-authority policies. A delegation matrix is a formal document assigning financial and other authorities to specific categories of managers. As in the example, the authority to approve expenditures up to a certain level would be defined in such a matrix. As part of the delegation matrix, the manager is assigned the authority to formally approve or sign for the transaction.

After-the-fact, or *ex post*, control involves a review process for decisions and expenditures that have already been made. In such circumstances, the actors, be they individuals or organizations, are fully responsible for the action because they had the authority to approve it and action was taken on the basis of their authorization. For example, a cheque may be issued on the authority of an individual, with no other review except to verify that it is the approved official who has that authority. Some form of control exists, through monitoring, sampling, summarized reporting, or variance analysis, to oversee the quality of decisions already made at either an individual or aggregate level.

Who is the Controller?

The next question to ask: who is the controller, and who is being controlled? This varies through the organization and may be a good example of the hierarchical rule that everyone in complex public-sector organizations is the ham in someone else's sandwich. **Figure 9.6** illustrates the scope of control that organizations may have to exercise in order to meet their objectives.

FIGURE 9.6
The Controller and the Controlled

Controller	Control Subject
Operational manager	Subordinate units
Divisional or senior manager	Operational manager
Corporate manager	Divisional or senior manager
Internal auditor	Operational manager
External auditor	Internal auditor
External auditor	Corporate manager
Corporate manager	Minister and/or legislature
Corporate manager	Board of directors
Legislature	Ministers, senior officials
Board of directors	Chief executive officer

Such a list could go on and on. The simple fact is that relationships between controller and controllee exist at many levels and operate in many ways. They are also imperfect and often clouded by other matters, be they operational, financial, or political. This imperfection of control relationships means that the reason for control – to effectively achieve the organization's goals – will not be ideally met in some circumstances.

The Array of Control Tools

The internal control environment comprises both the control environment and control procedures. The environment addresses issues of an ethical culture and the role of trust in setting control standards. Control procedures can be classified into two broad categories or systems with respect to what they do: one is to protect the resources and the other is to facilitate their effective use. Facilitative or strategic controls enable the achievement of program objectives. Protective controls are meant to protect public funds from being spent improperly or imprudently and to protect public assets from loss, theft, and damage. To express it another way, protective controls are input-oriented and facilitative controls are output-oriented.

The control framework should be set out in internal control policies, a key part in setting the tone and having an impact on the culture as well. Some of the policies needed are:

- general control framework,
- risk management,
- accounting systems,
- policies on disbursement of funds,
- contracting,
- procurement and purchasing,
- conflict of interest,
- travel,
- security of assets and personnel,
- records, and
- authorities and delegation.

We will be returning to some of these matters below.

The Control Environment: Trust and Ethics and Setting the Tone

Sound integrity and ethical values are critical to internal control. All controls are built around two notions:

- the trust the controller places in the organization or in persons with authority and responsibility, and
- the culture of ethical behaviour in the organization.

The core elements of a successful control environment that build from these notions are:

- consistent leadership and the modeling of ethical behaviour;
- an emphasis on building the competencies for effective control;
- governance processes that emphasize the solving of problems, building on lessons learned from errors, and handling errors in a corrective way;
- risk assessment; and
- monitoring of both control outputs, but also of the controls themselves to reduce complacency.

Trust

In cases of organizational control, trust is not a matter of feelings or emotion. Whether individuals are inherently trusting or trustworthy is not the matter at hand. Rather, trust is a calculation that is made by the organization about its own people, about other organizations, and about other people, as well as its leadership. Here, the waters can become murky as such calculations inevitably become mixed up with personal feelings, history, and calculations about the gap between stated intentions and capacity to actually deliver. Making trust calculations public and transparent is not easy, and it is seldom done. Nonetheless, it plays an important role in how an organization develops its approach to control.

Trust is also an important element in balancing the desire for full assurance through control (no surprises, no errors) with the cost or improbability of achieving it. In the end, more control systems, however technologically sound or detailed, depend on the people who run them. Therefore, a degree of trust is necessarily extended to operators of the systems, on the assumption that their intentions are sound and their track record indicates that such trust is deserved, taking into account what was written above – trust is conditional and rightly subject to monitoring.

Over that time, confidence and trust are built up. Organizations value their reputation and work hard to maintain it. Talking about it very seldom cuts it: it takes a proven record. For example, a long-term, dependable supplier of service with a proven track record for good delivery and sound management is a valued asset to any organization. But trust relationships can collapse any time. In the public sector, governments often forget the importance of these relationships when they over-react, by immediately moving to enact draconian measures of control. At that point, trust just flies out the window.

An Ethical Culture

All of this control could be happening while, with the wrong values in play, serious intrusions into public trust could be accruing. This could be either through misappropriating public funds, using them for purposes not intended, or diverting them to personal uses. It is axiomatic that public-sector organizations and the people within them have to act in an ethical manner. Therefore, ensuring that the ethical framework of the organizations and their personnel is sound is yet another form of control, one that is essential to the success of all other efforts. As the auditor general of Canada has noted:

> The promotion of values and ethics is an essential part of a good governance framework that needs to be continually and systematically addressed to help ensure probity and the long-term viability of federal entities.[5]

Individual managers and decision makers are often faced with ethically challenging situations that require them to make some form of judgement, often with competing goods to be achieved. Sorting through such dilemmas is not simple. When public funds are at stake as well as adherence to the law, the stakes can be high and the pressures great.

An ethical framework for effective financial management is closely linked to how the organization is managed

overall. Therefore, in thinking about the role of ethics in this one area, it is important to see that ethical behaviour is to be valued in all aspects of the organization's behaviour.[6] There is no room for "Do as I say, not as I do." That is what is meant by tone at the top.

Some of the tools that public-sector organizations use to ensure that they are promoting ethical behaviour are:

- establishing codes of conduct or ethics;
- supporting sanctions for ethical misconduct;
- using merit principles in hiring and promotion;
- employing a wide variety of training initiatives on ethics for both new employees and those already in position;
- identifying high-risk positions (not persons) where either special training on ethical challenges or special surveillance is called for;
- disclosing any conflicts of interest and policies to support this, noting that this becomes more important the higher the level of the position;
- creating mechanisms to report misconduct of superiors and adequate safeguards for those reporting (i.e., confidential channels and whistleblower legislation);
- establishing ombudsman positions;
- providing ethical counsellors, trainers, offices; and
- involving professional associations, such as the CICA, to develop ethical guidelines for membership.

Clearly, control does not happen without adequate values and ethics to support it. As Washington and Armstrong note:

> By definition, the management of ethics and conduct is not just about monitoring and policing behaviour. It is also about promoting integrity and good conduct. It is about seeking some consensus on what is good behaviour and giving public servants some guidance as to how they should act, make decisions, and use discretion in their everyday work.[7]

Therefore, addressing ethics as part of an overall control strategy makes good sense and is probably less costly than additional regulatory measures.

Facilitative or Strategic Control

Facilitative controls are closely linked to the strategic outcomes of the agency. They are aimed at ensuring that the organization maintains an effective alignment between its operations and its desired outcomes. Therefore, they focus on building the capacity to control positively to correct variance at that level. Facilitative-control systems are exemplified by financial planning and forecasting systems, and by integrated financial and non-financial performance systems. They alert managers to the need to revise plans and take actions so as to correct identified problems or to take advantage of newly identified opportunities. This category includes controls designed to collect, record, and process financial data and prepare timely reports. People do not usually think of data collection, processing, and reporting as part of their organization's internal control system, but without an effective information system, there will be no evidence that the controls are working. In addition, facilitative controls are concerned with having the right people with the right skills in the right jobs. They also have a strong governance element: is their effective managerial oversight, direction and the capacity to redirect resources adequate to make corrections or adapt as risks are identified?

Controls in the facilitative category include:

- A governance system that regularly reviews risk, sets priorities, assigns accountabilities and reviews the results.
- Policies to address the issues listed above and provide consistent guidance.
- An audit oversight process that focuses on key risk areas with external advice.
- Policies assigning responsibility for various information-gathering tasks to various parts of the organization, such as the financial officer, the financial analysis group, or a performance-monitoring group.
- Reports defining the information the organization wishes to receive and analyze on a regular basis.
- Reports created so they are understood by senior managers or board members and management. Overly complex or simplistic reports will result in poor communication of financial data.
- Financial performance information is communicated, along with, and clearly connected to, operational information and comparisons with plans and budgets, so that the information can be used for making decisions and achieving program objectives.
- Sound financial reporting – both external and internal – is accompanied by the use of standard analytical tools such as forecasting, use of historical data, ratio analysis, effective cash management, and quality of financial reports.
- Qualified staff is trained on control mechanisms.
- Conflict of interest guidelines exist.
- Regular monitoring of control systems to test their effectiveness, and providing checklists on key activities guide staff and suppliers on the required steps for proper compliance.

Protective Controls

Protective controls run the gambit of established practices and controls unique to the business of the agency, department or government. Because they are connected, some of the preventive controls that might be part of a control framework are not strictly financial but contribute to financial security. The principal categories of protective control activities are:

- a delegation matrix that clearly defines financial authorities for individuals in the organization and also limits their authority, thereby requiring the approval of a higher level position or cross-check with another officer;
- adequate separation of duties;
- proper authorization of transactions and activities;
- measures to control theft or fraud;
- background checks on employees in sensitive areas;
- password protection protocols;
- regular and required software protection testing;
- adequate documents and records;
- physical control over assets and records along with regular inventories;
- reconcilliation of financial and related statements, variance analyses, physical inventories and audits;
- independent checks on compliance, accuracy and performance;
- establishment of error tolerances and gates that require a higher level of review;
- active supervision, including inspections; and
- controls to verify financial records (monthly reviews and annual audits).

These examples will involve a mix of manual and automated controls. Increasingly, first level checking of error patterns, authorization overrides, or increased incidents of correction are captured within analytical data systems that generate reports to higher level supervisors as alerts.

Testing the Controls

Having a control framework in place can create a sense of trust and confidence. It can also create complacency. As control is driven by risk and risk is such a dynamic variable in the organizational environment, the controls themselves need to be monitored to make sure they are working, are addressing the real risks and can be trusted. It is not wise to assume that, if controls are strong enough, there will be no fraud, or that errors will be captured and the financial statements will be accurate. The reality is that controls provide reasonable, but not absolute, assurance that objectives are being met. In the end, controls rely on the people who operate them, even when they are themselves subject to technological review of their actions. Aside from the need to audit control systems on a periodic basis, there are signs that controls are not fully effective. Some of these show up and should be taken for signals that controls might need to be rethought:

- Regular evidence of inadequate knowledge of the control requirements, as in "I didn't know that" when they should have.
- Inadequate segregation of duties, as in "We trust Mr. X who does it all so well that we need not worry." Evidence is very clear that most fraud is committed by long-term, trusted employees.
- Evidence of inappropriate access to assets. Passwords on stickies on computers, offices open inappropriately, files left lying around.
- Control as form over substance, as in "I always just sign this stuff off. No worries."
- Your senior financial advisor says, "Don't worry, be happy. I've got it all under control."
- Control override, as in "I don't care how this happens, just do it."

Finding the Balance Between Control, Discretion and Cost

There is a tension between the level of control exercised over managers and the degree of freedom or discretion that they have to actually do the work that they are there to do. This involves many dimensions of management: decision scope, the capacity to reallocate funds, and the ability to respond to emerging situations. The key elements of control are the amount of delegated authority, reporting requirements, actual discretion, and what is seen as the time and money burden of control. The challenge is how to maintain accountability while ensuring that service is being given.

Control is not costless. It is a normal part of the administration of an organization but cost is a major factor in determining the amount of control. Further, governments can transfer control over some costs to other organizations when they contract with them to perform services, accompanied by reporting requirements at a level of detail that either increases overall project costs or else diverts funds from direct program delivery to supporting control functions.

Risk and public interest will drive the degree of control that an organization will want. It will also determine whether the controls should be *ex ante* or *ex post*. In general, *ex ante*

controls are more costly in that they apply to whole categories of expenditures, all of which must pass through the gate to be authorized. Further, they increase costs in the sense that they generally slow down processes, reducing the efficiency of the operation and, by implication, reducing services to the recipient. Ways can be found to expedite such processes, such as defining gates at a risk level that permits some payments to go through automatically and some to be held because of risk factors, such as high cost. Sometimes this will involve a dollar threshold below which a certain amount does not require authorization or pre-audit while amounts above it involve some form of supervisory or second-opinion review. This is an example of how costs can be mitigated, even in a high-risk environment that demands *ex ante* forms of control.

Controls can also be costly in that they may limit managerial discretion to respond to unique circumstances. This discretion is usually sought in the name of improved client service or adaptation to special needs in a specific community. Another variant on this is that managers may have to pursue higher-cost solutions to problems because policies demand certain processes even though there may be advantages to moving more quickly to find low-cost solutions. Consider a manager seeking to stretch her funds, who sees a sale of office furniture at costs significantly below the standing offers that she is required to draw from. Procedures do not permit her to take advantage of such savings. She could, however, use her authority to make local purchases with a government credit card to make a number of lower-cost purchases from this sale, meet her office needs, and maximize the budget potential. This would improve the office environment and, hopefully, productivity. Is this breaking the rules or applying them creatively? Managers often have to confront controls that they see as constraints that increase costs and reduce their budgetary potential.

Another cost of controls derives from their demands on managerial attention. What is the appropriate balance between focus on the client or program objectives and focus on taxpayers' rights to sound financial management of their resources? This rhetorical overstatement of the issue does serve to illustrate the dilemma facing many managers and organizations: when is there enough control, and at what point does it begin to reduce organizational effectiveness? There is no clear answer to such questions. While it is trite to say that a proper balance must be struck, in the public sector, control too often wins out. Of course, this is followed by accusations of mindless bureaucracy running rampant at the cost of service. Similarly, bureaucrats can become preoccupied with controls as a way of protecting themselves against criticism, or worse, when something goes wrong. This obsession with control, repeated often enough, makes it become the actual work of the organization, instead of the work for which it was created.

Things to watch for as indicators that there are excessive or inappropriately placed controls:

- Too many details make it impossible to see the larger picture.
- More time is being spent on feeding information into control systems than is spent serving the client.
- Control systems take too narrow a focus, being too financial or quantitative, to serve their strategic need.
- There is a glass ceiling on variance and problem areas in that senior managers do not give it enough attention.
- Controls are not trusted.

Finally, third-party deliverers of public services can suffer when government controls become excessive. In contracting, part of the goal is to transfer many of the administrative burdens to the deliverer, but contracting agents often demand a level of reporting detail that effectively turns the third party into an arm of government control. Part of what is contracted is the ability to deliver the public good. Organizations, especially in the voluntary sector, often face a reporting burden that distracts personnel from their ability to deliver the goods contracted for.

Whatever the control framework, it must be weighed against what it costs to operate and its effect on the organization itself and its delivery systems. It also has to be weighed against what constitutes reasonable expectations of return; that is, measuring good control against risk and political necessity. Is it worth the money? In the public sector, factors of politics enter very quickly into this calculation. That is perfectly valid, and a part of the democratic process. Hopefully, such calculation is informed and considered and not simply rapid knee movements.

The Concept of Controllership in Government

Increasingly, governments, especially larger ones, are organizing to develop centres of policy and oversight, known as controllership offices. These are intended to strengthen the government's capacity to set government-wide policies to meet the strategic control needs across departments. Some of the activities that these offices are concerned with drive right to the heart of effective control. In fact, the modernization of financial reporting and improvement of systems to support that are key control improvements

that government has been able to achieve. Therefore, a controller will be preoccupied by:

- the establishment of accounting standards and the adoption of standard definitions and interpretations to permit the comparison of financial performance information;
- creation of policies for risk management and assurance that it is implemented in operating units within government;
- policies for key asset management practices such as procurement, management of assets and liabilities;
- development of a competent control community of employees within government, serving as a focus for knowledge and training development; and
- integrating financial with other strategic performance information to give a full picture of performance.

A report of the provincial auditor of Ontario noted the impact of these changes on control frameworks:

> Public-sector controllers have historically focused primarily on establishing basic accounting systems and financial controls to, for example, ensure that government spending is within the levels approved by the Legislature. However, over the last decade there have been a number of initiatives at the federal and provincial government level to expand this traditional role of the controller.[8]

At the heart of the efforts by several governments to improve their controllership was a recognition that a disconnect had occurred, as discussed above, between the goals of the organization and the available means to exercise the necessary levels of controls. Part of that disconnect is the inadequacy of the financial community in understanding the program goals of many public-sector organizations and align the control framework to achieve them in a cost-effective and legal manner. Historically, the controllers' philosophy has been that one size would fit all, regardless of the risk, the understanding, and competence of the staff and the form of the organization. Modern public-sector controllers have had to make a major transition from the public accounting techniques of the past and also from controllership practices.

This modernization process is certainly consistent with the objectives of effective control – of an organization being "in control" rather than simply "under control." The main elements of this effort have focused on training, staffing standards, and quality of information. Many governments have moved forward with efforts to keep up with the pace of change in public-sector management in general. One of the tools introduced in the process of the modernization of controllership is the capacity checklist, which is one way to ensure an organization is keeping pace with changes and that its financial and control functions are supporting the goals of the organization effectively. Such checklists have been developed for nonprofits and governments. An example can be found in **Appendix 3, Federal Government Controllership Capacity Checklist** and **Appendix 4, The Financial Management Capability Model: Auditor General of Canada.**

Chapter 10
Cash Management: In-Year Budget Control and Monitoring

Chapter Objectives:

- Defining cash management
- Understanding its role in budget-management processes
- Developing and applying a cash-management cycle
- Using forecasting and analytical tools to better manage the approved budget

As we saw in the last chapter, control of public resources is a continuous process. While the characterizations of active *ex ante* and *ex post* controls are important, managing resources within the current year requires additional tools that involve financial condition analysis as well as projections about future behaviour and plans. This is real-time control, which seeks to answer, and then do something about, questions such as:

- What has happened to our budget plan so far this year?
- Are we are on target for our budget projections?
- What do we project is going to happen for the remainder of the budget year?
- How do we explain the variances?
- Where can we find funds to meet some short-term demands that are well within our mandate and authority, but for which we have not allocated funds?
- What will we do with a surplus resulting from an unanticipated drop in program levels?
- Is this a permanent or temporary situation?
- What does this tell us about our managers' performance?

By answering such questions and then taking steps to address gaps, change strategies, reallocate funds or take corrective action, managers can better ensure that resources are available to support the level and quality of services and programs for which they are responsible.

Defining Cash Management

This chapter focuses on what is needed to help answer such questions, a process that we call cash management. This term is, admittedly, used somewhat idiosyncratically here by comparison with its use in other accounting and financial-management texts. In some definitions, cash management can refer to the tools to manage money at hand: the treasury or liquidity-management functions. This would encompass banking policies, investment strategies and practice, and policies for safeguarding the funds.

In essence, then, cash management as discussed in this text embraces a broad range of control practices associated with the monitoring of financial performance within the current fiscal year (in-year) to ensure that adjustments can be and are made to accommodate changes with respect to the plan and budget. The following definition covers the goal and scope of cash management:

> *Cash management is the formal system which compares actual expenditures against unit spending plans for a given financial year, identifies risks and variances and enables the adjustment of resource allocations to reflect changed circumstances in the that year.*

The objectives of creating a system for organizational cash management are to:

- have funds to pay the bills (i.e., sufficient liquidity) and meet budget targets;
- use budgeted resources for their program purposes, and not leave needed funds unspent and program goals unmet;
- keep within the appropriated or authorized budget;
- have the organizational and resource capacity to react to changes in plans;
- reallocate available funds to meet emerging, short-term priorities; and
- assess managerial performance, correct errors, adapt to unplanned shifts, and learn from this to adapt future budgets and program parameters.

Cash management is not a way to re-open the budget decisions but to adapt to changing circumstances. It encompasses the various elements necessary to effectively manage the assigned budget of a unit within the year over which it is to be implemented. This means that some of the keys to good cash management are:

- Effective cash-flow projections and forecasting in order to assess the organization's performance against plan and budget.
- Reports to the appropriate authorities to alert them to changes, confirm that the budget will be spent according to plans, release surplus funding for reallocation, and monitor managerial performance to make adjustments in the short term.
- Governance procedures to ensure timely review of financial and performance information and to make decisions to adjust programs, reassess budgets, or find alternative strategies such as increasing cash available or reallocating unneeded funds.

This definition stresses that cash management is a formal process or system. In our personal finances, most of us keep an eye on how much money we have, how much we need, and whether there is a gap. We also look to build savings or other non-current assets to deal with contingencies, emergencies or opportunities as they arise. For most budget managers, the same is true. They generally know what their budget is, how they expect to spend it, and whether or not they have the funds, resources, or cash to meet their obligations as part of that plan. Like a private individual, many public sector managers, especially those in smaller agencies, depend on transfers from funding governments or a fee-based income flow, and will also keep an eye on their liquidity to, as noted above, simply be able to meet payroll and pay the bills.

Of course, cash-management strategies can be more complex and formal than the actions of a single prudent manager. They involve the systems that organizations use to manage their in-year budgets to maximum effect. They range from the manager's concerns, as just outlined, to the preoccupation of the financial advisor or controller with ensuring that adequate monitoring of budget behaviour based on reliable financial and operational information will properly signal to the senior manager that those in the organization are operating within their funding authorities, that the plans laid out in the approved budget are unfolding as anticipated, that changes are being managed or recognized, that surpluses are identified for reallocation, and that managers are performing well. Hence, there is a need for formal reporting and structures. Cash management, for all this, is part of the overall management framework of an organization. **Figure 10.1** suggests the relationship of key factors in understanding the budget position in-year of an organization. There is clearly no single measure that can completely describe the relative financial position of an organization. Further, as the cash management process combines past performance relative to budget, an assessment of the current financial and risk situation, and projections about future behaviour, all the factors in this framework are coming into play, as we will see when we describe the cash management process itself. The framework makes the key point that effective cash management requires a sensitivity to the environment as it changes, to program parameters that are in flux, to changes within the organization – here we mean the unit, department and government – that will change the rules of the game, and finally, to the financial condition based on emerging performance data, financial reports and analyses.

Before we take a closer look at cash management strategies, it is probably wise to be reminded of what can go wrong. To that end, **Figure 10.2** offers some scenarios that are best avoided if possible. In addition, this, like budgeting, is part of financial management that if rife with gaming. Therefore, Appendix 6 describes *The Cash-Management Games People Play.* While both are offered in a somewhat tongue-in-cheek manner, the point is serious: how you manage resources put into your hands reflects upon your reputation as a manager and your credibility as a seeker of more resources, expanded scope, or support in risk taking.

FIGURE 10.1
Framework for In-Year Budget Management

FIGURE 10.2
Some Cash Management Scenarios Most Public Managers Would Like to Avoid

Topping the Pinocchio Index	This index is the work of the C.D. Howe Institute,* which annually reports overall budget overruns at the government level. Its 2011 report claims that governments have overspent approved budget plans by $82 billion over the previous ten years.
Overspending the budget and knowing about it	This can be a form of risk management or a commitment to a program objective regardless of the costs. The degree of forgiveness will vary dramatically across governments.
Overspending the budget and not knowing it	This is a sign of negligence and bad management. Surprise is not a healthy part of financial management.
Underspending the budget but not meeting program needs	This is a situation that requires some nuanced analysis before coming to conclusions, as there may well be legitimate reasons for this. It remains, for the most part, something to avoid.
Underspending the budget and not knowing	See above, but dumb and dumber seems to coalesce here.
Getting financial information too late to be able to do anything about it	This places the manager in a bind, reduces organizational flexibility and brings into question the quality of financial advice.
Commitments that mask potential surpluses for reallocation	This is seen as a protective defensive measure, but hardly a corporate move.
Too little, too late	Funds arrive too late to spend. This leaves a surplus that may or may not be available for profiling in future years.

* Retrieved at http://www.cdhowe.org/pinocchio-index-shows-governments%E2%80%99-budget-overruns-total-82-billion-c-d-howe-institute/14694.

In-Year Cash Management Versus Budget Planning

Budget planning and in-year cash management are different, although linked, as it is only through effective cash management that budget plans are realized. **Figure 10.3** offers some illustrations of those differences, some of which we will review in more detail. The focus of cash management is on the current fiscal year: how to ensure that cash is available, how to ensure that the budget plan or budget is being carried out, and how to react and adjust when it is not. One exception to this would be a flexible-budget organization, one that is so dependent on earnings that it has to constantly adjust its program in response to those changes. Such would be the situation of an organization with no reserves or base funding that is totally dependent, for instance, on fees income. No amount of budget planning will avoid the need for rapid response in this instance. On the other hand, even in this rather extreme example, the organization will have a concept of the desirable service level and some form of plan or budget to achieve with the funds available. Most organizations in the public sector, however, have budgets that are known and relatively stable. For them, cash management plays an essential role in completing the budget process.

Second, the objective of cash management is not to change budgets on the run. Rather, it is to use the approved budget plans as a tool of control to compare actual performance with the plan. Any gaps between these two

can lead to challenges: find funds, use or deploy funds that are not needed, or reallocate. More will be said about these processes later, but managers will use such controls reluctantly, only if they feel they will not permanently lose surplus funds that become available from temporary program changes. In fact, to avoid losing funds, they may well commit them as having been spent, so as not to be penalized by losing surpluses at the end of the fiscal year. This has led to all kinds of aberrant end-of-year spending as organizations try to come in just on budget without "leaving money on the table."

The one exception to this is a budget change arising from legislative or policy changes during the year. As noted in the discussion of budget processes, most governments employ a supplementary estimates or budgeting process throughout the fiscal year that allows the approval of appropriations for such changes. In such instances, the manager may receive new permanent funding. For governments, the gap in time between initiating a new cost stream by way of policy or legislation and approving the appropriation may be significant, especially for large expenditures, but there may well be strong political pressure to get the changes up and running. That is when the government as a whole has a cash-management problem: finding the funds to provide interim financing. Larger governments tend to have contingency and reserve funds to cover some shortfalls. Alternatively, they can increase borrowing.

FIGURE 10.3
Differences Between Budgeting and Cash Management

	Budgeting	Cash Forecasting and Management
Objective	Allocates resources, sets authorizations, limits and targets.	Project and manage gaps between budget projections and actual results.
Process objectives	Lock in and secure resources.	Maximize use of resources through corrective management or reallocation.
Main preoccupations	Government and agency priorities Projected targets for performance and restraint Sources of revenue Optimal allocation	Current situation Variance: why and significance relative to cost and risk Action to correct and adapt Interim reallocation
Time horizon	Long term and permanent	In-year and adaptive
Variability and frequency of change	Linked to annual planning cycles, but subject to interim adjustment.	Can be highly variable within year depending on risk and volatility.
Work timeframe	Done in advance of year and with considerable notice.	As current as possible and needed Frequent updates

Third, good cash management does affect future budgeting and may well expose the inadequacy of the current budget relative to the organization's planned outputs. Managers may signal shortfalls that, upon examination, turn out to be of a permanent nature. An important question in variance analysis is whether the cost surge is temporary or permanent. As well, if budgets are consistently underspent, the organization may, over time, question if the amounts budgeted are too high.

A Budget in Hand: Good First Step

What follows is a discussion about how to establish an effective system to forecast, monitor, and manage cash throughout the budget year. This is built on the simple – and perhaps somewhat hopeful – assumption that the manager has a budget in hand to manage. One of the challenges of financial management in the public sector is that this is not always the case. It is a sign of sound management within the organization, and of good political or board leadership as a whole, when budgets are approved and distributed to operating units on time, i.e., in advance of the beginning of the organization's fiscal year. When they are not, it creates uncertainty and difficulty for operating managers. It reduces their capacity to develop an adequate understanding of budget limitations and possibilities. It also loses valuable time in the cash-management cycle of the fiscal year. Managers will be reluctant to declare surpluses if they are uncertain of receiving all the funds they believe they need. Similarly, as a precautionary measure, they may declare the potential that they will not have sufficient funds, as a means of protecting themselves, should their full budget not arrive.

There are many causes for delays in finalizing budget distribution. The agency may be uncertain about its own financial position. It may be dependent, as is the case in so much of the health care sector, on more senior government funding decisions. In such a situation, moving into the new fiscal year with current staff and program levels may create the potential for a cash crisis. Not doing so can create a program crisis. In other instances, it is possible that a department or agency of government has its budget, but has not completed an internal distribution, for many reasons: disputes over distribution, conflict between distributed funding and centrally held reserves or special funds, disputes over budget levels affecting potential operating levels, new cost formulae, etc. Operating managers are often left to go into the first quarter of the fiscal year without knowing the exact budget. As so many of them have, they carry on as if they had the money.

Another source of such discontinuity lies in intergovernmental transfers and governmental funding of major public institutions such as universities and hospitals. Often these institutions are left in highly ambiguous positions on costing formulae and are unable to establish a base budget. There may also be multiple sources of funding that affect an operating unit or program. For instance, the organization may have a complex matrix-type structure in which certain funds are held by functional specialists and distributed separately from the main operating budget. One example of this is information technology, in which both capital and support functions are managed centrally. This becomes a problem when funds are distributed from such functional specialists to the operating manager, who must negotiate the best equipment and service levels for his unit. This may or may not take place in a timely manner.

As mentioned, the ideal state is that operating managers know their budgets at the beginning of the fiscal year. Unfortunately, organizations tend to repeat themselves: they develop a culture that accepts such delays as a way of doing business. While this clearly devalues good financial management in the organization and probably prevents the organization from maximizing its resources, such repetition also makes it relatively risk-free for managers to assume that, all things being equal, last year's budget, along with any changes they are aware of, is probably what will be the final product. This would at least enable operating managers to begin making projections, since this is in their interest as good managers. In all probability, an organization that cannot get its act together to adopt a budget will also accept some slippage on its cash forecasts – and wonder why funds were left unspent at the corporate level.

Establishing a Cash-Management System

Any cash management system is built on three questions, shown in **Figure 10.4.**

A cash-management system will have the following elements:

- an appropriated budget;
- changes and modifications to the approved budget to create an adjusted budget;
- projections over the budget period on how the money will be spent: the in-year cash flow or expenditure plan, a system of measuring actual financial performance in relation to the projected plan;
- a system of monitoring performance, identification of variances, and reporting results at the appropriate level.

- the capacity for management discussion and analysis of the results and variances; and
- a governance mechanism that would review the results, assess variances, determine necessary adjustments, and make decisions needed to effect those adjustments.

FIGURE 10.4
The Three Big Questions in Cash Management (and in Most Financial Control)

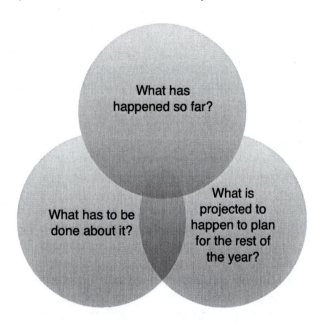

These elements of the cash-management system are tied together in graphic form in **Figure 10.5.**

In this cycle, organizational roles and responsibilities will vary, but any system for forecasting, monitoring, and management of cash will involve a combination of interests and tasks:

- Senior management sets budgets and program direction.
- Line managers manage within the resources they are given to carry out programs.
- Financial advisors must provide information to budget-setters for their decision making, as well as advice to line managers about their budgets.
- Financial advisors provide information and analysis to identify variances, offer comparisons and further analysis of budget performance, and make recommendations to line managers and senior managers.
- Financial advisors prepare reports to enable senior managers to make decisions.

- Line managers respond to variances against plans, with explanations, solutions, and alternatives.
- Senior managers determine what actions to take on the basis of these two sets of inputs.

Preparing a Cash-Management Plan

Once there is sufficient certainty about the resources available for the year – that is, the approved or appropriated budget – the challenge becomes how the funds will flow over the course of the year. Depending on the organization, there may be emphasis on both inflows (revenues) and outflows (expenditures) or a focus on expenditures only. For instance, where an organization that is dependent upon a series of cash inflows from donations, grants, and government transfers to set an in-year financial plan in place, it has to make some assumptions about exactly when the funds will arrive and be available for program use. Knowing how and when funds flow into this type of organization is not as precarious an exercise as might be thought. In fact, most organizations can, indeed, predict their cash inflows based on:

- Previous patterns of inflow in the past year; for example, donations tend to peak regularly, during major fundraising events; major government funding tends to flow twice a year, provided the grants are approved in advance.
- Anticipation of any changes that might cause such a flow to be altered; for example, the organization decides that it will change its fundraising campaign to a different type and a different time, or a major donor adjusts some criteria and is reviewing its procedures, which may create delays.
- Timing of the maturity of investments or endowments in various funds may be a factor. Restrictions governing particular funds may not permit the movement of money from one fund to the other, but the availability of cash in one fund may be important if some form of inter-fund borrowing or temporary transfer is permitted within the organization's rules for fund management.
- Awareness of the timing of cash outflow requirements is necessary to match them up with inflows. For example, major capital expenses are anticipated for the summer, thereby necessitating a surge in demand for cash outflow in late summer.

For many government organizations, the question of cash inflows is not one that they have to address. Budgets are set, and the manager does not have to be concerned about finding the money to meet the obligations. As already

FIGURE 10.5
The Cash-Management Cycle

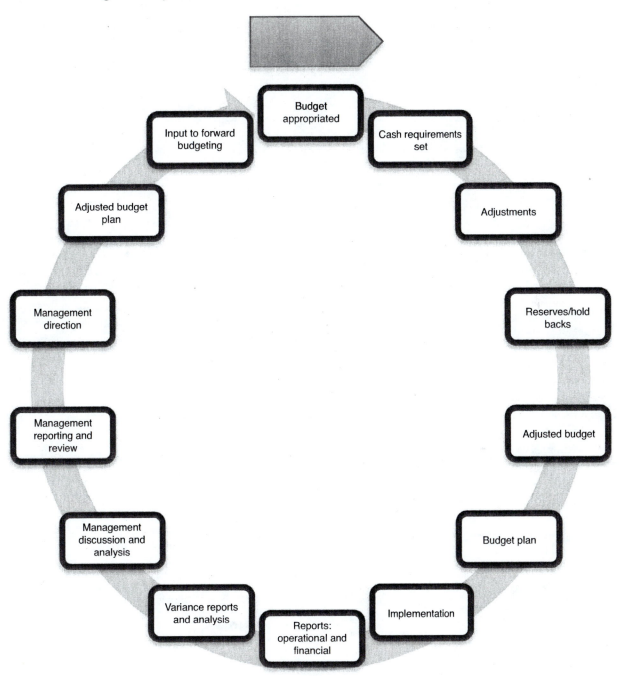

noted, management of revenue inflows through taxes and other means is a treasury function that is attended to on their behalf. Their focus, then, will be on the other side of cash flows: the expenditure side.

This chapter is concerned with the cash management of expenses that are detailed in the organization's operating budget. This usually encompasses funds for staff salaries and benefits, supplies, equipment, and operational funds, whether they are for disbursements to individuals, various elements of the care and support to clients, or the purchase of services to meet program objectives. Although cash-flow planning for individual capital projects is not included in this, the principles remain similar.

Managers often see budget-plan forecasts as difficult to make and, to some extent, unrealistic. They also characterize them as straitjackets in which managers are held to account for the financial performance of their operations despite many unpredictable and uncontrollable elements. In other words, forecasts are seen as meeting some financial needs, but having very little to do with the real world of day-to-day operations. There can be some truth in this, which makes it important to build reporting systems that are both useful and realistic. This takes the collaborative efforts of managers, senior leaders, and financial advisors working together over time, with respect for the challenges each faces. Through this process, they can arrive at a consensus about the forecasting efforts, their use and relevance, and their continuing credibility. Such an effort can be hard work for an organization that faces operational and financial challenges. Failure to make the effort means loss of control over one of the key elements of getting the work done – the money.

Managers who are asked to submit budget forecasts are really estimating the work flow that they can achieve with the funds they have. They are assessing the environment, measuring risks and setting in place their best predictions of how resources will be spent. Unfortunately, in many cases, such information is not used beyond being entered in the financial reporting system and used to compare actual performance to budget without sufficient managerial attention. In some cases, not even this happens. Some managers simply adopt the divide-by-twelve approach, which amounts to little more than filling in the blanks. Organizations that act this way might as well not waste their time even trying to manage their cash. They lose significant opportunities to ensure that budgetary fluctuations are managed effectively or that overages or underages demand or permit reallocation to meet priorities. In other words, they lose real control of their limited resources to forces they do not care to pay attention to.

In a refreshingly open acknowledgement of the importance of good forecasting, a school in the United Kingdom stated:

It is essential to closely monitor the budget because:

- The school may realize extra funding during the year leading to a larger surplus than expected, in which case the school may wish to meet some requests for additional funding that had previously been put on hold.
- Unexpected expenditures may occur, e.g., building works in the summer may overrun budget, or additional members of staff may be required.

- There may be a shortfall in expected income, such as lettings or bank interest.
- The number of pupils arriving in September may be more or less than estimated on the January PLASC return.
- Initial assumptions in preparing the annual budget could be wrong.[1]

It is therefore vital that organizations create rules for budget forecasting that make sense, that are based on solid facts and data, not just derived by dividing by twelve.

It has often been argued that establishing a plan for expenditures over the year is an unrealistic exercise. This may be true for organizations that do not take their financial management seriously. Nevertheless, failing to do so misses potential opportunities to use unneeded funds. It also shows that the organization is not ready to put in place control systems to monitor behaviour and adjust resources accordingly. Rather, it becomes a victim of events that it might have anticipated. As a first step in this process, the cash-management plan sets out predicted expenditure flows based on budget limitations. How this is distributed will depend on the organization.

Spending Plan: Estimating Budget Performance for the Reporting Period

The degree of detail needed: Should the plan be based on the approved line items in the budget? Should it be at the level of the responsibility centre head, or more disaggregated or aggregated? For instance, the responsibility centre head may have four units performing essentially the same duties, but in different locations, and with somewhat different staffing patterns, and may want to project expenditure patterns on a unit-by-unit basis to permit better monitoring of each unit's management of its resources. She, in turn, may only be asked to prepare a plan for all her units.

The period frequency: Is the plan to be built on a monthly or quarterly basis? In high-risk areas, the reporting may need to be even more frequent. Here, the issues are risk and materiality: just how important is it to know the pattern of expenditures at this level of time detail?

The treatment of one-time expenditures: Not all expenditures flow on a periodic basis over the year. Certainly expenditures like salaries and disbursements and grants do, but most budgets have one-time expenditures as well. For example, the purchase of computers may be a budget item for data-processing centres in the organization. Whether it is material to know if these purchase are going to be made all at once or throughout the year will depend once again on the organization. The treasury people will definitely want to know when the orders will be filled and the accounts become payable. Those for whom this is less relevant have two options: book the expenditures in the plan as a one-time event at the beginning of the year, thereby committing the full funds, or schedule the purchases in the plan so that they can be reflected in financial monitoring later on.

The role of budget caps or conditions: One challenge for budget managers is that the senior line or staff managers at the corporate level may intervene in the approved budgets to limit the manager's discretion, or higher authorities within the organization may set an expenditure target below what the manager budgeted. In general, most budgets are not approved by legislatures at a level of detail that would reflect individual units within organizations. In fact, they are generally at the program level.

Similarly, while formal budgets may be approved by the corporate level of the organization for reporting and accounting purposes, senior management may choose to set reduction targets in certain areas to ensure that funds will be available for other purposes, or that areas of special concern are addressed as a management priority. Suppose that, in its strategic planning, the organization decides that it will need 1 percent of operating funds to meet an emerging political need for more support to communications initiatives of concern to the minister. Instructions may flow that all units will target their salary and other operating budgets at 99 percent of the approved budget. In another instance, the organization may be greatly concerned about the level of overtime caused by staff absenteeism, especially staff working shifts in continuous operations. It may target a reduction in overtime expenditures of 5 percent over the year.

In either example, the budget plans have to take such adjustments to their budget into account. In fact the 99 percent mentioned above becomes the new 100 percent for the responsibility centre manager. She will have to manage that reduction and distribute it within her plan. It would be folly to have a budget plan that spends the full original 100 percent, even when the budget manager feels she needs all those funds to meet her current obligations. What she must do in such instances is ensure that it is understood in the organization that she will operate in a different way because of a decline in the resources that are available. This is often a source of tension within organizations because some senior managers come to the view that efficiencies and better management should make

it possible to deliver the same level of program or better. In some instances, this is indeed true. In others, it is not.

Reserves or hold-backs: Does the organization distribute the full budget to the responsibility centre managers or is some held in reserve to be distributed later in the year, on the basis of need and merit? This is a complex cash-management question. Organizations follow many different routes with an eye to enforcing good management and also to having flexibility to respond to emerging issues at the corporate level. Such issues in the public sector are often political and short-term in nature. Others are catastrophic events demanding massive and timely resource responses.

The existence of a central pot of funds, often called a reserve or contingency fund, has many implications for the organization. These will be discussed further below. However, with an eye to the creation of a cash-management plan, the real question is whether a portion of the responsibility centre manager's budget is being held back for this reserve within the year being planned. Reserves are often a permanent element of the organization's budget, but as we see further on, the reserve can be a useful tool in resolving cash-management issues for the organization.

The issue of hold-backs is somewhat similar to that of caps or expenditure limitations but less directed at specific managerial action to reduce cost flows over the year. Rather, monies within the responsibility centre manager's budget may be held back for other purposes; for example, a certain portion of grant funds or supply money may be held back to permit pooled purchases, so that they can be managed either centrally, with other units, or as a pool. There is also the question of whether the amount received will really be needed over the period, given anticipated changes to policy or the law or flows of demands. For instance, while the grants portion of the budget may reflect previous years, a recent decision to limit eligibilities to certain organizations and thereby eliminate others may mean that the program will shift considerably. The hold-back would then be used as a form of protection for the funds by a senior manager to ensure they are available for other purposes. It is also implied that the funds held back would become available should they actually be needed.

Arriving at an Adjusted Budget

Before coming up with a cash-management plan, the manager must know the exact budget he is working with. This involves making adjustments for some of the elements that we have described that affect the cash available. Budgets can be adjusted any time of the year if they are affected by either the addition of new budget funds, changes in programs through policy or law, or mandated reductions. For the purposes of creating a budget plan, however, the initial adjusted budget should closely resemble the approved budget, unless any hold-back factors come into play. The most important quality of an opening adjusted budget is that it should fairly represent to all who will use it the actual funds available to the manager for use in the program.

Figure 10.6 provides an example of a budget that has been adjusted to take into account funds held back and funds transferred for use within the manager's responsibility centre. In this case, there were a small number of adjustments that reflected some managerial concerns: the level of overtime use, some use of pooled resources to reduce costs of the purchase of equipment, and the creation of a small reserve.

Now that these initial adjustments are made, the manager is ready to begin the actual work of forecasting the financial activity over the year.

Tools of Forecasting

Use of Historical Data

Operational managers in the public sector often face demands that they cannot predict. While this is true, the exercise of in-year budget forecasting is to deal not with exceptions but rather with rules. Rules include those imposed by the organization for how the manager will manage funds in the coming year. Not to be overlooked is the rule of history, which is that, all other things being equal, organizations will repeat their behaviour unless they make specific moves to change it. That is, the best predictor of how funds will be spent in the future is how they were spent in the past.

FIGURE 10.6
Adjusted Starting Budget for Budget Plan Forecasting

	Adjusted Starting Budget for Budget Plan Forecasting Emergency Response Unit Provincial Department of Public Safety Grey Oaks Unit, Grey Oaks, Alberta				
Line Item	**Original Budget Amount**	**Hold Back, Reduction Target or Reserve Adjustment**	**Transfers In**	**Transfers Out**	**Adjusted Starting Budget**
Staff	230,000	(35,000)[a]	45,000[b]		240,000
Overtime	85,000	(10,000)[c]			75,000
Call-out expenses	20,000		5,000[d]		25,000
Training – contracted	25,000				25,000
Training – in house	20,000		5,000[e]		25,000
Equipment: operational	50,000			(50,000)[f]	
Equipment: administration	40,000				40,000
Communications	25,000				25,000
Supplies: operational	75,000	(5,000)[g]		(20,000)[h]	50,000
Supplies: administration	25,000				25,000
Total	595,000	(50,000)	55,000	(70,000)	530,000

Notes:
[a] One support position was not funded because it is under review by the department.
[b] An additional response officer (junior) was transferred from a pooled allotment held at headquarters to permit more training relief.
[c] Management reduction target set by the ER director.
[d] Grey Oaks is designated as an isolated area, so call-out costs (mileage, etc.) are higher: additional funds from a special HQ fund.
[e] Funds available for travel to this isolated area.
[f] All operational equipment is managed centrally to reduce purchase costs. Transfer to HQ.
[g] HQ has established an equipment reserve fund by means of a levy on all units.
[h] Central purchasing of supplies will reduce costs: funds are transferred out of the unit, but all the supplies it has budgeted for will go to the unit.

In addition, in many public operations, there are seasonal patterns to how funds are spent. There are peaks and valleys of activity within programs that can be predicted using established historical patterns, an understanding of how the program works, and awareness of the operating environment. While many organizations have fairly steady flows of activity, e.g., pension entitlements tend to be stable on a month-to-month basis, some have definite season peaks, e.g., emergency welfare assistance may peak in the winter months when seasonal employment dips. Historical data within the organization should serve as a guide for forecasting future behaviour.

Let us look at two examples, one in the voluntary sector and one in a government operation, to see why this is important. The voluntary organization provides emergency shelter for families in distress. As the manager assesses her budget for the coming year, she needs to forecast her workflow and thus predict how her available budget will be spent over the year. In doing so, she looks at past demand for shelter services as an important indicator. **Figure 10.7** illustrates admission patterns over the past three years. There appears to be a consistent pattern of higher seasonal use.

Even with the higher demand in 2003, the seasonal pattern remains consistent over the years. This is one indicator for the manager about her resource expenditures for the year. It can be expected that variable costs (food, clothing, housekeeping, etc.) will rise in the winter months. Given the small variation in numbers, it is highly unlikely that the manager's fixed costs would change much; the cost

of permanent staff is probably a constant (a fixed cost) and therefore relatively stable whether the demand is 35 admissions per month or 40.

This voluntary organization's financial officer will want to see if the revenue flows are timed to meet the increased need during winter. In an operation of this size, it is likely that everyone is familiar with the patterns and that contingencies are made to meet the winter demand.

There are two factors that may help frame the predictions that may underlie the manager's budget planning. She may be aware of changes in the environment that might affect the pattern of the previous three years. For instance, unemployment may have become worse in the area, leading to more family violence and higher shelter admissions. Evidence to date is anecdotal but sufficient to cause some concern. Such information would be a basis for forecasting that she may or may not choose to link to her budget plan, depending on the degree of her confidence in the information and the organization's past experience during spikes in unemployment. The second factor is that the current adjusted budget may be inadequate to meet even past demand. Therefore, while the above information may permit her to program her funds, she must also make note of the shortfall.

Use of Formulae, Average Costs, and Revenues at Shady Gulch

The second example illustrates how a government operation may use historical data in preparing cash forecasts

FIGURE 10.7
Shelter Admissions: Historical Patterns

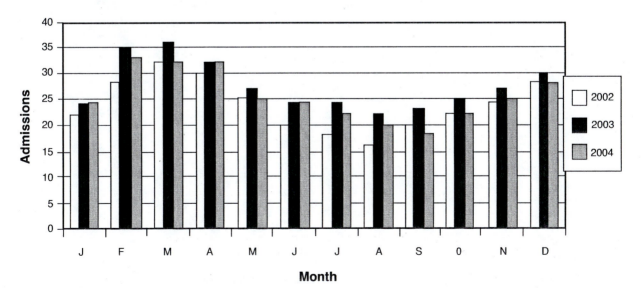

for the current year. All parts of the public sector depend on revenue flows. For most government entities, that means dependency on the government's overall taxation and income strategy, not the agency's own ability to raise revenue. As fees become more common, and as revenue dependency becomes a fact of life for many government services, the calculation of revenues is becoming a vital aspect of cash-management forecasting, so it is useful to look at both the revenue and expenditure sides of forecasting.

Three steps that are followed in the example of Shady Gulch Provincial Park are instructive in building a revenue forecast:

1. **Basis of Calculation:** uses formulae, averages for past usage and cost formulae, usually taken from historical data that apply directly to this park or supplied by a central office.

2. **Detailed Projections of Revenues for the Planning Year:** applies the formulae and makes assumptions about the coming year.

3. **Summary Document.**

Figure 10.8 provides the data that the park manager has been given or has calculated himself to form the basis of his projections. Most of this information is historical, based on three-year averages. Three years is a good number because it provides some comparative data and also identifies years that may be anomalous – either very high or very low – as a result of unusual circumstances. **Figure 10.9** then outlines, in detailed form, how these figures are applied to the estimated revenues for the coming year.

The manager of the park has chosen to do a straight-line projection of revenues. It is based on the assumption that use will continue to be based on historical patterns and

FIGURE 10.8
Shady Gulch Provincial Park: Detailed Calculations of User Volume and Income

Revenue Data Source	Previous Years' Usage		Average
Average vehicle permits sold	2004 2003 2002	1,468 1,216 1,240	1,308
Group camping rate	N/A		58
Group campsites – days leased	2004 2003 2002	125 117 125	122
Backcountry camping sites – ages 18+	2004 2003 2002	1,419 1,496 1,225	1,380
Backcountry camping sites – ages 6 to 17	2004 2003 2002	672 611 522	601
Laundry concession	2004 2003 2002	2,417 2,021 1,867	2,102
Canoe rentals	2004 2003 2002	3,4191 3,1661 31,329	32,393
Reservations	2004		5,804
3-year averages only: a. Campsites occupied b. Bus permits c. Seasonal vehicle permits d. Daily vehicle permits e. Firewood sales			17,289 16 159 3,284 38,000

FIGURE 10.9
Projected Camp Use Revenues, 2005: Shady Gulch Provincial Park

	Period	Sold or Occupied	Rate $	Subtotal $	Total $
Camping fees (all site types)					
Subtotal		17,289		$496,799.50	$496,799.50
Additional vehicle fees	May 13 – Oct. 10	1,308	$8.50	$11,118.00	$11,118.00
Group camping	May 13 – Oct. 10	122	$58.00	$7,076.00	$7,076.00
Subtotal				$18,194.00	$18,194.00
Interior/backcountry					
Ages 18+	May 13 – Oct. 10	1,380	$7.50	$10,350.00	$10,350.00
Ages 6–17	May 13 – Oct. 10	601	$4.00	$2,404.00	$2,404.00
Child			$0.00	$0.00	$0.00
Subtotal – interior/backcountry		1,981		$12,754.00	$12,754.00
Vehicle permit fees					
Subtotal		3,284		$30,704.50	$30,704.50
Summer vehicle permits	May 13 – Oct. 10	159	$70.00	$11,130.00	$11,130.00
Winter vehicle permits			$50.00	$0.00	$0.00
Annual vehicle permits			$110.00	$0.00	$0.00
Bus permits	May 13 – Oct. 10	16	$60.00	$960.00	$960.00
Subtotal				$12,090.00	$12,090.00
Reservation fees					
Reservations booked	For 2005 season	5,804	$12.00	$69,648.00	$69,648.00
Reservations cancelled/changed	For 2005 season	1,161	$9.00	$10,447.20	$10,447.20
Subtotal					$80,095.20
Total					**$650,637.20**

that any changes in cash-flow projections (in this case, revenues) will be based on a change in fees, not the rate of use. Why would he do so? First, there is little information to suggest any changes will occur. At least, none is known. For instance, there are no indicators that volume will be down in the coming years – inquiries have already started for camping sites, even with snow on the ground. Second, the park is at maximum use already. It is a popular site and can be expected to operate at maximum demand capacity with no growth in supply, so projecting growth on a straight-line basis is reasonable under the circumstances. The manager has not been asked to either expand the scope of the camping, which would violate a policy commitment on size and scope of camping facilities in a natural setting such as Shady Gulch, or to increase fees. Should there have been a fee increase that would have been incorporated into the calculations. It would not have

affected the volumes unless the manager felt that such a fee increase would reduce demand.

The final summary report, **Figure 10.10** reflects the results of the first two steps, but at a less detailed level. This report will be used by the administrators of the entire park system to estimate their revenues. Note that the final figure in this report includes both the detailed calculations of use of camp facilities and the other income sources, such as laundry and sale of firewood, that were contained in **Figure 10.8**.

This example offers a good and intentionally detailed illustration of how one would go about estimating revenues for the purposes of cash forecasting. It is a sound basis for any form of expenditure calculation as well. The key is having relevant historical data that establish a pattern, which the manager and financial advisor feel is valid,

FIGURE 10.10
Summary of Revenue Estimates: 2005–06

Category	Revenue Forecasted
Camping and day use fees	$650,637.20
Seasonal leasing	0.00
Pay and display	0.00
2004 capital projects	
Hydro sites 2004	
Firewood sales	38,000.00
Kindling	
Leases/LUPs	
Cabins, yurts, staffhouses	
Capital development 2005 (new)	
Customer service projects	
Operation of stores	
Sale of provincial park merchandise	
Other (specify)	
Laundry	2,102.00
Boat/canoe rental	32,393.00
Picnic shelter rental	
Commissions and concessions	
Total	**$723,132.20**

applying them in a systematic fashion to the anticipated flow of work over the period, and then providing a summary of the information for purposes of decision making.

Another helpful feature of this example is that it illustrates the involvement of several parts of the organization in the creation of these estimates. While the line manager is front and centre in finalizing any estimates, he is only one user of this information. Similarly, he is only one party who has a stake in having accurate information. For example, line managers at the regional and provincial level will want to understand this information to give them a systematic story of revenue flow. They may also want to front-end load the formulae and calculations to ensure that revenue expectations are met, or that programs are changed to better reflect their objectives. Therefore, they may actually ask the park manager to plan for and estimate a growth in campsite use of, say, 5 percent. This is more than just a number. It is, in fact, a direction to the manager to increase the use of the facility. Such a direction may, and should, lead to the manager considering whether or not he can produce such a result, what he would need to get there, and how it can be accomplished. The projection thus moves naturally into the management and planning cycle.

This information will also be used by those responsible for monitoring program performance and its bridge to the financial-reporting, analysis, and cash-management processes of the organization. Therefore, there may be planning staff who monitor and generate some of the formulae being used by the front-end manager. Similarly, financial analysts will be providing information at the local, regional, and national levels to line managers who generate the actual figures used. The park manager may have a financial advisor or have regular access to the financial-information system that is generating information for him on the Shady Gulch's incomes and costs. It should be noted that the interests of the financial advisors and analysts extend beyond just providing the historical data. They will use the information to support and advise, but also to control and analyze. The forecasts that are developed here become part of the monitoring of financial performance over the year. They serve as the base comparator with actual performance to assess cash management within the year; that is, to assess whether the park is performing as projected by the park manager. The data enter the financial-management information system and become part of regular reports to senior managers, as well as feedback on performance to the park manager.

In this instance, the park manager will also be preparing another set of projections: those associated with expenditures. Here, decisions on such issues as staffing, supplies, capital projects, and rentals will be dictated not by the revenue flows but by the funds allocated to the park by the central offices.

The revenue flows are obviously a concern to the organization in this example. In most government organizations, there is little relation between a revenue pattern and this expenditure-budget process. Rather, revenues are placed into the consolidated fund for the government as a whole and distributed through the government's budgeting system. Given the level of detail and the amount of work that raising revenue represents for the park manager, senior managers, planners, and financial advisors, the provincial park organization obviously treats this revenue as an important goal. In addition, those parks that earn high revenues will probably be rewarded in the budget-planning process with resources to ensure that revenue levels remain high. Nevertheless, the individual parks and, in all likelihood, the entire park system, will not retain the funds they earn. Rather, they will go into the consolidated revenue fund of the province.

Monitoring Financial Performance and Variance Analysis

The purpose of all this detailed planning and projecting is to equip the organization to respond to changes in its environment, deal with unexpected outcomes, and maximize the use of the resources at its disposal. To do so, it must have information about what is going on, how it is performing relative to expectations, and where it has to focus its corrective capacity should one area face a critical situation that requires changes to be made.

This monitoring focuses on financial performance and the use of financial information, but it requires much more than that to be effective and relevant to making judgements about variance and deciding what to do about it. It examines how the organization is delivering on its core programs and its objectives for the period under consideration. Operational information must be combined with financial information. This will let the organization assess its financial condition in the real world: does it need funds to deal with unexpected events, or will it have the time and opportunity to readjust its spending and use funds that will not be spent for the line item for which they were originally allocated? How this process of variance analysis unfolds is well illustrated in a guide from the Australian National Audit Office in **Figure 10.11.** This is a good illustration of how accountability, both personal and organizational, play continuously to answering the questions implicit in this process. How did this happen? What went wrong? How do we correct? What have we learned about the future?

The organization therefore must establish and use reporting systems that provide information for making decisions about in-year budget management. Usually, this will be coordinated by the central financial group, along with whatever staff support units have a strong interest in such decisions. In large organizations, this information rolls up to the central office, often through intermediary structures, e.g., regional offices, shared services or headquarters, which also add some measure of analysis and decision making. Since some organizations will expect the operating unit to manage some of the variances and shortfalls within that unit, what gets reported will vary, and the front-end operating unit may report information based on its overall performance. Internally, there may be subunits on which the local manager is gathering information regularly in order to manage the operations. Further, large regional structures may also be expected to deal with many of their cash requirements through delegations from national headquarters. Depending upon the materiality of the issue being measured, it may be that only regional totals are wanted for higher-level consideration. The essential features of a typical organization's review process are summed up in **Figure 10.12.**

FIGURE 10.11
Framework for Analyzing and Explaining Budget Variances

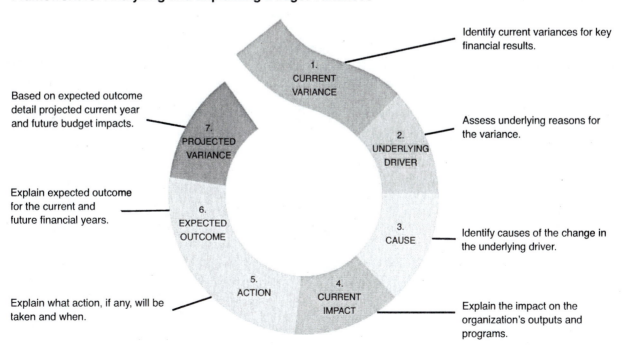

Source: *Developing and Managing Internal Budgets: Better Practice Guide,* Australian National Audit Office, 2008.

FIGURE 10.12

Qualities of the Cash Management (In-Year Budget) and Financial Performance Review Process

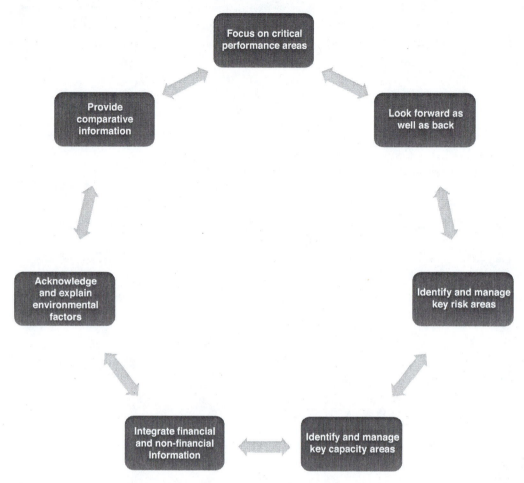

Source: *Reporting Principles*, Canadian Comprehensive Audit Foundation, 2003.

Cash-management reports must answer several questions:

- Are we going to be within our budget allotments?
- Are we operating according to our budget plan?
- How does our performance compare with relevant historical data?
- Does this performance mean that more funds may be necessary or that some funds may become surplus in this area and thus available for reallocation?
- What are the variances, and why have they occurred?
- What is the responsibility centre manager going to do about negative variances?
- Are positive variances within a retention range for the local manager, or are they available for needs outside the unit elsewhere in the organization?
- Do we have the needs and authorities to reallocate these funds?
- What does this information tell us about the performance of the manager in this unit?

- What does this information tell us about the long-term funding?

Questions like these should form the basis for a checklist of key steps in effective in-year budget cash management.

Governance

The cycle of cash-management reporting should coincide with how the organization governs itself. If timely financial performance information is provided to senior management, they should be in a position to do something about it in a useful manner. Receiving quarterly reports, but not having them analyzed and considered for decision making, may meet some bureaucratic need but produce few results, so reports should position senior management to ask, and get, answers to the types of questions that are listed in the previous section.

From a broad organizational point of view, the cycle of cash-management reporting[2] should be such that it can feed into the budget cycle of the government. Most governments have a cycle of supplementary estimates designed to approve appropriations for departments to deal with new programs, program changes, and sudden cost increases within the fiscal year. The organization can use the supplementary-estimates process only if it has adequate information about its current financial situation. That being said, most governments will have little sympathy with departments that have cost overruns which they can generally be expected to manage within their own authorities and allotments.

Setting Up a Monitoring Timetable

All organizations receive regular financial reports. Setting them up and linking them to operational data varies with need, risk, and the general way managers work within the organization. For example, some organizations will want to monitor high-risk budgetary items more frequently than those that are seen as stable and lower risk. A major overtime problem within an organization, as often occurs with operations operating 24 hours a day, 7 days a week (24/7), may be subject to intensive review and reporting – even weekly if a critical stage has been recognized. It is certainly possible to set up a budget plan to track weekly expenditures on such items, but how realistic the plan is will depend on the quality of historical information and the ability to gather information on a timely basis. Most organizations will want to establish a pattern of review that makes it possible to gather performance and financial data on a regular basis with some certainty and in a standard format. Developing the right format takes some time and experimentation. Generally, a quarterly review is frequent enough to permit the organization to identify areas of both cost overruns and potential surpluses.

For the Eastbrook Correctional Facility, the federal facility in the example that is developed here, the fiscal year begins on April 1, so the first quarterly review is at the end of June. Subsequent formal reporting would be required at the end of September, December, and March. For most organizations, the first review does not establish trends for that year, but certainly permits comparison with previous years. Because it is so close to the beginning of the financial year, it is too early in the financial cycle for any major changes to have occurred relative to the opening budget plan. Even at this early stage, though, some aspects of the budget process do lend themselves to projections. For instance, a major capital piece of equipment approved in the budget is expected to arrive in December. The manager

has set up his budget to plan for it to be expensed at that time, and paid for then as well. This will be a one-time expenditure, not a continuing one. Early in the year, he learns that there will be a major delay in getting the equipment, so the funds might be available for other uses. This permits the organization to reprofile the equipment expenditures. Reprofiling is a means of either reallocating funds within a fiscal year or moving an expenditure to future years. The essential balance of the budget is maintained, but plans are reprofiled to reflect the new reality. The manager should not be penalized for offering up surplus funds. Rather, because he was upfront about the delays, he should be assured that the major equipment will be part of his budget next year. An incentive of this kind is vital to getting honest and open reporting.

Performance Reports

The nature of the financial-performance reporting will vary. In some cases, the information will simply be a quarterly comparison of budget plan to actual performance. Others will provide more detailed operational information. The example in **Figure 10.13** looks in detail at two particular line items at the Eastbrook Correctional Facility: custodial staff costs and overtime.

FIGURE 10.13
Budget Figures

Eastbrook Correctional Facility Eastbrook, Nova Scotia Quarterly Financial Report, December 2007 Staffing and Overtime, Custodial Staff Only	
Total staff (custodial)	225
Average salary	$61,000
Total budget cost	$13,725,000
Adjusted salary budget (operating target = 211.5 FTEs*)	$12,900,000
Total overtime hours budgeted	54,900
Total overtime budget (full allocation)	$2,745,000
Average cost per overtime hour	$50

* FTE = Full-Time Equivalent.

In this instance, the first line of the quarterly financial statement shows that there are 225 custodial staff on strength, which would cost $13,725,000 for the year. Facing adjustments that reduce the overall budget, the facility finds itself effectively overstaffed and must therefore reduce overall staff costs to meet its actual adjusted budget allocation. From a cash-management perspective, this means actually reducing staff to an average of 211.5 over the year because the facility has started the year above the target. In order to meet this average staff level target, the plan, as indicated in **Figure 10.14**, envisages a dip below the target to achieve the average outcome.

FIGURE 10.14
Staffing: Budget Plan Versus Actual

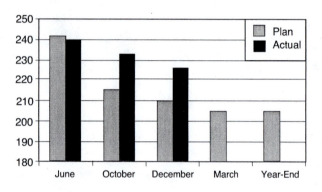

Figure 10.14 thus presents a report on performance against the figures in the budget plan. This form of report determines if there is a variance against plan but provides little explanation with respect to its origin.

In operational terms, the manager has not been able to get his targeted staffing levels down to the desired levels. This will have operational impacts that may also lead to increased overtime costs as staff are hired to fill positions left vacant due to the staffing shortfall. In fact, at this point in the year, it is safe to predict that the target will not be met. Cash management has to start at the beginning of the year, not at some point during it, especially when adjusted targets impose the need to change staff levels.

Variance Reports

When information is submitted in the format above, it raises many questions. Normally, the organization will indicate if there is a difference between the planned expenditures and actual budgets. This is called the variance report. It identifies differences in financial and operational behaviour from what was expected by the organization. There are three types of variance reports that could be used here:

1. a forecasted versus actual report, as shown in **Figure 10.14**;

2. an analysis of key variances report; or
3. a historical variances report.

Forecasted Versus Actual Report

Only material and substantial variances should be reported and submitted for action, either by the responsible manager or by superior levels of the organization. There are no easy rules for judging the seriousness of the variance against plan. It requires that all parties in the process have some awareness of, and sensitivity to, the context of the variances. In the example of the correctional facility, the front-line manager has been given a staffing target below the planned operational needs of the organization. Whether or not this is appropriate depends on both historical trends and the fiscal and strategic direction of the facility and its senior management. Further, the materiality will also be judged by the immediacy of the problem and the organization's overall flexibility. In some cases, variance is only reported if it exceeds a certain percentage of the established budget plan for the year. Managers on the front line and those higher up, as well as the financial advisors, should all have roles in assessing the materiality of the variance and the actions that might be taken. A variance report by itself is of limited use. It must be accompanied by information that explains the situation.

Analysis of Key Variances Report

Due to the need for such contextual information, forecasts of plan versus actual must be accompanied by an analysis of why differences or variances occur or are anticipated. From the financial side, a number of analytical tools are useful to set the variance in context:

*   historical comparisons, to be discussed below;
*   the cost of the variance to date (i.e., how much of the actual budget has been spent);
*   the projected variance if nothing changes (i.e., the straight-line projection);
*   the variance in comparison to similar units in the system; and
*   relevant financial ratios.

The manager of the correctional facility must also analyze:

*   what caused the gap between expectations and results (e.g., fewer retirements or transfers than planned);
*   workload determinants that changed in actual performance (e.g., inmate population increases and opening of a closed housing unit to accommodate an emergency influx of inmates);

- cost drivers that need attention (e.g., excessive posts);
- limitations of the budget itself; and
- actions that could be taken to correct the situation.

A manager who fails to meet budget plans may be put under the gun (for a wry look at this, see Appendix 7). Examining variances is also a key accountability tool for senior management. It is incumbent on the organization to determine the materiality of variances, the risks they pose and what steps it might take to rectify the situation. The following are some considerations for senior managers when looking at variance reports.

- Is this trend in the right direction?
- Is this isolated to this unit, or is it a general phenomenon?
- Did we set realistic targets?
- Can we fund the shortfall that we see emerging?
- Is this manger delivering? If not, is this enough to force us to take some action, such as removing him and finding some else?

Historical Information

This chapter has already discussed the utility of historical comparisons in looking at predictions about future spending and in examining variances. Such information takes many forms. **Figure 10.15** provides such information. One interesting fact that emerges from having this information and combining it with performance over one year is that, even though we know the actual staff levels are higher than planned this year, they are actually the lowest they have been for several years.

FIGURE 10.15
Historical Staffing Patterns (Custodial Only): Year-to-Year Average

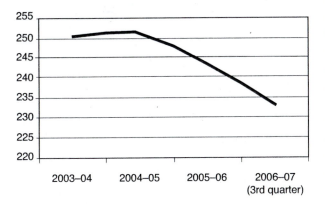

The relevance of this information is that the reduction in salary costs that senior management wants is, generally, on track although the evidence for the current year suggests some worry. The risk for senior managers is that the targeted outcome may never be reached because of delay and external resistance. That is a judgement that only senior line managers can make. In the short term, however, the financial advisor must comment on the need for more salary funds to make it through this year if the current information is correct in suggesting expenditures will not be on target. It would appear that, at this point in the year, the facility's custodial staff is costing an average of \$13.7 million, based on the current complement. To come in on budget for staffing, the manager would have to significantly cut staff in the last quarter. If the manager relies only on a strategy of retirements and transfers, without actually reducing staff levels through redundancies, it is highly unlikely that he can reach his targets. In addition, the highly unionized public-sector environment involves lengthy processes of seeking alternative employment or expensive severance packages that must be taken into account. If, on the other hand, the salaries are being paid to temporary employees, it might be feasible to reduce staffing levels in such a short period of time. Therefore, even if senior managers choose to accept that the longer-term trends are in the right direction, there is a need for an immediate cash infusion to meet the salary budget.

Reallocation and Readjustment

The final phase of the cash-management cycle involves adjustments to the available cash or funds for the manager's use based on the variance reporting and analysis. This is a governance function that makes the process truly a financial-management exercise and not simply a matter of providing financial reports that do not get used. It is also a way for organizations to manage themselves over the course of a financial period to meet demands or circumstances that no amount of sound planning and budgeting can accomplish. Therefore, not only must variances be identified, but the organization must have a very good notion of its actual capacity to reallocate. Should it find itself facing extraordinary costs due to unforeseen catastrophic circumstances – for example, the Armed Forces are called into peace-keeping missions in extraordinary numbers, or medical officials face outbreaks such as SARS in Ontario in 2004 – then the organization may not be able, in and of itself, to carry the cost burden. That is why the supplementary-estimates process is so important. Similarly, for voluntary organizations, there was no expectation in 2005 that the Red Cross could simply find existing monies to mount the large-scale tsunami relief that it did so effectively. Rather, it created a separate fund and sought public support, which it received in abundance.

These exceptions of catastrophic events aside, larger governmental organizations are generally expected to make every effort to build in sufficient capacity for managing financial variance themselves. Similarly, voluntary organizations can, over time, invest in reserves to meet unexpected needs. They would, as cash is available, create contingencies for unanticipated cash-flow challenges.

Authority to Reallocate

Large public sector budgets are seldom approved at a detailed level, thereby permitting some flexibility to move funds from one line item to another. As we have seen, rules exist to limit this, but it remains a possibility. For example, general administrative funds are not broken into operating units by the legislature. They are distributed by the departmental senior management and so can be reallocated. Certain barriers to reallocation may exist and may create situations where the organization has funds to meet needs but cannot use them. Some examples of such rules are:

- funds specifically voted for a single program;
- rules created by central agencies that forbid the reallocation of certain funds, such as the movement of capital funds to cover operating expenses, or the transfer of supplies or equipment funds to salary dollars;
- a specific ministerial or political commitment that funds designated for a specific program will be used only in that program; and
- restricted funds created by special-purpose endowments, or with rules that the monies cannot be moved from one fund to another.

The senior management of the organization has to know not only the formal rules governing the reallocation of funds but also the dynamics of reallocation. This requires some judgement as to the reaction of specific stakeholder groups to the redirection of funds that were designated to an area of interest to them. This is likely to be negative despite the fact that the funds would not have been spent in any event, because there is one reality that both stakeholders and internal managers confront when they see and hear of reallocation – the potential for permanent loss of the funds.

Freeing Up the Funds

Cash projections involve two factors: actual performance and the ability of managers to forecast expenditures and thereby commit the funds. Committing the funds means that the manager, in a cash environment, will indicate that the funds will be spent.

The nature and firmness of these commitments are matters that the financial advisors in the organization need to consider. Suppose that a manager commits that all grant funds are going to be spent within the fiscal year. That gives the manager maximum protection from raids by the money-seeking financial folks, let alone his boss, who probably could use the money elsewhere. Sometimes, the manager is reporting truthfully and the commitments are real: grant applications have been received, they are being processed in a timely way, and the demand for grants meets or exceeds the supply. Thus, the manager sees a full year for the program. Sometimes, the manager is less than truthful: applications are low, and the processing has ground to a halt due to delays in ministerial staff approvals. The money just is not moving, but the manager resists giving it up, especially if he fears permanent loss of funds or even in-year flexibility.

It is at this point that the challenge function by controllers or financial advisors becomes important to the organization. The challenge function is often difficult to define exactly but involves an informed questioning of the interpretation that managers put on information, and even on the decisions they make, by staff within the organization who are in a position to assess that information on the basis of their financial, planning, and operational expertise. This task often falls to the financial advisor, especially when it comes to cash forecasting. Organizations depend on this function as a form of control to temper excessive short-term enthusiasms or ensure that financial information is interpreted accurately. Therefore, should a manager have a history of committing funds and then lapsing or seeking internal reallocations within his unit, then those analyzing the reports must bring this to the attention of senior managers.

Similarly, senior management, facing a series of financial challenges, may ask managers to review their commitments to see what funds can be freed up. In parallel, they may ask the financial advisors to review these same commitments, to make use of that challenge function.

As well as looking at individual manager's budgets within the organization for reallocation, there is the possibility of using such tools as reserves with controls on the release of funds and corporate hold-backs that hold a certain percentage of the funds until need is well established. Reserves are generally created to give senior management some flexibility. The question of when to free them up is one of timing and competing demands. One problem with using them up too early is that it reduces flexibility later in the year.

Finally, senior management will have to make some risk decisions about reallocating funds. Risks are not always dangers, but are also opportunities. However, once money is reallocated, either from a general reserve fund or from one program to another, it is not available for other uses, at least in the short term. Therefore, in considering a reallocation, even with the best variances reports and information, a number of risk factors should be taken into account:

- Can the situation be brought under control within the year?
- Can it be brought under control better than it is now?
- Would moving funds from manager A's budget to manager B's create a new program risk?
- Would this reallocation exacerbate or create a dependence on central reserves?
- Would this model managerial behaviour that is not wanted in the organization, such as rewarding poor management, discussed below?
- Will any reallocation reduce our overall flexibility? Are we going too far? What redundancy do we have to respond to changing circumstances?
- Are we confident in our overall reading of the situation?
- Will this increase or decrease the danger of coming in over or under budget?
- Would this just be a bandage, covering up a real problem that we should be addressing now? Would it buy us time to fix the underlying issue?
- Will this create political and stakeholder problems?
- Will this create the appearance or accusation of misuse of funds for purposes for which they were not voted?
- Will this create inter-agency problems or transfer costs to other agencies of government? Can we tolerate that?

The Danger of Rewarding Bad Management

When an operating variance emerges, one question always comes up: "Is this a bad manager? Are we just rewarding bad management if we step in to help?" Financial information on cash management is an important tool for senior management in evaluating organizational and individual performance. It is often a case of finding funds to meet urgent needs and, at the same time, assessing whether the manager could have managed better to improve financial performance. Senior managers are often in the position of allocating or reallocating funds even when they feel there is bad management. The reality is that they must meet short-term, high-risk needs, even if it sometimes means giving money to a bad manager. When this becomes a pattern, then senior management does have to address the manager's individual performance. Failure to do so will be noticed by other managers, who will become even more reluctant to give up their flexibility when they feel bad management is being rewarded.

Building Incentives and Protecting Budget Integrity

As evidenced in Appendix 6, **The Cash Management Games People Play,** it is possible for both an organization and individual managers to play a lot of games to protect their turf and avoid losing funds that may actually be needed elsewhere. The agency or organization can act in ways that enhance the disincentive for (a) honest forecasting and reporting if it consistently appears to reward bad management, and (b) poor forecasting by meeting the short-term cash needs these often create. There is little disincentive if there are no obvious consequences for the bad managers involved or if the budget and management structures that seem to perpetuate the problems are left intact. There are a number of behavioural and structural ways for an organization to prevent its cash-management system from falling into gamesmanship and thus losing its usefulness and credibility. The first is for consistent governance. The second is to get the reporting right, combining financial and operational data on a basis that everyone understands and uses. The third is to ensure that bad management is punished, even if short-term financial help is needed where things really go wrong. The fourth is a system of training and cultural practices that foster honesty and collegial support (We help you this year; you help out next.)

The Crucial Relationship Between Line Manager and Financial Advisor

Organizations cannot rely solely on either their line managers or their financial advisors for all the information they need to assess and manage their performance. As noted several times, highly reliable financial information is predicated on a budget plan based on the operational plans and expectations of the organization. However, there is a basic tension in setting up a cash-management plan based on this budget. Line managers, with the help of the financial advisor, will establish and agree to the budget plan upon which they will be assessed. Those managers then run the operation within that budget.

Financial advisors play a number of roles, at times at odds with each other:

- **Challenge Function or a Controllership Role**: This is often vested in special units in large organizations, usually called analytical units. The reporting where this occurs is typically in the variance reporting and the analysis that accompanies it. This analysis may or may not directly challenge the manager's version of the results. For instance, if the manager says that a performance problem is an isolated incident that will not recur, the financial advisor may point out that, according to an analysis of the historical data, this is the third year of such overages. It is up to senior management to determine the significance and reliability of these two versions of the same events.
- **Information Support:** They provide the support function of ensuring that financial information is provided and linked to operational information, and that regular reporting is on time and of good quality.
- **Technical Advisor to Managers:** All managers in the agency need the advice of their financial advisors. They can be helpful in sorting out solutions, finding sources of funds and recommending ways to free up funds. This problem-solving ability comes with experience and an understanding of the operational side of the business.

It is also, to a degree, incumbent on both the line manager and financial advisor to inform each other of their positions and try to arrive at a shared understanding of events that reflects their information and views. In the end, organizations depend on this inherent tension between line and functional advice to bring out hard truths to enable good decision making.

Summing Up

Cash management is a skill that involves both the manager and the financial advisor. It is essential in ensuring the best use of scarce funds to achieve public goods. The following are important attributes of an effective cash-management system.

Establishing and Using Effective Governance

Careful attention to in-year budget performance has to start at the top, and be consistently practiced with

consequences. "Nobody's ever asked us before to focus on it" is a very simple way of saying that the senior leadership in the organization does not care about its cash situation – it has other concerns. Because no one cares, no one measures, and no one manages. To ensure good cash management, the organization has to set up ways of governing the process. Organizations that have tight budgets or highly volatile operational or program demands are more likely to do this than those that seem to have excess capacity to meet emerging needs.

The degree of risk and need will probably dictate the kind of cash and budgetary monitoring that occurs throughout the year. In addition, the degree of interest by senior management in financial issues will also indicate the amount of time that they want to spend on it. Nevertheless, effective public management means being increasingly aware of the relationship between resources and their use. Using the transactional, lower-management element of a financial-management system without the other element – the oversight and governance – sends signals within the organization that effective use of resources is not considered important. It also invites deal making among managers just to survive. Eventually the web of these deals will mean that senior managers have lost effective control of their resource base. Further, as pressure on governments mounts to find funds to reallocate to higher priorities, knowledge of the cash situation and use patterns becomes an integral part of the capacity of senior managers to make effective decisions.

For a cash-management system to be effective, it must be seen to have the attention and support of senior managers. While the danger always exists that such processes will drag senior managers into too many details of operations, they must have information at the right level to make decisions about the cash situation of the organization. This means that there is tremendous pressure on financial advisors at the senior level to communicate this information in a meaningful way. A quarterly review of a department's financial situation cannot bury the participants, let alone the CEO or deputy minister, in details. Therefore, the form of reporting must be appropriate to the needs of the level reviewing it. It must also lead to relevant decision making in which the focus of the most senior group may be on a small number of sensitive areas that require it the most. This is the heart of exception reporting of variances.

Giving Assurance to Good Management

Not all cash-management problems result from bad management. Similarly, not all surpluses mean that the managers are performing well. In fact, they may not be meeting their program objectives, but rather managing money in such a way as to save it rather than benefit the program. Nevertheless, the cash-management system must provide some assurances to managers who have surpluses or commitments that they might be able to shift into another financial period, so that they will not end up losers overall. How can this happen? They could lose funds that they have declared surplus, so their budgets could be lowered the next year. They could hold funds and lose them at the end of the financial period without being able to use them. They could see their funds be used, but get no help when they face pressures.

While it is difficult to set up the ideal system to prevent such things from happening, some techniques are available. First, rules can be set in place within the organization to permit some retention of surpluses from one financial period to the next. In smaller public-sector organizations, this is not an issue, because funds are self-financing and retained funds are simply kept. In larger governments, the annual appropriation system ensures that all funds not used within the financial period return to the consolidated fund. That is changing now, as an incentive to avoid excessive year-end spending of surpluses and to reward good management. Often governments permit a form of carry-over of some percentage of the year-end surplus. This encourages a more open declaration of surpluses, to some degree, as some assurance of carry-over can be built into the system. Further, the organization can reward good management of funds by distributing the carry-over on a corporate basis to those whose financial performance is good.

It is always difficult to incorporate protections against the potential loss of future budget levels. The simple reality is that a continued pattern of under- or overuse of funds may signal the need for budget adjustments. The budgetary cycle of well-managed public-sector organizations should be long enough that single events do not trigger a decision of this kind, but as patterns emerge, they must be responded to.

Rigorous Review of Commitments

It has already been noted that commitments are an important part of cash forecasting and management, and offer managers assurance that funds can be committed (even though not actually spent) and thus protected for their intended use. Commitments can also be abused and can be misleading to senior managers; for example, if a manager simply commits all discretionary funds without a specific plan, this is a form of protectionism that may distort the manager's actual needs and probable use of resources.

It is at this point that the challenge role of the financial advisor comes into play. The advisor should monitor and question commitments to test their firmness and accuracy. Commitments should be treated not as money already spent but as what they are: intentions to spend money. Thus, they can become de-commitments under review or challenge. As well, faced with a major challenge, senior management may direct that managers review their commitments to see which ones are binding and which are flexible.

Chapter 11
Confirming Control: Accountability and Reporting

Learning Objectives

- Distinguishing different types of public-sector accountability
- Understanding the relationship between financial and non-financial information in accountability
- Examining various means to report and be accountable

Accountability: Big Idea with a Broad Reach

Accountability is a tough concept. It is often associated with blame and punishment. Scandals abound. So do headlines about them. Here we will take a deeper look, but with a focus on the role that financial information and reporting play in supporting accountability. Accountability is an essential part of delivering public goods and policies. Accountability is a concept with a broad and positive reach for public-sector organizations. It encompasses operational processes, management control, the effectiveness of those controls, the efficiency with which the organization carries out its work and its adherence to the laws and requirements for probity. These elements form the basis of what is called executive accountability, applied to the internal management of organizations. However, accountability also applies to external entities such as the third party delivery agents, a board of directors, and external agencies of review, most notably legislative auditors. Here the accountability is to render an account of one's duties and report to that authority on the execution of the responsibilities that you have received from them. In this context, it also means to be subject to scrutiny, questioning, and formal review. Accountability also extends to relationships with service providers both within the public sector and into the private sector through contracted services, contribution agreements, and funding supports. These relationships include some form of reporting or accounting for the funds.

To demonstrate control and adherence to due process, as well as ensuring the efficient and effective realization of the organization's objectives, is often challenging. Accountability can also be costly, adding to the overall cost of administration and, in some instances, straining the skills and abilities of the personnel within the organization to provide the kinds of accountability demanded of them. However, cost or inconvenience provides no excuse to avoid accountabilities in public organizations. There have been a number of developments in the past decade to increase overall government transparency in financial reporting. As well, technology has driven an increased capacity to derive more and more analytical, forward-looking information from financial and operational reporting. This development, only now emerging as a powerful public sector tool, will certainly change the nature of performance reporting, as the early evidence has already shown.

This chapter will focus on the mechanisms for accountability in public organizations. However, throughout, the principal objective is to focus on how public organizations can build, nurture and sustain sufficient trust to be able to operate with adequate managerial flexibility while maintaining credible accountability. The same concern applies to organizations that provide governmental services through third-party arrangements, as they must account to the government contracting with them. These can be complex contractual relationships, none of which diminish the public organization's ultimate responsibility to account to its legislature or board. The need, therefore, to ensure that there is an unbroken thread of accountability within these relationships is a preoccupation of governments as they broaden their use of third party delivery options.

The Public Sector Accountability Landscape: Accountable for What?

Modern concepts of accountability for public finances are widening and deepening. In **Chapter 1**, we looked at a number of features, mentioned in the CICA *Public Sector Acounting Handbook* that distinguished government from business. Most pertinent to this chapter is that "Governments are held to a higher standard of accountability than a business or a not-for-profit organization."[1] To develop some further precision around that concept, the Public Service Accounting Standards Board, in its 2012 Consultation Draft Paper, ***Measuring Financial Performance in public Sector Financial Statements,*** suggested that there are three broad accountabilities expected regarding the financial affairs of a public sector entity:

1. **Performance:** The extent to which the entity performed in accordance with its financial plan by providing information on actual versus budgeted results.

2. **Forward Impacts:** The extent to which current activities and results have an effect on future activities and results, including inter-period equity, sustainability of policies and programs, annual accumulated surplus or deficit, and risks inherent or created by present behaviour.

3. **Financial Condition:** Based on accurate financial reports, reporting on key aspects of financial condition, including net assets, cash and cash flows, debt and other liabilities, capital assets etc. Further, reporting on the sustainability of the entity, the risks associated with its financial position and the annual and accumulated surplus or deficit.[2]

Suffice it to say that all public organizations face accountability challenges. These challenges are both internal and external, as we will see below. Further, public organizations tend to be confronted with an array of accountabilities that, in the strictest sense of this concept, are not really formal accountabilities, but rather a series of requirements to deal with stakeholder concerns, media demands and other issues. In any event, accountabilities in the public sector contain the following characteristics:

- **Transparency:** Virtually all of the accountability systems within government are subject to various forms of scrutiny or access rules that ensure that all information on performance, financial probity, results and evaluative information becomes public. In the not-for-profit sector, there is less structural or legislative guarantee of transparency, but, for the most part, the sector embraces transparency as a value. Further, effective boards govern in a transparent manner. Additionally, those who contribute through taxes or donations are increasingly demanding transparency from these organizations.

- **Multiplicity of Accountabilities:** Very few public organizations have what might be called a straight-line accountability to a single owner, board, or set of shareholders. Rather, they have formal and informal accountabilities to legislatures or boards, but also to users of the services, clients, the public in general and others. There is also a multiplicity of forms of accountability. While the focus of this text is financial management, it has recognized throughout that public organizations work to achieve a number of concurrent ends: good policy, adherence to the law, and financial probity and proficiency. Attempting to report on, and be accountable for, all these ends is a challenge. Certainly, financial statements cannot by themselves provide enough information to measure all these different areas of accountability.

- **Hierarchical and Horizontal Nature of Accountabilities:** There are accountabilities strictly within an organization: these are hierarchical in nature. Similarly, there are reporting and accountability requirements to legislatures and boards of directors. These, too, are hierarchical. However, at the same time, there are accountabilities that involve collaborative work among organizations that are working towards a common goal. Similarly, as governments move increasingly to using shared service organizations within the government to provide administrative services to all departments from one source, they also begin to experience the challenge of internal service accountabilities.

These kinds of horizontal accountabilities can be rife with tensions and challenges. As Susan Phillips and Karine Levasseur of Carleton University pointed out recently with respect to the increasing problems of relations between the Canadian federal government and voluntary sector service providers:

The federal government is thus trying to do two seemingly contradictory things in its relationship with the voluntary sector: be a collaborator and partners, on the one hand, and hold a tight rein over performance contracting, on the other. Can the two coexist, or does the control exerted by the accountability regime undermine attempts at collaborative relationships?[3]

Qualitative and Quantitative

The goal of sound financial management is to produce high quality reliable, verifiable and trustworthy financial information that is linked to the performance goals of the organization. Is that enough? Not in the public sector. All the best financial data in the world about a bad policy and a set of numbers that show how well it has been administered does not make it a good policy. That is why quantitative information must be supplemented with qualitative information to get a full understanding of the impact of a particular policy.

Further, at a lower level in the accountability grid, many of the accountabilities are also soft or fuzzy, both code words for qualitative rather than quantitative. For example, it has been well established that staff morale is an important factor in the success or failure of an organization. While this can be quantified to a certain extent, it is more qualitative in nature as it looks at elements or organizational culture, which is hard to put into exact numbers.

- **Focus on Both Results and Compliance:** In the public sector, the "how" in achieving organizational goals is often as important as the "what." The "how" is focused on compliance with rules, probity, equity, fairness and adherence to procedures. The "what" – the achievement of a public good – often means some adaptability to circumstances for individual cases, a measure of innovation and entrepreneurship to reach the goals, some tolerance of error to permit learning and adaptation to improve. The tensions here are evident. In accountability terms, it can mean, in practical terms, sacrificing one for the other. Unfortunately, it can also mean trying to pursue both at the same time.
- **Complexity:** It is clear from the above that there is a complex accountability landscape in the public sector. This applies to both the operations of the organizations themselves – the internal accountabilities – and the external accountabilities to legislatures, boards of directors, memberships and the general public.

What public sector managers are accountable for starts with some top-tier elements:

- effectiveness of the program,
- efficiency of delivery,
- sustainability of future delivery, and
- probity in delivery and reporting.

What financial reporting has to contribute also has several elements:

- accurate formal financial statements to match actual to budget;
- timely information within the budget year to enable a firm understanding of the financial position of the unit or agency, and adjust through cash management;
- linking the cost to the program outcomes; and
- accuracy and transparency in reporting to ensure confidence in the numbers being reported.

What Accountability Means

At this point, we move from the general view of accountability to the specific nature of accountability within the public sector and how financial management plays key roles, most notably on the reporting side. Let us look at two definitions of accountability that address many important elements of public-sector accountability.

The Panel on Accountability and Governance in the Voluntary Sector (hereafter, the Panel), defines accountability in the following way,

> Accountability is the requirement to explain and accept responsibility for carrying out an assigned mandate in light of agreed-upon expectations. It is particularly important in situations that involve public trust. However, a commitment to accountability should be thought of not only as answering to external audiences, but also as a constructive tool for organization, development, enhancing management practices, self-evaluation, and strategic planning.

The application of accountability involves three elements:

- taking into consideration the public trust in the exercise of responsibilities;
- providing detailed information, showing how responsibilities have been carried out, and what outcomes have been achieved; and
- accepting the responsibility for outcomes, including problems created, or not corrected, by an organization or its officials and staff.[4]

Another view of how accountability could be defined is from Professor Janice Stein of the University of Toronto, in her book, ***The Cult of Efficiency***:

> Accountability is about evaluating performance, meeting legitimate standards, fulfilling legitimate commitments, and holding responsible those who fail to meet the standards. The right to judge government performance flows naturally from the role of citizen, as does the right to sanction those who fail to meet the standards.[5]

Finally, Christine Ryan and Peter Walsh of Queensland University of Technology, in their review of shared accountabilities, note that:

> An inherent feature of accountability in the governmental context is that some identifiable individuals or defined groups are held responsible for a set of activities that correspond to their actual span of control and capacity to act.[6]

What, then, are the principal characteristics of accountability relationships in the public sector, regardless of their complexity?

- **Assignment of Authority, Power and Resources:** This is the downward delegation of duties to an individual or organization. This can be by law, by policy, by way of formal delegation matrices, or by the completion of an organizational work plan, budget distribution, and performance contracts. It can also be implicit or indirect, such as using formal position descriptions to describe duties that have delegations of authority in them and a statement of expected duties to perform and, possibly, outcome expectations.
- **Accountability for Performance and Results:** In accepting the authority, power and resources, the individual or organization also takes on the responsibility to perform the work and account for the results.
- **Assignment of Duties:** In assigning duties formally, the granting authority also provides clear direction, legislative or regulatory guidance, and resources consistent with the expectation.
- **Requirement to Report:** The necessity to report in a formal way, often prescribed by the granting authority, deals with thee elements:
  - results achieved,
  - compliance to legal and procedural requirements, and
  - efficiency.
- **Judgement Exercised:** At some level, be it within the organization and with the public at large, public sector accountability involves the right of the granting authority to make judgements about how the accountability has been exercised and act on that judgement. In the ultimate test, in a democracy such as ours, that may mean the downfall or re-election of a government. In more mundane terms, it may be a clean bill of health on a financial statement by a legislative auditor.

These characteristics are illustrated graphically in **Figure 11.1, The Accountability Dynamic.**

FIGURE 11.1
The Accountability Dynamic

Unless the two sides of this dynamic are in place, an individual or organization cannot be held accountable. To be accountable, they must be given the direction, authority, power, and resources to do something. However, in this dynamic, there is a reciprocal duty to account for, explain, and report to those conferring those powers. One cannot happen without the other.

Many terms are used, with varying degrees of precision, in the discussion of accountability in the public sector. We have looked at a few definitions of accountability and examined how the dynamic of accountability works. The late Arthur Kroeger, a former federal deputy minister, made a presentation to the Public Accounts Committee of the House of Commons in which he drew a distinction among accountability, responsibility and answerability. It was an important contribution to understanding accountability, since there is the danger of various forms of accountability spread in the public sector, a situation described above, in which public organizations face many groups who feel, legitimately or not, that there is an accountability relationship, when it is something else. Further, in the public sector, maintaining an understanding of whom one is accountable to is important in maintaining democratic institutions and also the appropriate authority relationships in voluntary organizations. Mr. Kroeger describes three obligations of ministers, but notes that they extend to any public official:

Responsibility: "To be the Minister responsible for a department of government means that you are in charge of it. … If you are the Minister in charge of a department, then you have an obligation to oversee and direct what it does … What responsibility does not mean is that you are required to know and control everything that is happening at all times."

Accountability: "An accountability relationship beings with a conferral of authority by one party on another. When authority is conferred on you, you also acquire an obligation to account for how you used that authority. In a strict sense your accountability is only to the person or institution that conferred the authority on you."

Answerability: "People in positions of authority may be called to explain themselves and justify their conduct to many different parties [to whom they are not accountable] … This type of obligation for people in authority can best be described as 'answerability'."[7]

A Continuum of Accountabilities

Accountability takes place at different levels and for different results. **Figure 11.2** presents a grid of accountabilities that we would typically find in an agency of government. These accountabilities move from operational or input-oriented accountabilities within the organization to performance and results, external ones to legislatures, councils or boards.

It shows that organizations are accountable for a full range. For instance, within an operating unit, there are operational accountabilities. These would involve the day-to-day operations of the unit, ensuring that both operational requirements are met and that all safety, production targets are met. Then there are managerial accountabilities, often closely linked to the operations. For instance, is the unit experiencing program pressures that will affect its overtime budget? Is staff hired to fill all positions? As can be seen in the figure, information supporting these questions is closely related to what we call managerial coefficients, the measuring of activities, inputs and relationship to budget expectations. Financial accountabilities are an inherent part of any set. They will take in compliance with financial procedures, the establishment of controls and their active use, staying within budget and providing the required reports to support all of that. Moving along the continuum, the accountability array begins to take on both an internal and external orientation. In the area of compliance, an important element in many public sector organizations, internal and external standards or prescribed processes, often mandated in law or regulation, will have to be measured and assurance of compliance given.

The last two rungs in this grid deal with more external pre-occupations. Outputs are the products, services or facilities that result from an organization's activities. Accountability here is to deliver the public good as promised in the budgeting and planning processes. Outputs relate directly to the objectives of the agency. For example, a social agency may plan to provide literacy training to up to 1,500 clients over a fiscal year. The output goal becomes 1,500 clients receiving that service. The performance indicator developed from that could be the ratio of the number who received the services over 1,500. In financial performance terms, it could be that the percentage of the assigned budget was spent for the intended services, or the average cost of the individual service in relation to a benchmark service cost that compares with agencies in other municipalities.

Outcomes relate to the policy goal of the activity. Outcomes are the impact of these outcomes on a broader policy goal that may involve many contributors. Here the preoccupation is with the program goals of the organization and how they contribute to a policy outcome. No one public sector organization is solely responsible for this complex public good. For instance, taking the literacy training example from above, the policy outcome could be that individuals with poor literacy are able to read better and are, therefore, more ready for the job market. The short-term outcome is literacy capability, which may relate directly to the training fairly well. The medium and long-term goal of employment may be a much more complex set of issues. Literacy may be one impediment to employment. There may be many others. Therefore, while the output of the agency in literacy training may contribute to the ultimate outcome, it is not the sole contribution attributable to accountability in this complex equation.

Governments and agencies therefore try to make sure that there is an understanding of the degree to which what they do contributes to outcomes. They do this through building a policy model that links its chosen outputs to a desired outcome, to limit the degree of attribution to what that agency actually feels it can do to affect the desired outcome and to continuously re-evaluate the underlying assumptions of that model.

All these forms of accountability occur within an agency at one time. The degree of focus and use of the information needed to support them will vary with the focus of the individuals within the organizations. For instance, a unit manager in a mental health facility may have a strong operations focus but with budget and compliance responsibilities as well. Her preoccupation will be on the left side of the chart – operations and management.

FIGURE 11.2
A Continuum of Accountabilities

Continuum of Accountabilities					
Internal ➡					**External**
Operations	Management	Financial	Compliance	Outputs	Outcomes
Measures focus on managerial and financial concerns	➡				Measures focus on program information and finances
	Financial Information Needed in Each Accountability Set				
• Costing • Spending within authorities • Procurement compliance	• Budget in place • Authorities and delegations in place • Performance against budget	• Financial reports – internal • Variance analysis and reports	• Procedures followed • Risk profiled and controls in place • Delegations in place	• Budget set against target • Audit clearance on program • Financial statements • Indicators of performance	• Program expenditure profile • Value for money

A corporate planner in the same facility may, however, be focused on overall results and future planning. Her orientation will be on the results achieved by the hospital and, to a certain degree, the impact these results have on broader desired outcomes.

Every part of this continuum has to work. Organizations need operational and financial information as part of the way they manage. This search for information in useful formats can lead to some conflicts and a heavy expenditure of resources when the external reporting, often to a central agency or external oversight body, places an undue burden on the organization. There has to be a balance in this continuum and how accountabilities are exercised. Information has to match up to those accountabilities. Getting the information right and well balanced for internal operations, control and decision making should be the priority. After-the-fact external performance reporting will reflect the internal robustness.

The Relationship of Accountability and Financial Reporting

The Treasury Board of Canada defines financial reporting in the following way:

> Financial reporting refers to financial reports and disclosures that are both internal and external to a department. Internal financial reporting can include

financial information that supports decision-making, planning, budgeting, resource allocations, accounting, performance assessments and reports. External reporting includes all financial statements, reports or disclosures, including those prepared for Parliament or to be made public.[8]

Financial reporting is an important tool of accountability. They also indicate how the individual or organization has provided good management and stewardship of funds. They can provide information on the results achieved, although only in limited ways. For example, financial data will tell the user if the budget as approved was spent and for the types of uses prescribed. It cannot say how effective those expenditures were. They can, once audited and certified by the responsible manager, provide assurance that the organization has managed its funds within the procedural requirements. Combined with program results, they can provide information on the relative efficiency with which the objectives were achieved. At that point, the report becomes a performance report with financial and performance data combined and linked.

Good financial management, therefore, is at the heart of establishing accountability. One of the features of public sector accountability is that it is transient and volatile, often shifting as events occur, become political and controversial. It is therefore really important that the core accountabilities be tied down, well measured and consistently reported. Much depends on trust in those providing the information. Having sound financial systems that produce reliable data is a means of establishing such trust. Janice MacKinnon, Saskatchewan's minister of finance during a time of real crisis in that province, relates how important good financial information was in making decisions about the crisis:

> In the 1990s accountability for public finances improved dramatically. All government agencies were required to make regular and timely public reports; many provinces moved to an accrual accounting system, which meant that public costs have to be recorded as soon as commitments were made, rather than allowing such expenses to be moved forward to some future date; and all provinces moved to "summary financial statements" – a single financial statement that included the financial results from all government agencies. The latter was extremely important in preventing governments from hiding deficits by moving money around among different government agencies... At least in the future, taxpayers would be fully aware of their government's fiscal situation.[9]

This shows the importance of effective financial statements in gaining and retaining confidence in what is being reported. Performance information, built around financial and operational information, has to be able to answer questions of trust, probity and confidence, such as:

- Has the agency provided its services in an efficient and effective manner?
- How did the agency finance its activities and meet its cash requirements?
- Were revenues from current-year taxation and the agency's other resources sufficient to cover the cost of current-year services?
- Was part of the burden of paying for current services shifted to future-year taxpayers?
- Did the agency's ability to provide services improve or deteriorate compared with the previous year?
- What resources are currently available for future expenditures and to what extent are resources reserved or restricted for specified uses?

An important quality of financial information is that it has to meet the needs of many different users and for a variety of purposes. **Figure 11.3** outlines the dynamic relationship of types of financial information with meeting accountability requirements as well as affecting key business processes such as planning and future budgeting.

FIGURE 11.3
Financial Information: Multiple Users, Multiple Needs

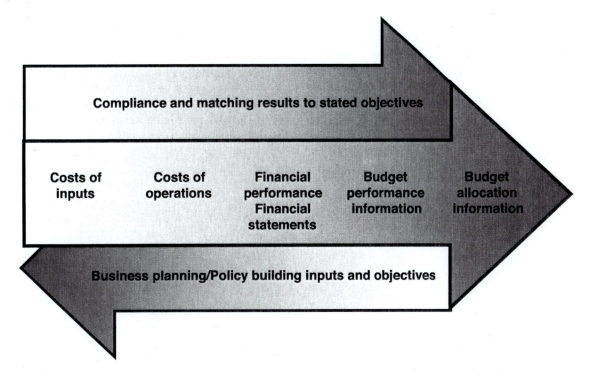

The Users of Financial and Performance Reports

Public agencies, organizations and governments have a number of audiences for whom financial performance reports are prepared. There are, however, two reasons to report performance: to account, both internally and externally, and to manage, with a strong but not exclusive emphasis on the internal. Often performance reports serve both purposes. For instance, formal financial statements have a universal draw in terms of both internal and external attention. However, monthly operational and financial data will be a concern to internal managers. Some of the users of them are:

- **Citizens:** The ultimate accountability for governments is the citizens they serve. They are, after all, the prime funders of governments. More importantly, they elect the governments.
- **Media:** From time to time, the media will need to look at a statement of financial position or, at least, some of the reports on performance in key areas of their concern.
- **Interest Groups:** Those who represent recipients of services, advocates for particular causes, or those who serve as general watchdog bodies will want to use financial information that the organization provides as a way to understand what is going on, to assess the organization's effectiveness or determine if their group's interests were met.
- **Research Bodies:** The Canadian Tax Foundation[10] is a nonprofit body that conducts extensive research into the tax system. In doing so, it provides more insight into financial management issues.
- **Legislatures and Boards of Directors:** These are the authorizing and legislating bodies that retain ownership of the organizations in legal terms. They set the rules. They have the ultimate accountabilities – to citizens or organization members.
- **External Oversight Bodies:** While we will deal more fully with external auditors and other oversight bodies later on in this chapter, they play an important role in serving the legislatures that create an organization, and as independent reviewers of financial information and the maintenance of accounting principles, appropriate financial management practice, as well as issues of efficiency and effectiveness.
- **Internal Oversight Bodies:** Similar to the above, organizations will create internal audit and evaluation groups to monitor and assess financial reports.
- **Central Agencies of Government:** Central agencies must take what is termed a "whole of government" view of financial information and performance audits. However, their role in providing this view is dependent upon the quality of the information that is provided by the many departments and agencies of the government.
- **Senior Managers within Agencies and Government:** Financial information and reports are used internally as well as externally. Therefore, there are users within organizations that have a strong interest in both the integrity of the information for monitoring, decision making, and tracking performance. See the next paragraph for more detail on this group.
- **Senior Governments or Agencies that contract out services or are responsible for other delivery agencies within the government:** This is a growing field of government concern. As governments devolve the delivery of specific services to specialized agencies within government, usually under the oversight of policy-setting departments or ministries, they remain fully accountable for these agencies. Reviewing their performance data is an essential part of their continuing oversight responsibilities. Similarly, in large, complex and long-term contractual relationships, government agencies as the buyer of the services will have a legitimate interest in the financial performance of the supplier.
- **Individual Donors and Funding Organizations:** It is highly unlikely that funding organizations will provide more funding when they lose confidence in the organization's ability to manage its finances. Similarly, some public organizations may have direct oversight and control roles in relationship to other public organizations. This is most prevalent in the government/voluntary sector interface. Financial reporting and its quality may have an effect on the long-term financial support that is given.
- **Creditors and credit-rating organizations:** Applying to both government and the voluntary sector, one of the first concerns of any lender will be the financial condition of the organization.

As noted, financial and performance data is also part of reporting to management. This is the provision of reports in a timely manner for internal use. Often this information is provided more frequently, is less structured, and more attuned to monitoring resource flows within a specific period. Some of the users of these reports are:

- **Line Managers:** Line managers need to know what is going on for control and cash management purposes. They need to be able to make adjustments in operations and budgets based on these.

- **Senior Management:** Go back to the cash management cycle as well as the budget cycle in previous chapters and the need for information on performance is clear.
- **Internal oversight bodies:** This category includes two groups: central units that advise the senior management and pull together overall corporate information, most notably the central finance office, and internal audit groups that have a duty to identify risk and make recommendations for improving errors and validating the quality and trustworthiness of internal reporting
- **Staff:** Employees need to know how the organization is doing. They need feedback on performance at an individual level, but also at a unit or corporate one.

The Objectives of Financial and Performance Reporting

At the heart of good reporting is meeting the accountability contract that the individual or agency has with its authorizing body. Such reporting will be based on the direction, resources and delegations that were received to do the job. Providing reports therefore, should, make it possible for the users of this information to assess the discharge of the accountability taken on, and make decisions about the public good, the means of delivery, the resources allocated to it, and the political consequences of all of this.

To do this, effective public-sector financial and performance reporting should effectively:

- demonstrate the organization's accountability that enable users to asses that accountability in a manner that is mutually understood;
- assess the financial and operational performance against budget and plans;
- provide sufficient information to permit users to assess the financial condition of the agency, to assess whether current revenues and expenses will meet program objectives, or impose future liabilities on taxpayers;
- show that the agency is compliant with its legal financial reporting and contractual requirements; and
- provide information about the organization's level of service and capacity.

In 2002, the Canadian Comprehensive Audit Foundation (CCAF) published ***Reporting Principles: Taking Public Performance to a New Level.***[11] It defined some key concepts:

At its core, "performance" is about how well an entity or program is accomplishing what is intended as measured against defined goals, standards or criteria. More broadly, performance may also relate to efforts, capabilities and intent. Terms such as organizational performance, program performance, financial performance, environmental performance, or the conduct of public business are sometimes used to circumscribe the scope of performance matters being dealt with.

"Public performance reporting" refers to the formal mechanisms that a government uses to communicate with the public and legislatures in accordance with agreed guidelines. It is the formal response to a desire or need to report performance to those who have a legitimate interest in knowing, understanding and assessing performance, and then acting on this information.

In the report, CCAF also recommends nine principles to provide direction for public performance reporting in Canada.

These principles reflect a unique integration of the differing perspectives of legislators, managers and auditors – three groups with an important stake in public performance reporting. Taken as a set, these core principles provide a guide to judgment in the preparation of reports (but not a template for what they will say or deal with).

The general principles recommended by CCAF are:

1. **Focus on the few critical aspects of performance:** Reports need to bring out the most important and highest risk elements of performance. Performance reporting should be at the right level of generality, not so detailed as to overwhelm the user of the information. Performance reports should address what the organization had identified as its priorities in its planning documents or accountability contracts.
2. **Look forward as well as back:** The report stresses the need to link results to previously set expectations and to report past and future projected information in a consistent manner to facilitate user understanding of where the organization has been and where it is heading.
3. **Explain key risk considerations:** The general state of effective risk management among public-sector organizations has already been discussed. The report suggests *"Reporting should identify the key risks as viewed by management, explain the influence of risk on choices and directions and relate achievements to levels of risk accepted."*

More recently, PSAB's *Standards of Recommended Practice*, have identified certain key risk areas upon which combined financial and non-financial reports should provide information:

- **Sustainability** – The degree to which an organization can maintain its existing financial obligations with respect to both service commitments to the public and financial commitments to creditors, employees, and others.
- **Vulnerability** – The degree to which an entity is dependent on sources of funding outside its control or influence, or is exposed to risks that could impair its ability to meet its existing financial obligations, with respect to both service commitments to the public and financial commitments to creditors, employees, and others.
- **Flexibility** – The ability to meet service and other obligations if circumstances change; for example, the ability to respond to reductions in revenues or increased costs.[12]

4. **Explain key capacity considerations:** The CCAF report highlights the importance of informing stakeholders about resource allocation implications on the ability to achieve goals and strategic objectives.

5. **Explain other factors critical to performance:** Increasingly public sector organizations are finding new ways to address the factors that contribute to their success or that can deter it.

6. **Integrate financial and non-financial information:** This will be discussed in the following section.

7. **Provide comparative information:** *"Information about the results of comparable organizations helps show the reasonableness of performance expectations and the potential for improvement."*

8. **Present credible information, fairly interpreted:** Reports should be credible and reliable. Using standards of reporting is key to making this happen.

9. **Disclose the basis for reporting:** Users of financial and performance reports need to understand why reporting is being done the way it is. They need to know the basis of accounting in financial reports. They need to know how performance measures were arrived at, how they are relevant, and how they compare year to year.

To conclude this section on the objectives of financial performance reporting, here are five questions that individuals and organization should ask when they set up their reporting structure:

1. Does the measure support the organization's strategic goals?

2. Does the measure support the organization's operational processes?
3. Is the measure easy to understand?
4. Can the measure be found in obtainable data?
5. Is the measure a good indicator of the organization's performance?

Integrating Financial and Non-Financial Information

Public-sector organizations generate and receive a lot of information about how they are performing. They pursue a large number of objectives and activities that are the source of this information. Some are inputs – e.g., how many people are employed and where. Some of these are processes – e.g., number of applications reviewed. Some involve outputs – e.g., number of kilometers of roads repaved. Some involve a direct or indirect contribution to outcomes – e.g., reduced crime, a healthier public. Public-sector organizations are measured in a variety of ways, often by different groups or interests. In the public sector, while there is a general desire to address results as the primary focus of organizational behaviour, the means used are important in the public sector as well. The means asking how things are done; answers questions such as: Were the legal requirements met? Were resources distributed equitably? Were entitlements met? Therefore, there will be a series of measurements that involve both operational and financial information.

Bringing together all this performance information into an integrated whole is seldom seen because of the ambition of the undertaking and it can be very costly. Very few public sector organizations have realized full integration. The realistic test becomes deciding what measures are needed and useful to allow the organization to meet its requirements. One of the best efforts to bring such data together in a useful way for both internal management and external reporting has been some variation of a balanced or holistic approach to reporting. In this, information about finances, operations, clients and organizational learning are balanced to provide a complete picture of organizational performance. Here, too, organizations have experienced challenges to sustain a balanced approach as it is challenging to find an array of measures that, in the end, provide the meaningful information that managers need.

Integration of financial and non-financial data does not mean that all data must look like financial data. Similarly, not all the information that managers need to manage needs to be of the kind that financial data must pass. No one single measurement – a sort of amalgamated number or, even worse, colour code – is going to do it for complex public agencies. In turn, organizations that place too much stock in financial reporting alone have a distorted picture of their performance. This can also place an inordinate burden on the CFO to act as if she or he is the sole purveyor of performance information that meets all the needs of the organization.

There is an important set of connections between financial and other performance information. That is, the ability to know what things cost, to understand the nature of those costs, and to apply that information in the continuing management of them. In other words, reviewing operational information without a sense of the full costs of the operations means not fully appreciating the inherent risks, the potential for budgetary distortions, or the creation of opportunities such operational information can produce.

Another example of connecting non-financial and financial information is in the so-called softer areas of performance management: client satisfaction, public opinion, and the vital issues of organizational capacity, ranging from infrastructure costs to staff alignment. Even in these areas, financial information plays an important role. For example, where issues of public service are involved, there are also often questions of the equitable distribution of resources, either regionally or by category of entitlement. Such information will have a financial base.

With regard to infrastructure and organizational capacity, two important examples highlight the role that financial information plays. The first is the ability to cost staff training, development and other investments in people. The second is the ability to use the potential that accrual accounting and budgeting gives to overall infrastructure costing in terms of planning and costing changes. This will help the organization determine its capacity to continue to deliver the same or better levels of service.

Figure 11.4 shows how financial information integrates with other forms of information as part of the input measures for each category.

Financial performance information has been used for decades as a surrogate for overall organizational performance. Because financial performance can be readily measured, it has been readily available. However, it seldom tells an organization how it is performing with respect to its public policy objectives. As Norman and Gregory have noted,

> The emphasis on gathering information for accountability purposes has resulted in a flood of safe, measurable, financial information about assets that are relatively trivial components in the production of outputs. Information about human capital issues, which is crucial for ensuring success in people-intensive service organizations, is relatively scarce. Similarly, public sector organizations have had legal financial reporting requirements well before any requirements to report on results.[13]

Ideally, a fully integrated system of performance measurement would have financial and cost performance – along with operational performance – information combined with a longer-term set of measures that relate to overall policy outcomes, stakeholder interests, public support, and organizational development.

Reports and More Reports: A Sampler

It is impossible to give a definite list of the kinds of reports that make up a performance-reporting regime. They vary considerably. There are standardized

FIGURE 11.4
Relationship of Financial Information with Other Performance Data

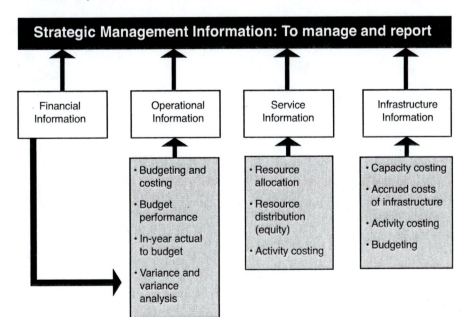

reports such as consolidated financial statements as well as less formal, but equally rigorous, internal reports for management use. The following lists offer a sample of the kinds of reports that one would normally expect to see in any agency of any size in the public sector. It is not definitive, although as we will see in discussing the annual reports of agencies and governments, certain statements are essential.

Examples of external reports are:

- Statement of Financial Position
- Statement of Operations
- Statement of Change in Net Debt
- Statement of Cash Flow
- Quarterly reports
- Public accounts
- Annual reports
- Audit reports
- Results-based reports
- Performance measurement reports

Examples of internal reports are:

- Operational data
- Actual to budget reports
- Variance analysis
- Financial ratios
- Efficiency measurements
- Scorecards/Dashboards
- Cash Flow projections
- Audit reports

Annual Reporting

Format and appearance vary so dramatically that it would be impossible to display even a representative number of annual reports that public sector organizations produce. In general, all jurisdictions in Canada require their governments to produce annual financial statements. Increasingly, as Janice MacKinnon noted, these increasingly resemble the financials statements we examined in previous chapters, but with considerable textual embellishment. Most governments produce forms of performance reporting, based either on government-wide performance targets or targets for individual departments.

Most standard-setting accounting organizations for both government and the voluntary sector recommend that annual reports contain information that addresses the following:

- Management Report: Introductory information and management's discussion and analysis

- Consolidated Financial Statements
- Auditor's Report
- Notes on the Financial Statement

Many public organizations meet the standards of reporting described above, but increasingly try to link the financial information to performance and risk issues. As this has developed, annual reports have become longer, more linked to the stated objectives of the organization and often with more of a publicity orientation in order, it is argued, to increase readability. In essence, organizations see this as a way to "tell their story."

Reporting can take many formats and is not restricted to an annual report. As mentioned, increasingly, a successful reporting system for a government or a not-for-profit organization will link the financial results and the program or policies objectives. As this develops, it is even more important to ensure that the basic financial information is sound and does not get lost with all the other information provided.

Larger governments will separate detailed financial information from their performance reports and will only report summary data in them. However, they do provide such information through their public accounts documents, which are submitted to their legislatures on an annual basis. Similarly, these entities will also separate their auditor's reports and attestation or exceptions, as these are usually part of the role of the legislative auditor, to be discussed below. Smaller organizations, be they towns or charitable organizations, will usually have an external auditor's statement contained in the report.

Audit and Financial Management

Effective internal and external audit systems exist to serve the need for public accountability. However, these systems do not provide accountability itself. That rests with the individual or agency that has taken on the responsibilities and powers to do something and must account publicly. Audits, in their various forms, are control tools to be used in both assessing performance and holding those accountable responsible for compliance to both their own objectives and the means approved to achieve them. There is a tendency to see audits as part of a blame-game culture in government. That can happen, especially when egregious mismanagement or misuse of public money is found. For the most part, audits, whether they be from the internal audit service or the external auditor, are important ways to make corrections, identify trends and build trust in the quality of performance reports.

The Canadian Comprehensive Audit Foundation (CCAF) defines audit in the following way:

> Audit serves an accountability relationship. It is the independent, objective assessment of the fairness of management's representations on performance or the assessment of management's system and practices, against criteria, reporting to a governing body or others with similar responsibilities.[14]

Who or what the governing body is depends upon the accountability relationship. It can be a board of directors, internal management at superior levels, a minister, city council, or other governing body.

The need for audits has been with us for a very long time. In fact, the ancient Egyptians used auditors to control transactions for the royal treasury. They also established detailed records of their work and the resulting transactions. Thus the notion of using people and systems to safeguard public funds and provide a check against corruption runs deep in our culture.

In describing the public sector accountability process and where audit fits into it, Wayne Cameron, former auditor general of Victoria State, Australia offers this diagrammatic view of the process in **Figure 11.5**.

FIGURE 11.5
The Audit Triangle

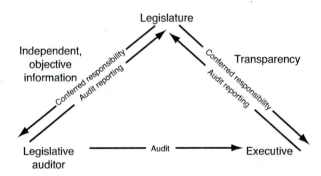

Source: Wayne Cameron, "Public Accountability: Effectiveness, Equity, Ethics," *Australian Journal of Public Administration* 63, no. 4 (December 2004): 59-67.

This triangle shows the dynamic nature of accountability and audit. And, as Mr. Cameron points out, audit does not replace the need for managers to account. Rather it is a key form of risk mitigation and assurance:

> For the minister and departmental officials, the key channel of accountability remains the chain of responsibility, upwards through the departmental hierarchy to the secretary and the minister and, via the minister, to parliament and the public. This central channel is supplemented by a number of other accountability mechanisms, including the accountability of public servants to respond to enquiries by parliamentary committees, to those agencies, which through their statutory roles, reinforce public accountability such as the Auditor-General, the Ombudsman, tribunals and the courts, as well as freedom of information.[15]

Auditing is part of the control framework for any agency and a significant part of oversight by governing bodies for external audit. How much audit there is depends on the size, complexity and amount of public money involved. The greater the complexity, and the greater the risk, the more there is a need for an internal audit function, in addition to a separate external function.

Virtually all governments have a form of external audit office, reporting either to the legislature or council or the government directly. The former is the norm. They will also create specialized oversight agencies with audit functions where the public policy requirements exist. For example, the Office of Official Languages for the federal government of Canada regularly audits departmental compliance with the *Official Languages Act*.

At the heart of the use of audit is the need for public and independent assurances on two fronts:

- **Attestation** that management's information is fairly and completely represented, be it financial information (for the most part it is) or any other information that management offers, and that it is presented in conformance to practice, standards and rules.
- **Assessment** and reporting on management's performance in comparison to the approved purposes of the program, its stated objectives and goals, as well as the need for economy and efficiency.

Auditor-General Cameron describes this as the difference between *conformance* and *performance*. In any case, audit plays an important role within the accountability framework. **Figure 11.1,** at the beginning of this chapter, presented an accountability framework. **Figure 11.6** incorporates audit into this framework to illustrate the dynamic nature of the interaction and underline again the basic fact that audit oversight has to be driven by the degree of power, resources and authority conferred, and the risk, both inherent and episodic, in each program.

FIGURE 11.6
Audit Supports and Monitors Accountability

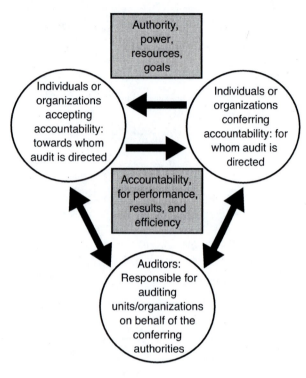

Categories of Audits

There are three ways to categorize audits:

- **Occurrence:** Does the audit take place before or after the activity of the organization takes place?
  - An audit that occurs before the activity is an *ex ante* or pre-audit. This is designed to determine the propriety and correctness of the transaction before it is completed in order to reduce risk to an absolute minimum. It will deal with such matters as the authority of the individual to authorize the transaction, the correctness of the calculations and the adherence to requirements.
  - An audit, regardless of purpose, that occurs after the individual transaction or the accounting period for the organizations is an *ex post* or post audit. This can be performed by internal or external auditors. It can also focus on a much wider range of audit concerns such as meeting objectives, efficiency in doing so, effectiveness, etc.
- **Internal or External**: Is the audit conducted by the staff of the organization (or auditors under contract to the organization), or by an external auditor?
  - An internal auditor will perform a range of audit functions but the client is the senior management of the organization.

- An external auditor will usually report to the authorizing institution of the organization.
- **Scope of the Audit:** In both internal and external audits, the scope can vary from strictly financial to broad outcome concerns.
  - **Financial**: this involves attestation of accounts, confirmation of actual expenditure to planned spending and compliance with accounting procedures, true representation of costs, full reconciliation of all accounts.
  - **Economy**: Comparisons of planned input costs to actual input costs is one form of economy audit. For example, in the purchase of equipment, was the estimated cost of a large and complex piece of equipment what was actually paid? If not, why not?
  - **Efficiency**: Was the goal of the organization met at the lowest cost possible?
  - **Effectiveness**: What were the actual results in comparison to the planned ones? Did the organization provide the right services?
  - **Sustainability**: This has two dimensions that will preoccupy many organizations:
    - Is the organization in a position to achieve its desired results over time, and
    - what are the impacts in terms of the social, economic and environmental costs associated with attaining the goals of the organization?

Internal Audit Functions

The management of a public agency has to demonstrate that it can control its resources. For government, however, especially for those agencies of government that have many financial transactions, either in the area of entitlements (pensions, social assistance, etc.) or grants and contributions, the internal capacity to review, either *ex ante* or *ex post*, is an important one for internal control.

Some of the functions of an internal audit are to:

- review and provide advice on the adequacy control systems of the organization by testing them and reporting on results;
- assess project control capacity for large, high risk projects where risks are high;
- ensure that adequate measures are in place to minimize theft, fraud or misrepresentation;
- monitor and evaluate the risk management processes;
- ensure that grant and entitlement decision-making processes reduce errors to a minimum to prevent overpayment and the need for recovery;

- ensure that regulations covering how funds are spent, recorded, and controlled are adhered to; and
- attest to the accuracy and integrity of the information in the financial and reporting system.

One of the most important roles that an internal audit performs is to provide assurances to senior managers that the control systems they have put in place are working.

Risk and Materiality in Determining What to Audit

Audit resources are scarce. What an agency chooses to audit will be driven by two factors: materiality and risk. We have addressed both factors elsewhere, most notably in discussing control. From an audit perspective, materiality is the extent, either quantitatively or qualitatively, of an omission or misstatement in accounting information: error rates – or an impact of error – that would create a misrepresentation of the financial condition of the reporting entity, or represent a distortion of the anticipated performance results. Clearly, the degree of potential distortion or impact on the agency is important. While some tolerance of error is to be expected in any enterprise, some things just have to be right. In other instances, management can build in tolerable variances, above or below which further actions need to be taken.

Some of the areas in which an audit may be required as a result of materiality are:

- misstatement of financial statements, thereby requiring a restatement;
- financial transactions above certain predetermined levels;
- highly visible items, e.g., international travel; or
- areas where the failure of compliance can lead to significant harm to the public, the agency, or its political oversight.

Audit risk is the risk that an auditor may unknowingly fail to provide an accurate opinion on financial statements. This involves such risks as poor sampling, which fails to provide an adequate picture of areas of error or misstatement. In determining risks that might lead to audit action, one that has been mentioned, but that is pertinent in this context, is control, i.e., the failure of the existing control framework to function as planned or to take into account a shifting risk environment.

Taken more broadly, the risks inherent in the financial, human resources, and operational activities of the organization as discussed in the section on control apply in determining the audit program.

Need for Independence

Internal audit generally has to have a significant degree of independence, and be seen to be able to exercise that independence in order to be effective. While it clearly serves the needs of the organization and, in particular, the chief executive officer, it must be able to function without interference with its audit activities. Therefore, the internal audit should be sufficiently independent of the activities that it audits to enable auditors to perform their duties in a manner that facilitates impartial and effective professional judgements and recommendations. The auditors should have no executive responsibilities. This means that they should not be operating or managing any activities that will themselves be subject to an audit in the future. Further, their involvement in the management structure of the organization should be sufficiently distant from both line and staff functions such that they can readily audit either.

For many years, especially as governments downsized, some organizations reduced the size and scope of internal audits. Moreover, they integrated it into other corporate functions, thereby creating a potential conflict of interest between those who audit on behalf of the organization and those who manage. In general, most audit standards suggest that internal auditors report to the organizational head, to ensure direct access and independence. Many organizations dilute this relationship by burying the function below the level of direct reporting to the CEO. That often reflects the individual orientation of the departmental or organizational head. Where reporting relationships are not intended for internal audit, some additional efforts have to be made to assure independence.

Similarly, there is a tension between the role of the auditor, in examining and reporting, and the role of the audit advisor, providing advice on risk, materiality and program design that would prevent financial or program errors. The latter is forward orienting, centred on planning and engagement with line managers and staff within the organization. The later is retrospective, and fits with a much more traditional view of the internal audit function. The reality is that public agencies need both kinds of audit services. The challenge is to ensure the integrity of the retrospective function while still being a team player in broader corporate activities.

The advantage of a good internal audit system is that it enhances control for the organization. It permits the organization to think about its risks, sets up a system for auditing risks suited to its needs, and gets at the errors before external oversight bodies do. These are valuable assets in the control of complex public organizations. The disadvantage of the internal audit function is simply that it is limited as the auditors, even with independence, still serve the departmental or organizational head. They are, in fact, part of the organization. Hence, it can be argued that their independence is somewhat constrained. While the organization will always be the ultimate arbiter of how to direct an internal audit and use its reports, it can put in place tools to ensure that there is adequate governance of the internal audit to ensure that its independence is safeguarded. This would be the role of the audit committee.

Audit Committees

The creation of audit committees in the public sector has been driven by the failure of governments to effectively use internal audits to prevent misuse of funds. It has also been driven by private sector scandals involving poor internal oversight tools leading to major accounting errors, misuse and fraud.

An audit committee is generally a committee of the executive group of the organization. Generally, it is chaired by a non-financial line manager, or what is known in the private sector as an independent board member.[16]

Some of the functions of the audit committee are to:

- establish, for approval by the executive committee, the terms of reference for internal audit;
- advise the executive committee on the effectiveness of the internal audit strategy;
- review and recommend the resources allocated to internal audit;
- assess the periodic work plans of the internal audit, any material changes to these plans, the head of internal audit's annual and interim audit report(s), and any implications arising from their findings;
- ensure that the independence of the internal audit function is maintained;
- assess and advise on the adequacy of management's response to internal audit advice and recommendations;
- oversee the arrangements made for co-operation between internal audit, external audit, and other review bodies; and
- ensure that selection, monitoring, and training are in place to meet the requirements for the post of the head of internal audit.

In some governments, internal audit has become a centralized and shared service among departments. For instance, in 2003, the Alberta Government Deputy Ministers created a central function called the Office of the Chief of

Internal Audit, with an audit charter. In this instance, the Audit Committee is made up of senior deputy ministers, including the deputy minister of the Cabinet Office, the most senior administrative position. The Audit Committee reports to the Deputy Minister Executive Council. It conducts or contracts for all internal audits as well as for cross-governmental internal audits.[17]

One role that the internal auditor plays is that of liaising with external auditors, as well as central agencies that usually provide policy guidance on internal audits. Of course central agencies and external auditors value their own independence. However, having an auditor talk to an auditor is a good communications strategy for explaining how the organization manages its control frameworks. Hopefully, this can be a means of reducing effort and duplication, especially when the plan for internal audits effectively addresses high risk issues.

External Audit: The Legislative Auditor

The role of the external auditor is similar in form to the internal auditor, but that person serves a different master. Rather than being a service to the agency and its executive to provide assurance on financial and effectiveness matters, the external auditor reports to the authorizing body, either a legislature or council or to the board of the agency. It is intended to provide an independent and public eye on the soundness of financial practices and whether the agency or government, for that matter, are achieving the best value for the money being spent.

Originally, many legislative auditors were created as the sole government audit function, essentially being the internal auditor. The functions today are quite different, as illustrated in **Figure 11.7.**

From the view of legislators, the value of legislative auditors has not simply been in their technical expertise on the financial side, but on their increasing focus on the efficiency and effectiveness of government spending, known as value for money.

In terms of the role of external auditors in assessing the state of the agency or government's financial statements, they have three principal tasks. The auditor must provide an opinion, contained in the financial statements themselves, as to whether the accounts of the government:

- are true and fairly presented according to accounting standards,
- ensure that money approved by the legislature was used for the purposes intended, and

FIGURE 11.7
Role Statement of the Provincial Auditor of Saskatchewan

The Lieutenant Governor in Council appoints an auditor to audit our Office. The auditor must be an accountant who is a member in good standing of a recognized accounting profession that is regulated by an Act. The auditor can not be employed by a Government department, a Crown agency, a Crown-controlled corporation, or by the Office of the Provincial Auditor.

Annually, the auditor reports to the Legislative Assembly whether, in his opinion:

- our financial statements are reliable;
- we have adequate management systems and practices;
- we have complied with laws that govern our Office;
- our reported costs of auditing government organizations are reliable;
- our reported actual time employees spend on tasks are reliable; and
- the assumptions underlying our request for resources (annual budget) are suitably supported and consistent with our goals, objectives, strategies, and action plans, and that the assumptions provide a reasonable basis for our request.

Source: Provincial Auditor of Saskatchewan: http://www.auditor.sk.ca/paweb/aboutouroffice.html.

- represent financial transactions covered in the accounts are in accordance with the relevant authority that governs them.

A financial audit follows established criteria, usually applying standards set by the Public Sector Accounting Board. Certified accountants and auditors collect data from a sampling of financial transactions. The language of the findings is specific and limited. The attest, as it is called generally, finds that no errors were found based on the sampling technique. It does not state that all financial transactions were correct or well spent, rather that the sample conformed to the accounting rules. Where the auditor finds either an error or a disagreement on the application of specific accounting principles, the opinion will contain a reservation.

When external auditors focus on value for money, their studies focus not strictly on financial reporting, but on broader questions, such as:

- **Economy:** is the organization using the resources that it has in the best possible manner to achieve its objectives?
- **Efficiency:** were the objectives of the organization reached at the lowest cost?

- **Effectiveness:** were the results obtained consistent with stated goals?
- **Sustainability:** have the organization's actions and use of resources put it at risk of carrying on or being able to function effectively in the future? This is also called stewardship.

Independence

Independence – the state of being impartial and free from bias and conflicts of interest – is the cornerstone of auditing. Anything that impedes an honest and straightforward approach to the performance of an audit will reduce public confidence. The fact that this independence is backed by legislation instills public confidence in the process. For instance, were a legislative audit to reveal significant matters critical to government, those matters would, by law, have to be made known to legislators and the public.

To be independent in appearance, as well as in fact, legislative auditors have been granted the capacity to act without direction or interference from government. Any efforts to circumscribe that freedom are generally met with public opposition. In practice, and subject to statute and professional standards, this means that legislative auditors are able to determine when and how audits will be conducted and who will conduct them. They, for the most part, have the license to set the audit program for their jurisdictions, to choose the bodies to be audited, to determine the nature and scope of audits to be conducted, and to decide whether their own offices will carry out the work, or contract that work out to private sector auditors. They take direction from the public accounts committee of the legislature when it asks that a specific audit be conducted.

The practices used in the appointment of an auditor general vary across governments. However, in all cases, the legislature is involved in some way in ensuring their independence. In most Canadian jurisdictions, legislative assemblies have assured this independence in a number of ways:

- The legislature usually has some involvement in the appointment of the auditor.
- Appointments are generally for fixed terms, with removal permitted only for cause or incapacity.
- Remuneration of the legislative auditor is usually attached to a reference group, to prevent governments from changing pay levels when one too many bad reports comes in.

- Legislation provides legislative auditors with immunity from legal action.
- Legislation allows legislative auditors to decide how best to undertake audits (for example, by using in-house staff, contracted staff, or contracted firms).

Legislated Mandate

For most jurisdictions there is an act of the legislature creating the auditor's position and outlining the duties. **Figures 11.7** and **11.8** are illustrative of the auditor's mandate and duties. Some important elements that are usually included in legislation are:

- the scope of audit mandate, including all departments, and potentially including related organizations such as Crown corporations and arm's-length agencies;
- the authority and duty to report back to the legislature;
- the authorities to investigate without encumbrance (a guarantee of independence); and
- the identification of the legislative auditor as an officer of the legislature.

Accountability and Oversight of Arm's-Length Agencies and Contracted Services

The growth of arm's-length delivery arrangements through contracting with both the private and not-for-profit sector is a trend that started in the 1990s and one that will continue in the future. It advances a well-founded concept of multiple delivery channels for public goods, and the notion of partnerships of various forms and meanings.[18] However, as Gabriel Meagher and Karen Healey of the University of Sydney point out:

> Paradoxically, the ideal of partnership is being inscribed in public policy at a time when managerial reforms threaten to intensify the tensions between government and non-government agencies.[19]

Third-party arrangements do pose additional challenges to meeting the accountability requirements of public-sector financial management. However, their existence does not in any way diminish accountabilities and the need to report on both performance and conformance. Rather, it changes the ways in which this might be done and distributes the burden of design, assignment of responsibilities, and measuring, monitoring and reporting results differently. The current literature makes it clear that this is a work in progress. As Donald F. Kettl has pointed out, governments have to learn how to be more contract management savvy than they have been in the past.[20] Similarly, a series of public controversies about contracts, grants, and contributions,

FIGURE 11.8
Duties of the Auditor General of the City of Toronto

As approved by City Council, the Auditor General is empowered:

a. To conduct, or cause to be conducted, audits on behalf of City Council in the areas of compliance, financial (excluding attest), program or value-for-money, information technology infrastructure, environment, and sustainability; and other audits as appropriate;

b. To undertake forensic investigations including suspected fraudulent activities;

c. To oversee the work of external auditor(s) performing financial statement/attest audits;

d. To examine problems and carry out special assignments identified by the Auditor General, or approved by 2/3 majority resolution of Council;

e. To provide assurance that the information technology infrastructure contains adequate controls and security by ensuring the existence of such controls in existing systems, assessing overall computer security including business continuity (emergency) planning;

f. To coordinate audit activities with internal auditors and any contracted work to ensure efficient and effective use of audit resources;

g. To manage the fraud hotline; refer issues to departmental management and the Internal Audit Division as appropriate.

Additional powers

a. The Auditor General shall have access to any records necessary to complete audit work.

b. Staff of those organizations within the Auditor General's scope have a duty to co-operate with the Auditor General and to not obstruct audit activities.

Mandate

The mandate for the Auditor General's Office was approved by Council and empowers the Auditor General to assist City Council in holding itself and its administrators accountable for the quality of stewardship over public funds and for the achievement of value for money in City operations. It establishes that the Auditor General shall be responsible for carrying out financial (excluding attest), compliance and performance audits of all programs, activities, functions of all City departments, agencies, boards, and commissions, and the offices of the Mayor and members of Council.

most notably the HRDC political firestorm of the early 2000s have led to what is commonly called a "contract chill" in which process measurement and control has taken precedence over the results.

Contracting for services is hardly new to government. However, over the past twenty years and closely associated with the new public management[21] phenomenon in various countries, it has increased. Third party delivery by private or nonprofit entities has increased in a range of government services. Many governments view this flexibility in delivery as positive. They believe that they can realize savings in buying rather than building service delivery tools. Further, through the integration of "back room" services, i.e., those support functions that generally have no public profile, they can realize the benefits of both centralization and, to some degree, out-sourcing. Finally, these arrangements can allow governments to decentralize and localize service delivery to the public through contracting that matches local circumstances.

However, despite the many benefits, the accountability questions raised through contracting for services and using third parties are many. Some are:

- Do the same standards of accountability that apply to government also apply to non-governmental providers?
- Are reporting requirements the same when the objective of contracting is to focus on results, not process?
- Is the public agency doing the contracting less able to be accountable for financial probity and conformance to rules? If yes, how does it ensure this takes place?
- Does the public agency managing the contract become a form of auditor as well as a buyer of services?
- Do private or public-sector financial standards apply?
- What is the cost and burden of reporting?

As Robert Mulgan[22] points out, there are two factors that have an impact on accountability practices once a third party arrangement is in play:

- differing accountability practices between the contracting organization and the contractor, and the limits of adaptability; and
- alteration of the management methodology from one of internal, hierarchical organizational relationship to a new contractual relationship that involves both a buyer/seller relationship and a continuing, partnership-type arrangement.

There are also a number of private-sector concerns with contracting arrangements:

- Commercial confidentially usually has to be negotiated into the contract to protect the firm from competitors: this often leads to some information being masked from public view.
- Private financing of government activities through arrangements for lease-back, long-term risk sharing, and/or build-and-lease arrangements are also different forms of activity that are not well understood in the public realm.

- The extent to which the private service provider or project manager must adapt and use public sector values that involve transparency, equity and access, which would not occur in the private sector, is a concern.
- The basis of accounting and differences that arise may be difficult.
- Costs of reporting, monitoring and auditing need to be limited to the bare essentials.
- Governance that can produce resolutions to problems when they arise, that reduces the risk of project "creep" when the contracting government tries to add services or change terms of reference in mid stream may cause problems.

Establishing effective contract management to enable good financial administration demands that certain features of the relationship be well structured. Some of these are:

- a clear understanding of the desired outcomes or deliverables;
- clear definitions of accountabilities of all parties involved;
- good costing, not only of the services or goods delivered, but also the oversight costs;
- appropriate contract design and contract process administration, including the addition of probity audits in real time for high risk contracting processes;
- clear guidelines on reporting requirements by both parties;
- an agreed cash flow arrangement;
- effective contract governance to enable problem solving; and
- appropriate post-contract evaluation.

Audit concerns for contracted arrangements should include questions that ask the following:

- Has a due diligence enquiry (including consideration of issues such as financial stability, training programs, management style, and insurance coverage) of any potential service providers been performed?
- Are the risks, which will be created through entering into a service provider arrangement, understood, and are there processes in place for managing these?
- Have service level agreements (or similar) been documented and agreed to by both parties?
- Do the service level agreements adequately identify the respective roles and responsibilities of the agency and the service provider?
- Do the service level agreements include monitoring, reporting (including against key performance indica-

tors), escalation, and conflict resolution clauses to ensure that issues can be addressed appropriately?

- Has the agency confirmed that the selected provider has controls to ensure the privacy and security of the agency's data?
- What controls and security practices does the provider enforce to provide assurances that critical information is handled appropriately?
- Is there ongoing communication between the agency and the service provider about the work performed?
- Are there documented processes for raising issues of unsatisfactory performance with the service provider?
- Are there processes to ensure that any fees charged by the service provider are appropriate based on the services provided, contracted costs, and service-level agreement requirements?
- Does the department obtain sufficient and appropriate assurance from the service provider for the chief finance officer's annual statement to the accountable officer?

Third party contracting in no way dilutes the accountabilities of pubic officials for the public good. It complicates that accountability, however. The costs of these new forms of accountability have to be factored into the overall assessment of the use of a third party in service delivery. However, the same has to be said for the cost of effective accountability with the traditional structures of the public sector. Neither is free.

Summing Up

For the financial manager, having clear accountabilities backed up with assurance through tools such as an audit are essential. This chapter focuses on the notion that accountability is essentially a contractual relationship. Of course, it would be naïve not to acknowledge how that concept gets very messy when we add in politics and the media. From the perspective of trying to get the financial and organizational tools in place, however, the notion is robust and useful.

There are five elements of accountability inherent in this chapter:

1. the delegation of responsibilities, ideally based on agreed expectations and standards;

2. the provision of authority, resources, and a reasonably supportive environment to allow for the fulfillment of those responsibilities;

3. the obligation of the accountable party to answer for the performance of responsibilities based upon the provision of comprehensive, valid, and balanced information on performance;

4. the obligation of the authorizing party to monitor performance, and to take (or require to be taken) corrective action when performance problems or shortcomings are identified; and

5. the bestowal of rewards and penalties based on performance, which can include non-monetary rewards such as publicity and other forms of recognition for superior performance.[23]

An effective system of accountability, and having tools like audit as well as operational controls, is important for a number of reasons. As we have pointed out throughout this text, it is not your money; it is the public's money. Given the complexity of the task and work environment, clarity is essential before we can be held to account. Getting that clarity is a difficult task. So, too, is there risk when we delegate powers. There is also risk inherent in what we do in government. Mitigating that risk through constant monitoring and control to make corrections is an inherent element of accountability. That is why there is an increasing interest in using learning and feedback tools to correct for error, or for unanticipated shifts in program, cost, and behaviour. Those shifts are inevitable and organizations without a sufficiently resilient accountability and control regime will not be supple enough to respond to them. Finally, accountability and audit are not about blame. Accountability is the ability to discern and attribute individual and collective results. Blame is about who is going to pay the price for problems. If there's no clear accountability (and even if there is), you can blame anyone for problems. But fear of being the whipping boy isn't going to help you build a productive, learning organization. Both accountability and blame have roles to play in good management. You have to be able to use both, but not confuse them. Remember, generally in the media or with Mad Men bosses, when you hear "What we need here is more accountability" really means, "What I need is someone to blame." A boss who says there is not enough accountability is actually criticizing him or her self.

Appendix 1
The Budget Games People Play[1]

The point has been made several times in this text that budgeting can be a process of competition for scarce resources. Therefore, the potential for winners and losers is always there. No manager wants to lose the budget game. Often, winning is just holding your own and not incurring losses in budget levels. Sometimes, it can mean additions to existing programs or the addition of some program enhancement for which the manager has been fighting for some time. Alternatively, it can mean budget reductions, driven by overall government reductions, program changes or shifting priorities.

The budget game has real consequences. Skilled players will win for their cause. That means that they have to develop plays and execute them well. Often it means having just the right timing, with the right set of proposals well thought out, to fill a gap or need. There can be trade-offs with other players. All budget cycles involve a series of accommodations and compromises leading to a set of fairly narrow decisions by the top leadership, be it a prime minister or a city council or a board of directors.

Parties to the game should be aware of the plays that have developed in many bureaucracies. What follows is a *tour d'horizon* of such ploys. They break down into four categories:

1. Getting new programs funded.
2. Defending existing programs.
3. Resisting cuts.
4. The senior manager's defence.

In a number of these, an appropriate response by senior managers is suggested as well.

Getting New Programs Funded

1. Creeping Incrementalism

How It Works: Sell a modest program initially; ignore its real magnitude until after it has gotten under way and build client and constituency support for the program. In many cases, float ideas on a pilot project, demonstration project or "seed funding."

Example: One provincial official suggested to her federal counterpart that it would be a good idea to make immigrants with landed immigrant status eligible for unemployment insurance. While all agreed that this would be a good thing and decided to go ahead with it, no one did the ultimate costing, which grew dramatically over the years and transferred budget costs from the provinces to the federal level. Once the higher costs were fully understood, it was politically impossible for the federal government to back down.

Resistance: Reject the proposal up front as poorly conceived and use the **thin edge of the wedge** counter-ploy, as in: "This could just be the TEOTW (The End of the World) and who knows where it will end." Another good phrase to use is, "This could be a slippery slope."

Build in sun-setting provisions with evaluative procedures before approving any further funding: most good bureaucrats will have a counter-strategy for that, but they will have had to work for it.

2. Chinese Box

How It Works: Bury certain politically undesirable budgetary expenditures inside a larger, more palatable program to slip it under the nose of senior management.

Example: This has been done so many times, examples simply seem unnecessary: burying administrative embellishments in program improvements, e.g., a new financial system to support a new federal-provincial child-care agreement.

Resistance: Demand detailed break down programs so that such items become visible. Demand cost break-downs and more detailed information.

3. Split Infinitive: Divide and Conquer

How It Works: Seek approval or sponsorship of a budget proposal from more than one source to a point at which there is commitment tied down or it would be difficult to withdraw approval. How to do that is a book in itself.

However, any two-parent family with children will be able to see it in action most bedtimes.

Example: A common trick in large, complex organizations that have line and staff structures, is, for a line manager, to get some staff support and then go to her line boss with that approval, suggesting a virtual *fait accompli*. Once line commitment is secured, the manager then returns to the staff side and firms up support.

Resistance: This will depend on the organization. In some instances, as long as the manager keeps the lines of communication open, in particular with her boss, seeking multiple supporters for a budget proposal is just what is needed to get it in the budget. However, putting the ultimate budget manager in a squeeze like this deserves to be punished. Good planning and strategic thinking around budget proposals and a no-surprises policy is what works in the end.

4. Get the Tail to Wag the Dog

How It Works: Get budget approval for a specific item that is part of a larger program, which has not yet been approved. This then creates a stronger argument to approve the whole program.

Example: Seek approvals for systems upgrades in computer systems to improve client services to a new standard. The standard is not part of any new departmental policy, just a planning concept that the manager strongly supports. However, it is not approved. Should the systems upgrades be approved, the larger direction is, *de facto*, approved.

Resistance: This is difficult in many cases, as the overall objective or standard is often hard to argue with. As well, forcing the sponsoring manager to go back to basics and obtain the policy approval will meet with resistance. However, that is the only real solution.

5. Using Magic as an Accounting Device: the Shell Game

How It Works: Propose a budget item or change with an assumption that the real cost to the organization will only be a portion of the end cost and that the other funds will come from (get ready for a stream of bureaucratic clichés here): partnership funding, equal sharing, matching funds, etc.

Example: This is an oft-used Canadian government tradition in which the federal government offers what are called 50 cent dollars, i.e., for a program, it will pay half the costs if the province pays the other half. Similarly,

for the volunteer sector, this becomes a trap in which the donor agency, often government, will match funds raised for a program in which it has a highly visible role. This then puts the volunteer agency in the fund-raising mode.

Resistance: Senior management must be aware that close cost analysis is crucial here. Similarly, ensuring the sources of funding are there and verifying them is important.

6. The Gift Horse – It's Free!

How It Works: Obtain budget approval based on funding coming from another source.

Example: Under intense community pressure, a federal government MP finds capital funds for an MRI machine for the local hospital. The equipment is purchased and announcements are made. The hospital now has to operate and maintain the machine, costs that no one has factored in, but which will, over the usable life of the machine, be much greater than the cost of the machine.

Resistance: Look the gift horse in the mouth and check out long-term costs. Include these in the package costs that are presented to the enthusiastic donor or sponsor so that the whole cost of the program is funded.

7. The Word Came Down

How It Works: Imply to your boss that you had direction, or at least implied direction, from your boss's superior or higher level sponsors. This is similar to the Split Infinitive technique.

Example: Inform your boss that the budget item idea is not really yours, but one that some superior to your boss wants to push. This can be at the political level (minister's office), a board member, another senior official or someone in a central agency. Imply that your boss's unit would be favourably seen if it pushes this.

Resistance: The boss should try to get some form of formal support to back up this claim. Of course, the boss can simply pick up the phone and find out if the claims are true. The boss who doesn't see this one coming should be sent back to boss boot camp.

8. The End Run

How It Works: This is the reverse of No. 7. In this case, the sponsoring manager goes around his immediate superior and starts to lobby for a budget item or change in the hope of winning allies to pressure the boss.

Example: Use a briefing with ministerial staff to raise a possible budget increase in allowance for certain departmental clients. Say that it is to test the waters, sound out the minister's views and get a go-ahead to look into it. Take the conversation back to your boss as a direction.

Resistance: This is a major corruption of the decision-making process. It often puts the players in very difficult positions, unsure of whom to believe, and distrustful when the idea seems to be resisted afterwards. Anyone attempting an end-run of a decision-making process needs to be brought to task.

9. I'm OK, You're at Fault

How It Works: Find an error in budget instructions, their timing, or lack of direction on the boss's part. Use this error to lobby for more money for your budget on the grounds that the instructions made it impossible to properly present the case. Imply that things have gone on so long that the idea has to be approved.

Example: A really effective ploy here is to indicate that the budget instructions and limitations in them failed to take into account the direction found in the minutes of the board executive committee to factor in a certain issue in plans, even if the minutes were quite vague about the budgetary implications.

Resistance: This can be messy and can be a major gamble, especially if the boss is a reasonable person. It may pay to be unreasonable and stick to the holy grail of budgetary restraint. Alternatively, the boss can play the **Turn the Tables** ploy and instruct the manager to factor the budgetary items into her budget, but retain the overall budget levels found in the instructions. Then the manager is stuck with delivering something with no new funding to do it with.

10. Only the Best

How It Works: This ploy is often used when there are alternatives and the manager wants the higher quality or higher cost solution. One sees this in organizations with a large rank and file with strong public support. Here, the manager appeals to corporate pride: we are the leaders and so we need this enterprise management system, which is "world class," "best of breed," or "leading edge technology."

Example: A small organization wants to buy into a leading computer system, even though it really does not need the level of complexity and functionality that it offers. However, it is "the best and we should use the best."

Resistance: A couple of tactics work here: the **Scrooge Ploy** and the **Analysis Torture Ploy**. The former puts the boss or decision maker into the nay-sayer role. The latter forces the emotional thrust of this argument through the sieve of committee review, a sure way to kill emotional appeals if there ever were any.

11. Show Me Yours

How It Works: This is really a question of what the neighbours have and you wanting to have it, too. The manager uses comparative techniques to embarrass the organization into supporting new budget items.

Example: Without arguing the merits of each item, police services are well known for checking out each other's equipment and using examples from other regions to get more budget funds to improve theirs.

Resistance: Resisting the contagion factor around some equipment purchases is tough. In some cases, the upgrades are necessary to avoid liability issues, and in others they are genuinely needed. However, using these comparisons on a regular basis without really knowing the benefits of these new items, and without standard setting, is dangerous.

12. Ahead of the Curve

How It Works: The manager argues that the budget item will put the organization at the forefront of one of... client service, technology, science, leadership, and the beat goes on. The operative phrase is "at the forefront." This is an appeal to organizational pride.

Example: A manager wants to equip all park staff with GPS equipment so they know where they are and can gather more accurate data on species counts, trail maintenance and repairs. Then, all this data will be assembled and analyzed.

Resistance: It pays to be confident in what you do as this will often work with the insecure senior manager who wants to look good. A more secure manager would demand a clear notion of the real benefits of these purchases. Further, they may use the counter ploy – **What Are You Going to Do With It?** – a tactic questioning what use this refined data would be and who would pay for maintenance.

13. The Pre-emptive Strike

How It Works: The budget sponsor implies that if this is not done, someone else will do it and look good or hinder the organization from getting involved.

Example: The manager agues that if the department does not start its own program for employee assistance, a central agency will come in, write the rules, build in all kinds of oversight and possibly even make the department pay for it. However, by doing this, the department will be able to design the program itself.

Resistance: There will be a long list of requests for budgetary items like this, as they appeal to the organization's desire to protect its interests. Normal evasive techniques can work here, especially ones that delay or seek to clarify the other organization's intentions. Sending the manager out to find out the other organization's plan is one such technique.

14. Rebranding the Sows' Ear

How It Works: The manager uses appealing labels to sell a program. This may not be entirely misleading, but they do distort information.

Example: Most budget controllers will resist any attempt to add administrative support to a program. They will also resist adding capital to a program change. However, when the manager puts forward a program with part of the budget being for service delivery, and the other part for administration and capital, the intention is to distort exactly what it being bought and sell it under a better name.

Resistance: Senior managers have to have high **BS Factor Analysis Skills.** (Of course, in this instance, BS stands for blatantly superfluous.)

15. Send in the Experts

How It Works: Managers use experts to justify their budget increases.

Example: The use of experts from universities, consulting firms, or professional organizations in defending program changes is so pervasive that examples hardly seem necessary.

Resistance: The best technique senior managers employ is to use the **Dueling Experts** approach; i.e., bringing in counter views, which usually abound. Alternatively, discredit the expert, implying bias and poor research, or question credentials and suggest that the expert's work is inconclusive.

Holding the Fort: Protecting and Growing the Current Budget

1. Placards and Protests

How It Works: Most programs have clients, recipients or interest groups. Mobilizing them to do the work of fighting off budget cuts is a tried and true tradition in an organization. Whether this is done through manipulation by the manager or simply as an outcome of the review process, the result tends to be the same: heightened political tension, media interest, or possible retrenchment.

Example: During a recent cycle of budgeting in a large Canadian city, faced with cuts, the city decided to close a number of neighbourhood libraries. This led to protests in those localities that eventually saw the restoration of part of the proposed cuts. Community mobilization can work.

Resistance: This is often a test of political, rather than bureaucratic, will. However, such reactions are predictable and a legitimate part of democratic decision making. The key is ensuring that the political level understands and accepts the risk of public reaction. Whether it holds firm or caves to public pressure in the end is a challenge, as that level holds the decision-making authority. Another tactic is for the senior manager to thoroughly understand the interest groups involved in any budget move, and not to let these interests work solely with one manager. Rather, the senior manager would want them to have a higher-level contact, even the senior manager.

2. Spam Your Budget Increase Request

How It Works: Any increase you request will be supported by massive amounts of data, extensive presentations, and too much information for the senior manager to absorb. The *force majeur* of the quantity is supposed to drive out the real content. (This actually does work sometimes.)

Example: In order to get more funds for maintenance of information technology, include all repair and upgrade requests, all data on repair work, detailed schematics of the system as it is now (just to scare people), or a large, unprioritized list of change requests, even if they are upgrades. Bunch all of this together into a lump sum and present it as though it is barely enough that "will just keep you afloat."

Resistance: This is a good place to use the **Give Me Your Top Five** tactic. Given that the senior manager cannot sort through all the data, let alone make sense of it, she should just say, give me the top five priorities and we will see how much that costs. If this merits more attention, then ask for year-to-year comparisons and ask what has changed. Suggest that this kind of data might be worth a review by an outside expert – your outside expert. That will certainly cause sober second thought.

3. Time Ambush

How It Works: Rush submissions in at the last minute, thereby avoiding intensive scrutiny, claiming that the budget process itself was so much work that you had to come in past the deadline but, miraculously, before the final submission had been signed off by the senior manager.

Example: The senior manager set herself up here. She asked for complete information in all change requests. The manager needed to build up his maintenance budget for vehicle repair and wanted ten more vehicles. He knew this would not be popular. So he held back and rushed it in at the last minute. He claimed the information requirements forced him to do comparisons with other departments and that the senior manager's office was late in making the contacts for it.

Resistance: This is a setup, pure and simple. Often the request might be quite legitimate. Therefore, some sort of compromise might resolve the problem. But it is important to remember that budget cycles come around again. Therefore, the senior manager should put in place **The Pain I can Inflict is Greater than the Pain that you can Inflict** tactic so that the manager feels the wrath caused by the time ambush sufficiently that he will not repeat it. For instance, while agreeing to the change, the senior manager could hold the funds in a special fund that she controls.

4. The Sacred Base

How It Works: The manager argues that last year's base cannot be changed without dire consequences. She uses the argument that the budget exercise is only about how much the increment or increase should be.

Example: While the senior manager wants to find as much flexibility in the budget as possible, one effective form of resistance is to treat the base as unchangeable. This is generally supported by volume data that shows no change in demand for the service. Further, cost increases should flood in to show the need for more.

Resistance: In fact, it is often the case that the base is not under question. It will depend on the degree of need in the budget process.

5. Aim High, Settle for Less

How It Works: The manager pads the budget requests to a level higher than really needed or than what he expects to receive. The reductions by senior management take him to where he expected to be.

Example: The manager inflates prospective fuel increases and volume demand projections to justify higher budgets in those areas. The senior manager reduces these projections, but leaves the rest alone. Mission accomplished.

Resistance: Senior managers should never accept large unsupported cost inflation projections; they should build them into their guidelines and permit no deviation.

Resisting Cuts

1. Paralysis by Analysis

A key tool, but a dangerous one in the hands of skillful managers, is to call for a study when budget cuts are being proposed. Certainly, the use of external sources to study an issue has the immediate effect of subjecting the budget defender to scrutiny. However, a flawed study – and it will be a flawed study in someone's eyes – can often lead to problematic results. Careful control is needed. Such a study will have to be carefully designed, or it will be dismissed.

2. A Pyrrhic Victory

In the face of budget cuts, especially across-the-board ones, managers can propose changes that will either cost more to implement, e.g., getting rid of staff with high pay-out costs, or be politically problematic. The classic example is the perennial story, never actually documented, of the RCMP. When faced with budget cuts, offering up the Musical Ride, a wildly popular but hardly mission-central aspect of their activities was the ploy. Of course, this would be politically unpopular, so the RCMP ends up with what it wants – no cuts. There is, for the record, no documented evidence that this ever happened, but it is a good illustration of how this ploy can work.

3. Unleash the Clients

Once again, this has already been factored in above, but it involves bringing in affected clients to oppose the changes.

Counter-Attack: Senior Management's Responses

Some of the counter-measures that senior managers can use have already been mentioned in the *Resistance sections*. Already cited have been the following tactics:

- Thin Edge of the Wedge
- Turn the Tables
- Scrooge Ploy
- Analysis Water Torture Ploy
- What Are You Going to Do With It?
- BS Factor Analysis Skills
- Dueling Experts
- Give Me Your Top Five

- The Pain I Can Inflict is Greater than the Pain You Can Inflict.

What follows are some other tactics that senior managers can use to ward off, or manage, budget tactics and games.

1. Hold Back

The senior manager ensures that various budgets do not get too independent of his control. Various means to do this are to not distribute all funds at the beginning of the year, thereby both holding more control, but also seeing if the funds are really needed. Another is to hold capital funds in a controlled reserve and distribute on request.

2. Count the Pennies

Effective delegation notwithstanding, an important way to be in a position to judge budget needs and the potential for cuts is effective cash management information and control of the current budget. Letting go of an awareness of how money is spent is bad management. Letting go of spending authorities based on a good plan is effective management. But it is still important to keep a window on what is happening.

3. The Madman Theory: Just Cut Across the Board

When resistance is at the maximum and there is a stalemate in the decision-making process, across-the-board cuts may be the only answer. Since the potential exists for paralysis by analysis and a lot of time wasted in a variety of defensive moves, the counter-argument that such cuts distort policy intent will just have to be swallowed in comparison to the costs of being reasonable.

4. The Devil Made Me Do It

Often, it pays to have an evil twin or another boss to blame. This is, in fact, often the case. No senior manager really has all that much unfettered discretion. However, if this argument is used, it may reduce the amount of defensive ploys for managers. Of course, it may not do much for the esteem of the senior manager.

5. Meet You Half Way

The senior manager offers to cut a deal and fund part of the program. The pressure has to be on in this instance in order to end the process. In that way, the senior manager sounds half decent.

6. Let's See the Boss

This is a variant on No. 4: offer to go with the manager to discuss this item with the senior manager's boss or, even worse, with the executive committee. While some managers may leap at this chance for exposure, others will rightly see this as a very risky proposition. The manager may find herself out on a limb and hear the chainsaw – possibly in her own boss's hands – taking over her career planning.

Appendix 2
A Brief History of Budgeting and Financial Management Reform in North America

"Surely, it is not asking too much that a lot of reform be preceded by a little knowledge." – Aaron Wildavsky[1]

Progressives and Budget Rationality

Over the past century, public sector budgets have changed dramatically. In fact, the very creation of a single government-wide budget was a reform in itself, the assertion of central control over ministries and departments to reduce their independence and the role of special interests. Control not only over taxation but also on expenditures was the objective of many of these changes. Much of this reform came from the United States and, in particular, reforms at the city level as a result of widespread corruption in city governments. The Canadian experiences have tended to mirror or, in some cases such as PPBS (discussed below), have tended to mimic the American.

Budget reforms also emerged as the roles of governments and public sector organizations changed. They became more involved in the lives of citizens, more interventionist in general, and thus subject to greater accountability. Budgets became, first, a consolidated statement of the government's financial plans, and then grew to be used as statements of government policy and accountability.

The reform trend led to the adoption of increasingly complex budget formats, following, in a variety of paths, the movement from simple line-item budgets, through to program budgets, from zero-based budgets to performance budgeting.

In the United States, under the influence of the Progressive Movement,[2] a broadly based political movement for reform of government institutions to reduce the influence of corrupt party bosses, modern budgeting came into being. As a reaction to this, public interest groups as well as business leaders demanded that governments clean up their acts and become more efficient. Budget reform became part of these reforms and has continued to evolve in the United States and Canada ever since. They have focused on making revenue and expenditure policy for the government prior to the beginning of the fiscal year, enhanced executive control, better management, and greater planning.

The focus on creating government-wide budgets was primarily driven by a desire for cost control and accountability to fight against corruption. Influential reformers like Woodrow Wilson in the early twentieth century argued in favour of strengthening the executive authority in government through budgetary process reform.[3] He successfully championed the progressive income tax system. He also argued that there should be a budget prepared by the executive arm of government. The history to date had been legislatively driven with the budget being the sum of its parts in that individual departmental budgets were approved, but no overall budget. Such was the political resistance to such a move, that it took until 1921 before Congress passed legislation creating a budget office in the executive branch.

Similarly, in Canada, while the legislative process was much more driven by the government of the day sitting in Parliament, a single integrated budget was not the norm. Ministers led the expenditure planning process such as it was. The Department of Finance played more of an accounting role than a fiscal, tax and budgeting policy one.

While the idea of having a budget planned in advance of its execution may seem normal from today's perspective, it was revolutionary in its own day. It served to remove control from individual government entities and their advocates and to turn it over to central controlling functions. It also linked a basic public sector budgeting principle – tying expenditures to revenues – for the first time.

It was not until 1937 that the Government of Canada created a standardized form for departments to use in the creation of their **Estimates**.

While the budgetary statement of the minister of finance receives the most press attention, it is the Estimates that are the detailed and formal spending plans of the government as a whole. These are usually published the day of the budget speech, which will highlight the main changes. However, prior to 1937, the lack of a standardized format for the Estimates meant that Parliament approved the votes of individual departments using a non-standardized process. As told by Donald Gow:

> Prior to 1937, the votes in the Estimates had no standard principle of organization. For example, some votes covered pensions to individuals; others covered the purchase of specific things, e.g., books, magazines and binders for the Supreme Court. Some votes covered a whole program, such as soldier settlement; others covered activities operating in support of a particular subindustry (sic), such as dairying (sic). ...
>
> In the details of the Estimates, or rather in the "details of civil government," there was a listing on every continuous position in the government service. Also, each department had an item called "contingencies," which often was a very mixed bag indeed. For example, under the Secretary of State it covered clerical assistance, postage and stationery, the administration of the *Companies Act*, sundries and the Patent and Copyright Office. That is to say, the details were broken down partly into things in which money was spent and partly into particular organizations or purposes.[4]

An Order-in-Council was passed by Cabinet instructing that the 1937–38 Estimates be reformed to adhere to the following principles:

1. There was to be an item for each distinct project, service or grant.
2. Items of a general character were to be eliminated.
3. Items were to be assembled, by and large, under the responsible departments.
4. Statutory items, which should be subject to annual review, were to be put in the Estimates.

5. An effort was to be made to furnish the total cost of construction projects that would not be finished during the year but would be covered by the Estimates.[5]

With an increased focus on control as a primary objective, budget formats such as line-item budgeting stressed guaranteeing agency accountability by ensuring that the agencies used the money provided to them only for the stated policy established by law. Audit provisions were added and later strengthened to enhance central control, confront corruption, and prevent public employees from being unchecked in their decision making.

The line-item budget has come to dominate public-sector budgeting, enduring many so-called reform efforts. As anticipated by its creators in the Progressive Movement, it has made the task of monitoring inputs, i.e., costs, a relatively straightforward one. It has proven remarkably compatible with other types of budgeting such as performance budgeting and program budgeting. As Janet M. Kelly has pointed out:

> Line-item budgeting is an easy format to manage when one has limited information, a time deadline, and a political system that makes adjustments on the margins. This first budget form, reflecting both the need for monitoring and control and the facilitation of management decision making, was a reflection of the desire for efficiency in government fostered by the Progressives.[6]

Underlying this trend towards close scrutiny at the line-item level was the deep distrust in the United States of public servant discretion in spending. Linked to this was the fact that most hiring was patronage based, thereby guaranteeing a built-in bias towards certain politicians and a poor quality of public servant. It is therefore significant that at the same time public service reform movements leading towards the introduction of such principles as hiring based on merit, and free of political interference, were being championed and introduced under the same progressive movement influence, so, too, were budget reforms.

Parallel developments were occurring in Canada. While the Tammany Hall[7] level of corruption was never seen as of equal concern in Canada, in the late 19th century, there were a series of administrative reforms at the federal level, often mirroring the American experience of the previous decades. Again, budget reforms based essentially on line-item budgets and strong input control were first introduced. However, legislative control over line items, as seen even today in the United States, were never put in place, reflecting the stronger executive role in Canada.

John Lorne McDougall, a former member of Parliament,[8] was appointed the first independent auditor general of Canada in 1878. The job was previously performed by a government official, the deputy minister of finance. This can be seen as the beginning of the separation of legislative auditing from the executive functions of government. This step was tentative because the auditor general of that day had two main functions: to examine and report on past transactions and to approve or reject the issue of government cheques. Today these would be seen as two quite distinct functions and their separation seen as a necessary element of the separation of duties according to the principles of accounting.[9]

The Auditor General's Annual Reports to the House of Commons in this early era were weighty documents, sometimes as long as 2,400 pages. They listed every single government transaction, from the purchase of bootlaces, to contracts for bridge building. This reflected two elements of the early line-item budget processes:

1. A focus on input rather than outputs or linkage to programs, and
2. a high control orientation at the pre-expenditure point rather than assessing expenditures after the delegated officials had used the resources.

Of course, while parliamentarians may argue, as they often do today, that they lacked sufficient information to understand how public monies were being spent, the amount of detail they were initially given was overwhelming.

The progressive era budget reforms included such changes as: annual budgets, comprehensive budgets, detailed line-item budgets (at least in the current year operational budget), and program and performance budget formats for management and policy makers. In that regard, the notion of an annual budget is a relatively recent phenomenon.

During the progressive era in the United States, the strong executive power over the legislature grew and was reflected in budget reforms. The federal budget process was largely centralized with the United States Office of Management and Budget (OMB) playing the key role. In Canada, both at the federal level and in the provinces, the central responsibility for budget formulation rested with the Ministry of Finance or Treasury. At the municipal level, this process was more prosaic, with the mayor being in the lead, but not fully in command, of the budget process. This has lead to extensive involvement by individual councillors in these processes.

In the United States, some of the major budget and related progressive reforms that influenced the strong executive are as follows:

1. 1950: The Hoover Commission successfully recommended the *Budgeting and Accounting Procedures Act* and championed Performance Budgeting (PB).
2. 1961: The Department of Defense installed the Planning Programming Budget System (PPBS).
3. 1965: The Johnson administration mandated that all federal agencies use PPBS.
4. 1971: The Nixon administration required all federal agencies to use Zero Based Budgeting (ZBB).
5. 1981: The Reagan administration rescinded ZBB.

Once again, various efforts in Canada, especially at the federal level, copied these ideas, often with the same results, or lack thereof. However, the Canadian history[10] shows how the overall expenditure management system has gradually evolved over time, with each new system or budgetary technique building upon the existing system. Not only does one see features of the budget that survive over time but also some new budgetary reforms that are developed as a reaction and adjustment to some of the shortcomings of previous reforms.

Major Budgetary and Expenditure Management Reforms in Canada

Prior to 1962, the federal government undertook "line item" budgeting with a focus on resource and administrative inputs as opposed to program or departmental outputs and outcomes. In 1962, The Royal Commission on Government Organization (Glassco Commission) recommended that:

- the government do away with "line-item" budgeting and adopt a program approach to budgeting in the form of a Planning, Programming and Budgeting System (PPBS) in order to strengthen the "central direction of government;"
- greater authority be delegated from central control agencies to departments and agencies to administer their programs and expenditures.

This was best described in terms of the slogan, "Let the managers manage." The government established the Bureau of Government Organization (BOGO), headed by a deputy minister to coordinate the implementation of the Glassco recommendations. The Treasury Board instructed departments to submit five-year forecasts of departmental expenditures.

In 1966, the Treasury Board was separated from the Department of Finance and became a separate department with responsibilities for, among other things, managing the government's expenditure budget. However, the lead on creating the government budget remained with the Department of Finance. Several provinces take a similar organizational approach – separating the decisions on the level of expenditures and economic policy (Finance) from internal management of the government and its budget (Treasury Board). The Treasury Board is a committee of Cabinet and the only one created in law. The Treasury Board continues to be supported by the Treasury Board Secretariat (TBS) to guide the expenditure management process.

In 1968, the federal government adopted PPBS as a government policy. It strengthened the role of the Treasury Board and its Program and Planning Branches in expenditure management. Under PPBS, policy and expenditure decisions were separated, with the Cabinet committees deciding on programs and the Treasury Board deciding on expenditures.

The Treasury Board issued a guide to departments and agencies on how PPBS was to be implemented. The key concepts include:

- setting of program objectives,
- systematic analysis to clarify objectives and assess alternative ways to achieve them,
- framing the budgetary programs to achieve objectives,
- future projections of the costs of programs,
- plans for the year-by-year achievement of programs, and
- information by program to monitor achievement of program objectives, and to reassess objectives and programs.

In 1970, The Treasury Board introduced the concept of "A-B-X" budgets to support the program review function of PPBS. The "A" budget consisted of those expenditures required to finance existing programs at their current level of service. The "B" budget consisted the financing required for new programs or to expand existing ones. The "X" budget consisted of expenditure reductions to existing programs to finance any new programs.

In the late 1960s, major changes were implemented to the way the expenditure Estimates were presented to Parliament:

- Expenditures were to be presented by departments on a program-by-program basis with a statement of objectives.
- Each program was to be broken down into activities and total costs and displayed in terms of objectives of expenditure.
- Non-budgetary items (loans, investments, and advances) were to be individually displayed by program.

- Estimates by program presented for the coming year were to be compared to the forecast of expenditures for the fiscal year just ending, and to the actual expenditures of the previous year,
- Grants and capital expenditures in excess of $5 million were to be segregated into separate votes.
- Salary data was replaced by data on authorized and planned person-years.
- The number of standard objects of expenditure were reduced.

Many features of these reforms remain in the main budgetary documents of Canadian governments to this day.

In 1974, the Treasury Board, in response to difficulties that departments were having in developing measures of program effectiveness and operational performance for PPBS, put in place a framework of operational performance management systems (OPMS). OPMS proposed a comprehensive analytical framework for tracking program outputs in relation to program inputs. The Treasury Board Secretariat promoted management by objectives (MBO) in an effort to assess results achieved against pre-determined program goals.

However, in spite of reform efforts, the results were not convincing, especially for Canada's legislative auditor. The auditor general, in his 1976 annual report to Parliament, declared that, "Parliament and indeed the government has lost, or is close to losing, effective control of the public purse."[11]

In response, the government strengthened the expenditure decision-making process of Cabinet in an effort to increase control of government spending and to ensure that government expenditures would increase no more rapidly than the growth in GDP. Also, the government established what came to be called "the Treasury Board referral system." Prior to this, new spending initiatives were increasingly being approved by Cabinet committees, then considered by Cabinet, and only afterwards being referred to Treasury Board for consideration of the resources. The new "referral system" required that new spending proposals be considered by Treasury Board prior to consideration by Cabinet.

The government also established the Office of the Comptroller-General within the Treasury Board whose responsibilities were to significantly strengthen financial management and program evaluation within government.

In 1979, the government passed an amendment to the *Auditor General's Act* establishing a legislative basis for **"value for money audits."** This ushered in a new era of independent performance reviews of departmental management and programs undertaken by the auditor general who reports to Parliament.

In 1979, the Royal Commission on Financial Management and Accountability (the Lambert Commission)[12] recommended measures to "avoid waste in government" and "strengthen accountability," including an overhaul of central agencies.

In February 1980, the government established the policy and expenditure management system (PEMS). Under PEMS it was intended that policy and expenditure decisions be integrated at the macro level by the Cabinet Committee on Priorities and Planning, and at the micro level by Cabinet policy committees who manage their budgetary envelopes.[13] Budgetary envelopes were established by the Priorities and Planning Committee of Cabinet on the recommendation of the minister of finance, with input from policy committees.

To help implement PEMS, departments and agencies were required to prepare multi-year operational plans setting out the ongoing costs of existing programs for consideration by Treasury Board. Departments and agencies also prepared strategic overviews setting out the policy rationale and expenditures associated with new initiatives for consideration by Cabinet committees.

PEMS rapidly took on many of the characteristics of budgetary and financial fads: great enthusiasm in the announcement of it, little follow through, and an increase, not decrease, in the burden to implement. It came under considerable strain as:

- policy committees of Cabinet found it difficult to achieve consensus in order to make real and significant savings to fund new programs;
- the minister of finance increasingly earmarked a portion of new money in the envelope specifically for certain programs and ministers, thereby undercutting the role of the policy committee to determine specific program priorities within the context of government-wide priorities and the overall envelope levels for the sector, and
- there were concerns about the large, expensive, and elaborate organizational structure, in the form of the ministries of state which were required to support the system and the policy committees of Cabinet.

In the early 1980s, steps were taken to simplify PEMS with the prime minister of the day indicating that it was "too elaborate, too complex, too slow, and too expensive." The supporting ministries of state for economic and regional development and for social development were eliminated

and their combined staffs of several hundred people were redeployed to departments and agencies.

In 1986, the Neilsen Task Force, involving 19 separate study groups, reported its findings recommending expenditure reductions and the elimination of tax expenditures of between $7 billion to $8 billion.[14] There was considerable focus on eliminating subsidies to agriculture, fisheries, transportation, business, and regional development. The government did not implement any of the major recommendations. This failure to act on this review and the continuous across-the-board cuts served to significantly undermine any form of systematic budget formulation system within government.

In this period, the Treasury Board implemented increased ministerial authority and accountability (IMAA), another attempt to "let the managers manage," by negotiating memoranda of understanding between the Treasury Board and departments to increase authority and flexibility in delivering programs while establishing an accountability framework for measuring performance.

In 1989, the prime minister created the Expenditure Review Committee chaired by the deputy prime minister in an attempt "to ensure that the government's expenditures continue to be directed to its highest priorities, and that expenditure control continues to contribute to deficit reduction." The Operations Committee of Cabinet served as a gatekeeper with spending decisions being made by the Cabinet Committee on Priorities and Planning.

In 1990, the government launched "Public Service 2000"[15] in an effort to reform and modernize the way in which the public service manages and administers government programs. The primary factor that led to this initiative to reform the public service was a growing frustration that "managers were being undermined by a culture based on rules." Four expenditure management tools for departments were put in place:

- single operating budgets for departments to increase the flexibility between salary and operating budgets,
- the elimination of person-year controls on departments,
- year-end carry forward of up to 5 percent of operating expenditures for departments, and
- increased retention for departments of funds raised from cost recovery.

The Treasury Board introduced shared management agendas with departments in an effort establish a joint agenda between Treasury Board and each department on specific departmental performance and on the administrative and managerial flexibilities required by departments.

In the mid-1990s, a major global recession and the impact of debt accumulation hit the federal and other governments hard. In 1993, the government launched the Program Review as it moved to reduce the ballooning deficit. The minister of finance promised to "review all government spending."

The questions, which would form the basis for the review within departments, and by central agencies and by the Coordinating Group of Ministers were:

- **Public Interest Test:** Does the program or activity continue to serve the public interest?
- **Role of Government:** Is there a legitimate and necessary role for government in this program area or activity?
- **Federalism Test:** Is the current role of the federal government appropriate, or is the program a candidate for realignment with the provinces?
- **Partnership Test:** What activities or programs should, or could, be transferred in whole or in part to the private or voluntary sector?
- **Efficiency Test:** If the program or activity continues, how could its efficiency be improved?
- **Affordability Test:** Is the resultant package of programs and activities affordable within the fiscal constraint? If not, what programs or activities should be abandoned?

Notional targets for reduction by departments were established by the Department of Finance and communicated by the deputy minister of finance to departments. The notional targets were not scientific but were broadly divided into three categories: very significant reductions over 50 percent (for example, in Transport Canada), substantial reductions of about 25 percent for many departments, and smaller reductions of less than 15 percent.

In 1995 the government established a new expenditure management system" (EMS) which incorporated a number of features aimed at more rigorous expenditure restraint by ensuring that:

- programs continued to be reviewed on an ongoing basis,
- expenditure and deficit targets were achieved on a step-by-step annual basis, and
- any new expenditures proposals were considered within the context of the tight fiscal framework and as part of the minister of finance's budget.

Specifically the features of the new expenditure management system included:

- Improved expenditure planning by requiring the review and reallocation of expenditures within the budget process.
- Treasury Board changed its role from "funder to banker" by reducing the size of its central "operating reserves" to focus on departmental investments to yield future year savings or cost avoidance.
- Central "policy reserves" were formally eliminated, with any new initiatives to require greater scrutiny and to be funded through reallocations.
- Departments were to focus on performance and program results with increased public accountability.
- Departmental business plans were established to focus on strategic changes in departmental programs to achieve the budget targets.
- Some increased administrative and budget flexibility was provided to departments to encourage more effective management and delivery of programs within the context of significantly reduced resources.
- Establishing departmental "Outlook" documents to assist the House of Commons' standing committees in reviewing departmental expenditure planning by focusing on future expenditure trends and priorities.
- Each fall, the minister of finance was to publish an economic and fiscal update as the basis for setting fiscal and economic parameters and assumptions within which the spring budget was to be developed.

In 1997, the government reported on its *Panel on Modern Comptrollership*.[16] The Treasury Board was to be "reoriented to play an enhanced role as the government's management board." This involved a greater emphasis within government on results-based management and strengthening results-based accountability.

One result of this was that the Treasury Board published *Results for Canadians,* a framework and agenda for management within the federal government. The key features of the framework were:

- building a "citizen focus" into the management of government activities and services,
- highlighting the importance of sound public service values,
- focusing on the achievement of results for Canadians, and
- promoting discipline, due diligence and value for money in the use of public funds.

As can be seen, the Canadian experience has been driven more by trying to manage deficit challenges than deal with managerial modernization. Reforms to how it managed began to emerge once the great budget crunch of the 1990s provided the need to build better internal controls and reinforce the capacity of the centre of government to manage the whole house to get it in order.

Looking at Some of the Higher Profile Budget Reform Efforts: In Search of the Ultimate Acronym

In the history of various budget reforms, there have been some which have been commendable and an improvement in both process and results, but also those that seem to have demanded much and delivered little. While these have already been mentioned, a bit more detail should serve as adequate caution.

PPBS: Planning-Programming-Budgeting System

Very few reforms, or attempts at change that are characterized as reform, have names so firmly attached to them as PPBS: Robert McNamara, former president of Ford Motor Company and secretary of defense in the Kennedy and Johnston administrations of the 1960s. PPBS was introduced into the Department of Defense in 1961 and imposed upon the remainder of the American federal government in 1965. It was declared dead in 1969 and given a proper bureaucratic burial – by way of memorandum – in 1971. As with so many change efforts, it was meant to accomplish a great good: introducing consistent analytical tools to examine in detail all options available before making budget choices. The theory was that good quality examination of alternatives to produce a specific program outcome would yield better decisions. Such an examination would be supported through new and deeper levels of analysis, generally free of politics and the kind of trade-off politicking that accompanies budget making. The reality was that such a system demands a huge amount of information leading to various forms of paralysis by analysis. Similarly, it is uninformed by the very political framework and trade-offs that it attempted to circumvent. It also required a solid agreement on the objectives to be achieved and a wide tolerance for nuance among the choices.

Fundamentally, PPBS was a policy wonk's dream world. It was also a huge bureaucratic burden, often taking senior managers away from their actual work and burying them in volumes and volumes of paper (at that time). The Canadian experience, as noted above, was one of up-front enthusiasm for PPBS followed by a quiet wake.

While it was never formally abandoned in the Canadian government, it can be argued that it only came to life in form but not in substance.

Management by Objectives

As a budgetary process reform that emerged in 1970s, management by objectives (MBO) has left a modest, but useful legacy. Based in broad-brush strokes on Peter Drucker's 1954 book, ***The Practice of Management***, it was an attempt to better align budgetary information with the objectives to be reached for the program. In this way, it was hoped that it would readily identify costs that were not objective-oriented. This process foundered on the difficulty in clearly stating objectives, especially in the absence of political inputs which always guide and nuance so-called scientific objective setting in the name of democracy. Second, it opened the door for many of the bureaucratic and organizational games that are described in Appendix 1. Bureaucratic behaviour shifted to finding language and texture to match existing programs with newly stated objectives.

Zero-Based Budgeting (ZBB)

This has already been described in the previous chapter in some detail. Like PPBS, this proved over its short life, to be labour intensive and difficult to implement. Further, it accomplished little that a simple line-item/program budget could not, i.e., control. It also did nothing to halt the growth of government, which was a dominant concern of North American governments by the 1990s.

Budgeting for Retrenchment

Faced with citizen tax revolts in the United States and public debt ratios approaching third world levels in Canada, governments, for ideological and pragmatic reasons, began further budgeting reforms as the twentieth century ended. This era focused on how to cut costs, if not programs. In fact, both conservative and liberal governments moved the bar well into the realm of cutting programs, entitlements and transfers to reduce the overall size of the budget, the tax burden, and the debt-to-GDP ratio, a key fiscal indicator of the Government of Canada.

Two trends emerged at this time: The first is the process of fundamental, cross-departmental reviews that characterized in the Government of Canada's Program Review of 1995 and its Expenditure Review of 2004–2005. Governments increasingly have cut across traditional budget processes, driven by internal planning with a strong bottom-up approach. They have begun to subject departments and expenditures to more intense scrutiny, often with specific reduction targets in mind.

The second trend has been that of re-organizing and improving government services as a means to reduce costs. In the United States, the National Performance Review under then Vice-President Al Gore, inspired by the popular concepts of re-inventing government,[17] sought to do government differently, and, by implication, more cheaply. Similar efforts in Canada such as Public Service 2000 and a series of relative and subsequent administrative reform efforts were closely linked to the emerging budget cutback culture.

Summary

This brief history of budgetary reforms and processes suggest that there have been many developments in public sector budgeting. However, some fundamentals have been established that appear to be holding firm:

1. Accountability comes, first, in the form of controls over inputs and then, with increasing focus in various ways, on results, which are a major preoccupation of public-sector budgeting.
2. Line-item/program budgets remain the most generally understood forms of budgeting, even with their input orientation.
3. Budgeting is seen as an important tool of public policy where aspiration meets capacity.

Appendix 3
Federal Government's Comptrollership Capacity Checklist[1]

Comptrollership Capacity Check

KPMG Consulting has developed a suite of capacity check diagnostic tools to help public service executives assess the capacity of their organizations to meet the goals that they and their ministers have set. One of the keys to achieving these goals is sustained and effective controllership. The *Report of the Independent Review Panel on Modernization of Comptrollership in the Government of Canada* has concluded that controllership must be situated within the everyday decision making of managers. It notes that, traditionally, government has focused on financial controls and accounting, creating a system of controllership based on command and control. It recommends that the government should strive for a "loose/tight" model of controllership, which combines a strong commitment to central standards and the achievement of results, with flexibility regarding processes and operational approaches. The federal government's *Comptrollership Capacity Check* is intended to help government departments and agencies assess the state of modern management practices within their organizations in order that they can develop a model of modern management practices which combines a commitment to standards and management flexibility. The seven key areas of the *Comptrollership Capacity Check* are:

1. strategic leadership,
2. motivated people,
3. shared values and ethics,
4. integrated performance information,
5. mature risk management,
6. rigorous stewardship, and
7. clear accountability.

Strategic Leadership

- *Leadership commitment*
  Awareness and commitment of deputy head and senior management to establishing and implementing a modern management practices environment.

- *Managerial commitment*
  Awareness of managers of their modern management practices responsibilities, and commitment to implementing them.
- *Senior departmental functional authorities*
  Extent to which senior departmental functional authority and supporting organization are used for objective commentary and independent advice.
- *Planning*
  Strategic, business and operational planning, and the linkages between them and to resource allocation.
- *Resource Management*
  Mechanisms for ranking program options, identifying funding requirements and allocating resources, and budgeting and forecasting.
- *Management of partnerships*
  Partnerships are used extensively by the organization in support of service delivery by leveraging the capabilities of external stakeholders, partners, and other government organizations.
- *Client relationship management*
  Commitment to consciously strengthening relationships with client organizations, and to integrating and coordinating how client services are developed and delivered.

Clear Accountability

- *Clarity of responsibilities and organization*
  Clarity of assignment of responsibilities and accountabilities throughout the organization.
- *Performance agreements and evaluation*
  Extent to which the achievement of financial and operating results is embedded in performance agreements.
- *Specialist support*
  Availability of top-flight counsel to help managers make judgement calls on modern management and operational issues.

- *External reporting*
  Extent to which parliamentary, central agency and key stakeholder information reporting requirements are met.

Shared Values and Ethics

- *Values and ethics framework*
  Leadership of policies and activities that visibly support the ethical stewardship of public resources and give priority to "modern management practices."

Mature Risk Management

- *Integrated risk management*
  Measures are in place to identify, assess, understand, act on, and communicate risk issues in a corporate and systematic fashion.
- *Integrated management control framework*
  Appropriateness of management controls in place, and linkages between controls through an integrated control framework.

Integrated Performance Information

- *Integrated departmental performance reporting*
  Key measures exist to monitor overall organization-wide performance and best-value results.
- *Operating information*
  Measures and systems to monitor service quality and efficiency of program delivery.
- *Measuring client satisfaction*
  Utilization of client survey information on satisfaction levels, and importance of services.
- *Service standards*
  Monitoring against client service standards and maintaining and updating standards.
- *Evaluative information*
  Utilization of non-financial information related to program effectiveness and outcomes.
- *Financial information*
  Reliable financial information is available in a timely and useful fashion.
- *Cost management information*
  Mechanisms for using activity and product/results-based costs.

Motivated People

- *Modern management practices competencies*
  Extent to which modern management practices competencies are defined and whether managers have access to training.

- *Employee satisfaction*
  Mechanisms in place to monitor employee morale and staff relations.
- *Enabling work environment*
  Practices for communication, wellness, safety, and support that enable staff to provide client-focused delivery while reaching their full potential.
- *Sustainable Workforce*
  The energies of staff are managed wisely to help sustain the organization's viability.
- *Valuing peoples' contributions*
  Extent to which the organizational culture fosters staff participation, team building, sharing of ideas, risk taking, innovation, and continuous learning, and rewards or provides incentives for such behaviour.

Rigorous Stewardship

- *Business process improvement*
  Extent to which processes are clearly understood, are conducted in a uniform fashion, and are continuously improved in line with best practices.
- *Management tools and techniques*
  Range of analytical techniques (e.g., cost-benefit, sensitivity, life cycle, benchmarking) are available to managers.
- *Knowledge management*
  Performance/management information is readily accessible to internal and external users via technology, and lessons learnt are shared across the organization.
- *Accounting practices*
  Records of financial transactions are kept on a consistent and useful basis for purposes of audit and reporting, and are consistent with generally accepted accounting practices and the financial information strategy (FIS)[2]
- *Management of assets*
  Assets are managed and utilized efficiently based on a lifecycle approach; records of assets are maintained, and assets are accounted for, on an accrual basis according to GAAP/FIS.
- *Internal audit*
  Strong internal audit program is in place, and audit results are a critical input to management decision making.
- *External audit*
  Process for ensuring adequate attention to results and recommendations of external audits of department operations.

Appendix 4
Internal Control Checklist

The following checklist was developed using the COSO publication, *Illustrative Tools for Assessing Effectiveness of a System of Internal Control,* September, 2012, available at www.coso.org/ic.htm. It has been adapted to a shorter format, with only certain elements of the suggested documentation. While application is general, this template has been targeted at public sector institutions. References to a board are relevant as boards figure significantly in the governance of many public sector agencies and institutions, and play an important role in creating and monitoring the control environment. Otherwise, the reference to governing authority is meant to encompass legislative oversight, executive, political, and bureaucratic oversight, including the role of central agencies/head offices of governments and departments in the overall management of control.

As is the case with all checklists, these tools provide invaluable ways to develop a complete analysis of the needs and leading practices in many areas. They are also dangerous in that they invite what is known as check-off behaviour: got the form, created the policy, things must be fine. The thing about checklists is that you have to keep checking.

Control Environment		
Control Principle	**Summary of Controls**	**Deficiencies and Risks**
1. Demonstrates Commitment to Integrity and Ethical Values—The organization demonstrates a commitment to integrity and ethical values.		
Management and oversight bodies set tone at the top.		
Establishes standards of conduct.		
Evaluates adherence to standards of conduct.		
Addresses deviations in a timely manner.		
2. Exercises Oversight Responsibility — The governing authority demonstrates independence from management and exercises oversight for the development and performance of internal control.		
Oversight responsibilities are clearly defined.		
The oversight body operates independently.		
Sets expectations and targets to create a system of internal control.		
3. Establishes Structure, Authority, and Responsibility—Management establishes, with board oversight, structures, reporting lines, and appropriate authorities and responsibilities in the pursuit of objectives.		
Management takes all structure of the entity into account in developing controls.		
Clear lines of reporting are established and used.		
Management defines, assigns and limits authorities and responsibilities.		

Control Environment		
Control Principle	**Summary of Controls**	**Deficiencies and Risks**
4. Demonstrates Commitment to Competence — The organization demonstrates a commitment to attract, develop, and retain competent individuals in alignment with objectives.		
Policies and practices reflect expectations of competence, standards and qualified staff.		
Performance and competence are regularly evaluated, and shortcomings are addressed.		
Adopts, uses and evaluates means to attract, develop, and retain high quality employees.		
Plans and prepares for succession.		
5. Enforces Accountability — The organization holds individuals accountable for their internal control responsibilities in the pursuit of objectives.		
Accountability is set through structures; authorities and responsibilities are documented and acted upon.		
Performance measures, incentives, and rewards are established.		
Performance measures, incentives, and rewards are evaluated for ongoing relevance and effectiveness.		
Expectations are balanced with work impact, workload and capacity of units, and individuals to deal with the array of pressures such systems can impose.		
6. Risk Assessment — The organization specifies objectives with sufficient clarity to enable the identification and assessment of risks relating to objectives.		
Risk tolerances are considered in setting objectives.		
Does the organization consider both operational and financial performance goals?		
Are operational objectives linked to resource allocation?		
Is materiality defined and used in reviewing financial information?		
Is there a formal risk assessment process?		
7. Identifies and Analyzes Risk — The organization identifies risks to the achievement of its objectives across the entity and analyzes risks as a basis for determining how the risks should be managed.		
What is the process for identifying and assessing risks to the entity, as well as subsidiary and key supply entities?		
Does the organization examine both internal and external risks?		
Is there engagement of appropriate levels of management, expertise, and front-end workers?		
Are risks fully reviewed on a continuous and open basis?		
How does management develop and control risk responses?		
Are there regular inspections, audits, and reviews of fraud and threat risk?		

Control Environment		
Control Principle	**Summary of Controls**	**Deficiencies and Risks**
8. Identifies and Analyzes Significant Change — The organization identifies and assesses changes that could significantly impact the system of internal control.		
How are changes in the external environment assessed?		
Does the organization assess its current business model and the impact of changes, major or minor, to its control capacity?		
Are changes to leadership assessed, especially with respect to risk tolerance and control issues?		
9. Selects and Develops Control Activities — The organization selects and develops control activities that contribute to the mitigation of risks for the achievement of objectives to acceptable levels.		
A direct link to risk assessment and mitigation has been created.		
Relevant business processes are targeted for control.		
A mix of control activities have been created, and are balanced with each other.		
The costs, capacity, and necessary degree of controls are evaluated regularly.		
Control levels are monitored, and are reaffirmed or changed as needed.		
Segregation of control duties at operational and corporate levels are monitored for compliance.		
Specific controls over technology acquisition, use, protection and data, and privacy protection are developed.		
10. Deploys through Policies and Procedures — The organization deploys control activities through policies that establish what is expected, and establishes procedures that put the policies into action.		
A relevant suite of policies and procedures are created for risk management and control.		
Responsibility and accountability for executing polices and procedures are clearly assigned.		
Personnel competence is ensured through selection, training and effective supervision.		
Policies are reassessed on a regular basis.		
11. Uses Relevant Information — The organization obtains or generates and uses relevant quality information to support the functioning of other components of internal control.		
Information requirements have been identified.		
Internal and external sources of information have been captured in a structured, predictable way.		
Information has been provided in a useful and relevant way.		
The costs and benefits of the reporting load on the organization have been considered.		

Control Environment		
Control Principle	**Summary of Controls**	**Deficiencies and Risks**
12. Communicates Internally — The organization internally communicates information, including objectives and responsibilities for internal control, which are necessary to support the functioning of other components of internal control.		
Managers communicate regularly with personnel and key stakeholders.		
Managers communicate with governing authorities in meaningful and useful ways.		
Managers create separate communication lines to protect sources, e.g., whistleblowing.		
Managers build in, and use, listening channels that go beyond formal reporting.		
13. Conducts Ongoing and/or Separate Evaluations — The organization selects, develops, and performs ongoing and/or separate evaluations to ascertain whether the components of internal control are present and functioning.		
A mix of evaluations has been created.		
External expertise is used to assess internal controls.		
A point in the planning cycle has been created to re-evaluate control framework.		
Managers communicate deficiencies in controls, and monitor corrective actions, which are assessed.		

Appendix 5
The Financial Management Capability Model: Auditor General of Canada[1]

Background

The Financial Management Capability Model (FMCM) is based on an adaptation of the Software Engineering Institute's "®Software Capability Maturity Model."[2] The Institute developed the model as a tool for assessing an organization's ability to build software applications. We saw that this approach could be used to create a model for assessing the financial management capability of government departments.

The FMCM is a framework that describes the key elements of effective financial management. It sets out a path that an organization can follow to develop progressively more sophisticated financial management practices as needed. It shows the steps in progressing from a level of financial management typical of a start-up organization to the strong, effective, financial management capabilities associated with a more mature and complex organization.

In addition to its use in auditing, the Financial Management Capability Model also provides a tool that a government organization can use to:

- determine its financial management requirements according to the nature, complexity, and associated risks of its operations;
- assess its existing financial management capabilities against the requirements it has determined; and
- identify any gaps between those requirements and its existing financial management capabilities. Having identified these gaps, an organization can then address any significant ones and work toward developing the appropriate level of financial management capability.

Structure of the Financial Management Capability Model

The Financial Management Capability Model is a framework for strengthening financial management through many small evolutionary steps. The model illustrates the stages through which an organization can evolve as it defines, implements, measures, controls, and improves its financial management processes. These steps have been organized into five progressive "capability levels." Each level represents a well-defined stage toward developing a mature financial management regime.

The following are the five levels of the Financial Management Capability Model:

- start-up,
- control,
- information,
- managed, and
- optimizing.

Each capability level consists of a cluster of key process areas (KPAs). When an organization has instituted all of the KPAs associated with a given level of financial management capability, it may be considered to have achieved that level. Note that each KPA has a purpose and one or more goals. Certain activities and results or outcomes are also associated with every KPA. Essentially, therefore, KPAs are the main building blocks that determine the financial management capability of an organization. They identify what must be in place at that capability level before the organization can advance to the next level.

The Start-Up Level

The start-up level describes the financial management characteristics of an organization that has not yet established its key policies and practices or its control framework. At this level, in the absence of established practices, the organization's ability to achieve its business or program objectives depends on the often-isolated efforts and accomplishments of individuals. In these circumstances there is no certainty that such accomplishments would be repeatable or sustainable.

This situation might exist if an organization has experienced dramatic changes in its operations – for example, if it has implemented a new program or policy, amalgamated with another department, or relocated its operations. If it has not effectively managed the increased risks associated with the change, the organization could be at the start-up level of financial management capability.

The lack of repeatable, sustainable practices of financial management and control means that any data produced may not be complete, accurate or reliable. Similarly, without an adequate control framework in place, assets may not be adequately protected or resources adequately controlled.

The key challenge the organization faces in progressing to level 2 is to develop realistic, useful financial and operational business plans and to establish a basic control framework that allows it to monitor and control resources and safeguard and protect assets.

The start-up level, unlike other levels in the Financial Management Capability Model, is not a stable environment in which it is desirable to remain.

The Control Level

At the control level (i.e., level 2), the focus is on ensuring that adequate resources are available, assets are safeguarded, data are reliable, and operations are monitored and controlled, and conducted with prudence and probity. Organizations at the control level are able to meet statutory and regulatory reporting requirements.

Organizations that have instituted the key process areas for this level have established a control framework that provides a stable environment and ensures that control practices are repeatable and sustainable. The control framework includes financial, operational and management controls. When these basic controls are operating as intended, they will help the organization to control or reduce risks and to produce complete and accurate financial and operational data.

With sound financial and operational data, the organization can carry out its basic stewardship responsibilities and meet its reporting obligations. The integrity of the data supports operational planning decisions and monitoring activities. It ensures that sufficient funds have been obtained to meet budget and cash-flow requirements, and it satisfies statutory and operational reporting requirements.

An organization at the control level will be able to answer "Yes" to the following key questions:

- Do we have a control framework to ensure that our assets are safeguarded, our data are accurate and reliable, and our operations are conducted with prudence and probity?
- Are transactions processed and controlled in accordance with applicable legislative and/or regulatory requirements?

The primary activities that the organization's finance group performs at the control level involve the traditional accounting functions – processing transactions, bookkeeping and general accounting functions. Finance focuses on ensuring that controls over the financial systems are adequate to produce complete, accurate and timely financial data and to provide functional guidance to operational groups as required.

At the control level, operational managers play a role in achieving basic financial management capabilities. This involves establishing realistic financial plans based on expected results, and estimating the resources required to achieve those results. At level 2, the data on which these plans are based are typically historical in nature, drawn from past experience. At this level, operational managers would also track actual progress and resource use against planned results.

At the control level, reliable historical data are available. However, they are not generally available as "information." Although ad hoc analysis can be carried out, the effort to collect information may be extensive and time-consuming because it may be fragmented, scattered and not easily accessible.

The Information Level

At the information level (i.e., level 3), key process areas focus on integrating the organization's financial and non-financial systems, practices and procedures to provide information that can be used to manage resources with prudence and probity, and in an efficient and economical manner.

At level 3, an organization will be capable of both measuring and managing its risks, and can tailor management practices within its various operating units to manage and reduce risk cost-effectively. At level 3, the organization will have information on the cost of producing a product of a given quality or delivering a service at a given level.

A key aspect of level 3 is the changing role of the finance department. The role begins to move away from performing only the traditional accounting functions to performing as a team player providing valuable support to operational managers. Finance works with operational managers to develop a financial structure that provides them with cost-effective controls and information that meets their day-to-day needs – for example, information on product costs.

At the information level, operational managers have a broader understanding of their financial management responsibilities. They also recognize their responsibility to contribute to the organization's financial management capabilities.

Critical to achieving this level of capability is a climate that institutionalizes financial management practices throughout the organization's culture. This would require that senior management explicitly demand and promote effective financial management and demonstrate its value. Such a culture is developed by formalizing financial management policies and practices across the organization and supplementing them with appropriate training – and instituting a system of rewards, recognition, and sanctions that reinforces the culture.

In addition to being able to answer "Yes" to the control level questions, an organization at the information level will be able to answer "Yes" to the question, "Do we have the financial management systems, practices, and information that we need to measure and monitor the cost and quality of our outputs and the use of our resources?"

At the information level, organizational standards for all processes and activities have been established to allow for measurement and comparison between similar business units across the organization. These standard financial management practices can be tailored to each unit's nature and unique risks.

One of the key processes at the information level is to provide consistent and comparable financial and operational (non-financial) information and reports that meet the needs of managers. This information provides a basis for developing performance indicators, cost, and quality measures, and monitoring performance, to ensure that intended results are being achieved and to demonstrate accountability.

The Managed Level

At the managed level (i.e., level 4), the organization uses the information developed at level 3 to balance two competing objectives: using its resources economically and efficiently, and producing cost-effective results – for example, goods or services of acceptable quality. The organization understands the financial implications of the choices and trade-offs it makes among these objectives. Such information also allows the organization to better account for the way that it uses the resources entrusted to it.

An organization at the managed level can better manage its financial and operational performance because it has – and uses – the "right" information. It has information and analyses on the relative costs of different approaches to achieving its objectives. An organization with level 4 capabilities uses that information and impact analyses to make informed decisions on cost versus quality, and risk versus opportunities, or decisions on levels of service.

An organization with level 4 financial management capabilities also has mechanisms for measuring the impact of variables such as cost, quality, productivity, and degree of success in achieving its stated objectives. This capability flows from a history of having measured and managed organizational performance, which includes, for example:

- managing the organization's information and knowledge resources as assets, so that information needed to make informed decisions is available (for example, by using simulations, historical trends and manipulating variables to see how they affect results);
- defining the relationships among variables that affect cost, quality, and level of service, and understanding how they impact on the organization's desired results;
- using information to make informed choices among competing objectives like cost, quality, and schedule;
- understanding the financial implications of decisions before making them, and monitoring their outcomes;
- using quantitative information to control variances (for example, fluctuations or changes) in the organization's production or service delivery processes; and
- using quantitative information to balance among competing business line objectives (for example, to reduce cost, increase productivity, improve quality, reduce risk, or increase opportunities).

An organization at the managed level will be able to answer "Yes" to the question, "Do we know what it costs to achieve a given result, and did we follow the most cost-effective approach in achieving it?"

The Optimizing Level

An organization at the optimizing level (i.e., level 5) uses information from inside and outside the organization to set and achieve strategic targets or objectives for improvement. Achieving these targets enables the organization to increase the value of its services or products to clients or consumers.

Thus, at the optimizing level the focus is on continuous improvement. The organization uses what it has learned from past experience to identify areas for future improvement. This involves:

- developing prospective information to anticipate both internal and external changes that may affect the organization's performance (instead of reacting to changes) and making the necessary strategic or tactical decisions to manage their effects;
- measuring the organization's performance against that of others in the same industry and setting strategic targets for improvement;
- finding best practices and learning from other organizations (benchmarking); and
- finding ways to minimize costs and maximize revenues, and to improve the quantity and quality of outputs, by introducing new technology or improving existing processes.

The key question that an organization at the optimizing level asks itself is, "How can we as an organization improve our performance?"

Appendix 6
The Cash Management Games People Play

Hidden deep in the heart of every financial manager is a poker player. Once the game of getting the best budget deal possible is in play, the time comes to manage the money, manage it well, manage to your best advantage, and manage to guard it carefully. This calls for both defensive and offensive strategies. Sometimes using these strategies has worthwhile results, other times not. Managers will take risks and make predictions about their spending behaviour that, at times, are right on and at other times are not. Knowing how managers might behave is an important element of managing cash management outcomes.

The following describes a number of ploys that often occur in bureaucracies when managers are trying to defend their turf from intrusion, to guard their financial flexibility within their budget year, and still make sure that they will carry on next year with the same resources. Of course, woven into this is another series of ploys used to defend off-target behaviour and financial outcomes, i.e., when they go over-budget and a deficit looms on the horizon.

Every manager has an evil twin. This twin shows up at odd times. When money is involved and the possibility exists that the manager may lose some in the current fiscal year and that this might just cast doubts on next year's budget, this is the time when the evil twin comes out.

A reader might ask, is this any different from the games that have already outlined around budget formulation? In general, the tactics and strategies do indeed parallel each other. However, in-year budget management is a separate, but linked, task so can take on slightly different elements. Hence, this section is offered to outline these. In addition, as before, some potential managerial responses are suggested.

Disclaimer

By outlining such ploys, some of which involve questionable ethics, the author is not advocating their use. However,

an alert manager will recognize that they are used regularly and will be ready to respond to them. In the end, however, good cash management is a matter of balancing the need to get the job done, the need to control both programs and costs, along with the need to meet the corporate goals of the organization as well.

One factor that all these ploys have to take into account is that very few public sector organizations will rely solely on the responsible financial manager for cash forecasts and spending projections. While practice varies considerably, and there is clearly no one way to do effective cash forecasting, the financial advisors at both the unit and corporate levels will be expected to either bring together all the line managers' projections into a single document or also offer their own projections. Often, organizations with relatively weak line financial management capacity will rely solely on the financial advisor to bring together the projections. Regardless of what the routine is, there will be some form of interaction that takes place which may challenge the line manager's projections or call them into question. After all, sound management of a hard-earned budget is a performance issue for managers.

Pre-Emptive Moves

These are ploys that seasoned managers will use to either over-play or underplay their cash situation on a regular basis. While they will comply fully with projection requirements and prepare all the forecasts that the system calls for, they will build into that work some ways of portraying the information that essentially mask their true spending performance and leave them with ample margin to manoeuver throughout the year.

1. Commit All the Funds Up Front

Rather than projecting a budget based on actual expectations or historical trends, simply take a stand that all your funds will be spent for the program and no surpluses will be available over the year. This will involve making a simple declaration, offering some evidence, and also making specific commitments of funds for special projects.

2. Reduce the Money's Visibility

This is not about stealing money. It is about making it less visible and less open to scrutiny by corporate line managers or financial advisors. It is a bit risky. For instance, monies could be transferred to a reserve fund or a specialized fund that is generally regarded as restricted. Though a side deal, it could be transferred back or spent for program purposes without actually accounting for it in the cash forecast for the program. Rather, it is, to all intents and purposes, not in view when the time comes to make decisions.

3. The Sky is Falling: Claim Under-Budgeting

Start your forecasting report with a claim that you do not have the funds you need to meet program needs, that you were under-budgeted, and now must scrape along as best you can. This gives the impression that you will need everything you have.

When Budgets Go Over

Naturally, no manager wants to go over-budget and be blamed for it. So the ploys in this area often involve a lot of finger-pointing – away from the defensive manager. These ploys also involve a certain amount of plea bargaining to get help. It might be argued that the best course of action is simply to admit to, and project, a budgetary pressure early and deal with it. It sounds so simple you wonder why it does not happen all that often. However, there are many pressures inhibiting managers from admitting that they have problems: reputation, power, and protection of turf being only three of many. The nature of the alarm that an over-budget forecast sets off will vary from organization to organization. Often the urgency is magnified by the fact that such trends are not caught early enough through the poor use of forecasts at the corporate level. This exacerbates the situation and adds to the panic.

1. Blame Someone Else

Variance from planned expenditure patterns can be explained in many ways. Finding another party, preferably someone not in the room, or involved in the process, is a means to transfer responsibility. If the transfer of blame is believed, it may make the organization more amenable

to helping you out. For example, stating that the action of central agencies have increased your costs in a way you could not possibly have forecast is a good ploy. Everyone hates central agencies. Be careful that you are not alone in making such a claim. Outside agencies that are slow to pay, or have caused increased costs, are a good ploy to use as well. Be careful with the use of this ploy because it will only be put up with so many times.

2. Live Above It

"I just can't stop serving my clients." – a noble phrase that puts you above the fray. Generally, when caught with external service cost overruns, you can use this kind of thing. Of course, you have to be able to clearly point to the unforeseen nature of this event.

3. The End Run: The Minister Made Me Do It

Claim that your costs were caused by political pressure that you did not resist. For example, you could say that to maintain a good relationship with a ministerial assistant, you gave in to pressure to fund a pet project in the minister's riding. Be ready for denials out of the ministerial assistant, of course. However, you can also do this by claiming the high road of having avoided political embarrassment through some assiduous expenditure that put pressure on your budget but saved the day politically.

4. Attack the Bean Counters

A good opener to this one is "Where did these numbers come from? They don't look like the ones that we use. What did you people in finance do to distort the situation like this?" Another ploy is to claim false comparisons in analytical reports. This works really well if there are inter-regional or inter-unit comparisons. Your defence is that your circumstances are not the same as the other region's, and that it is obvious that these numbers are not clean.

A good defence is for finance to get all reports signed off several times before submitting them. The battle to produce data that is not open to attack is a real one in organizations, and often is subject to phony attacks like the ones above.

5. The Sky is Falling

Claim that the organization just doesn't understand the kinds of pressures it has created for your program. The internal program pressures have been intense as well. All of this has worn out your staff and distracted you and your managers from numbers to manage all this pressure and panic. If there is not some relief it will only get worse and more visible.

Money About to be Left on the Table

One of the fundamental reasons for sound cash forecasting and management is so that funds budgeted will be used for the purposes intended. Unforeseen circumstances will affect the desired outcome either positively or negatively depending on the circumstances. Sound financial management practice seeks to identify whatever flexibility might emerge in the budget of the organization and use it to deal with these unforeseen events or demands. As well, there is always a positive use for additional funds, should they become available. It is a mortal sin to let money lapse that could otherwise be used within the organization. Some might argue that funds should be spent solely for the purposes intended. Indeed, such is the case. However, as we have already seen in discussing budgets, line-items, and program parameters, there can be a great deal of latitude built into budget plans and authorities, usually intended to enable the organization to respond to fluctuations within the program. Operating legally and ethically within that room to manoeuver still permits the temporary reallocation of funds within a fiscal year to meet short-term demands.

For the manager who may "lose" such funds, this could be very threatening because the funds may be reallocated permanently to another budget. She may also have her own list of small projects and needs that she wants to use the funds for. Being a corporate player and donating to the greater good is just fine in theory, but not necessarily in practice, especially when you are the manager affected. One challenge for senior managers is to ensure that rewards systems are put in place to recompense those ready to give up funds for reallocation. Unfortunately, seasoned managers have been through too many situations when this has not happened, so defensive positions are built up.

1. Make a Side Deal

Lend money to another program that can use it this year with an understanding that they will pay you back next year. Of course, this requires having the authority to transfer the funds or to make expenditures on behalf of another program. This is easier than one would think, especially if the amounts are not highly visible. For example, you could buy 10 computers for a fellow director and then get her to buy 20 Blackberries for you the next year. All within your authority. All program related. This can result in money being protected from the vultures at corporate who want to help out the chump manager who is in real program trouble.

2. Attack the Bean Counters

Just keep at it. Suggest that they have not properly worked out your hold-back authorities and that you should retain the funds because of their poor calculations. Claim that the reallocations proposals are little more than a poorly concealed resource grab that will distort your program and rain down embarrassment on the minister. In the case of a decision, argue that the funds are just a loan, which you are making for the corporate good, and that you will need the funds back next year.

3. Extract Some Future Wiggle Room

Question what will be done with the reallocated money. Extract assurances that this is not a permanent loss of funds. Instead of fighting it, offer to make a loan to corporate (this requires you holding to the position that this is your money even though it truly is all corporate in the end) this year and, in exchange, you will get special authorities or consideration next year.

4. Pull in the Stakeholders

Make sure that your key stakeholders know that you might be losing money this year (and don't overly assure them about next year) for their program. This, of course, takes the gall of ignoring that you are probably doing all the program expenditures you can already and that the funds really are available. This is a very tricky ploy; one that might backfire. For instance, the stakeholders might turn on you and demand to know, quite legitimately, why the funds were not being spent. In another instance, your boss or the minister might get a highly politicized blast from the stakeholders and angrily turn to you for an explanation. This one takes brass.

Notes

Introduction to the Second Edition

[1] This quotation is attributed anecdotally to Tommy Douglas, former Premier of Saskatchewan and former Leader of the New Democratic Party, who was reputed to have said in reference to his dealings with some federal government officials, "When they say that it's not about the money, but about the principles involved, it's all about the money."

[2] There can be much confusion in defining this part of the public sector. The scope of reference used in this text comprises those organizations that are referred in the 2003 report by Statistics Canada: *National Survey on Nonprofit and Voluntary Organizations*. For its own purposes, the agency defined this sector as "incorporated nonprofit organizations, which are defined as: organizations that are nongovernmental (i.e., are institutionally separate from governments); non-profit-distributing (i.e., do not return any profits generated to their owners or directors); self-governing (i.e., are independent and able to regulate their own activities); voluntary (i.e., benefit to some degree from voluntary contributions of time or money); and formally incorporated or registered under specific legislation with provincial, territorial or federal governments. The report does not include grassroots or citizens' groups that are not formally incorporated or registered with provincial, territorial, or federal governments."

[3] An excellent discussion of these tools and their implications for public-sector governance in the future is the work of Dr. Lester Salamon, editor, *The Tools of Government: A Guide to the New Governance* (New York: Oxford University Press, 2002).

[4] *The Five Pillars of Effective Governance*, Centre for First Nations Governance, retrieved at http://fngovernance.org/publications.

[5] This section is based on an article I wrote for the *FMI*IGF Journal* (Spring 2013).

Chapter 1

[1] A good source of insight into this thinking is T.W. Plumptre, *Beyond the Bottom Line: Management in Government* (Halifax: Institute for Research on Public Policy, 1988).

[2] The term "enterprise management system" (EMS) refers to complex software applications that support the operations of an organization, along with financial and, generally, human resource and inventory systems in a more or less integrated fashion.

[3] Statistics Canada, "Public Sector Statistics," No. 68-213-XIE.

[4] Statistics Canada, "Highlights of the National Survey of Nonprofit and Voluntary Organizations," No. 61-533-XPE.

[5] Paul C. Light, *The True Size of Government* (Washington, DC: Brookings Institution Press, 1999).

[6] Dr. Lester Salamon, editor, *The Tools of Government: A Guide to the New Governance* (New York: Oxford University Press, 2002).

[7] Lester A. Salamon, "Rethinking Public Management: Third-Party Government and the Tools of Government Action," *Public Policy* 29, no. 1 (Summer 1981), and Lester A. Salamon and Michael S. Lund, "The Tools Approach: Basic Analysis," in Lester A. Salamon, editor, *Beyond Privatization: The Tools of Government Action* (Washington: Urban Institute Press, 1989), 23-50.

[8] Salamon, *The Tools of Government*.

[9] Ibid., 605.

[10] An excellent review of the history and context of the fiscal imbalance issue in Canada can be found in Robert Gagne and Janice Gross Stein's report for the Council of the Federation, entitled, "Reconciling the Irreconcilable: Addressing Canada's fiscal imbalance," available at http://www.councilofthefederation.ca/pdfs/Report_Fiscalim_Mar3106.pdf.

[11] The work of these agencies is publicly available through the exposure drafts that they set out for all to see. For the PSAB, these can be found at http://www.frascanada.ca/publicsector-accounting-board/index.aspx and for the IFAC, the main site is http://www.ifac.org/.

[12] For a good overview of New Public Management, see Salamon, *The Tools of Government*; Colin Talbot and Christopher Pollitt, editors, *Unbundled Government: A Critical Analysis of the Global Trend to Agencies, Quangos and Contractualisation* (London: Routledge, 2003).

Chapter 2

[1] CICA, "Financial Reporting by Governments" (Scott Report), 1980.

[2] E.S. Browning and Jonathan Weil, "Burden of Doubtful: Stocks Take a Beating As Accounting Worries Spread Beyond Enron," *The Wall Street Journal*, 30 January 2002, p. A1.

[3] This material is based on George J. Murphy, "A Chronology of the Development of Corporate Financial Reporting in Canada: 1850 to 1983," *The Accounting Historians Journal* (Spring 1986).

[4] Ibid.

[5] Much has been written on this topic. A quick overview of the impact on churches involved in making these settlements can be found at http://www.anglicanjournal.com/canada/residential-schools/004/article/courts-approve-residential-schoolssettlement/.

[6] A wealth of detailed information is available on Sarbanes-Oxley. For a quick overview, the material in Wikipedia is accurate and general. See http://en.wikipedia.org/wiki/Sarbanes-Oxley_Act.

Chapter 3

[1] There is considerable discussion of capital budgets and planning later in the text. Capital is often treated separately in financial management. Capital assets are defined as tangible properties, such as land, buildings, and equipment, and intangible properties such as copyrights with value. Buildings or equipment with useful lives extending beyond the year in which they are purchased or put into service are also referred to as long-term investments, capital items, capital investments, or capital acquisitions.

[2] This material is based on steps that can be found in various presentations. For example, see http://www.netmba.com/accounting/.

[3] www.ifrs.org.

[4] Ibid. p. 49, IFRS.

[5] CICA, *Not-for-profit Reporting Guide,* Standard 4400-22.

[6] Ibid.

[7] Accounting Standards Framework Implementation Guide for SAIs: Management Discussion and Analysis of Financial, Performance and Other Information, Issued by the Committee on Accounting Standards, October 2001.

[8] CICA, *Not-for-profit Financial Reporting Guide.*

[9] In large organizations, even in the public sector, these would be called business lines.

Chapter 4

[1] Ian Ball, Tony Dale, William D. Eggers, and John Sacco, "Reforming Financial Management in the Public Sector: Lessons U.S. Officials Can Learn from New Zealand," Policy Study No. 258, Reason Public Policy Institute, May 1999.

[2] Organisation for Economic Co-operation and Development, Public Management Service, "Accrual Accounting and Budgeting Practices in Member Countries: An Overview," International Accrual Accounting and Budgeting Symposium, Paris, 13-14 November 2000.

[3] Robert B. Denhardt and Janet Vinzant Denhardt, "The New Public Service: Serving Rather than Steering," *Public Administration Review* 60, no. 6 (2000): 549-559.

[4] There is a large array of literature on public-private partnerships and the financing of such projects. The following are suggested reading only:

- Rob Ball, Maryanne Heafey, and David King, "The Private Finance Initiative and Public Sector Finance," *Environment and Planning C: Government and Policy* 20, no. 1 (2002): 57-74.
- Paul Grout and Margaret Stevens, "The Assessment: Financing and Managing Public Services," *Oxford Review of Economic Policy* 19, no. 2 (2003): 215-234.

[5] Allan Barton, "The Use and Abuse of Accounting in the Public Sector Financial Reform Process," Australian National University, National Institute of Economics and Business Public Lecture, June 2003.

[6] Jon Blondal, "Accrual Accounting and Budgeting: Key Issues and Recent Development," *OECD Journal on Budgeting* 3, no. 1 (2003).

[7] Sheila Fraser, *Public Accounts of Canada* (2002), Volume 1.

[8] Marc Robinson, "Accrual Budgeting and Fiscal Policy," *OECD Journal on Budgeting* 9, no. 1 (2009): 1-29.

[9] Barton, "The Use and Abuse of Accounting."

[10] Noel Hepworth, "Preconditions for Successful Implementation of Accrual Accounting in Central Government," *Public Money and Management* 23 (2003): 37-44. Available at SSRN: http://ssrn.com/abstract=381677.

[11] Adapted from Noel Hepworth, "Preconditions for Successful Implementation of Accrual Accounting in Central Government," a paper published by the Chartered Institute of Accountancy and Public Finance (UK), January 2003.

Chapter 5

[1] Evert A. Lindquist, "Citizens, Experts and Budgets: Evaluating Ottawa's Emerging Budget Process," in Susan D. Phillips, ed., *How Ottawa Spends 1994-95: Making Change* (Ottawa: Carleton University Press, 1994), 91-128.

[2] Aaron Wildavsky, *The Politics of the Budgetary Process* (Boston: Little Brown, 1974).

[3] A responsibility centre is a part of the organization, such as a department or a unit, for which a manager is assigned responsibility. These are often set up in a hierarchical fashion within an organization, with varying degrees of delegated authority to spend and approve expenditures.

[4] Aaron Wildavsky, *The Politics of the Budgetary Process* (Boston: Little Brown, 1964).

[5] Unless such entitlements are established in specific legislation.

[6] Jerome B. McKinney and Lawrence C. Howard, *Public Administration: Balancing Power and Accountability* (Oak Park, IL: Moore Publishing, 1979).

[7] Robert N. Anthony and David W. Young, *Management Control in Nonprofit Organizations* (Homewood, IL: Richard Irwin, 1984), 359.

[8] The terms department and agency are used interchangeably to define those parts of the government that are created, usually in law, to carry out specific functions of government.

[9] Kenneth Kernaghan and David Siegel, *Public Administration in Canada: A Text* (Toronto: Methuen, 1987).

[10] Ontario, Ministry of Municipal Affairs and Housing, *Municipal Capital Budgeting Handbook* (undated).

[11] In fairness to governments, sudden shifts in program demand are usually accommodated through contingency or emergency funding or requests for additional funding authorization from the legislature. In addition, some fluctuating programs are structured as special funds with the capacity to use residual cash reserves in a year when demand is high and then retain income during years when it is low.

[12] Government of Quebec, Expenditure budget, 2013-2014, available at http://www.tresor.gouv.qc.ca/fileadmin/PDF/budget_depenses/13-14/3-Special_Funds_Budget.pdf.

Chapter 6

[1] Aaron Wildavsky, *Budgeting: A Comparative Theory of Budgetary Process*, 2nd edition (Transaction Books, 1986).

[2] A good source of background on the concept of wicked problems is available in a publication of the Australian Public Service Commission, *Tackling Wicked Problems*, available at http://www.apsc.gov.au/__data/assets/pdf_file/0005/6386/wickedproblems.pdf.

[3] Adapted from Barry Blom and Salomon A. Guajardo, *Revenue Analysis and Forecasting* (Chicago: Government Finance Officers Association, 2001), 11.

[4] The Chartered Institute of Public Finance and Accountancy (U.K.), "A Question of Cost," 1995.

[5] Steven A. Finkler, editor, *Financial Management for Public, Health and Not-for-Profit Organizations* (Upper Saddle River, NJ: Prentice Hall, Inc., 2001), 97.

[6] Ibid.

[7] A good example of a well-articulated policy on direct and indirect costs for contract services costs is the University of Victoria's policy; available at http://web.uvic.ca/uvic-policies/pol-1000/1170ESCP.html.

[8] Samuel L. Baker, "The Costs of Providing Screening Mammography," University of South Carolina Arnold School of Public Health, Department of Health Services Policy and Management, HADM J712 Sept. 4, 2002.

[9] Finkler, *Financial Management*, 99.

[10] Ibid.

[11] Wildavsky, *Budgeting: A Comparative Theory of Budgetary Process*, 12.

[12] For a useful recent overview of public-sector fund reallocation, see Joanne Kelly and Dirk-Jan Krann, *Reallocation: The Role of Budget Institutions* (Paris: OECD Publishing, 2005).

Chapter 7

[1] Available at http://www.lethbridge.ca/City-Government/Financial-Documents/Pages/Capital-Budget.aspx.

[2] The OECD defines social capital as "networks, together with shared norms, values and understandings which facilitate cooperation within or among groups": S. Cote and T. Healy, *The Well Being of Nations: The Role of Human and Social Capital* (Paris: OECD Publishing, 2001).

[3] J.M. Mintz and R.S. Preston, *Capital Budgeting in the Public Sector* (Kingston, ON: Queen's University, 1993).

[4] http://www.pir.gov.on.ca/userfiles/page_attachments/Library/4/IPFP_Complete.pdf?N_ID=4.

Chapter 8

[1] This term is hardly new, attesting to some degree, to the fact that governments have long struggled with how to cut. The phrase gained prominence in the following article: Robert D. Behn, "Cutback Budgeting," *Journal of Policy Analysis and Management* (pre-1986) 4, no. 2 (Winter 1985).

[2] From http://www.tompeters.com/dispatches/010836.php.

[3] Canadian Parliamentary Budget Office, *Budget and Expenditure Reporting to Parliament: Strengthening Transparency and Oversight in an Era of Fiscal Consolidation*, 25 April 2012, retrieved from www.parl.gc.ca/pbodpb/RedirectDocument.aspx?Url=/Macintosh%20HD/Users/AG/Downloads/Budget_and_Expenditure_Reporting_EN.pdf.

[4] K. Matthew Gilley and Abdul Rasheed, "Making More by Doing Less: An Analysis of Outsourcing and its Effects on Firm Performance," *Journal of Management* 26, no. 4 (2000): 763-90.

[5] C. Harland, L. Knight, R. Lamming, and H. Walker, "Outsourcing: Assessing the Risks and Benefits for Organizations, Sectors and Nations," *International Journal of Operations & Management* 25, no. 9 (2005): 831-850.

[6] W. Moore, W.F. Baber, and R.V. Bartlett, "Loss Aversion and Rationality in Cutback Management," *Public Finance and Management* 12, no. 3 (2012): 237-260. Retrieved from http://search.proquest.com/docview/1095379000?accountid=6180.

Chapter 9

[1] COSO Internal Control – Integrated Framework, December 2011, retrieved from www.coso.org/documents/coso_framework_body_v6.pdf.

[2] Shahid Ansari, "Systems Theory and Management Control," teaching note, 2004; available at http://faculty.darden.virginia.edu/ansaris/Systems%20Theory%20and%20MCS-TN.pdf.

[3] Lori Bender and Andrew Graham, "Risk Management: Moving the Framework to Implementation" (Ottawa: The Conference Board of Canada, 2004). This study clearly identified a reluctance by senior managers to actually implement a system of risk management. It also examined a number of public-sector jurisdictions where this had been done and the results that were realized.

[4] This concept has its origins in the United Kingston. A good explanation of its application can be found at http://www.hse.gov.uk/risk/theory/alarpglance.htm.

[5] Canada, *October 2000 Report* (Ottawa: Office of the Auditor General of Canada, 2000).

[6] Sally Washington and Elia Armstrong, "Ethics in the Public Service: Current Issues and Practice," Public Management Occasional Paper, No. 14 (Paris: OECD, 1996).

[7] Ibid., 11.

[8] *Towards Better Accountability*, Report of the Provincial Auditor, 2003, Chapter 2.

Chapter 10

[1] United Kingdom, Department of Education and Skills, "A Guide for Preparing Budget Monitoring Reports," April 2004, Department of Education and Skills, United Kingdom.

[2] Terminology to describe cash management can be vexing. Many organizations simply do not use the term, using instead such terms as "financial performance reporting," "performance against budgets reports," or simply "financial report."

Chapter 11

[1] CICA, Public Sector Handbook.

[2] Retrieved through www.frascanada.ca/standards-for-public-sector-entities/.../item68525.pdf.

[3] Susan Phillips and Karine Levasseur, "The Snakes and Ladders of Accountability: Contradictions between Contracting and Collaboration for Canada's Voluntary Sector," *Canadian Public Administration* 47, no. 4 (Winter 2004): 451-474.

[4] Panel on Accountability and Governance in the Voluntary Sector, "Building on Strength: Improving Governance and Accountability in Canada's Voluntary Sector," 1998, p. 11.

[5] Janice Gross Stein, *The Cult of Efficiency* (Toronto: House of Anansi Press, 2001).

[6] Christine Ryan and Peter Walsh, "Collaboration of Public Sector Agencies: Reporting and Accountability Challenges," *International Journal of Public Sector Management* 17, no. 7 (2004): 612-631.

[7] Statement by Arthur Kroeger to the Public Accounts Committee of the House of Commons, 21 February 2005 – with permission of the author.

[8] Treasury Board of Canada Policy on Financial Resource Management, Information and Reporting, retrieved at www.tbs-sct.gc.ca/pol/doc-eng.aspx?id=18796&section=HTML.

[9] Janice MacKinnon, *Minding the Public Purse* (Kingston, ON: McGill-Queen's University Press, 2003).

[10] http://www.ctf.ca.

[11] Canadian Comprehensive Audit Foundation, *Reporting Principles: Taking Public Sector Performance Reporting to a New Level* (Ottawa: Canadian Comprehensive Audit Foundation, 2002).

[12] Cited in Jason Reid, "Reading the Story in Public Sector Financial Statements and Annual Reports"; Beyond Numbers, February 2013, retrieved at http://www.ica.bc.ca/kb.php3?pageid=5265&mobileSession=70f2b41f663d0fa248fa5e2118ff18d3.

[13] Richard Norman and Robert Gregory, "Paradoxes and Pendulum Swings: Performance Management in New Zealand's Public Sector," *Australian Journal of Public Administration* 62, no. 4 (December 2003): 35-49.

[14] Canadian Comprehensive Audit Foundation, *Comprehensive Audit Reporting – Concepts, Issues and Practice* (Ottawa: Canadian Comprehensive Audit Foundation, 1991), 32.

[15] Wayne Cameron, "Public Accountability: Effectiveness, Equity, Ethics," *Australian Journal of Public Administration* 63, no. 4 (December 2004): 59-67.

[16] An independent board member is one who has no employment or contractual relationship, nor a proprietary interest, in the organization on whose board she sits.

[17] The Charter of the Office of the Chief Internal Auditor and the Audit Committee can be found at http://www.gov.ab.ca/home/index.cfm?page=856.

[18] The term "partnerships" does indeed cover the waterfront of joint policy collaboration with the voluntary sector to very tightly negotiated partnership agreements with private firms to construct a bridge. It remains a term that is problematic as it implies something closer to a living arrangement than an exchange of goods and services.

[19] Karen Healy and Gabrielle Meagher, "Caring, Controlling, Contracting and Counting: Governments and Non-profits in Community Services," *Australian Journal of Public Administration* 62 (3), 2003.

[20] Donald F. Kettl, *The Global Public Management Revolution*, 2nd edition (Washington, DC: Brookings Institution Press, 2005).

[21] The literature on new public management is exhaustive. For a good overview of the most recent developments, see Salamon, *Tools of Government*. Similarly, Peter Aucoin, *The New Public Management: Canada in Comparative Perspective* (Montreal: Institute for Research on Public Policy, 1995) is a good early introduction. For a more retrospective look around the world, see Andrew Graham and Alasdair Roberts, "The Agency Concept in North America: Failure, Adaptation, and Unexpected Benefits," in Christopher Pollitt and Colin Talbot, editors, *Unbundled Government* (London: Routledge, 2003).

[22] Robert Mulgan, "Accountability Issues in the New Model of Governance," Technical Report Discussion Paper 91, Australian National University, 2002.

[23] Adapted from Paul G. Thomas, "Why is Performance-based Accountability so Popular in Theory and Difficult in Practice?" Paper presented to the World Summit on Public Governance: Improving the Performance of the Public Sector–Taipei City, 1-3 May 2007, retrieved from www.ipac.ca/documents/WHY%20IS%20PERFORMANCE1.pdf.

Appendix 1

[1] The structure of this section, and many of the titles, were adapted from Robert N. Anthony and David W. Young, *Management Control in Nonprofit Organizations* (Homewood, IL: Richard Irwin, 1984). Some Canadian refinements have been added and the examples updated.

Appendix 2

[1] Aaron Wildavsky, "Rescuing Policy Analysis from PPBS," *Public Administration Review*, 29, no. 2 (1969): 189-202.

[2] Thomas D. Lynch, *Public Budgeting in America* (Englewood Cliffs, NJ: Prentice-Hall, 1995).

[3] W.W. Wilson, "The Study of Administration," *Political Science Quarterly* 2 (1885): 197-222.

[4] Donald Gow, "The Progress on Budgetary Reform in the Government of Canada," Special Study No. 17, Economic Council of Canada, 1973.

[5] Ibid.

[6] Janet M. Kelly, "The Long View: Lasting (and Fleeting) Reforms in Public Budgeting in the Twentieth Century," *Journal of Public Budgeting, Accounting and Financial Management* 15, no. 2 (Summer 2003): 309.

[7] Tammany Hall was the name given to the Democratic Party's political machine that dominated New York City politics from

the mayoral victory of Fernando Wood in 1854 until the election of Fiorello LaGuardia in 1934. The eighty-year period between those two elections marks the time in which Tammany was the city's driving political force, but its origins actually date to the late 18th century and its fall from power was not truly complete until the early 1960s.

[8] For more information on the history of the auditor general of Canada, see http://www.oag-bvg.gc.ca/domino/other.nsf/ html/bodye.html#history.

[9] By the term "separation of duties," we mean that one person's work serves as a complementary check on another's. Implied in this definition is the concept that no individual should have complete control over any transaction from initialization to completion. Adequate segregation of duties has a major impact on ensuring that transactions are valid and properly recorded.

[10] http://www.aucc.ca/_pdf/english/programs/cepra/outline %20of%20annotated%20histor.pdf.

[11] Canada, Auditor General of Canada, *Report of the Auditor General* (Ottawa, 1976).

[12] Royal Commission on Financial Management and Accountability, *Final Report* (Ottawa: Department of Supply and Services, 1979).

[13] The resource envelopes define the financial resources that are available to a Policy Committee of Cabinet for a particular policy sector.

[14] Task Force on Program Review (Ottawa: 1986).

[15] For information on Public Service 2000, see Jack Stilborn, *Federal Public Service Renewal – The La Relève Initiative*, Political and Social Affairs Division, November 1998, Library of Parliament, available at http://www.parl.gc.ca/information/library/PRBpubs/prb987-e.htm.

[16] Treasury Board of Canada, *Report of the Independent Review Panel on Modernization of Comptrollership in the Government of Canada*, available at http://www.tbssct.gc.ca/cmo_mfc/resources2/review_panel/rirp_e.asp.

[17] David Obsorne and Ted Gaebler, *"Reinventing Government: How the Entrepreneurial Spirit Is Transforming the Public Sector* (Reading: Addison-Wesley, 1992).

Appendix 3

[1] Source: Treasury Board of Canada: http://www.tbs-sct.gc.ca/cmo_mfc/Toolkit2/cap_check/cap_check_e.asp.

[2] In explaining what the FIS is, the Government of Canada, states the following:

FIS is a government-wide initiative designed to enhance decision making and accountability across government, and improve organizational performance through the strategic use of financial and non-financial performance information. The three key components of FIS are:

Systems – the introduction of new modern integrated information systems;
Policies – the adoption of full accrual accounting similar to what is practiced in the private sector;
People – a cultural change focused on enhanced analysis and use of information.

Accounting is only the starting point. The greater goal of FIS is to bring about all the attendant changes in systems, policies and people. Ultimately, FIS aims at nothing less than changing the culture of resource management in the Government of Canada.

Source: http://www.tbs-sct.gc.ca/fin/sigs/fis-sif/faq/faq-fissif_e.asp#whatis.

Appendix 5

[1] Retrieved from http://www.oag-bvg.gc.ca/internet/English/meth_gde_e_19706.html#0.2.2Z141Z1.WKP23M.TXB89F.M.

[2] ® CMM and Capability Maturity Model are registered in the U.S. Patent and Trademark Office.

Glossary

Accelerated depreciation
Technique that allocates a higher portion of a long-term asset's cost as an expense in the earlier years of its useful lifetime and a smaller portion in the later years.

Account
A category of financial event that the organization deems sufficiently important to be listed as a separate category, which can be captured in reports.

Accountability
The obligation to render an account of, and accept responsibility for, one's actions, both ... the results obtained and the means used. – Report of the Auditor General of Canada, Chapter 7, March 2004. Accountability involves reporting results compared to agreed-upon expectations. Accountable people and organizations explain any differences between their planned and actual results: how much was spent, what was delivered, and what was achieved. – Annual Report of the Auditor General of Alberta, 2001–02.

Accountability framework
A process and potentially a document in which authorities are assigned to individual managers, along with specific objectives for the program, and measures to be reported upon for assessment purposes.

Accounting
A system for keeping track of the financial status of an organization, and the financial results of its activities.

Accounting controls
Methods and procedures for the authorization of transactions, the safeguarding of assets, and the accuracy of accounting records.

Accounting cycle
The accounting cycle is made up of the steps repeated each reporting period for the purpose of preparing financial statements for users. The net results of these steps is that the organization then has a set of procedures for analyzing, recording, classifying, summarizing, and reporting its financial transactions.

Accounting standards
Authoritative standards for financial accounting and reporting developed through an organized standard-setting process and issued by a recognized standard setting body that is independent of the organization to which the standards apply. Accounting standards specify how transactions and other events are to be recognized, measured, presented, and disclosed in government financial statements. The objective of such standards is to meet the needs of users of financial statements by providing the information needed for accountability and decision making.

Accounts payable
Amounts owed to suppliers.

Accounts receivable
Money owed to the organization or individual in exchange for goods and services it has provided, or for obligations such as taxes, fines, and duties.

Accrual basis of accounting
An accounting system that records revenues in the period in which they become earned (whether received or not) and the expenses in the period that resources are used. Therefore, the transactions and events are recorded in the accounting records and recognized in the financial statements of the periods to which they relate.

Accrual output budgeting
Form of budget system currently in use in the United Kingdom, New Zealand and Australia, based on performance budgeting, that places the entire budget for each department on an internal market or purchaser/provider basis. Governments purchase services and products from departments in market-type transactions. Departments treat government funding as revenue, and have their own profit and loss statements. This is intended to encourage competition and maximize the use of internal resources.

Activity statement
Financial statement that reports the results of operations over a period of time (revenues and expenses), as well as other changes in the net assets of the organization.

Activity-based costing
Cost measurement system that focuses on activities of the organization so that an understanding is developed of the costs of each type or service offered.

Aging schedule
Management report that shows how long receivables have been outstanding since an invoice was issued.

Allocations
Subdivisions of an **appropriation** into more detailed categories, such as business lines or responsibility centres, programs, or **objects of expenditure**. Sometimes, spending is further broken down into **allotments.**

Allotments
A system that allocates budget resources to specific time periods or for use only after a certain event occurs.

Amortization
The writing off, in a systematic manner over a pre-determined number of accounting periods, of a balance in an account.

Depreciation accounting is a form of amortization applied to tangible fixed assets.

Annuity

Series of payments or receipts each in the same amount and spaced at even time periods.

Appropriation

Approval by a legislative body of an organization's budget. Appropriations create the authorization for spending the amount in the budget.

Assets

Possessions which have value. In accounting, assets are resources owned, or in some cases, controlled, by an individual or organization as a result of transactions or events from which future economic benefits are expected to flow to that individual or organization.

Assurance

The conclusion provided by an auditor concerning a subject matter of interest to the user. Absolute assurance is not attainable because of factors such as the use of judgement, the use of testing, the inherent limitations of control, and the fact that much of the evidence available to an auditor is persuasive rather than conclusive in nature.

Attestation

A statement by an auditor undertaking to express an opinion on the reliability of assertions made by management in their financial statement, and that the statement conforms with the stated accounting practices of the organization.

Audit

Examination of the financial records of the organization to verify their accuracy, discover material errors, evaluate the internal control system or determine if financial statements have been prepared in accordance with **generally accepted accounting principles.**

Audit criteria

Reasonable and attainable attributes of adequate systems against which the systems being audited can be assessed.

Audit trail

A set of references that allows a person to trace back through accounting documents to the source of any financial transaction. It usually entails a formalized record keeping system.

Audited financial statements

Financial statements that have been examined by a certified accounting professional, who issues an opinion letter, called an auditor's report.

Average cost

Full cost divided by the volume of service units.

Bad debts

Amounts that are owed to the organization that are never collected, or that the organization recognizes it will never collect, so that it will "write them off" the financial records.

Balance sheet

Financial report that indicates the financial position of the organization at a specific point in time. Often referred to as the **Statement of Financial Position.**

Basic financial statements

Financial statements that must be included in an organization's annual report to comply with GAAP. The required statements are a **Statement of Net Assets**, a **Statement of Activities**, the **Statement of Financial Position** and **fund** financial statements.

Betterment

Betterments are enhancements to the service potential of a capital asset such as:

(1) an increase in the previously assessed physical output or service capacity,

(2) a reduction in associated operating costs,

(3) an extension of the estimated useful life, or

(4) an improvement in the quality of output.

Bottom-up budget

Budget prepared by **responsibility centre** managers, who inform the top management of their spending plans and needs.

Break-even analysis

Technique for determining the minimum volume of services or goods that a program or service must provide to be financially self-sufficient.

Budget

A plan that provides a formal, quantitative expression of management's or government's plans and intentions or expectations. It generally expresses the amounts that programs have to spend over a fixed period, normally a fiscal year. The legal authority to spend such funds and legal force that limits expenditures to those limits is the **appropriations** voted by the legislature.

Budget reserves

Amounts in the budget that are to be used for unanticipated expenses. These can be identified as contingency funds, reserves for prudence purposes, etc.

Budgetary Transaction

Transaction that affects the net worth of the government.

Business plan

Detailed plan for a proposed program, project, or service, including information to be used to assess the proposal's financial feasibility.

Capital assets

Tangible properties, such as land, building and equipment, and intangible properties such as copyrights with value. Buildings or equipment with useful lives extending beyond the year in which they are purchased or put into service; also referred to as long-term investments, capital items, capital investments or capital acquisitions.

Capital budget

Plan for the acquisition of buildings and equipment that will be used by the organization in one or more years beyond the year of acquisition. This is actually both a budget and a plan: often future year expenditures are not listed for approval, but for information, while the current or upcoming year is often more concrete and detailed, intended to be the actual expenditures for the period.

Capital equipment

Equipment that is expected to last more than one year, and is of significant replacement value, often with a depreciation schedule to assign value over its useful life. Equipment items of lesser value are often not treated as capital, but as supplies, e.g., computer printers.

Capital projects fund

Fund used to account for major acquisitions of plant or equipment.

Carrying costs of inventory

Capital costs and out-of-pocket costs related to holding inventory. Capital costs represent the lost interest because money is tied up in inventory. Out-of-pocket costs include such expenses as insurance on the value of inventory, annual inspections, and obsolescence of inventory.

Cash basis of accounting

Accounting system under which revenues are recorded when cash is received, and expenses are recorded when cash is paid.

Cash budget

Plan for the cash receipts and cash disbursements of the organization. This may be an important document for organizations with cash requirements above their on-hand resources or with organizations that may have to develop a borrowing strategy for the fiscal period.

Cash equivalents

Funds held in bank accounts, short-term certificates – any item that can be readily converted to cash.

Cash flow

Measure of the amount of cash received or disbursed over a given time period, as opposed to revenues or expenses, which frequently are recognized at a time other than when the actual cash receipt or payment occurs.

Cash flow statement

Statement of changes in financial position: statement that summarizes where cash came from and what cash was used for throughout the reporting period.

Cash held in escrow

A term likely to appear on a balance sheet statement when the organization has cash, usually held by a third party, that is reserved for a completed transaction which still requires further conditions to be met before it can be paid, e.g., clearing a regulatory review.

Cash management

This text's definition: Active process of monitoring financial and program activity within the budget of the organization to determine if budgetary requirements will be met, whether they might be deficits or surpluses, within the current year and determining what appropriate action to take in either case.

Alternative definition: process of planning for borrowing and repayment of cash or investing excess cash on hand: this is a more technical exercise of managing available funds to the best advantage of the organization. It is also the more common use of the term.

Chart of accounts

Accounting document that defines the structure of the financial recording and reporting system of the organization. It would define the elements into which the budget is divided for the organization; it would further assign an identifying number for each possible element of a financial transaction. Transactions are coded and reports generated in a manner consistent with this chart.

Chief financial officer

Manager who is ultimately responsible for all the financial functions in the organization.

Collateral

Specific asset pledged to a lender as security for a loan.

Collections

A capital asset, generally held by a not-for-profit organization or public gallery, consisting of works of art, historical treasures, or similar assets that are:

(1) held for public exhibition, education or research,

(2) protected, cared for and preserved, and

(3) subject to an organizational policy that requires any proceeds from their sale to be used to acquire other items to be added to the collection.

Combined balance sheet

Financial statement that presents the **balance sheet** information for all **funds** and account groups. Totals for each **asset, liability** and **fund balance account** across funds may be provided, but are not required.

Commercial assets

An asset, the costs of which are entirely met through the imposition of user charges (i.e., through payments by consumers), and which does not therefore require tax finance.

Commitments

Future obligations or intentions to spend that the organization has that do not appear on the balance sheet. Depending on their use within an organization, these should be taken together with **encumbrances** which are less formal.

Comparative financial statements

Financial statements that present financial information from more than one fiscal period.

Compound interest

Method of calculating interest in which interest is earned on not only the amount of the original investment but also the interest earned in prior periods.

Conservatism principle

Financial statement must give adequate consideration to the risks faced by the organization.

Consolidated balance sheet
Balance sheet that combines information from all funds, reporting information on an entity-wide basis.

Consolidated revenue fund
Term common to Canadian federal and provincial governments to describe the principal operating fund of the government. In principle, all revenues from all government activities are to be placed in this fund.

Constant dollars
Dollar amounts that have been adjusted for the impact of inflation.

Contingent liabilities
Obligations that will exist in the future if certain events occur, such as if the organization loses a lawsuit.

Continuous budgeting
System in which a budget is prepared on a month-to-month basis based on fluctuations in revenue and demand for services.

Contributions
Non-reciprocal transfers to organizations, generally not-for-profit, of cash or their assets or non-reciprocal settlements or cancellations of its liabilities. Government funding provided to a not-for-profit is considered to be a contribution. In the context of some governments, contributions entail some element of re-porting accountability back to the government giving the money.

Control
Systems put in place in an organization to ensure that the actual results come as close as possible to planned results. Control can also be systems for monitoring and reporting.

Control framework
The purpose of the **control framework** is to provide a clear definition of the roles and responsibilities of each party involved in making financial decisions in an organization with the overall goal of providing accurate, complete, useful and timely account-ing information which is used in the day-to-day decision-making process by all management levels of the organization. Such a document is part of the overall management control system of an organization. It lays out delegations, authorities, decision routes, and legal requirements as well as reporting requirements for the organization.

Cost
Amount spent on something. Costs have two stages: acquisition or, **unexpired cost** and **expired costs**. When some asset or service is purchased the price is considered to be the acquisition cost. If the item is an asset, the portion that has not been consumed will appear on the balance sheet at its unexpired cost. As the asset is used up, it becomes an expired cost, or an **expense**.

Cost accounting
A subset of accounting related to measuring costs to generate cost information for reporting and making management decisions.

Cost accounting system
Any coherent system designed to gather and report cost information.

Cost allocation
The process of taking costs from areas or cost objectives and allocating them to others in order to determine the overall cost of a service, product or unit. This will entail assigning indirect costs, such as information technology or administrative support, to line activities within an organization.

Cost centre
Unit or department in an organization for which a manager is assigned responsibility for costs.

Cost convention principle
Generally accepted accounting principle that requires assets to be valued at their cost at the time of acquisition.

Cost object
Unit of service, program, organization, or good for which the cost is desired.

Cost-plus or cost-based contract
A construction contract in which the contractor is reimbursed for allowable or otherwise defined costs and, in the case of a commercially-based contract, an additional percentage of the variable costs or a fixed fee.

Cost-benefit analysis
Measurement of the relative costs and benefits associated with a particular project or course of action.

Current assets
Resources the organization has that either are cash or can be converted to cash within one year or that will be used up within one year. Current assets are often referred to as short-term or near-term assets.

Current liabilities
Those obligations that are expected to be paid within one fiscal year.

Current ratio
Current assets divided by current liabilities; this liquidity ratio assesses the ability of the organization to meet its current obliga-tions as they come due for payment.

Debt
Liability – an amount owed by one individual or organization to another.

Debt to equity
Debt divided by net assets or fund balance; this leverage ratio considers the relative magnitudes of debt to equity of the organ-ization to assess the risk created by the use of leverage. This ratio is very important in the private sector in terms of the risk of seeking more debt, or the potential for lenders to provide it. However, it sometimes applies to the not-for-profit sector as well.

Decentralization
Delegation of decision-making autonomy downward within the organization, or to centres of service not in headquarters. Delegation should be accompanied by appropriate delegation matrices and accountability frameworks.

Deferral method

Under the deferral method of accounting, expenses of future periods are deferred and recognized as revenue in the period in which the related expenses are incurred. Endowment contributions are reported as direct increases in net assets. All other contributions are reported as revenue of the current period. Organizations that use fund accounting in their financial statements without following the restricted fund method would account for contributions under the deferral method.

Deferred charges

Assets that have been paid for, and have not yet been used, but that will not be consumed in this **fiscal year**.

Deferred contribution

A restricted contribution received or recorded as a receivable but carried forward to be taken into income in future periods.

Deferred maintenance

Any maintenance work not performed when it should have been. Maintenance work should be performed when necessary to ensure capital assets provide acceptable service over their expected lives.

Deferred inflow

A deferred inflow is to be used by the entity in one or more specified future reporting periods. An example of a deferred inflow is a multi-year grant transferred to the entity that does not meet the definition of a liability, but includes a stipulation by the transferor that it is to be used to finance the general activities of the entity over one or more specified future reporting periods. A decrease in a deferred inflow would be recognized as revenue.

Deferred outflow

A deferred outflow is to be used by the transferee in one or more future reporting periods. An example of a deferred outflow is a multi-year grant transferred by the entity that contains no conditions, but a stipulation by the transferor that it is to be used for the general activities of the recipient entity or party over one or more specified future reporting periods. A decrease in a deferred outflow would be recognized as an expense.

Deficit

The excess of spending over receipts or budget; excess of expenses over revenues.

Defined benefit pension plan

A plan that specifies either the benefits to be received by employees after retirement, or the method for determining those benefits.

Delegation matrix

A formal document assigning financial and other authorities to specific categories of managers. For example, the authority to approve expenditures up to a certain level would be defined in such a matrix.

Depreciate

Decline in value or productive capability through the allocation of the asset (usually a fixed or long term asset) over the periods it is used or consumed.

Depreciation expense

Amount of the original cost of a fixed asset allocated as an expense each year.

Direct costs

1. Costs incurred within the organizational unit for which the manager has responsibility are referred to as direct costs of the unit.
2. Costs of resources used for direct provision of goods or services or activities that relate to the core mission of the organization are also referred to as direct costs.

Disbursement

Cash payment or transfer.

Discount rate

Interest rate used in time value of money analysis.

Discounted cash flow

Method that allows comparisons of amounts of money paid at different points of time by discounting all amounts to the present.

Donor-restricted funds

General class of funds that must comply with various requirements, that donors have placed at the time of the donation, which stipulate how the donations can be used.

Double-entry accounting

Refers to the fact that whenever a change is made to the fundamental accounting equation, at least one other change must be made as well to keep the equation in balance.

Encumbrance

An indication that a certain amount of money has been earmarked for a particular purpose, and is no longer available for other uses.

Endowment

Restricted fund that contains permanent assets that belong to the organization and that may not be spent; only earnings may be removed from this fund under normal conditions.

Endowment contribution

A type of restricted contribution subject to a donor-imposed stipulation specifying that the principal contributed must be held permanently, but may earn income through investment. This income would then be available for a restricted use.

Endowment fund

A self-balancing set of accounts which reports the accumulation of endowment contributions. Under the restricted fund method of accounting for contributions, only endowment contributions, and investment income subject to restrictions stipulating that it be added to the principal amount of the endowment fund, would be reported as revenue of the endowment fund. Allocations of resources to the endowment fund that result from the imposition of internal restrictions are recorded as inter-fund transfers.

Enterprise fund

Term seen in reference to a fund used to account for government services provided on a business basis. The operation of a municipal golf course may use such a fund for its accounting purposes.

Entitlements
Benefits that must be given to any individual who meets eligibility criteria specified in the law which created the entitlement.

Entity
Specific individual, organization, or part of an organization that is the focus of attention; accounting must be done from the perspective of the relevant entity and the definition of that entity must be applied consistently.

Enterprise Crown corporation
A corporation, which is not dependent on legislated appropriations, and whose principal activity and source of revenues are the sale of goods and/or services to outside parties. An enterprise Crown corporation is ultimately accountable to the legislature, through a minister of the Crown, for the conduct of its affairs.

Equities
The right-hand side of the balance sheet, i.e., the liabilities and net assets combined.

Equity
Ownership, e.g., the share of the house that is owned by the homeowner free and clear of any mortgage obligations, is the homeowner's equity in the house.

Estimates
The main estimates are government documents providing a detailed breakdown of government spending for the upcoming fiscal year. The main estimates for the Canadian federal government are issued with a blue cover and are often called the blue book.

Exception report
A report of individual items, such as cash forecast variances, that exceed a specified limit or planned expectation. Often such reports are "rolled up" into a summary report for senior management review.

Expenditure
Term used instead of expense in modified accrual systems to contrast timing of recognition from when the item is used (expense under accrual) to when an obligation is incurred to pay for the item using current financial resources (expenditure under modified accrual or cash).

Expense accrual
Term used to distinguish the accrual basis of accounting from the governmental modified accrual basis of accounting.

Expense or expensed
Decreases in economic resources, either by way of outflows, reductions of assets, or incurrence of liabilities, resulting from an entity's ordinary activities. Also, a cost that is properly identifiable with the operations of a period, or with revenues earned during that period, or that is not identifiable with the operations or revenues of a future period or periods.

External accountant
Accountant who is not an employee of the organization; often hired to perform an audit of the organization's financial records. In the public sector, this could be the legislative auditor, e.g., the auditor of the province.

Factoring
Selling or disposing of the organization's accounts receivable, usually for less than their face value. This will occur when it is easier to do this than collect the receivables in the usual way.

Fair market value
Amount of the financial consideration that would be agreed upon in an arm's-length transaction between knowledgeable, willing parties who are under no compulsion to act.

Favourable variance
Variance in which less was spent than what was budgeted. Such a variance may not been seen as favourable from the perspective of the program's objectives or the clients of the program.

Fee-for-service
System in which there is an additional charge for each additional service provided.

Fiduciary
Relating to holding something in trust; a trustee maintaining assets in trust on behalf of a person who is not yet old enough to determine how to spend them.

Fiduciary funds
Trust or agency funds used to account for resources held by a trustee or agent.

FIFO
See first-in, first-out.

Financial accounting
Financial accounting is concerned with providing information to stakeholders outside the organization in prescribed ways that establish credibility for the organization and determine compliance with applicable legal requirements. Often this is in the form of structured reports such as the balance sheet or cash flow statement.

Financial assets
Assets that could be used to discharge existing liabilities or finance future operations and are not for consumption in the normal course of government operations, e.g., cash, a realizable asset that is convertible to cash, a temporary investment.

Financial budget
The operating budget and the capital budget combined.

Financial condition analysis
An analysis of the financial status of a government organization based on a financial statement analysis as well as an evaluation of external factors that affect the financial condition of the government, or part thereof, such as the wealth of the popula-

tion, employment rates, interests rates, service demand, or the general economy.

Financial management

The part of management that focuses on the use, management, and effectiveness of financial resources to achieve objectives as well as the use of financial techniques and expertise to provide information for decision making, assuring optimal use of the resources and providing assurances of probity and propriety in their use.

Financial statement analysis

Analysis of the viability and effectiveness of an organization done by reviewing financial statements, including the accompanying management analysis and explanations, auditor's (both internal and external) reports, the use of comparative data, and taking environmental factors into account.

Financial ratios

The use of ratios to compare various elements of financial statements that enable analysis of the performance and relative position of the agency. Used consistently they provide temporal and organizational performance comparisons, and show a quick point of departure for first evidence on the overall financial position of the entity. Example: current ratio as defined as current assets divided by current liability, which measures the entity's capacity to meet current obligations.

Financial statements

Reports that convey information about the organization's financial position relative to its plans, objectives, obligations, and the results it is achieving.

First-in, first-out (FIFO)

Inventory costing method that assumes the oldest inventory is used first.

Fiscal capacity

The extent to which a government can raise money to provide goods and services to its citizens within its economic, legal, and political constraints.

Fiscal year

One-year period defined for financial and planning purposes. It may start at any point in the calendar year.

Fixed assets

Those assets that will not be used up or converted to cash within a fiscal year; referred to as long-term assets.

Fixed costs

Costs that do not change in total as volume changes within the **relevant range.** These costs do not normally increase or decrease as volume rises or falls with normal operating levels.

Flexible budget

Budget that is adjusted for volume of output.

Flexible budget variance

Difference between actual results and the flexible budget.

Flexible budgeting

Process of developing a budget based on different workload levels. Often used after the fact to calculate the amount that would have been budgeted for with actual workload levels that were attained.

Float

The interim period from when a cheque is written until it is cashed and clears the bank.

FTE

Full-time equivalent of one, full-time staff position. Often expressed as a dollar figure equivalent to either a specific staff position or an average number. Used to allocate funds to part-time or temporary forms of employment.

Full accrual

Accrual basis of accounting; term used to distinguish accrual accounting from government modified accrual basis of accounting.

Full cost

Total of all costs associated with an organizational unit or activity, including both direct and indirect costs.

Full disclosure

Generally accepted accounting principle that requires that information conveys material financial information that the financial statements do not adequately disclose.

Fund

An accounting entity with its own separate set of financial records for recording and reporting assets, liabilities, fund balance and changes in fund balance.

Fund accounting

Comprises the collective accounting procedures resulting in a self-balancing set of accounts for each fund established by the legal, contractual, or voluntary actions of an organization. Fund accounting involves an accounting segregation, although not necessarily a physical segregation, of resources. Movement of resources between funds is often restricted by specific rules, or requiring specific authority, perhaps even legislation or changes to budget provisions.

Fund balance

The equivalent of owner's equity or net assets in a fund accounting system; equal to assets, less liabilities.

Fungible

Interchangeable – subject to interpretation.

Future value

The amount a present amount of money will grow to be worth at some point in the future.

GAAP

Generally accepted accounting principles: set of rules that must be followed for the organization's financial statements to be deemed a fair representation of the organization's financial position.

General fund

A self-balancing set of accounts which, under the restricted fund method of accounting for contribution, reports all unrestricted revenue and restricted contributions for which no corresponding restricted fund is presented. The fund balance represents net assets that are not subject to externally imposed restrictions.

General journal

First place that financial transactions are entered into the accounting records; chronological listing of all financial events, e.g., sales, payments, receipt of transfers.

General ledger

Book of accounts; listing of the balances and all changes in each of the organization's accounts. This is more often a computer system than a physical book or file.

General operating fund

Unrestricted fund used for the routine and operational activities of the organization.

Going-concern principle

Generally accepted accounting principle that involves assuming that the numbers reported on an audited financial statement are those of an organization that will continue in business for the foreseeable future.

Goodwill

Intangible asset that represents a measure of the value of the organization that goes beyond its specific physical assets. Not normally applied to government operations.

Governance

Governance is a process and structure that brings together capable people and information to achieve goals. It guides an organization to achieve its goals and ensures the effective use of resources. The process and structure clearly define the organization's accountability systems.

Government business enterprise (GBE)

An entity that has all the following characteristics:
(a) It has the power to contract in its own name.
(b) Financial and operational authority has been assigned to carry on a business.
(c) In the normal course of its business, it sells goods and services to other entities at a profit or full cost recovery.
(d) It is not reliant on continuing government funding to be a going concern (other than purchases of outputs at arm's length.
(e) It is controlled by a public-sector entity.

There are many forms of GBEs in Canada. One good example is any Crown corporation.

Income statement (or earnings statement)

A financial statement that reports revenues and expenses for a given period of time. It is intended to portray cumulative operational results for a given period of time.

Incremental budgeting

An approach to resource allocation that simply adds a set percentage or amount onto the prior year's budget allocation.

Incremental costs

Additional costs that will be incurred if a decision is made to increase production, levels of service, or volume within an existing program.

Indirect costs

1. Costs that are assigned to an organizational unit from elsewhere in the organization are indirect costs for the unit, e.g., IT support.
2. Costs within a unit that are not incurred for direct provision of goods or services, i.e., core business or mission central, but are nonetheless needed to provide those services, e.g., logistical support, physical plant, or financial services.

Infrastructure

Stationary assets with extremely long life-cycles, e.g., bridges, tunnels, dams, roads, and similar assets.

Inputs

Resources used for producing the organization's output. Examples are labour and supplies.

Intangible assets

Assets without physical substance or form. This can include goodwill.

Intergovernmental fiscal transfers

Any resource flow from one level of government to another, including taxes shared by law.

Interim statements

Financial statements covering a period less than the fiscal year. Quarterly cash forecasts of budget performance, with both historical data for the period of the year that is already over, and projections to the end of the year with a comparison of performance against budget, are interim statements.

Internal accountant

Accountant who works as an employee of the organization, and performs accounting operations on its behalf.

Internal audit

An audit function within an organization that meets its internal auditing requirements, e.g., verifying transactions with pre- or post-expenditure attributes; conducts regular audits of functions on behalf of senior management.

Internal balances

Amounts that one part of the government owes to another part, e.g., central processing operations that charge back to departments their share of the cost for processing cheques on their behalf.

Internal control

1. A system of accounting and performance measurement checks and balances designed to minimize both error and the possibility of fraud or embezzlement.
2. A system of measures, both financial and non-financial, to ensure that the organization is achieving its objectives and targets.
3. The process and systems that ensure that decisions made in the organization are appropriate and have the appropriate authorization.

Internal rate of return

Discounted cash-flow technique that calculates the rate of return earned on a specific project or program.

Internal service funds

Funds established for elements of government that provide specific services to other government units, e.g., information technology.

Inter-period equity

Refers to the extent to which the government uses only revenues from the current period to pay for only services provided in the current period. A surplus for a given year implies that a government is taking resources from the current taxpayers to provide benefits for future taxpayers. A deficit implies that current taxpayers are consuming resources that will have to be paid for by future taxpayers. Thus, a surplus or deficit might be considered to create inter-period inequity.

Inventory

Materials and supplies held for use in providing services or making a product.

Journal entry

An entry into the general journal or a subsidiary journal.

Journal ledger or general ledger

A journal ledger, or journal, is the central recording device to record financial information for accounting purposes. It is a chronological listing of every financial event that affects the organization. It is considered the database, record, file, or book of original entry of information into the accounting system.

Justification

Explanation used in defending a proposed budget or in explaining variances that have occurred.

Just-in-time inventory

An approach to inventory management that calls for the arrival of inventory just as it is needed, resulting in zero inventory levels.

Last-in, first-out (LIFO)

Inventory costing method that assumes the most recent acquisitions are always used prior to inventory acquired at an earlier date.

Ledger

Accounting book or system that keeps track of increases, decreases, and the balance in each asset, liability, revenue, expense and fund balance or net asset account.

Legislative auditor

An external auditor created by law and generally reporting to the legislative body and not to bureaucracy with the purpose of overseeing government accounts and providing opinions on them, both in terms of compliance with law, policy, and their value for money.

Leverage

The use of debt as a source of financing. Debt increases the risk of the organization because of the requirement to make interest payments.

Leverage ratios

Ratios that examine the relative amount of debt the organization has; sometimes referred to as solvency ratios.

Liabilities

Legal financial obligations the organization has to outsiders. Essentially, this is money that an organization owes to someone.

Line function

Elements of the operation of an organization involved in direct delivery or service or the main reason for that organization's existence.

Line of credit

Prearranged loan to be given when, and if, needed by the organization in an amount up to an agreed-upon limit.

Line item

Any cost or expense that is listed separately on a budget, e.g., salaries, cost of rentals, etc.

Liquid

Refers to how quickly an asset can be converted to cash. The more quickly an asset can become cash, the more liquid it is.

Liquid assets

Cash or other assets that can quickly be converted to cash to meet the short-term liabilities of the organization.

Liquidate

Convert to cash.

Liquidity ratios

Class of ratio that examines the ability of the organization to meet its obligations in the coming year.

Long-range plan (or budget)

Plan that covers a number of budget years, generally outlining longer-term plans and budget projections.

Long-term liabilities

Liabilities that are not expected or required to be repaid within the fiscal year.

Long-term restricted funds

Funds that contain restrictions, which prevent them from being used for current operations, e.g., contingency funds, long-term capital investment funds.

Management control system

Complete set of policies and procedures designed to keep operations going according to plan.

Management letter

Letter from an internal or external auditor to the management of the organization outlining audit findings that are not reported in the formal audit reports; often these are minor items, or comments on matters of significance but outside the scope of the audit. Generally, these are not made public with the audit.

Management's discussion and analysis (MDA)

A part of the overall financial reporting that is used by government entities and other organizations to provide the analysis of financial information by line managers or their financial advisors to explain financial events and performance and generally recommend a course of corrective action where needed. This section of the financial report will also list general accounting policies of the organizations and explain any changes that have taken place from the previous reporting period.

Managerial accounting

The generation of financial information that is needed to assist managers in their responsibilities. This is not a special form of accounting, but rather the use of accounting techniques to accomplish the broader control goals of the organization.

Margin

At the edge; usually refers to the impact of adding one more unit of service.

Marginal cost analysis

The process of making decisions based on the marginal costs of the change, rather than on the full or average costs.

Marginal costs

The change in cost related to a change in activity. Includes variable costs and any additional fixed costs incurred because the volume change exceeds the relevant range for existing fixed costs.

Marketable securities

Marketable securities are any form of short-term investment, e.g., stocks, bonds, readily convertible mutual funds, investments or treasury certificates that can be converted to cash.

Master budget

Set of all the major budgets in the organization; generally includes the operating budget, long-range budget, program budgets, capital budget and cash budget.

Matching principle

For a given unit of service provided, the revenues arising from providing that service, and the expenses incurred in providing it, are recorded in the same fiscal period.

Material

1. Amount substantial enough that an error of that magnitude in the financial statements would cause a user of the statements to make a different decision than would have been made if the user had known the correct information.
2. Amount of sufficient political or program importance that either reporting on it, or keeping track of it, is worthwhile, e.g., small grant programs that attract much publicity.

Materiality

In the context of financial reporting, materiality may be judged in relation to the reasonable prospect of an item or the aggregate of items being significant to financial statement users in making decisions. In broader financial management application, it would be an amount substantial enough that an error of that magnitude in the financial statements would cause a user of the statements to make a different decision than would have been made if the user had known the correct information.

Maturity

Due date or end date of a loan arrangement.

Maturity value

The principal amount of a loan to be repaid at the ending date or maturity date of the loan.

Mixed costs

Costs that contain elements of both fixed and variable costs.

Modified accrual accounting

Accounting basis widely employed by governments for recording purposes for governmental funds. Under this basis of accounting, the primary focus is on financial resources. Typical financial resources are cash, investments and receivables.

Modified cash

Basis for accounting under which routine revenues and expenses are recorded on a cash basis, but capital assets are recorded as expenses gradually over the years they are used rather than all in the year the organization pays for them.

Monetary denominator principle

Generally accepted accounting principle that requires resources on the financial statement to be stated in terms of monetary value and in a consistent manner, e.g., same currency at all times.

Net assets/equity

The residual interest in an organization's assets once liabilities have been deducted. "Net assets/equity" is the term used to refer to the residual measure in the statement of financial position (assets less liabilities). Net assets/equity may be positive or negative. Other terms may be used in place of net assets/equity, provided that their meaning is clear.

Net book value

The unexpired, or unamortized, cost of an asset as carried in the accounting records of an organization. This is the original cost of the asset less the total accumulated depreciation for that asset and any other write-downs, or the original cost of the asset less the total **accumulated depreciation** for that asset.

Net cash flow

Net difference between cash receipts and cash payments.

Net income

Revenue less expense; also called profit in the private sector; could be considered **retained earnings** for the purposes of some not-for-profit organizations.

Net financial position

Net financial position is the aggregate of an entity's assets and deferred outflows less an entity's liabilities and deferred inflows at the reporting date and can be represented by:

assets + deferred outflows − (liabilities + deferred inflows) = net financial position.

Net present cost

Aggregate present value of a series of payments to be made in the future.

Net present value

Present value of a series of receipts less the present value of a series of payments.

Net realizable value

Estimated selling price in the ordinary course of business less the estimated costs of completion and sale.

Net working capital

Current assets less current liabilities and encumbrances or commitments.

Net worth

Owner's equity.

Non-budgetary spending

Items excluded from budgetary spending, mainly expenditures under trust accounts managed by the federal government for third parties, such as pension payments from federal government employees' pension plans. Also excluded from budgetary spending in Canada are expenditures under the Canada Pension Plan (CPP), which is administered jointly by the federal and provincial governments.

Non-budgetary transaction

Transaction involving offsetting financial assets and liabilities thus leaving net debt unchanged.

Non-capital asset

A non-capital asset is a physical asset that is below the accounting limit for recognition as a capital asset in the accounts. It is not controlled in the central capital asset register since it costs less than the approved limit. This does not mean that the asset does not have value, but only that it is not cost effective to account for its consumption over more than one financial year. Non-capital assets are often characterized by the fact that they are easily transportable and have general purpose use.

Noncontrollable

Those items over which a manager does not have the authority or ability to control, e.g., the cost of fuel, intake for entitlement programs, emergency room volumes.

Non-exchange transaction

Under a non-exchange transaction, an entity receives value from another entity without directly giving approximately equal value in exchange, or gives value to another entity without directly receiving equal value in exchange. In public sector finance, this means that a taxpayer will be taxed at a rate consistent with earnings, not the value of goods and services received from government.

Non-expendable funds

Funds where only a portion of the money within it can be spent.

Non-financial assets

Assets acquired, constructed or developed that do not normally provide resources to discharge existing liabilities, but instead are normally employed to deliver government services, may be consumed in the normal course of operation and are not for sale in the normal course of operations.

Notes payable

Written documents representing a loan that is reported on the balance sheet.

Not-for-profit organizations

Entities, normally without transferable ownership interests, organized and operated exclusively for social, educational, professional, religious, health, charitable or any other not-for-profit purposes. A not-for-profit organization's members, contributors and other resource providers do not, in such capacity, receive any financial return directly from the organization.

Object code

A numeric code that is part of the overall budget code structure of the statement of accounts used to identify the nature, purpose or object of each financial transaction. Codes are used in all budgeting and accounting systems for consistent reporting purposes.

Objective evidence principle

GAAP that requires assets to be valued based on objective, rather than subjective, information.

Objects of expenditure

Categories of expenditures required to provide goods and services, such as salaries, inventory, rent, equipment, transfers and other resources.

Off-budget

Items that are not included in the normal government budget process, e.g., revenue from the proceeds of the sale of surplus equipment, some self-financial programs.

On-budget

Items that are included in the normal government budget process, i.e., items for which appropriations would be sought.

Operating

Related to the normal routine activities of the organization in carrying out its primary purpose.

Operating budget

Plan for the day-to-day operating revenues and expenses of the organization, for which formal budget approval and appropriations are sought in government and for which fund raising and grant applications are formulated in the not-for-profit sector.

Operating fund

Fund used to account for the day-to-day operations of the organization and all of its resources, and is not subject to restrictions on their use; also called the general fund or current unrestricted fund.

Operating margin

Profitability ratio that compares the operating profit (operating revenue less operating expenses) with operating revenue. It assesses the profitability of each dollar of revenue generated by the routine activities of the organization.

Operating statement

Compares the entity's revenues and other support with its expenses for a period of time, such as a quarter or a year. Often referred to as an income statement, activity statement, statement of revenues and expenses, profit and loss statement.

Opinion letter

Letter or communication from an accountant to users of the organization's audited financial statements providing the accountant's expert opinion as to whether the financial statements are a fair representation of the financial position and the actual results of the operation of the organization.

Opportunity cost

A measure of cost based on the value of the alternatives that are given up in order to use the resource available. In other words, if an organization chooses one course of action, what does it give up, or is not able to do, as a result of that action?

Opportunity costs of inventory

Carrying costs or costs of having money tied up in inventory rather than in a more active program's use, or for revenue generation purposes in the private sector.

Outcomes

Outcomes are the results an organization tries to achieve. They focus on the goals of the organization.

Outputs

Outputs are goods and services actually delivered by an organization to achieve outcomes. They tell you "how much" and "how many."

Overhead

Indirect costs allocated to a unit or department from elsewhere in the organization both for services provided in support of the unit and as a contribution to common central costs such as central offices.

Owner's equity

Residual value after the liabilities of an organization are subtracted from the assets. In the public sector, this would translate as net assets.

Performance audits

Review of the organization's operations, consisting of economic and efficiency audits and program audits.

Performance budget

Plan that relates the various objectives of a cost centre with the planned costs of accomplishing those activities.

Performance measures

Method of assessing progress towards achieving a goal.

Period costs

Costs that are treated as an expense in the accounting period for when they are incurred, regardless of when the organization's goods or services are sold.

Periodic inventory

Inventory method under which the organization records only purchases and uses a count of inventory to determine how much has been used (sold) and how much is left on hand.

Permanently restricted net assets

Net assets that must be maintained in perpetuity because of donor-imposed restrictions.

Perpetual inventory

Inventory method under which the organization keeps a record of each inventory acquisition and sale.

Posting

Process of transferring all parts of a journal entry to the specific ledger accounts that are affected by the entry.

Prepaid expenses

Assets that have been paid for and have not yet been used but that will be used within the fiscal year. These include items such as fire insurance premiums and rent paid in advance of use.

Present value

Value of future receipts or payments discounted to the present value of the money.

Privatization

The legal transfer of ownership from public to private hands, e.g., the sale of Air Canada.

Pro forma financial statements

Financial statements that present a prediction of what the financial statements for a project, program or organization will look like at some point in the future.

Profit centre

A responsibility unit that is responsible for both revenues and expenses. Often referred to in the public sector as revenue centres.

Profit margin

Excess of revenue over expense divided by total revenue; an indication of the amount of profits generated by each dollar of revenue.

Program audits

Reviews of the organization's operations to check for effectiveness. They determine whether the organization's programs are accomplishing their objectives.

Public Accounts

Financial statements for the government that have been audited by the legislative auditor for that jurisdiction.

Public accounts committee

At the federal level, a committee of the House of Commons. Such committees exist in most provincial legislatures as well. In either case, they are responsible for overseeing government expenditures. Individual committees still review departmental estimates and expenditure plans, theoretically in greater detail. In general, as well, the legislative auditor, e.g., the auditor general, will report to the legislature through this committee.

Qualified auditor's opinion

An opinion that, except for the effect or possible effect of one or more particular aspects, the matters subject to audit are in accordance with the criteria against which they were assessed. It is expected that the auditor will clearly state what the qualifications are.

Quick ratio

Cash plus marketable securities plus accounts receivable, all divided by current liabilities. This liquidity ratio is a more stringent test of the ability to meet current obligations as they come due rather than the widely used current ratios. Sometimes called the acid test.

Rate variance

Price variance that relates to labour resources. In such cases it is typically the hourly rate that has varied from expectations.

Recognition

The point at which a financial event is considered to have occurred and can be recorded in the financial records of the entity. The time of recognition differs under the cash and accrual bases of accounting.

Representational statement

The expression of the opinion, usually by an auditor, that all the financial statements are accurate to the best of his or her knowledge and that they have been prepared in a manner consistent with the policies of the organization and GAAP.

Reservation, reservation of opinion

A generic term for an adverse, or a qualified, auditor's opinion.

Residual value

Estimated net realizable value of a capital asset at the end of its useful life to an organization.

Responsibility

Identifies the field within which a public office holder (whether elected or unelected) can act; it is defined by the specific authority given to an office holder (by law or delegation). – Government of Canada, Guidance for Deputy Ministers, 2003.

Responsibility centre

Part of the organization, such as a department or a unit, for which a manager is assigned responsibility. These are often designed in a hierarchical fashion within an organization, with varying degrees of delegated authority to spend and approve expenditures.

Restricted fund

Funds whose assets are limited in their use. A self-balancing set of accounts, the elements of which are restricted or relate to the use of restricted resources. Under the restricted fund method of accounting for contributions, only restricted contributions, other than endowment contributions, and other externally restricted revenue would be reported as revenue in a restricted fund. Allocations of resources that result from the imposition of internal restrictions are recorded as inter-fund transfers to the restricted fund.

Restricted fund method

Specialized type of fund accounting that involves the reporting of details of financial statement elements by fund in such a way that the organization reports total general funds, one or more restricted funds, and an endowment fund, if applicable.

Retained earnings

The portion of the profits of a for-profit corporation that has been earned over the years, and has not been distributed to the owners in the form of dividends.

Return on investment (ROI)

The ROI is a return ratio that compares the net benefits of a project, verses its total costs. For example, if a project has an ROI of 200 percent, the net benefits derived from the project are double those of the expected total costs to implement the project. As such, the ROI calculation represents the relative value of the project's cumulative net benefits (benefits less costs) over the analysis period, divided by the project's cumulative total costs, expressed as a percentage.

Revenues

Amounts of money that the organization has received or is entitled to receive in exchange for goods or services that it has provided.

Revolving fund

A revolving fund is a statutory parliamentary authority to use the revenues generated from an activity to finance it. This authority generally continues from one year to the next without further authority from Parliament. Although surpluses or deficits may occur from year to year, they are generally expected to balance out over time. A revolving fund should support increased cost effectiveness, optimal use of resources, responsiveness to clients and good business practices, when used in conjunction with other appropriate arrangements. Such arrangements include the legal and policy framework governing the provision of government services, leadership of the organization and the system of rewards and incentives.

Risk

Anything that affects an organization's ability to achieve its goals.

Risk exposure factor

Investment revenue, intergovernmental revenue, and transfers-in all divided by controllable tax revenue; this ratio assesses the relative share of a government's resources that come from sources it does not control, as compared with the share that comes from a tax base it does control.

Risk management

Systematic steps an organization puts in place to deal with the risks that it faces.

Rolling forecast

Forecasts can be plans for expenditures and revenues or a projection of the cash flow for a given period, normally a fiscal year. With a rolling forecast the number of periods in the forecast remain constant so that if, for example, the periods of the forecast are monthly for 12 months then, as each month is traded, it drops out of the forecast and another month is added to the end of the forecast so there is always forecasting for 12 monthly periods into the future.

Self-financing program
Program in which the costs of delivery are recovered through an autonomous revenue source, such as fees, that are not placed in the **consolidated revenue fund**, but retained in a special fund to pay for the program.

Sensitivity analysis
Process whereby the financial results are recalculated under a series of varying assumptions and predictions. This is often referred to as "what-if" analysis.

Sinking fund
Segregated assets to be used for replacement of plant and equipment, or the repayment of a long-term liability such as a bond.

Solvency
Ability to meet current and future obligations.

Specific authorization
Requirement that a person get written permission to override general authorization policies.

Spending variance
The equivalent of the price or rate variance for fixed and variable overhead costs.

Statement of activities
Statement that provides information about the revenues and expenses of the government as a whole, as well as other changes in net assets.

Statement of cash flows
Provides information about the sources and uses of cash by the organization in carrying out its operating, financing, and investing activities for the period.

Statement of changes in net assets
Provides information about change in the portions of net assets attributable to endowments, capital assets, and other internal and external restrictions.

Statement of financial position
Presents the organization's economic resources, obligations, and net assets at the reporting date. Financial report that indicates the financial position of the organization at a specific point in time. Often referred to as the **balance sheet.**

Statement of net assets
Balance sheet presented in a format of assets less liabilities which equal net assets.

Statement of operations
Presents information about changes in the organization's economic resources and obligations for the period.

State-owned enterprises
See **government business enterprise.**

Straight-line depreciation
Technique that allocates an equal portion of a long-term asset's cost as an expense each year.

Subsidiary journal
Detailed journal where original entries are first made, with only a summary total entry being made to the general journal.

Subsidiary ledger
Ledger where detailed information is recorded, with only a summary being posted to the general ledger.

Sunk costs
Costs that already have been incurred and will not be affected by future actions.

Systems (accounting)
A set of interrelated accounting control processes relating to revenue, disbursements, the preservation or use of assets, or the determination of liabilities.

Systems (management)
A set of interrelated management control processes that are designed to achieve business goals economically and efficiently.

Tangible capital asset
A non-financial asset having physical substance that:
(1) is held for use in the production or supply of goods and services;
(2) has a useful economic life extending beyond an accounting period; and
(3) has been acquired to be used on a continuing basis.

Tax expenditure
Loosely, a tax exemption or advantage, sometimes called an incentive or loophole; technically, a loss of governmental tax revenue attributable to some provision of federal tax laws that allows a special exclusion, exemption, or deduction from gross income or that provides a special credit, preferential tax rate, or deferral of tax liability. The tax exemption or advantage is usually intended to assist a certain group, or to encourage a certain activity, such as the purchase of homes.

Tax transfer
A federal tax transfer involves the federal government ceding some of its "tax room" to provincial governments. Specifically, a tax transfer occurs when the federal government reduces its tax rates to allow provinces to raise their tax rates by an equivalent amount. With a tax transfer, the changes in federal and provincial tax rates offset one another and there is no net financial impact on the taxpayer. Tax transfers represent a growing source of revenue for provinces since they increase in value over time with growth in the economy.

Time value of money
Recognition of the fact that money can earn compound interest and, therefore, a given amount of money paid at different points in time has a different value; the further into the future an amount is paid, the less valuable it is.

Time-series model
Forecasting approach that uses trends and seasonal patterns in the past as a predictor for the future.

Top-down budget
Budget prepared by top management.

Total debt-to-equity ratio
Total liabilities divided by fund balance. The higher this ratio, the less borrowing capacity the organization has available.

Total margin
Profitability ratio that compares the excess of revenues over expenses with total revenues to determine the overall profits earned, including all sources of revenues and expenses, per dollar of revenues.

Transfer Payment
A transfer of money from a government to an individual, an organization or another government for which the government making the transfer does not:
(1) receive any goods or services directly in return as would occur in a purchase/sales transaction;
(2) expect to be repaid in the future, as would be expected in a loan; or
(3) expect a financial return, as would be expected in an investment.

Transfer prices
The amounts charged to one responsibly centre for goods or services acquired from another responsibility centre in the same organization.

Unexpired costs
Costs of an asset that have not yet been used up.

Unrestricted funds
Funds whose assets may be used for any normal purpose; usually only the general operating fund is unrestricted.

Use variance
Another name for the quantity variance, so called because the quantity variance focuses on how much of a resource has been used compared to what was predicted or planned.

Useful life
The estimate of the period over which a capital asset is expected to be used by an organization, or the number of production units that can be obtained from the capital asset. The life of a capital asset may extend beyond its useful life to an organization.

Value added
Costs that directly affect the quality of the ultimate product or service provided.

Value-for-money audit
A comprehensive form of auditing to determine if funds spent achieved the best return on investment, or were spent in the most effective means possible and according to the stated objectives. This form of audit borders on formal evaluation and policy analysis and is well beyond the narrow definition of **audit** per se.

Variable costs
Costs that vary in direct proportion with volume.

Variance
The difference between the budget and the actual results. Also, the difference between projected costs or volumes and actual results.

Variance analysis
Actual results compared with the budget or projections (or previous similar reporting period), followed by investigation and reporting to determine the cause of the variance.

Working capital
The amount of capital, or current assets available, for use in operating the entity. Commonly calculated as the amount by which current assets exceed current liabilities. It does not include fixed assets or such matters and accounts receivable as they are not available to operate the entity.

Write-off
Eliminate an asset from the accounting records and record it as an expense: term often used in its place: taking a charge.

Zero-based budgeting (ZBB)
Budgeting approach that requires an examination and justification of all costs rather than just the incremental costs and that requires examination of alternatives rather than just one approach: each budget year starts at zero and is built up, rather than added to or modified based on previous years' budgets.

Index

Queen's Policy Studies
Recent Publications

The Queen's Policy Studies Series is dedicated to the exploration of major public policy issues that confront governments and society in Canada and other nations.

Manuscript submission. We are pleased to consider new book proposals and manuscripts. Preliminary inquiries are welcome. A subvention is normally required for the publication of an academic book. Please direct questions or proposals to the Publications Unit by email at spspress@queensu.ca, or visit our website at: www.queensu.ca/sps/books, or contact us by phone at (613) 533-2192.

Our books are available from good bookstores everywhere, including the Queen's University bookstore (http://www.campus bookstore.com/). McGill-Queen's University Press is the exclusive world representative and distributor of books in the series. A full catalogue and ordering information may be found on their web site (**http://mqup.mcgill.ca/**).

For more information about new and backlist titles from Queen's Policy Studies, visit http://www.queensu.ca/sps/books.

School of Policy Studies

The Multiculturalism Question: Debating Identity in 21st-Century Canada, Jack Jedwab (ed.) 2014. ISBN 978-1-55339-422-8

Government-Nonprofit Relations in Times of Recession, Rachel Laforest (ed.) 2013. ISBN 978-1-55339-327-6

Intellectual Disabilities and *Dual Diagnosis: An Interprofessional Clinical Guide for Healthcare Providers*, Bruce D. McCreary and Jessica Jones (eds.) 2013. ISBN 978-1-55339-331-3

Rethinking Higher Education: Participation, Research, and Differentiation, George Fallis 2013. ISBN 978-1-55339-333-7

Making Policy in Turbulent Times: Challenges and Prospects for Higher Education, Paul Axelrod, Roopa Desai Trilokekar, Theresa Shanahan, and Richard Wellen (eds.) 2013. ISBN 978-1-55339-332-0

Building More Effective Labour-Management Relationships, Richard P. Chaykowski and Robert S. Hickey (eds.) 2013. ISBN 978-1-55339-306-1

Navigationg on the Titanic: Economic Growth, Energy, and the Failure of Governance, Bryne Purchase 2013. ISBN 978-1-55339-330-6

Measuring the Value of a Postsecondary Education, Ken Norrie and Mary Catharine Lennon (eds.) 2013. ISBN 978-1-55339-325-2

Immigration, Integration, and Inclusion in Ontario Cities, Caroline Andrew, John Biles, Meyer Burstein, Victoria M. Esses, and Erin Tolley (eds.) 2012. ISBN 978-1-55339-292-7

Diverse Nations, Diverse Responses: Approaches to Social Cohesion in Immigrant Societies, Paul Spoonley and Erin Tolley (eds.) 2012. ISBN 978-1-55339-309-2

Making EI Work: Research from the Mowat Centre Employment Insurance Task Force, Keith Banting and Jon Medow (eds.) 2012. ISBN 978-1-55339-323-8

Managing Immigration and Diversity in Canada: A Transatlantic Dialogue in the New Age of Migration, Dan Rodríguez-García (ed.) 2012. ISBN 978-1-55339-289-7

International Perspectives: Integration and Inclusion, James Frideres and John Biles (eds.) 2012. ISBN 978-1-55339-317-7

Dynamic Negotiations: Teacher Labour Relations in Canadian Elementary and Secondary Education, Sara Slinn and Arthur Sweetman (eds.) 2012. ISBN 978-1-55339-304-7

Where to from Here? Keeping Medicare Sustainable, Stephen Duckett 2012. ISBN 978-1-55339-318-4

International Migration in Uncertain Times, John Nieuwenhuysen, Howard Duncan, and Stine Neerup (eds.) 2012. ISBN 978-1-55339-308-5

Centre for International and Defence Policy

Afghanistan in the Balance: Counterinsurgency, Comprehensive Approach, and Political Order, Hans-Georg Ehrhart, Sven Bernhard Gareis, and Charles Pentland (eds.), 2012. ISBN 978-1-55339-353-5

Institute of Intergovernmental Relations

Canada: The State of the Federation 2011, Nadia Verrelli (ed.), 2014. ISBN 978-1-55339-207-1

Canada and the Crown: Essays on Constitutional Monarchy, D. Michael Jackson and Philippe Lagassé (eds.), 2013. ISBN 978-1-55339-204-0

Paradigm Freeze: Why It Is So Hard to Reform Health-Care Policy in Canada, Harvey Lazar, John N. Lavis, Pierre-Gerlier Forest, and John Church (eds.), 2013. ISBN 978-1-55339-324-5

Canada: The State of the Federation 2010, Matthew Mendelsohn, Joshua Hjartarson, and James Pearce (eds.), 2013. ISBN 978-1-55339-200-2

The Democratic Dilemma: Reforming Canada's Supreme Court, Nadia Verrelli (ed.), 2013. ISBN 978-1-55339-203-3